Junior Worldmark Encyclopedia of Foods and Recipes of the World

2nd Edition

Junior Worldmark Encyclopedia of Foods and Recipes of the World

2nd Edition

VOLUME 1:

Algeria—Germany

Susan Bevan Gall, Editor
Kathleen J. Edgar, Project Editor

U·X·L
A part of Gale, Cengage Learning

**South Huntington Pub. Lib.
145 Pidgeon Hill Rd.
Huntington Sta., N.Y. 11746**

GALE
CENGAGE Learning

Detroit • New York • San Francisco • New Haven, Conn • Waterville, Maine • London

Junior Worldmark Encyclopedia of Foods and Recipes of the World, 2nd Edition

Susan Bevan Gall, Editor

Project Editor: Kathleen J. Edgar

Contributing Editor: Elizabeth P. Manar

Managing Editor: Debra Kirby

Rights Acquisition and Management: Leitha Etheridge-Sims

Imaging and Multimedia: John L. Watkins

Composition: Evi Abou-El-Seoud

Manufacturing: Wendy Blurton, Dorothy Maki

Product Manager: Douglas A. Dentino

Product Design: Kristine A. Julien

© 2012 Gale, Cengage Learning

ALL RIGHTS RESERVED. No part of this work covered by the copyright herein may be reproduced, transmitted, stored, or used in any form or by any means graphic, electronic, or mechanical, including but not limited to photocopying, recording, scanning, digitizing, taping, Web distribution, information networks, or information storage and retrieval systems, except as permitted under Section 107 or 108 of the 1976 United States Copyright Act, without the prior written permission of the publisher.</para>

This publication is a creative work fully protected by all applicable copyright laws, as well as by misappropriation, trade secret, unfair competition, and other applicable laws. The authors and editors of this work have added value to the underlying factual material herein through one or more of the following: unique and original selection, coordination, expression, arrangement, and classification of the information.

For product information and technology assistance, contact us at Gale Customer Support, 1-800-877-4253.
For permission to use material from this text or product, submit all requests online at www.cengage.com/permissions.
Further permissions questions can be emailed to permissionrequest@cengage.com

Cover photographs: Front cover, © Rob Ahrens/Shutterstock.com. Back cover: Chef making kebabs, © Ian Tragen/Shutterstock.com; bread making, © Thomas M Perkins/Shutterstock.com; woman grinding wheat, © Kailash K Soni/Shutterstock.com.

While every effort has been made to ensure the reliability of the information presented in this publication, Gale, a part of Cengage Learning, does not guarantee the accuracy of the data contained herein. Gale accepts no payment for listing; and inclusion in the publication of any organization, agency, institution, publication, service, or individual does not imply endorsement of the editors or publisher. Errors brought to the attention of the publisher and verified to the satisfaction of the publisher will be corrected in future editions.

LIBRARY OF CONGRESS CATALOGING-IN-PUBLICATION DATA

Junior worldmark encyclopedia of foods and recipes of the world / Susan Bevan Gall, editor ; Kathleen J. Edgar, project editor. -- 2nd ed.
    v. cm.
    Includes bibliographical references and index.
    Contents: v. 1. Algeria to France -- v. 2. Germany to Japan -- v. 3. Kazakhstan to South Korea -- v. 4. Spain to Zimbabwe.
    ISBN-13: 978-1-4144-9071-7 (set)
    ISBN-10: 1-4144-9071-2 (set)
    ISBN-13: 978-1-4144-9072-4 (v. 1)
    ISBN-10: 1-4144-9072-0 (v. 1)
    [etc.]
    1. Food--Encyclopedias, Juvenile. 2. International cooking--Encyclopedias, Juvenile. I. Gall, Susan B. II. Edgar, Kathleen J.
    TX349.J86 2012
    641.59--dc23
                                                            2011050620

Gale
27500 Drake Rd., Farmington Hills, MI 48331-3535

978-1-4144-9071-7 (set)	1-4144-9071-2 (set)
978-1-4144-9072-4 (vol. 1)	1-4144-9072-0 (vol. 1)
978-1-4144-9073-1 (vol. 2)	1-4144-9073-9 (vol. 2)
978-1-4144-9074-8 (vol. 3)	1-4144-9074-7 (vol. 3)
978-1-4144-9075-5 (vol. 4)	1-4144-9075-5 (vol. 4)

This title is also available as an e-book.
ISBN-13: 978-1-4144-9076-2   ISBN-10: 1-4144-9076-3
Contact your Gale sales representative for ordering information.

Printed in China
1 2 3 4 5 6 7 16 15 14 13 12

Table of Contents

Cumulative Table of Contents vii

Reader's Guide xi

Measurements and Conversions xv

Getting Started with Cooking xvii

Glossary xxi

VOLUME 1: Algeria—Germany
Algeria **1**
Argentina **13**
Australia **23**
Australia: Aborigines and Bush Tucker **35**
Brazil **45**
Brazil: Afro-Brazilians **55**
Cameroon **65**
Canada **75**
Canada: Aboriginals **85**
Canada: French Canadians **95**
Chile **105**
China **115**
Côte d'Ivoire **127**
Cuba **137**
Czech Republic **149**
Dominican Republic **159**
Egypt **169**

Table of Contents

El Salvador **179**
Ethiopia **189**
France **201**
Germany **211**

Further Study **xxxiii**

Index **xlix**

Cumulative Table of Contents

VOLUME 1: Algeria—Germany
Algeria 1
Argentina 13
Australia 23
Australia: Aborigines and Bush Tucker 35
Brazil 45
Brazil: Afro-Brazilians 55
Cameroon 65
Canada 75
Canada: Aboriginals 85
Canada: French Canadians 95
Chile 105
China 115
Côte d'Ivoire 127
Cuba 137
Czech Republic 149
Dominican Republic 159
Egypt 169
El Salvador 179
Ethiopia 189
France 201
Germany 211

VOLUME 2: Ghana—Mexico
Ghana 1
Greece 13

Cumulative Table of Contents

Guatemala **23**
Haiti **33**
Hungary **45**
India **57**
Indonesia **69**
Iran **81**
Iraq **93**
Ireland **105**
Islands of the Pacific **117**
Israel **127**
Italy **139**
Jamaica **149**
Japan **161**
Kazakhstan **173**
Kenya **183**
Lebanon **193**
Liberia **205**
Mexico **215**

VOLUME 3: Morocco—Tanzania

Morocco **1**
Mozambique **13**
Nigeria **25**
Pakistan **37**
Peru **49**
Philippines **63**
Poland **77**
Portugal **91**
Russia **101**
Saudi Arabia **113**
Slovenia **125**
Somalia **137**
South Africa **149**
South Korea **161**
Spain **175**
Sweden **189**
Tanzania **205**

VOLUME 4: Thailand—Zimbabwe

Thailand 1
Turkey 15
Ukraine 29
United Kingdom 41
United Kingdom: Scotland 55
United States: African Americans 65
United States: Amish and Pennsylvania Dutch 79
United States: Great Lakes Region 89
United States: Jewish Americans 101
United States: Latino Americans 113
United States: Midwest Region 125
United States: Native Americans 135
United States: Northeast Region 147
United States: Southern Region 159
United States: Western Region 173
Vietnam 185
Zimbabwe 199

Reader's Guide

Junior Worldmark Encyclopedia of Foods and Recipes of the World, 2nd Edition, presents a comprehensive look into the dietary lifestyles of many of the world's peoples. Published in four volumes and now in full color, entries are arranged alphabetically from Algeria to Zimbabwe. Several countries—notably Australia, Brazil, Canada, the United Kingdom, and the United States—feature entries for specific ethnic groups or regions with distinctive food and recipe customs.

Junior Worldmark Encyclopedia of Foods and Recipes of the World features more than 900 recipes in 75 entries representing 64 countries. New entries for this edition include Dominican Republic, El Salvador, Portugal, Somalia, and the United Kingdom's Scotland. In selecting the countries, culture groups, and regions to include, librarian advisers were consulted.

In response to suggestions from advisers to the editors of the first edition, the list of entries to be developed was compiled. For this second edition, new entries were selected to represent regions of the world and to describe the foods and recipes of countries that have had influence on the cuisine of the world. The editors sought, with help from the advisers, to balance the contents to cover the major food customs of the world. Countries were selected from Africa (Algeria, Cameroon, Côte d'Ivoire, Ethiopia, Ghana, Kenya, Liberia, Morocco, Mozambique, Nigeria, Somalia, South Africa, Tanzania, Zimbabwe); Asia (China, India, Indonesia, Japan, the Philippines, South Korea, Thailand, Vietnam); the Caribbean (Cuba, Haiti, Jamaica); Europe (Czech Republic, France, Germany, Greece, Hungary, Ireland, Italy, Kazakhstan, Poland, Portugal, Russia, Slovenia, Spain, Sweden, Turkey, Ukraine, United Kingdom); Central America (Costa Rica, El Salvador, Guatemala); the Middle East (Egypt, Iran, Iraq, Israel, Lebanon, Pakistan, Saudi Arabia); North America (Canada, Mexico, and the United States); Oceania (Australia and Islands of the Pacific); and South America (Argentina, Brazil, Chile, Peru).

For the United States entry, the advisers suggested preparing an innovative combination of five regional entries (including Great Lakes, Midwest, Northeast, Southern, and Western) and five ethnic/culture group entries (African

Reader's Guide

American, Amish and Pennsylvania Dutch, Jewish American, Latino American, and Native American). Researchers interested in other major American ethnic and cultural groups, such as Chinese American, German American, and Lebanese American, are directed to the entries for the home countries of origin (such as China, Germany, and Lebanon).

For this second edition, new recipes were added to every entry. Recipes were selected to reflect traditional national dishes as well as modern lifestyles. Persons familiar with the cuisines of the countries were consulted to ensure authenticity. The editors acknowledge the invaluable advice of these individuals, without whose help this encyclopedia would not be as authoritative: Thelma Barer-Stein; Stefanie Bruno; staff of Corky and Lenny's delicatessen, Beachwood, Ohio; Janet Dery Cox; David Eger of Earthy Delights; Clara Gonzalez, Aunt Clara's Kitchen-Dominican Cooking; Terry Hong; Marcia Hope; Solange Lamamy; staff of Middle East Restaurant, Cleveland, Ohio; staff of Pearl of the Orient, Shaker Heights, Ohio; John Ranahan; Christine Ritsma; Ana Doris Rodriguez, assistant to the ambassador and deputy chief of mission, Embassy of El Salvador; and Nawal Slaoui.

Profile Features

This second edition of *Junior Worldmark Encyclopedia of Foods and Recipes of the World* continues to follow the trademark format of the Junior Worldmark design by organizing each entry according to a standard set of headings. This format has been designed to allow students to compare two or more nations in a variety of ways.

Also helpful to students are the translations of hundreds of foreign-language terms (which can be found in italics throughout the text) to English. Pronunciations are provided for many unfamiliar words.

Each profile contains two maps: the first displaying the nation and its location in the world, and the second presenting the nation's major cities and neighboring countries. Each entry begins with a recipe table of contents guiding the student to specific page numbers. The four-volume set also includes more than 340 color photographs, richly illustrating selected recipes, people of various cultures preparing food, markets, ingredients, or cooking procedures.

Most entries feature approximately 12 recipes, including appetizers, main dishes, side dishes, beverages, desserts, and snacks. Recipes were selected to balance authenticity and ease of preparation. Wherever possible the recipes use easy-to-find ingredients and familiar cooking techniques. Recipes are presented with the list of ingredients first, followed by the directions in a numbered procedure list. Recipes that use hot oil and require adult supervision carry a note preceding the ingredients list. Likewise, recipes that feature raw meat or fish in the final dish also carry instructions, which precede the ingredients list.

All entries feature books and Web sites, which will support further study of the foods, recipes, and mealtime customs of the country or group being studied.

A complete glossary of cooking terms used in the entries, from allspice to zest, is included at the front of each volume. A bibliography is included near the back of each volume.

The body of each country's profile is arranged in seven numbered headings as follows:

1 Geographic Setting and Environment

Location, fertile/non-fertile areas, climate (temperature and rainfall), total area, and topography (including major rivers, bodies of water, deserts, and mountains), are discussed. Various plants (including crops) and animals may also be mentioned. The current state of the environment and the role agriculture plays in the country's economy are also covered here.

2 History and Food

The influences of early cultures, outside influences (such as explorers and colonists), and the origins of staple foods and preparation techniques are discussed. Historical dietary influences between various ethnic or religious groups may also be discussed.

3 Foods of the Country or Culture

Foods and beverages that comprise the staples of the country's daily diet, including national dishes, are presented. Foods are identified by social class and ethnic group, where applicable. May also discuss differences between rural and urban mealtime practices.

4 Food for Religious and Holiday Celebrations

Discusses dietary guidelines, restrictions, and customs for national secular and religious holidays, both in food and food preparation. Origins of holiday traditions may also be discussed. Traditional holiday menus for many holidays are presented.

5 Mealtime Customs

Customs related to consumption of food at home, at restaurants, and from street vendors; entertainment of guests for a meal; number and typical times of meals; and typical school lunches and favorite snacks are discussed.

6 Politics, Economics, and Nutrition

Statistics from international organizations, including the United Nations, the World Bank, and the World Food Programme, are presented. Discussion of the health status of the population, with a focus on nutrition and obesity rates of the nation's children, are presented. Food laws and current dietary issues are discussed, where applicable.

7 Further Study

Books and Web sites are listed alphabetically. Web sites were selected based on the authority of the hosting agency and accessibility and appropriateness for student researchers. Each Web site citation lists when the site was last accessed. A few entries include listings of feature films notable for the role food and/or dining played in the story.

Each volume contains a cumulative index that provides easy access to the recipes by title and menu category (appetizers, beverages, bread,

Reader's Guide

soup, main dish, side dish, snacks, vegetables, cookies and sweets, and desserts).

Acknowledgments

Special acknowledgement goes to the many contributors who created the first and second editions of *Junior Worldmark Encyclopedia of Foods and Recipes of the World*.

Sources

Due to the broad scope of this encyclopedia, many sources were consulted in compiling the descriptions and recipes presented in these volumes. Of great importance were cookbooks, as well as books dedicated to the foods of a specific nation or culture group. Travel guides, where food specialties are often described for a country, were instrumental in the initial research for each entry. Cooking and lifestyle magazines, newspaper articles, and interviews with subject-matter experts and restaurateurs were also utilized. Publications of the World Bank and United Nations provided up-to-date statistics on the overall health and nutritional status of the world's children.

Advisers to the First Edition

The following persons served as advisers to the editors and contributors of the first edition of this work. The advisers were consulted in the early planning stages, and their input was invaluable in shaping the content and structure of this encyclopedia. Their insights, opinions, and suggestions led to many enhancements and improvements in the presentation of the material.

> Elaine Fort Weischedel, Franklin Public Library, Franklin, Massachusetts
>
> Linda Wadleigh, Media Specialist, Oconee County Middle School, Watkinsville, Georgia
>
> Mary Mueller, Librarian, Rolla Junior High School, Rolla, Missouri
>
> Susan A. Swain, Cuyahoga County Public Library, Ohio

Comments and Suggestions

We welcome your comments on the *Junior Worldmark Encyclopedia of Foods and Recipes of the World*, 2nd Edition. Please write to: Editors, *Junior Worldmark Encyclopedia of Foods and Recipes of the World*, 2nd Edition, U•X•L, 27500 Drake Road, Farmington Hills, MI 48331-3535; call toll-free: 800-347-4253; or send e-mail via http://www.gale.com.

Measurements and Conversions

In *Junior Worldmark Encyclopedia of Foods and Recipes of the World*, 2nd Edition, measurements are provided in standard U.S. units of measurement. The tables and conversions below are provided to help the user understand measurements typically used in cooking. To convert quantities and cooking temperatures to metric units, use these equivalents.

Note: The system used in the United Kingdom, referred to as UK or British, is not described here and is not referred to in this work, but educated readers may encounter this system in their research. The British cup is 10 ounces, while the U.S. cup is 8 ounces; the British teaspoon and tablespoon are also slightly larger than those in the United States.

U.S. measurement equivalents

Pinch is less than a teaspoon.
Dash is a few drops or one or two shakes of a shaker.
3 teaspoons = 1 tablespoon
2 tablespoons = 1 liquid ounce
4 tablespoons = ¼ cup
8 tablespoons = ½ cup
16 tablespoons = 1 cup
2 cups = 1 pint
2 pints = 1 quart
4 cups = 1 quart
4 quarts = 1 gallon

Liquid measurement conversions from U.S. to metric

1 teaspoon = 5 milliliters
1 tablespoon = 15 milliliters
1 U.S. cup = about ¼ liter (0.237 liters)
1 U.S. pint = about ½ liter (0.473 liters)
1 U.S. quart = about 1 liter (1.101 liters)

Solid measurement conversions from U.S. to metric

1 U.S. ounce = 30 grams
1 U.S. pound = 454 grams
Butter: 7 tablespoons = about 100 grams
Flour: 11 tablespoons = about 100 grams
Sugar: 11 tablespoons = about 100 grams

Oven temperatures

Fahrenheit equals Centigrade (Celsius)
250°F = 121°C
300°F = 150°C
325°F = 164°C
350°F = 177°C
375°F = 191°C
400°F = 205°C
425°F = 219°C
450°F = 232°C
500°F = 260°C

Getting Started with Cooking

Cooking is easier and the results are better if you take some time to learn about techniques, ingredients, and basic equipment.

Techniques

There are three important rules to follow when using any recipe:

Be clean. Always start with very clean hands and very clean utensils. Keep your hair tied back or wear a bandana.

Keep your food safe. Don't leave foods that can spoil out longer than absolutely necessary. Use the refrigerator, or pack your food with ice in a cooler if it will be cooked or eaten away from home. Marinate ingredients in the refrigerator. Make sure to cook beef, chicken, and other meats thoroughly.

Keep yourself safe. Always have an adult help when using the stove, especially when a recipe involves hot oil. Never try to do something else while food is cooking. Keep burners and the oven turned off when not in use.

In addition to these rules, here are some helpful tips.

Read through the recipe before starting to cook.

Write down the list of ingredients. Check to be sure you have everything you need. Make a grocery list and purchase anything you need before beginning to prepare the recipe.

Get out all the utensils you will need for the recipe.

Assemble all the ingredients.

Defrost frozen ingredients, such as puff pastry, in advance.

Wash up as you go to keep the cooking area tidy and to prevent foods and ingredients from drying and sticking to the utensils.

If food burns in the pan, fill the pan with cold water. Add a tablespoon of baking soda and heat gently. This will help to loosen the stuck-on food.

If you follow these rules and helpful tips—and use common sense and ask for help and

Getting Started with Cooking

advice when you don't understand something—cooking will be a fun activity to enjoy alone or with friends.

The basic techniques used in the recipes in *Junior Worldmark Encyclopedia of Foods and Recipes of the World,* 2nd Edition, are described briefly below.

Baking. To cook in the oven in dry heat. Cakes and breads are baked. Casseroles are also baked. When meat is prepared in the oven, cooks may use the term "roasting" instead of baking.

Basting. To keep foods moist while cooking. Basting is done by spooning or brushing liquids, such as juices from the cooking pan, a marinade, or melted butter, over the food that is being cooked.

Beating. To mix ingredients together using a brisk stirring motion. Beating is often done using an electric mixer.

Boiling. To heat a liquid until bubbles appear on its surface. Many recipes ask that you bring the liquid to a boil and then lower the heat to simmer. Simmering is when the surface of the liquid is just moving slightly, with just a few bubbles now and then around the edges of the liquid.

Chopping and cutting. To prepare food for cooking by making the pieces smaller. **To chop,** cut the food in half, then quarters, and continue cutting until the cutting board is covered with smaller pieces of the food. Arrange them in a single layer and hold the top of the chopping knife blade with both hands. Bring the knife straight up and down through the food. Turn the cutting board to cut in different directions. **To dice,** cut the food first into slices, and then cut a grid pattern to make small cubes of the food to be cooked. **To slice,** set the food on a cutting board and press the knife straight down to remove a thin section.

Dusting with flour. Sprinkle a light coating of flour over a surface. A sifter or sieve may be used, or flour may be sprinkled using just your fingers.

Folding. To stir very gently to mix together a light liquid and a heavier liquid. Folding is done with a rubber spatula, using a motion that cuts through and turns over the two liquids.

Greasing or buttering a baking dish or cookie sheet. To smear the surfaces with butter or shortening (or sometimes to spray with nonstick cooking spray) to prevent the food from sticking during cooking.

Kneading. Working with dough to prepare it to rise. First dust the surface (countertop or cutting board) with flour. Press the dough out into a flattened ball. Fold the ball in half, press down, turn the dough ball one-quarter turn, and fold and press again. Repeat these steps, usually for 5 to 10 minutes.

Marinating. Soaking an ingredient, usually meat, poultry, or fish, in a flavorful mixture. Marinating may be done to introduce new flavors to the ingredient, to tenderize the ingredient, or to change the ingredient in some way. Marinating should be done in the refrigerator.

Separating eggs. To divide an egg into two parts, the white and the yolk. This is done by cracking the egg over a bowl and then carefully allowing the white to drip into the bowl. The yolk is transferred back and forth between the two shell halves as the whites drip down. There must be no yolk, not even a speck, in the white if the whites are to be used in a recipe. The yolk keeps the whites from beating well.

Turning out. To remove from the pan or bowl.

Ingredients

A trip to the grocery store can be overwhelming if you don't have a good shopping list. Cooking foods from other countries and cultures may require that you shop for unfamiliar ingredients, so a list is even more important.

Sources for Ingredients

Most of the ingredients used in the recipes in *Junior Worldmark Encyclopedia of Foods and Recipes of the World*, 2nd Edition, are available in large supermarkets. If you have trouble finding an ingredient, you will need to be creative in investigating the possibilities in your area. The editors are not recommending or endorsing any specific markets or mail order sources, but offer these ideas to help you locate the items you may need.

Ethnic grocery stores: Consult the "Grocers" section of the yellow pages of your area's telephone book or online. If the stores are listed by ethnic group, try looking under the country name or the region (such as Africa, the Middle East, or Asia) to find a store that might carry what you need.

Ethnic restaurants: Ethnic restaurants may serve the dish you want to prepare, and the staff there will probably be willing to help you find the ingredients you need. They may even be willing to sell you a small order of the hard-to-find item.

Local library: Some libraries have departments with books in other languages. The reference librarians working there are usually familiar with the ethnic neighborhoods in your city or area, since they are often interacting with the residents there.

Regional or city magazine: Advertisements or festival listings in your area's magazine may lead you to sources of specialty food items.

Internet and mail order: If you have time to wait for ingredients to be shipped to you, the Internet may lead you to a grocery or specialty market that will sell you what you need and ship it to you.

Basic Equipment

The recipes in *Junior Worldmark Encyclopedia of Foods and Recipes of the World*, 2nd Edition, typically require that you have these basic items:

Baking pans. Many recipes require specific baking pans, such as an 8-inch square baking pan, round cake pan, 9-inch by 13-inch baking pan, or cookie sheet. Make sure you have the pan called for in the recipe before beginning.

Knives. Knives for cutting must be sharp to do the job properly. It is a good idea to get an adult's help with cutting and chopping.

Measuring cups. Measuring cups for dry ingredients are the kind that nest inside each other in a stack. To measure liquids, cooks use a clear glass or plastic measuring cup with lines drawn on the side to indicate the measurements.

Measuring spoons. Measuring spoons are used to measure both liquids and dry ingredients. It is important to use spoons made for measuring ingredients, and not teaspoons and tablespoons used for eating and serving food.

Potholders. A potholder or oven mitt is important to use when placing dishes or pans into the oven. These must be used when removing a hot dish or pan from the oven.

Getting Started with Cooking

Saucepans and pots. These round pans are taller. They are generally used for cooking dishes that have more liquid and for boiling or steaming vegetables.

Skillets and frying pans. These pans are shallow, round pans with long handles. They are used to cook things on top of a burner, especially things that are cooked first on one side, and then turned to cook on the other side.

Work surface. A very clean countertop or cutting board must be available to prepare most dishes.

Glossary

A

Allspice: A spice derived from the round, dried berry-like fruit of a West Indian allspice tree. The mildly pungent taste resembles cinnamon, nutmeg, and cloves.

Anise seed: A licorice-flavored seed of the Mediterranean anise herb. It is used as an ingredient in various foods, particularly cookies, cakes, and candies.

Arugula: An aromatic salad green with a peppery taste. It is popularly used in Italian cuisine.

B

Baguette: A long and narrow loaf of French bread that is often used for sandwiches or as an accompaniment to a variety of dishes.

Baking soda: A fine, white powder compound often used as an ingredient in such recipes as breads and cakes to help them rise and increase in volume.

Basil: An aromatic herb cultivated for its leaves. It is eaten fresh or dried and is most frequently used in tomato sauces or served with mozzarella cheese. The sweet basil variety is most common.

Baste: To moisten food periodically with liquid, such as broth or melted butter, while cooking. Basting helps add flavor to food and prevents it from drying out.

Glossary

Bay leaf: A pungent, spicy leaf used in a variety of cuisines, including meats, vegetables, and soups. It is most often used in combination with other herbs, such as thyme and parsley. Bay leaves should always be removed before a dish is served because they should not be eaten.

Blini: A Russian pancake made of buckwheat flour and yeast. It is commonly served with caviar and sour cream.

Bouillon: A clear, thin broth made by simmering meat, typically beef or chicken, or vegetables in water with seasonings.

Braise: To cook meat or vegetables by browning in fat, then simmering in a small quantity of liquid in a covered container.

Bratwurst: A small pork sausage popular in German cuisine.

Brisket: A cut of meat, usually beef, from the breast of an animal. It typically needs longer to cook to become tender than other meats.

Broil: To cook by direct exposure to heat, such as over a fire or under a grill.

C

Canapé: A cracker or a small, thin piece of bread or toast spread with cheese, meat, or relish and served as an appetizer.

Caraway seed: The pungent seed from the caraway herb used as a flavoring and seasoning in various foods, including desserts, breads, and liquors.

Cassava: A tropical, tuberous plant widely used in African, Latin American, and Asian cuisines. It is most commonly used to make starch-based foods such as bread, tapioca, and pastes. It is also known as manioc or yucca (in Spanish, yuca).

Charcoal brazier: A metal pan for holding burning coals or charcoal over which food is grilled.

Cheesecloth: A coarse or fine woven cotton cloth that is often used for straining liquids, mulling spices, and lining molds.

Chili: A spicy pepper of varying size and color. It is most frequently used to add a fiery flavor to foods.

Cilantro: A lively, pungent herb widely used in Asian, Caribbean, and Latin American cuisines as a seasoning or garnish. It is also known as coriander.

Glossary

Citron: A large, lemon-like fruit with a thick aromatic rind, which is commonly candied and used in desserts such as fruitcakes.

Clove: A fragrant spice made from the dried, woody flower bud of an evergreen tree native to tropical climates. In Indonesia, where cloves are grown, cigarettes are made from the crushed buds. Cloves also describe a single bud of garlic, shallot, or other bulb root vegetable.

Colander: A simple piece of kitchen equipment that resembles a metal or plastic bowl with holes in it. It is used to drain foods, such as pasta or vegetables, that have been cooked in boiling water (or other liquid).

Coriander: See Cilantro.

Cream of tartar: A fine, white powder that is added to candy and frosting mixtures for a creamier consistency, or added to egg whites before being beaten to improve stability and volume.

Cumin: An herb cultivated for its aromatic, nut-flavored seeds. It is often used to make curries or chili powders.

Currant: A raisin-like colored berry that is commonly used in jams and jellies, syrups, desserts, and beverages.

D

Daikon: A large, Asian radish with a sweet flavor. It is often used in raw salads, stir-fry, or shredded for a garnish.

Dashi: A clear soup stock, usually with a fish or vegetable base. It is frequently used in Japanese cooking.

Double boiler: Two pots formed to fit together, with one sitting part of the way inside the other, with a single lid fitting on both pans. The lower pot is used to hold simmering water, which gently heats the mixture in the upper pot. Foods such as custards, chocolate, and various sauces are commonly cooked this way.

F

Fermentation: A process by which a food goes through a chemical change caused by enzymes produced from bacteria, microorganisms, or yeasts. It alters the appearance and/or flavor of foods and beverages such as beer, wine, cheese, and yogurt.

Glossary

G

Garlic: A pungent, onion-like bulb consisting of sections called cloves. The cloves are often minced or crushed and used to add sharp flavor to dishes.

Garnish: To enhance in appearance and/or flavor by adding decorative touches, such as herbs sprinkled on top of soup.

Gingerroot: A gnarled and bumpy root with a peppery sweet flavor and a spicy aroma. Asian and Indian cuisines typically use freshly ground or grated ginger as a seasoning, while Americans and Europeans tend to use ground ginger in recipes, particularly in baked goods.

H

Haggis: Traditional Scottish dish made from sheep organs (including heart, liver, lungs, and intestines), oatmeal, and spices.

Harissa: Spicy condiment made from hot red peppers used in the cooking of North Africa and elsewhere.

Hoisin sauce: A thick, sweet and spicy reddish-brown sauce commonly used in Chinese cuisine. It is made of soybeans, peppers, garlic, and a variety of spices. Once commonly called Peking sauce, it was named for the city of Peking, now known as Beijing, the capital of China.

J

Jalapeño: A very hot pepper typically used to add pungent flavor. It is often used as a garnish or added to sauces.

Julienne: Foods that have been cut into thin strips, such as potatoes.

K

Kale: Although a member of the cabbage family, the large leaves do not form a head. Its mild cabbage flavor is suitable in a variety of salads.

Kashrut: See Kosher.

Glossary

Knead: To mix or shape by squeezing, pressing, or rolling mixture with hands. Bread is typically prepared this way before baking.

Kosher: Following, or observing, the detailed dietary laws, known as the laws of Kashrut. These laws are based on text from the Old Testament of the Bible. Food that follows these restrictions is called kosher food.

L

Leek: As part of the onion family, it has a mild and more subtle flavor than garlic or onion. It is commonly used in salads and soups.

Lemongrass: Long, thin, grayish-green leaves that have a sour lemon flavor and smell. Popular in Asian (particularly Thai) cuisine, it is commonly used to flavor tea, soups, and other dishes.

M

Mace: The outer membrane of the nutmeg seed. It is typically sold ground and is used to flavor a variety of dishes.

Manioc: See Cassava.

Marinate: To soak a food, such as meat or vegetables, in a seasoned liquid for added flavor or to tenderize.

Marzipan: A sweet mixture of almond paste, sugar, and egg whites, often molded into various shapes.

Matzo meal: Ground unleavened (flat), brittle bread often used to thicken soups or for breading foods to be fried. It is widely popular in Jewish cuisine.

Mince: To cut or chop into very small pieces, typically used to prepare foods with strong flavors, such as garlic and onion.

Mint: A pungent herb that adds a refreshing and sweet flavor to a variety of dishes, either dried and ground or fresh. Peppermint and spearmint are the most common of over 30 varieties.

Miso: A thick, fermented paste made of cooked soybeans, salt, and rice or barley. A basic flavoring of Japanese cuisine, it is frequently used in making soups and sauces.

Glossary

Molasses: A thick syrup produced in refining raw sugar or sugar beets. It ranges from light to dark brown in color and is often used as a pancake or waffle topping or a flavoring, such as in gingerbread.

N

Napa: A round head of cabbage with thin, crisp, and mild-flavored leaves. It is often eaten raw or sautéed. Also known as Chinese cabbage.

O

Okra: Green pods that are often used to thicken liquids and to add flavor. It is commonly used throughout the southern United States in such popular dishes as gumbo, a thick stew.

Olive oil: Oil derived from the pressing of olives. Varieties are ranked on acidity. Extra virgin olive oil is the least acidic and is typically the most expensive of the varieties.

Oregano: A strong, pungent herb commonly used in tomato-based dishes, such as pizza.

P

Parchment paper: A heavy, grease- and moisture-resistant paper used to line baking pans, wrap foods, and make disposable pastry bags.

Parsley: A slightly peppery, fresh-flavored herb that is most commonly used as a flavoring or garnish in a wide variety of dishes. There are over 30 varieties of parsley.

Pâté: A seasoned meat paste made from finely minced meat, liver, or poultry.

Peking sauce: See Hoisin sauce.

Persimmon: Edible only when fully ripe, the fruit resembles a plum in appearance. It has a creamy texture with a sweet flavor and is often eaten whole or used in such foods as puddings and various baked goods.

Pimiento: A sweet pepper that is often finely diced and used to stuff green olives.

Glossary

Pinto bean: A type of mottled kidney bean that is commonly grown in the southwesten United States and in Spanish-speaking countries, including Mexico. It is often used to make refried beans.

Pintxos: A way of serving food that originated in the Basque region of Spain. Similar to tapas (see Tapas), pintxos are made with one or two slices of bread topped with a tasty food and held together by a toothpick.

Pistachio nut: Commonly grown in California, the Mediterranean, and the Middle East, the mild-flavored green nut is enclosed in a hard, tan shell. They are either eaten directly out of the shell or are used to flavor a variety of dishes.

Plantain: A tropical fruit widely eaten in African, Caribbean, and South American cuisines. Plantains may be prepared by frying, boiling, steaming, or baking. Although closely resembling a banana, it turns black when ripe and may be eaten at any stage of ripeness.

Prosciutto: A seasoned, salt-cured, and air-dried ham. Eaten either cooked or raw, it is often thinly sliced and eaten with a variety of foods such as melons, figs, vegetables, or pasta.

R

Ramekin: A small individual baking dish typically made of porcelain or earthenware.

Ramen: A Japanese dish of noodles in a broth, often garnished with pieces of meat and vegetables. An instant-style of this noodle dish is sold in individual servings in supermarkets.

S

Saffron: A golden-colored spice used to add flavor or color to a wide variety of dishes. It is very expensive, so it is typically used sparingly.

Sage: A native Mediterranean pungent herb with grayish-green leaves. Its slightly bitter and light mint taste is commonly used in dishes containing pork, cheese, and beans, and in poultry and game stuffings.

Sake: A Japanese wine typically served warm in porcelain cups. The sweet, low-level alcohol sake is derived from fermented rice and does not require aging.

Glossary

Saltimbocca: Finely sliced veal sprinkled with sage and topped with a thin slice of prosciutto. It is sautéed in butter, then braised in white wine.

Sashimi: A Japanese dish consisting of very thin bite-size slices of fresh raw fish, traditionally served with soy sauce, wasabi, gingerroot, or daikon radish.

Sauerkraut: Shredded cabbage fermented with salt and spices. It was first eaten by the Chinese, but quickly became a European (particularly German) favorite. It is popular in casseroles, as a side dish, and in sandwiches.

Sauté: To lightly fry in an open, shallow pan. Onions are frequently sautéed.

Scallion: As part of the onion family, it closely resembles a young onion before the development of the white bulb, although its flavor is slightly milder. It is often chopped and used in salads and soups.

Shallot: A member of the onion family that closely resembles cloves of garlic, covered in a thin, paper-like skin. It has a mild onion flavor and is used in a variety of dishes for flavoring.

Shortening, vegetable: A solid fat made from vegetable oils such as soybean or cottonseed oils. It is flavorless and is used in baking and cooking.

Sieve: A typically round device used to strain liquid or particles of food through small holes in the sieve. It is also known as a strainer.

Simmer: To gently cook food in a liquid at a temperature low enough to create only small bubbles that break at the liquid's surface. Simmering is gentler than boiling the liquid.

Skewer: A long, thin, pointed rod made of metal or wood used to hold meat and/or vegetables in place while cooking. They are most commonly used to make shish kebabs.

Soybean: A generally bland-flavored bean widely recognized for its nutritive value. It is often cooked or dried to be used in salads, soups, or casseroles, as well as in such products as soy sauce, soybean oil, and tofu.

Star anise: A pungent and slightly bitter tasting seed that is often ground and used to flavor teas in Asian cuisines. In Western cultures it is more often added to liquors and baked goods (such as pastries).

Glossary

Steam: A method of cooking in which food (often vegetables) is placed on a rack or in a special basket over boiling or simmering water in a covered pan. Steaming helps to retain the flavor, shape and texture, and vitamins and minerals of food better than boiling.

Stir-fry: A dish prepared by quickly frying small pieces of food in a large pan over very high heat while constantly and briskly stirring the ingredients until cooked. Stir-fry, which is often prepared in a special dish called a wok, is most associated with Asian cuisines.

Stock: The strained liquid that is the result of cooking vegetables, meat, or fish and other seasoning ingredients in water. Most soups begin with stock before other ingredients are added.

Sushi: Fish and vegetables prepared in bite-sized portions with rice. Fish is usually raw, but may be cooked. (Shrimp is typically cooked for sushi.)

T

Tagine: A dish common to Algeria, Morocco, and Tunisia in North Africa. The term describes both the dish, a rich, spicy stew, and the earthenware pot with a cone-shaped lid in which it is cooked.

Tamarind: A brown fruit that is about 5-inches long and shaped like a large, flat green bean. Inside the brittle shell, the fruit contains large seeds surrounded by juicy, acidic pulp. The pulp, sweetened, is used to make juices and syrups.

Tapas: Small portions of food, either hot or cold, most commonly served to accompany a drink in Spanish and Latin American bars and restaurants.

Tarragon: An aromatic herb known for its anise-like (licorice) flavor. It is widely used in classic French dishes including chicken, fish, vegetables, and sauces such as béarnaise.

Tempura: Batter-dipped, deep-fried pieces of fish or vegetables, originally a Japanese specialty. It is most often accompanied by soy sauce.

Thyme: A pungent herb whose flavor is often described as a combination of mint and lemon. It is most commonly associated with French cooking. Thyme is used to flavor a variety of dishes, including meats, vegetables, fish, poultry, soups, and sauces.

Glossary

Tofu: Ground, cooked soybeans that are pressed into blocks resembling cheese. Its bland and slightly nutty flavor is popular in Asia, particularly Japan, but is increasing in popularity throughout the United States due to its nutritive value. It may be used in soups, stir-fry, and casseroles, or eaten alone.

Turmeric: A spice, made from the root of a plant in the ginger family. The root is dried and ground into a powder for use in cooking. Turmeric gives dishes a deep yellow color.

V

Vinegar: Clear liquid made by bacterial activity that converts fermented liquids such as wine, beer, or cider into a weak solution of acetic acid, giving it a very sour taste. It can also be derived from a variety of fermented foods such as apples, rice, and barley and is most popular in Asian cuisines in sauces and marinades.

Vinegar, rice: Vinegar derived from fermented rice that is often used in sweet-and-sour dishes, as a salad dressing, or as a table condiment. It is generally milder than other types of vinegar.

W

Water bath: A small baking pan or casserole dish placed in a larger roasting pan or cake pan to which water has been added. The small pan sits in a "bath" of water in the oven while baking. The water tempers the oven's heat, preventing the contents of the small pan from cooking too quickly.

Whisk: A kitchen utensil consisting of several looped wires, typically made of stainless steel, that are joined together at a handle. It is used to whip ingredients, such as eggs, creams, and sauces.

Wok: A large, round metal pan used for stir-fry, braising, and deep-frying, most often for Asian dishes. Most woks are made of steel or sheet iron and have two large handles on each side. It is used directly on the burner, similar to a saucepan.

Worcestershire sauce: A thin, dark sauce used to season meats, soups, and vegetable juices, most often as a condiment. Garlic, soy sauce, vinegar, molasses, and tamarind are just a few ingredients that may be included.

Y

Yucca: See Cassava.

Z

Zest: The thin outer layer of the rind of a citrus fruit, particularly of an orange, grapefruit, lemon, or lime. The zest is the colorful layer of the rind, while the pith is the white portion. Most commonly used for its acidic, aromatic oils to season foods, zest can also be candied or used in pastries or desserts. The citrus fruit should be washed before the rind is used in recipes.

Algeria

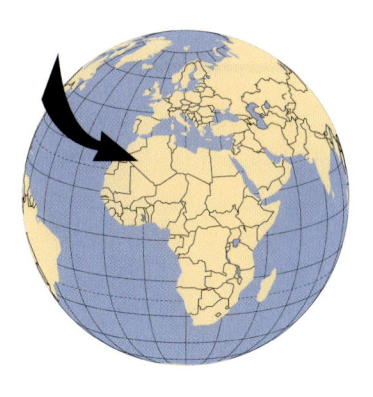

- Saffron and Raisin Couscous 3
- Smen Butter 3
- Fresh Sweet Dates 4
- Etzai (Mint Tea) 4
- Sahlab 5
- Banadura Salata B'Kizbara 5
- Sweet Couscous Dessert 6
- Stuffed Dates and Walnuts 6
- Algerian Cooked Carrot Salad 7
- M'hajeb 8
- Chlada Fakya (Fruit Medley) 8
- Cucumber & Yogurt Soup 9

❶ Geographic Setting and Environment

Algeria is located in North Africa on the Mediterranean Sea. The fertile and mountainous northern region is home to the olive tree, cork oak, and vast evergreen forests where boars and jackals roam. Fig, agave, and various palm trees grow in the warmer areas. The grape vine is native to the coastal plain. Central Algeria consists of high plateaus that contain salt marshes and dry or shallow salt lakes. The land becomes more arid (dry) the farther south one travels, eventually becoming the Sahara Desert. Roughly 80 percent of the country is desert, where vegetation is sparse. Camels are widely used to carry people and goods in this arid region. Jackals, rabbits, scorpions, and snakes are a few of the animals that also occupy the desert.

In the coastal region, the climate is typical of the Mediterranean region—pleasant nearly year round, with winter temperatures rarely falling below freezing (32°F/0°C). Rainfall is also abundant along the coast. Farther inland, higher altitudes receive considerable frost and occasional snow. Little or no rainfall occurs throughout the summer months in this region. In the Sahara Desert, rainfall is unpredictable and unevenly distributed.

Restaurants and cafés are found in the major cities—Algiers (the capital), Oran, and Constantine. In Algiers and Oran, food stands line the streets and offer brochettes, which are skewers of almost any kind of food imaginable. Popular brochettes are made of grilled lamb, kidneys, liver, or vegetables. Many food vendors and shops are located in the casbah in Algiers. Arabic for fortress, casbah refers to the ancient

Algeria

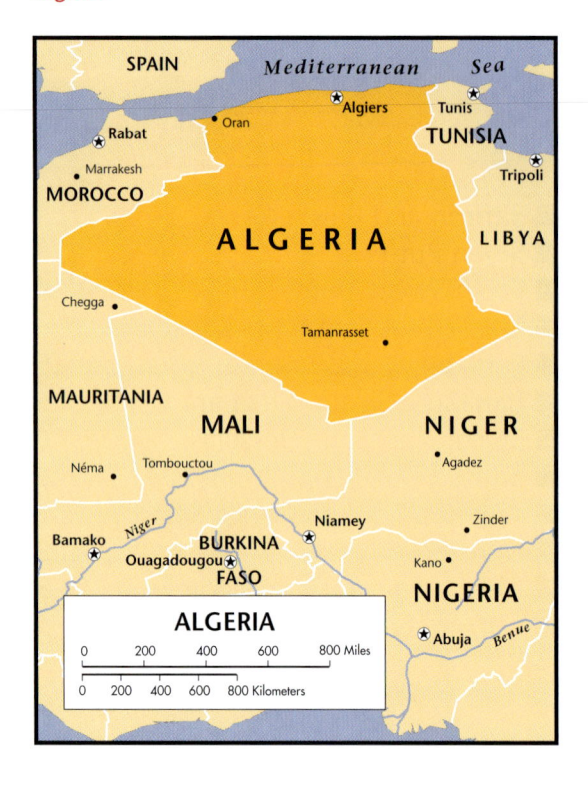

walled Islamic center of a city, especially in North Africa. The term is most often used to describe the walled section of Algiers. The casbah of Algiers has been designated as a World Heritage Site by UNESCO. However, the casbah's walls in Algiers are deteriorating and almost one-third of its buildings have collapsed.

2 History and Food

Algerian cuisine traces its roots to various countries and ancient cultures that once ruled, visited, or traded with the country. Berber tribesmen were one of the country's earliest inhabitants. Their arrival may extend as far back as 30,000 BC. Berbers introduced the cultivation of wheat. They also introduced such foods as *smen* (aged, cooked butter) and fruits, including dates. The introduction of semolina wheat by the Carthaginians (who occupied much of northern Africa) led the Berbers to first create couscous, Algeria's national dish. The Romans, who eventually took over Algeria, also grew various grains.

Muslim Arabs invaded Algeria in the 600s, bringing exotic spices such as saffron, nutmeg, ginger, cloves, and cinnamon from the Spice Islands of eastern Indonesia. They also introduced the Islamic religion to the Berbers. Islam continues to influence almost every aspect of an Algerian's life, including diet.

Algerians and their neighbors in Morocco and Tunisia enjoy spicy stews, called *tagines*. The dish is named for the special pot used in its preparation. The tagine pot consists of two parts, both made from heavy clay. The base of the pot is round and shallow. The top is a cone-shaped cover, which collects moisture during cooking. The moisture condenses and drips back into the stew, keeping it moist. When the stew is ready to serve, the top is removed and the base is carried to the table and used as a serving dish.

Olives (and olive oil) and fruits such as oranges, plums, and peaches were brought across the Mediterranean from Spain during an invasion in the 1500s. Sweet pastries from the Turkish Ottomans and tea from European traders also made their way into Algerian cuisine around this time.

In the early 1800s, Algerians were driven off their own lands and forced to surrender their crops and farmland to the French. The French introduced their diet and culture to the Algerians. Loaves of French bread were available in Algerian markets. French-style sidewalk cafés were established in Algerian cities. This French legacy remains evident in Algerian culture. In fact, Algeria's second language is French. (Arabic is the official language.)

Saffron and Raisin Couscous with Fresh Mint

Ingredients
2 cups water
½ teaspoon saffron
1 teaspoon extra virgin olive oil
½ teaspoon salt
2 cups couscous
¼ cup raisins
3 tablespoons fresh mint, chopped

Directions
1. In a saucepan, bring the 2 cups of water to a boil and add the saffron.
2. Return the pan to the heat, return to a boil, and mix in the olive oil, salt, couscous, and raisins.
3. Remove from the heat, cover, and let stand for 30 minutes.
4. Top with the fresh mint.

Makes 8 servings.

Tomatoes, potatoes, zucchini, and chilies, significant to Algerian local cuisine, were brought over from the New World.

Algeria ranks as one of the top 10 importers of grains, such as wheat and barley, in the world. Grain harvests in Algeria often fail because of lack of rain. Algeria experiences periods of drought, such as one in 2011, which cause crops to suffer. The government in the 2010s was looking for ways for the country to become less dependent on imported food.

However, during 2011, citizens in Tunisia and other neighboring Arab countries began to protest against their governments. The Algerian government wanted to avoid social unrest. To be sure that the population had enough food, the government increased food imports by almost 60 percent for the first half of 2011 compared to the same period in 2010.

Knowing that the country would need plenty of food for the holy month of Ramadan (August 11 to September 10, 2011), the government also arranged to almost double the amount of cereals, flour, and semolina during the first half of 2011. Reducing the country's dependence on imported food remained a long-term goal.

Smen Butter

Ingredients
2 cups (4 sticks) unsalted butter
2 teaspoons dried oregano leaves
1 tablespoon sea salt

Directions
1. In a saucepan, melt the butter over low heat.
2. Wrap the oregano in a piece of cheesecloth, tie, and set in the butter.
3. Keep the butter on low heat until it separates into a clear liquid and a milky mixture.
4. Strain the clear liquid into a warm glass jar.
5. Discard the milky mixture and the oregano.
6. Add the salt to the butter and mix until dissolved.
7. Cover the glass jar and let the butter sit until it turns into a thicker consistency. The butter is best, and most pungent, if it sits for about a week. Smen may be used in cooking, or spread on bread.

Serves 8.

❸ Foods of the Algerians

Traditional Algerian cuisine is a colorful combination of Berber, Turkish, French, and Arab tastes. It can be either extremely mild or packed with flavorful seasonings. Ginger, saffron, onion,

Algeria

garlic, coriander, cumin, cinnamon, parsley, and mint are essential in any Algerian pantry.

Couscous, the national dish, is actually a type of pasta, but it is often mistakenly considered a grain. The couscous pasta dough is a mixture of water and coarse, grainy semolina wheat particles. The dough is then crumbled through a sieve to create tiny pellets.

Algerians prefer lamb, chicken, or fish to be placed on a bed of warm couscous, along with cooked vegetables such as carrots, chickpeas, and tomatoes, and spicy stews. Couscous can also be used in desserts by adding a variety of ingredients, such as cinnamon, nutmeg, dates, and figs.

Fresh Sweet Dates

Ingredients

1 pound fresh dates
½ cup butter
¾ cup flour
1 teaspoon cardamom, ground

Directions

1. Remove the pits from the dates and arrange in 6 individual serving dishes.
2. Melt the butter in a heavy saucepan and stir in the flour.
3. Cook over medium heat, stirring constantly, until the flour turns golden brown. Be careful not to burn.
4. Remove the flour mixture from the heat and stir in the cardamom.
5. Remove from heat and allow to cool slightly, stirring occasionally.
6. While still warm, pour over the warm dates and allow to cool to room temperature before serving.

Makes 6 servings.

Etzai (Mint Tea)

Ingredients

1½ tablespoons green tea
Boiling water
3 tablespoons sugar, or to taste
Handful of fresh mint leaves

Directions

1. Put the tea in a teapot.
2. Pour in a cupful of boiling water, then immediately pour it out again. This is to wash the leaves.
3. Add the sugar to taste, then the mint leaves.
4. Pour in boiling water 12 inches away from the top (this oxygenates the tea) and stir well. Be extremely careful not to splash the boiling water.
5. Serve the tea very hot, again pouring it from a height of about 12 inches.

No Algerian meal would be complete without bread, normally a long, French loaf. Similar to Middle Eastern customs, bread is often used to scoop food off a plate or to soak up a spicy sauce or stew. More traditional Berber families usually eat flat, wheat bread.

Fresh or dried dates (shown here) may be used in recipes. Fresh dates are often used in Algerian recipes because they are widely available in the country. Fresh dates are not as sweet as dried dates. © ELIAS JAGUAR/SHUTTERSTOCK.COM.

Sahlab

Ingredients
3 cups (8 ounces each) milk
1 cup sugar
½ cup cornstarch
¾ cup water
¼ cup raisins
¼ cup coconut
¼ cup walnuts or pistachios, chopped
1 teaspoon cinnamon

Directions
1. In a small mixing bowl, dissolve the cornstarch in the water and set aside.
2. In a heavy saucepan, bring the milk to a boil over low to medium heat.
3. As soon as the milk boils, reduce the heat.
4. Stir in the sugar. Allow the milk to simmer until the sugar has dissolved (no more than 1 minute).
5. Slowly pour the cornstarch mixture into the milk, making sure to whisk rapidly to prevent the milk from sticking to the bottom of the saucepan. The milk will gradually thicken.
6. When it reaches the consistency of a thick gravy, remove from heat.
7. Pour sahlab into decorative small bowls, glasses, or mugs.
8. Sprinkle with raisins, coconut, chopped nuts, and cinnamon, if desired.
9. Serve hot.

Makes 6 servings.

Mechoui, a roasted whole lamb cooked on an outdoor spit, is usually prepared when a large group of people gathers together. The animal is seasoned with herb butter so the skin is crispy and the meat inside is tender and juicy. Bread and various dried fruits and vegetables, including dates (whose trees can thrive in the country's Sahara desert), often accompany mechoui.

Fresh mint is the preferred ingredient in mint tea. Fresh mint leaves are best used immediately after being harvested, but they may be stored for up to two days in the refrigerator.
© SKOWRON/SHUTTERSTOCK.COM.

Banadura Salata B'Kizbara (Tomato and Coriander Salad)

Ingredients
½ cup fresh coriander leaves, chopped
1 small hot chili pepper, seeded and finely chopped
5 medium ripe tomatoes, peeled
4 tablespoons fresh lemon juice
¼ cup virgin olive oil
1 teaspoon salt

Directions
1. Slice the peeled tomatoes and place in a bowl.
2. Sprinkle the chopped coriander over the tomatoes.
3. Mix the chopped chili pepper with the lemon juice and 1 teaspoon of salt.
4. Beat the olive oil into the chili-lemon juice mixture.
5. Pour over the tomatoes and coriander.
6. Let rest 15 minutes before serving.

Makes 6 servings.

Algeria

Sweet Couscous Dessert

Ingredients
1 cup plus 2 tablespoons couscous
⅔ cup warm water
⅔ cup fresh dates
⅔ cup ready-to-eat prunes
6 tablespoons butter, melted
¼ cup sugar
1 teaspoon cinnamon, ground
½ teaspoon nutmeg, ground
Rose petals, to decorate (optional)

Directions
1. Place the couscous in a bowl and cover with ⅔ cup warm water.
2. Leave 15 minutes to plump up.
3. Halve each date lengthwise, remove the seed and cut into 4 pieces.
4. Roughly chop the prunes.
5. Fluff up the grains of couscous with a fork, then place in a cheesecloth-lined sieve and steam over simmering water for 15 minutes until hot.
6. Transfer to a bowl and fluff up again with a fork.
7. Add the melted butter, sugar, dates, and prunes.
8. Pile the couscous into a cone shape in a serving dish.
9. Mix the cinnamon and nutmeg together and sprinkle over couscous.
10. Serve decorated with rose petals, if desired.

Makes 4 servings.

Stuffed Dates and Walnuts

Ingredients
12 fresh dates
½ cup ground almonds
2 tablespoons pistachio nuts, very finely chopped
2 tablespoons granulated sugar
Orange flower water (found at specialty stores)
24 walnut halves
Powdered sugar, to decorate

After the pit is removed from a date, pit-sized nuggets of filling fill the cavity to make a stuffed date, which may be served on a dessert tray. Algerian meals are often finished with nuts and fruit. © EPD PHOTOS.

Directions
1. With a sharp knife, make a slit down the length of each date and carefully remove the seed.
2. In a bowl, mix together the ground almonds, chopped pistachio nuts, and granulated sugar.
3. Add enough orange flower water to make a smooth paste.
4. Shape half of the paste into 12 nuggets the size of date seeds and use to stuff the dates.
5. Use the remaining paste to sandwich the walnut halves together in pairs.
6. Sift a little powdered sugar over the stuffed dates and walnuts. Algerians would serve these with rich coffee.

Makes 4 to 6 servings.

Beverages such as mint tea are a favorite in all the countries of North Africa. Tea is usually offered to visiting guests, though coffee flavored with cardamom is another option. With the abundance of fruits year round, fresh juices are plentiful and children tend to favor apricot nectar. *Sharbats*, fruit or nut-flavored milk drinks, are enjoyed by people of all ages. *Sahlab*, a sweet, milky drink, is especially popular. Traditionally, drinks were made with goat milk, although cow milk is now available. *Basbousa* (Egyptian semolina cake), *tamina* (roasted semolina with butter and honey), and sweetened couscous are just a few sweets enjoyed by the Algerians.

4 Food for Religious and Holiday Celebrations

The overwhelming majority of Algerians, about 99 percent, follow the beliefs of Islam, the country's official religion. (Christians and Jews make up 1 percent of the population.)

The Algerian observance of Ramadan, the ninth month of the Islamic year, is the most celebrated of all holidays. During the month-long observance, Muslims are required to fast (avoid consuming food and drink) between sunrise and sunset, although young, growing children and pregnant women may be allowed to eat a small amount. At the end of each day during Ramadan, families join together for a feast, sometimes as late as midnight.

During Ramadan in Algeria, the historic French influence in the country is apparent. The evening meal during Ramadam typically includes loaves of French bread (or wheat bread) and pots of hot mint tea.

Algeria has a number of popular pastries. M'hajeb is a traditional, filled pastry often enjoyed during Ramadan.

The holiday that marks the end of Ramadan, Eid al-Fitr, is celebrated with an important feast. It almost always begins with soup or stew. Lamb or beef is most often served as the main dish, although families living close to the Mediterranean in northern Algeria may enjoy a variety of seafood.

In most Algerian homes, a bowl of fresh fruit is placed on the table at the end of the meal. Traditionally, each person is responsible for peeling and slicing his or her own fruit. However, on special occasions such as Eid al-Fitr, the host will often serve the fruit already peeled, sliced, and flavored (most often with cinnamon and various citrus juices).

Other popular holiday celebrations are Labor Day (May 1) and the anniversary of the revolution over French control (November 1). Two local festivals that are celebrated every spring are the cherry *moussem* (festival) in Tlemcen and the tomato moussem in Adrar.

Algerian Cooked Carrot Salad

Ingredients
1 pound carrots
3 garlic cloves, chopped
Pinch of salt
Pinch of sugar
Lemon juice
¼ teaspoon salt
½ teaspoon cayenne pepper
¼ teaspoon cumin
Parsley, chopped

Directions
1. Scrape the carrots and cut them into four pieces lengthwise.
2. Cook in a little water with garlic and a pinch of salt and sugar for 15 minutes.
3. Drain and chill the carrots.
4. Just before serving, cover with lemon juice, and sprinkle with salt, cayenne pepper, and cumin.
5. Sprinkle with chopped parsley.

Makes 6 servings.

Algeria

M'hajeb

Ingredients
4 onions, chopped
2 tablespoons tomato puree
2 green peppers, chopped
2 tablespoons olive oil, divided
Salt and pepper
4 cups semolina
2 cups plain flour
Water

Directions
1. *Make the pastry filling:* Heat 1 tablespoon olive oil in a frying pan.
2. Add chopped onions and peppers and cook until softened.
3. Add tomato puree, salt, and pepper.
4. Cook for five minutes, or until onions and peppers are very soft.
5. Put filling mixture aside.
6. *Make the pastry:* Mix semolina, flour, and salt.
7. Make a hollow space in the mixture, and add water ¼ cup at a time, until a dough forms.
8. Knead the mixture until it becomes smooth, adding more water as needed.
9. Break the dough apart and roll into golf-ball size pieces.
10. Oil the dough and then, with your hands, flatten the balls into large squares. Make the dough as thin as possible (around ⅛ inch).
11. Place the filling in the center of the dough. Fold in all four sides of the dough to make a square shape, with the filling completely wrapped in the center.
12. Heat 1 tablespoon of olive oil in a frying pan.
13. Carefully lift the pastry and place it into a frying pan.
14. Cook on medium to high heat, until golden brown. Carefully turn and brown the other side. Serve.

Serves 10.

A Typical Holiday Menu

Cucumber and yogurt soup

Stuffed dates and walnuts

Roast stuffed leg of lamb

Tomato and raisin-stuffed eggplant

Potato & chickpea salad

Cooked carrots

Fresh fruit medley

Chlada Fakya (Fresh Fruit Medley)

Ingredients
½ cantaloupe, peeled, seeded, cut into bite-sized pieces
½ honeydew melon, peeled, seeded, cut into bite-sized pieces
1 cup strawberries, cut in half, stemmed, washed
2 bananas, peeled and thinly sliced
5 seedless oranges, peeled and thinly sliced
½ cup orange juice
Juice of 2 lemons
2 tablespoons sugar
1 teaspoon vanilla extract
1 teaspoon cinnamon

Directions
1. In medium serving bowl, carefully toss cantaloupe, honeydew melon, strawberries, bananas, and oranges.
2. In a small bowl, mix orange and lemon juice, sugar, vanilla, and cinnamon, and pour over fruit.
3. Toss gently, then refrigerate until ready to serve (at the end of a holiday feast, for example). Toss again before serving in individual bowls.

Makes 6 servings.

Cucumber & Yogurt Soup

Ingredients
1 large cucumber
2½ cups plain yogurt
2 cloves garlic, crushed
1 lemon rind, finely grated
2 tablespoons fresh mint, chopped
Salt and freshly ground black pepper
⅔ cup ice water
Mint leaves, to garnish

Directions
1. Rinse the cucumber and trim the ends. Do not peel.
2. Grate the cucumber into a bowl.
3. Stir in the yogurt, garlic, lemon rind, and chopped mint.
4. Season well with salt and pepper.
5. Cover the bowl and chill 1 hour.
6. Stir in ⅔ cup ice water. Add more water if the soup seems a little thick.
7. Adjust the seasoning, then pour into chilled soup bowls.
8. Garnish with mint leaves.

Makes 6 servings.

5 Mealtime Customs

Arabs are hospitable and encourage family and friends to share their food. Even an unexpected visitor will be greeted warmly and offered coffee (often flavored with cardamom) while the women and girls of the household prepare the meal. Cooking continues to be considered a woman's duty, as it has been in the past. Historically, recipes and cooking customs were passed down through generations by word of mouth when women gathered together to prepare meals.

All meals (normally three a day) are leisurely and sociable, although there are varying degrees of structure and etiquette (polite behavior). Diners are seated at a low table (*tbla* or *mida*); food is traditionally eaten with the thumb, forefinger, and middle finger of the right hand (the left hand is considered unclean). To use four or five fingers is considered to be a sign of overeating and should be avoided.

The dining atmosphere in a middle-class family may be a bit more elegant. A servant or young family member might visit each individual at the table, offering a bowl of perfumed water to diners for washing their hands before the meal is eaten.

The country's capital, Algiers, and popular coastal towns tend to have a wide variety of restaurants, featuring French, Italian, and Middle Eastern cuisine. In Algiers, the Mediterranean waters provide seafood, and the hustle and bustle of trade brings many different types of foods. In Algerian towns, souks (markets) or street stalls offer take-home products, such as spicy brochettes (kebabs) on French bread for those on the run. With the exception of an occasional fast-food burger, school lunches often consist of such traditional foods as couscous, dried fruit, stews, and sweet fruit drinks.

Southern Algeria is less populated and menus do not include as much seafood. Southern Algerian menus usually begin with either a soup or salad, followed by roast meat (usually lamb or beef) as a main course, with fresh fruit, especially dates, commonly completing the meal.

6 Politics, Economics, and Nutrition

Malnutrition has been one of the principal health problems in Algeria in the late 20th and early 21st centuries. Refugees from the Western

A produce vendor sells vegetables to a customer at a market in Ghardaia, Algeria. © ROBERT HARDING PICTURE LIBRARY LTD/ ALAMY.

Sahara territory in Morocco have lived in camps in northern Algeria since around 1975. The United Nations World Food Programme (WFP) provides food aid to the refugees. During 2011, the WFP distributed date bars and low-fat milk to 30,000 school children living in the camps.

About 5 percent of the population of Algeria is classified as undernourished by the World Bank. This means they do not receive adequate nutrition in their diet. Of children under the age of five, about 13 percent are underweight, and nearly 18 percent are stunted (short for their age). Very little land in Algeria is cultivated (only 3 percent), too little for the country to be self-sufficient and feed its own people.

However, in 2008 about 95 percent of the population had access to adequate sanitation: nearly 100 percent of those in urban areas and 88 percent in rural areas. Safe drinking water was available to about 83 percent of the population that year. Free medical care was introduced by the Algerian government in 1974 under the country's Social Security system.

7 Further Study

BOOKS

Brennan, Georgeanne. *The Mediterranean Herb Cookbook*. San Francisco, CA: Chronicle Books, 2000.

Crocker, Pat. *159 Best Tagine Recipes*. Toronto: R. Rose Inc., 2011.

Dunlop, Fiona. *The North African Kitchen*. Northampton, MA: Interlink Publishing, 2008.

Mallos, Tess. *North African Cooking*. North Clarendon, VT: Periplus, 2006.

Webb, Lois Sinaiko, and Lindsay Grace Roten. *Holidays of the World Cookbook for Students*. Santa Barbara, CA: Greenwood, 2011.

Winget, Mary. *Cooking the North African Way*. Minneapolis: Lerner Publications, 2004.

WEB SITES

CookingLight.com. http://www.cookinglight.com/ (accessed on February 2, 2012).

Epicurious: Algerian Flatbread. http://www.epicurious.com/recipes/food/views/Algerian-Flatbread-241505 (accessed on February 2, 2012).

Mediterranean Creole: Algerian Cuisine by Chef Zadi. http://www.chefzadi.com/ (accessed on February 2, 2012).

Algeria

Saudi Aramco World: Couscous Crossroads. http://www.saudiaramcoworld.com/issue/201101/couscous.crossroads.htm (accessed on February 2, 2012).

Whats4Eats: Algeria Recipes and Cuisine. http://www.whats4eats.com/middle-east/algeria-cuisine (accessed on February 2, 2012).

FILMS

Samia, by Philippe Faucon. (Official selection at the 2000 Venice Film Festival.) Samia is a teenage girl of Algerian descent living in Marseille (southern France) with her family. At home, Samia and her two sisters live in an Algerian culture. They speak the language, eat Algerian food, and observe the customs of their Muslim religion. But, as youngsters, they are torn; despite their parents' objections, they want to fit in with the rest of society. To be a young girl in this environment is even more difficult because her family's traditions have society believing that she has no independence. As she begins to spread her wings, the quick-witted and attractive Samia soon finds herself in conflict with her family. (In French and Arabic with English subtitles.)

Argentina

- ■ Ñoquis 14
- ■ Carbonada Criolla (Stew) 15
- ■ Empanadas (Little Meat Pies) 16
- ■ Chimichurri (Dipping Sauce) 16
- ■ Fruit Salad with Frozen Yogurt 18
- ■ Bocaditos (Finger Sandwiches) 18
- ■ Milanesa 19
- ■ Submarino 20
- ■ Alfajores de Maizena (Cookies) 20
- ■ Dulce de Leche (Milk Jam) 21

1 Geographic Setting and Environment

Argentina is a wedge-shaped country, the second largest (after Brazil) in South America. Although the Andes Mountains are located in the west, the majority of Argentina's land is low. Because Argentina lies in the Southern Hemisphere, the winter months are May through August, and the warmest summer month is January. Argentina has a temperate climate and rich, lowland regions, which make the country strong in agriculture.

More than 50 million head of cattle were raised by Argentine cattle ranchers in 2009. Argentina is also South America's largest producer of honey, an ingredient that makes its way into many delicious Argentine desserts. Argentine farmers began growing soybeans on a large scale in the 1990s, after the government approved the cultivation of genetically modified soya in 1996.

About $1.2 billion in seafood harvested from the ocean waters along the long coastline is exported each year. Hake (a type of fish related to cod), shrimp, squid, and scallops are among the main products exported.

2 History and Food

Native Indians lived in Argentina many years before the European explorers arrived. Members of an Indian tribe in the northern part of Argentina were farmers who grew squash, melons, and sweet potatoes. Spanish settlers came to Argentina in 1536. Between 1880 and 1890, nearly one million immigrants came from Europe to live in Argentina. Most were from Italy and Spain. The Italians introduced pizza, as well as all kinds of pasta dishes, including spaghetti and lasagna. *Ñoquis* is a popular potato dish introduced by the Italians. British, German, Jewish, and other immigrants also settled in Argentina, all bringing their styles of cooking and favorite foods with them. The British brought tea, starting the tradition of teatime. All of these cultures influenced the dishes of Argentina.

13

Argentina

Ñoquis

Ingredients
6 baking potatoes
Dash of salt
2 eggs
1 cup ricotta cheese
2 to 3 cups flour
Tomato sauce
Grated Parmesan cheese

Directions
1. Quarter potatoes and boil them in water with a pinch of salt, until tender. Drain well.
2. Mash the potatoes, gradually mixing in eggs and about 2 cups flour.
3. Stir in ricotta cheese and mix until the texture is smooth, adding extra flour if needed.
4. Pat the mixture into a rectangle on a smooth surface, such as a cutting board.
5. Cut the mixture into strips, and then again into rectangles. Use a fork to add a design (optional).
6. Heat a pot of salted water until it boils. Carefully drop the ñoquis into the boiling water. They will sink at first. When they rise to the top, they are done.
7. Remove ñoquis from the water, using a slotted spoon.
8. Serve with tomato sauce and Parmesan cheese.

Serves 6.

The country was historically famous for the quality of its grass-fed beef, which was usually served grilled. While beef is still served grilled, as of 2012, it is much more common to be served grain-fed beef. In the past, cattle roamed over large grazing pastures, known as the pampas. However, since the late 1990s more farmland has been dedicated to growing soybeans and more cattle are being raised in feedlots as a result. Still, the Argentine diet includes large amounts of beef, and the people consume nearly 154 pounds per capita—almost 3 pounds per person per week—each year.

3 Foods of the Argentines

Beef is the national dish of Argentina. The country was known for its huge cattle ranches, and the gaucho, or Argentine cowboy, is a well-known symbol of Argentine individualism. The gaucho image may still be seen in Argentina, but most ranches now feed their cattle on grain and grow other crops, such as soybeans on their land.

Many dishes contain meat, prepared in different ways. A favorite main course is *parrillada*,

Argentina

a mixed grill of steak and other cuts of beef. Grilled steak is called *churrasco*, a beef roast cooked over an open fire is called *asado*, and beef that is dipped in eggs, crumbs, and then fried is called *milanesa*. Carbonada is a stew that contains meat, potatoes, sweet potatoes, and chunks of corn on the cob.

Because many Argentines are descendents of the Italian immigrants who came to Argentina in the late 1800s, Italian dishes are found throughout the country. Some favorite Italian dishes include pizza, all kinds of pastas (such as spaghetti and ravioli), and ñoquis (gnocchi—potato dumplings) served with meat and tomato sauce.

Carbonada Criolla (Stew with Meat, Vegetables, and Fruit)

Ingredients
3 tablespoons olive oil
2 pounds of stewing beef, cut into 1-inch chunks
4 large tomatoes, chopped thick
1 green pepper, chopped thick
1 large onion
3 cloves garlic, minced
2 bay leaves
1 teaspoon oregano
2 cups canned chicken stock
3 potatoes, diced into 1-inch cubes
3 sweet potatoes, diced into 1-inch cubes
2 ears of corn, cut into 1-inch widths (or use 2 cups of frozen corn)
2 zucchini, diced into ½-inch pieces
2 peaches in ½-inch pieces
2 pears in ½-inch pieces

Directions
1. Heat oil in a heavy pot.
2. Brown beef in separate batches so that all of it gets cooked. Remove from the pot and set aside.

A variation of carbonada is shown here, placed inside a carved pumpkin. This version also features rice. © ANALIA VALERIA URANI/SHUTTERSTOCK.COM.

3. In that same pot, cook tomatoes, pepper, onion, and garlic until soft.
4. Add bay leaves, oregano, and chicken stock, and bring to a boil.
5. Return beef to the pot, and add potatoes and sweet potatoes. Cover and simmer 15 minutes.
6. Stir in zucchini and corn. Simmer 10 more minutes, or until vegetables are almost soft, then add the peaches and pears.
7. Cook 5 more minutes. Remove bay leaves.
8. Serve hot.

Makes 6 to 8 servings.

In addition to being beef-lovers, Argentines also love fruit. They eat more fruit than almost any other group of people in the world. Favorite

Argentina

fruits include peaches, apricots, plums, pears, cherries, grapes, and tuna (the fruit of a prickly pear cactus).

Empanadas (Little Meat Pies)

Ingredients

For Filling:
1 pound ground beef
½ cup onions, chopped
8 green olives, chopped
1 teaspoon salt
¼ teaspoon oregano

For Pastry:
2½ cups flour
1 egg yolk
½ cup water
¼ cup butter, softened
1 teaspoon vinegar
½ teaspoon salt

Directions

For Filling:
1. Brown the ground beef and onions in a frying pan until meat has lost all its pink color.
2. Stir in the remaining ingredients.
3. Drain the mixture well and allow it to cool.

For Pastry:
1. Preheat oven to 400°F.
2. In a bowl, mix the flour, butter, egg yolk, and vinegar together, stirring to combine.
3. Stir the salt into the water and sprinkle water, a little at a time, over the flour mixture.
4. Knead the dough until it is smooth. (To knead, flatten the dough on a surface that has been dusted with a little flour. Fold the dough in half and flatten again. Turn. Repeat the process for about 15 minutes.)
5. For each empanada, roll ¼ cup of dough into a 9-inch circle.
6. Put ½ cup filling on the circle, and fold the dough circle in half.
7. Press the edges of the dough together, and poke a small hole in the top using a toothpick. Place on a cookie sheet.
8. Repeat process until all the dough and filling are used up.
9. Bake 10 to 15 minutes.
10. Serve hot with chimichurri.

Chimichurri (Dipping Sauce)

Ingredients

½ cup olive oil
2 tablespoons lemon juice
⅓ cup fresh parsley, minced
1 clove garlic
2 shallots (or 2 small onions), minced
1 teaspoon minced basil, thyme, or oregano (or mixture of these, if preferred)
Salt and pepper to taste

Directions

1. Combine all ingredients in a bowl and let sit for at least 2 hours before serving with empanadas.

Empanadas, little pies usually stuffed with beef, vegetables, and cheese, are a favorite dish. These are eaten by hand and they are often enjoyed as a snack, or may be carried to school for lunch. *Chimichurri*, a dipping sauce, is usually served with empanadas. Because the sauce has to sit for two hours before eating, it is prepared before the empanadas.

❹ Food for Religious and Holiday Celebrations

Lent is the 40-day period preceding Easter in the Christian year. During the week before Lent, a large festival, El Carnaval del Pais (Carnival), is

Argentina

Empanadas, both homemade or purchased from a street vendor, are popular for lunches or as snacks. Popular fillings include chicken, beef, pork, or whatever the cook has on hand. © DANIEL KORZENIEWSKI/SHUTTERSTOCK.COM.

celebrated in many parts of Argentina. During Carnaval, people dress up in costumes and dance. They eat spicy food, including corn stew and *humitas en chala* (corn patties wrapped and cooked in their husks). It is a tradition to eat a cake in the shape of a large ring. On Easter, children eat chocolate eggs with tiny candies hidden inside.

Because it is a tradition in the Roman Catholic Church not to eat meat during Lent, Argentines eat more seafood dishes during this time. *Bocaditos* (finger sandwiches), made with shrimp, are a popular lunch or snack food during Lent.

On Christmas Eve, celebrated on December 24, Argentines eat a late meal of cold beef, chicken, or turkey, and fruit salad. Because Christmas occurs during summertime in South America, Argentines often eat the meal outside on decorated tables. After dinner, they eat almonds, dried fruits, and *pan dulce*, a sweet bread that is similar to fruitcake but has fewer fruits and nuts.

In many areas of Argentina, people hold festivals to honor aspects of the environment. For example, a city on the Atlantic coast celebrates the seafood harvest that is brought in from its fishing grounds. It is tradition for people to eat a

Argentina

seafood feast of shrimp, crab, and scallops. After the feast, a parade with people dressed in sea-creature costumes is held. Someone dressed as The Queen of the Sea leads the parade, sitting in a giant seashell. In San Antonio de Areco, November 10 is the Día de la Tradición (Day of Tradition), which celebrates Argentina's gauchos with cowboy-type activities, elaborate and simple beef dishes, and other traditional foods and beverages.

Fruit Salad with Frozen Yogurt

Ingredients
- 3 tablespoons honey
- 3 tablespoons lemon juice
- 1 medium apple, cored and chopped
- 1 medium plum, pitted and sliced
- 1 large orange, peeled and sliced into ¼-inch rounds
- 1 large grapefruit, peeled and sectioned
- 1 medium banana, peeled and sliced into rounds
- 1 quart frozen vanilla yogurt

Directions
1. In a large bowl, whisk together the honey and lemon juice.
2. Stir in the fruit and serve topped with a scoop of frozen yogurt.

Bocaditos (Finger Sandwiches)

Ingredients
- 12 thin slices French bread
- 1 container (3-ounce) cream cheese with chives
- ½ cucumber, thinly sliced
- 4 to 6 precooked shrimp
- 4 cherry tomatoes, sliced

Directions
1. Trim crusts from the bread.

With honey and lemon juice in the dressing, this fruit salad offers a refreshing balance of sweet and tart flavors. It may be served with a topping of frozen yogurt. © EPD PHOTOS.

2. Spread a thin layer of cream cheese on each slice of bread.
3. Place cucumber slices, tomatoes, and shrimp on one slice, and cover with another slice of bread to make a sandwich. (Any combination of these ingredients may be used.)
4. Cut into triangles or rectangles.

Serves 8 to 10.

❺ Mealtime Customs

Argentine families, like families everywhere, are busy. Because everyone is on a different schedule, they aren't able to eat every meal together. *Desayuno* (day-sigh-OO-noh, breakfast) is often a light meal of rolls or bread with jam and coffee. Most working people in the cities have a small *comida* (coh-MEE-dah, lunch) such as a pizza from a cafeteria. A farmer eats a hot dish for lunch, carried out to him in the field, of beef, potatoes, and chunks of corn-on-the-cob. Upper-class city families usually eat a large midday meal of meat, potatoes, and green vegetables.

Parrillada, a favorite among Argentines, features steak and other cuts of meat. Beef is the national dish of Argentina. © ANALIA VALERIA URANI/SHUTTERSTOCK.COM.

Milanesa

Note: This recipe involves hot oil and requires adult supervision.

Ingredients

1 pound top round, sliced thinly into about 6 steaks
½ cup flour
2 teaspoons oregano
1 teaspoon salt
½ teaspoon pepper
1 cup bread crumbs
2 eggs
Vegetable oil for frying

Directions

1. Mix the flour, oregano, salt, and pepper together in a bowl.
2. Whisk the eggs lightly.
3. Place each steak into the flour mixture, coating both sides.
4. Dip each steak into the egg, then place into the bread crumbs, coating both sides thoroughly.
5. Heat oil, about ½-inch deep, in a large skillet on medium-high heat.
6. Fry each steak for about 3 to 4 minutes on each side, or until breading is crispy and steak is cooked to desired doneness.

Serves 6.

Argentina

Submarino
(Milk with Chocolate Syrup)

Ingredients

1 glass of cold milk
1 teaspoon chocolate syrup

Directions

1. Place the spoon with the syrup in the cold milk, but don't stir it.
2. Drink a little milk, then lick some of the chocolate off the spoon.
3. Continue until glass is empty.

A market stall in Tigre, Argentina, shows a variety of items for sale, including breads, cheeses, and meats. © PETER HORREE/ALAMY.

Alfajores de Maizena
(Corn Starch Cookies)

Ingredients

2½ cups corn starch
1⅔ cups flour
½ teaspoon baking soda
2 teaspoons baking powder
¾ cup sugar
1 cup (2 sticks) butter or margarine, softened
3 egg yolks
1 tablespoon vanilla extract
Grated lemon peel

Directions

1. Preheat oven to 350°F.
2. Sift the corn starch with the flour, baking soda, and baking powder in a bowl.
3. Beat margarine and sugar, and add the egg yolks one at a time. Mix well.
4. Add dry ingredients a little at a time.
5. Add vanilla and lemon peel. Mix to form a stiff, elastic dough.
6. Stretch until the dough is about ½-inch thick over surface covered with flour.
7. Cut into circles using the rim of a drinking glass or a round cookie cutter and put the circles on an ungreased cookie sheet.
8. Bake for about 15 minutes. Let cool.
9. Spread some dulce de leche (see following recipe) on one cookie and sandwich with another cookie. Repeat with the rest of the cookies.

In the late afternoon, Argentines have a snack of tea, sandwiches, and cake to hold over their appetite until dinner (*cena,* SAY-nah), typically eaten around 9 p.m. The teatime tradition comes from the British immigrants, who brought tea to Argentina in the late 1800s.

Argentina

Dulce de Leche (Milk Jam)

Ingredients
1 can sweetened condensed milk

Directions
1. Preheat oven to 425°F.
2. Pour the sweetened condensed milk into an 8-inch round or square pan. Cover the pan with foil.
3. Place the pan in a larger, shallow pan filled with one inch of water. Bake for one hour.
4. Allow to cool; eat with bananas or as a cookie filling.

Vendors sell food on the streets (the equivalent of "fast food"). Ice cream vendors sell *helado*, Argentine ice cream, and warm peanuts, sweet popcorn, and candied apples. Some vendors sell *choripan* (a sausage sandwich) and soda pop.

Empanadas, little pies stuffed with beef, chicken, pork, or vegetables, are a popular snack. Children can take vegetable-filled empanadas to school for lunch.

A favorite drink is a *submarino*, or milk with chocolate syrup. A spoon with chocolate syrup is placed into the glass, but the syrup is not mixed into the milk. Instead, the chocolate syrup is licked from the spoon between sips of cold milk.

The dinner meal has several courses, including meat dishes, and ends with dessert. *Dulce de leche* (milk jam) is a favorite dessert for many Argentine children. It is often eaten with bananas or as a filling in *alfajores* (corn starch cookies).

6 Politics, Economics, and Nutrition

Government policies, which encouraged growing crops for export, raised the cost of food

Considered one of Argentina's traditional deserts, this layered cake uses "Dulce de Leche" (milk jam) as an icing. © ANALIA VALERIA URANI/SHUTTERSTOCK.COM.

gradually through the early years of the 21st century. In 2011 alone, food prices were raised three times. Cattle raising was traditionally one of the main activities of Argentine farmers, but cultivation of soybeans was growing rapidly. From 1990 to 2011, the soybean crop quadrupled. Soybean fields in 2011 covered more than one-half of the country's farmland. Exports of soybeans generated about $25 billion annually. Growing soybeans is done on large farms, many of which were formerly devoted to cattle-raising.

Argentina

Some observers believe that the shift from small to large farms has changed rural life in Argentina. Small farmers, who grew basic foods, such as grains and vegetables, were being squeezed off their land by large farms. This contributed to rising food prices.

Most people in Argentina receive adequate nutrition in their diets, although the World Bank classifies a small percentage as malnourished. About 97 percent of the population has access to safe drinking water and sanitation (hygienic conditions and safe disposal of waste products). A small percent of children under age five are underweight (about 2 percent) or stunted (are short for their age, 8 percent). These children are from the poorest Argentine families and may live in cities or rural areas.

7 Further Study

BOOKS

Brooks, Shirley Lomax. *Argentina Cooks!: Treasured Recipes from the Nine Regions of Argentina*. New York: Hippocrene Books, 2001.

Castro, Lourdes. *Latin Grilling*. Berkeley, CA: Ten Speed Press, 2011.

Fleetwood, Jenni. *South American Food and Cooking*. London, UK: Southwater, 2005.

Greenberg, Arnold. *Buenos Aires: And the Best of Argentina Alive!* Edison, NJ: Hunter Publishing, 2000.

Webb, Lois Sinaiko, and Lindsay Grace Roten. *Holidays of the World Cookbook for Students*. Santa Barbara, CA: Greenwood, 2011.

WEB SITES

Argentour: Argentina Food. http://www.argentour.com/en/argentina/argentina_food.php (accessed on February 2, 2012).

Global Gourmet. http://www.globalgourmet.com/destinations/argentina/ (accessed on February 2, 2012).

Latin American Recipes. http://www.ma.iup.edu/Pueblo/latino_cultures/recipes.html (accessed on February 2, 2012).

South America: Typical Food of Argentina. http://www.southamerica.cl/Argentina/Food/Guide.htm (accessed on February 2, 2012).

Whats4Eats: Argentina Recipes and Cuisine. http://www.whats4eats.com/south-america/argentina-cuisine (accessed on February 2, 2012).

Australia

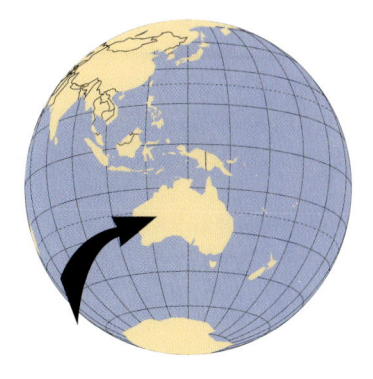

- Macadamia Nut Dukkah 24
- Carrot, Apple, and Raisin Salad 26
- ANZAC Biscuits 26
- Pikelets 27
- Australian Meat Pie 27
- Lamingtons 28
- Christmas Shortbread 29
- Pavlova 30
- Quick No-Cook Mini-Pavlova 30
- Chocolate Crackles 31
- Toast with Vegemite 32

❶ Geographic Setting and Environment

Australia is the world's smallest continent. Lying southeast of Asia between the Pacific and Indian oceans, its diverse landscapes and climates are home to a wide variety of plants and animals.

It is generally warm and dry all year round, with no extreme cold and little frost. Average annual rainfall is 17 inches (42 centimeters), much less than the mean for all the countries of the world, which is 26 inches (66 centimeters). Coastal areas receive more rainfall. Livestock, especially dairy and beef cattle, are raised, especially in the southwest. Areas where there is less rainfall can support sheep grazing. Sheep are raised for wool and for meat. In some years, insufficient rainfall can cause droughts that threaten to destroy crops. During the first decade of the 2000s, Australia experienced its worst drought in 100 years. The year 2011, however, was one of the wettest years on record in Australia.

The country's limited rainfall can also cause problems with water quality and availability. Because Australia produces most of its own food, a water shortage for plants and animals can cause agricultural production to suffer. Western Australia is especially affected by drought. In 2010, the government launched a pilot program to find the best way to help farmers during periods of drought. The government hoped to help farmers plan for the possibility of drought, instead of responding to drought when it happens. The new test programs were planned to continue until 2014 and include financial aid and free counseling for farmers and their families.

❷ History and Food

British Captain Arthur Phillip (1738–1814) established the first modern settlement in Australia in January 1788. The settlers were not very experienced as farmers and early agricultural practices were disastrous. Crop failure caused food

Australia

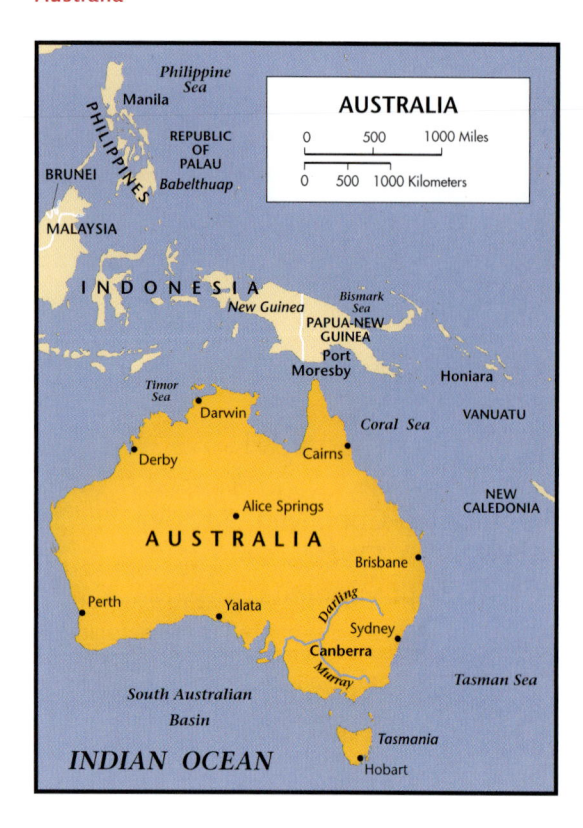

shortages and even starvation. Settlers depended on goods imported from Great Britain—such as tea, flour, beef, oatmeal, and cheese—to survive. They also learned to eat foods they found around them, such as fish and wild fruits and nuts.

The Australian diet has been heavily influenced by peoples from all over the world. The Potato Famine of the 1840s in Ireland led many desperate starving Irish people to leave their homeland, seeking relief in Australia (as well as Canada, the United States, and elsewhere). Gold was discovered in Australia a few years later, bringing more people to the country. Following World War II (1939–45), Europeans and Asians arrived in greater numbers. As a result, cuisines from other countries, such as Italy, Greece, and Lebanon, became popular. Europeans introduced tea, cocoa, coffee, fruits, and a variety of cheeses, and Asians introduced new spices and the technique of stir-fry.

Macadamia Nut Dukkah

Ingredients
½ cup raw, unsalted macadamia nuts
¼ cup raw, unsalted pine nuts
¼ cup raw sesame seeds
2 tablespoons coriander seeds
2 tablespoons cumin seeds
½ teaspoon salt
Pepper, to taste
Fresh crusty bread for serving
Extra virgin olive oil for serving

Directions
1. Lightly toast macadamia and pine nuts in a pan over medium heat for 1 to 2 minutes.
2. Chop nuts until they are crumb size.
3. Toast the sesame seeds in pan for 1 to 2 minutes, remove and set aside.
4. Toast the coriander and cumin seeds in the pan, stirring frequently for 1 to 2 minutes or until they begin to pop.
5. Crush the coriander and cumin until they become a fine powder.
6. Add the crushed spices, salt, and pepper to the nut mixture; mix well.
7. Brush the bread with olive oil and sprinkle the nut dukkah on top.

Serves 5 to 7

Australia is known for its seafood, fruits, beef, and lamb. Its dairy products, especially cheeses, are also very popular.

❸ Foods of the Australians

The end of World War II brought about significant change in Australian cuisine. People from

Australia

A wide variety of fruits and vegetables is shown for sale at a market in Queensland, Australia. © SHAUN ROBINSON/SHUTTERSTOCK.COM.

Europe and Asia brought new crops, seasonings, and cooking methods with them.

Wheat, rice, oranges, bananas, and grapes are just a few of the crops that grow in abundance throughout the country. Meat has always been a large part of the Australian diet, although Australians (like others around the world) began to be concerned about controlling cholesterol and fat in their diet. As such, they began to decrease their consumption of meat slightly at the end of the 20th century. Kangaroo, though once a popular meat in Australia's early history, is no longer widely consumed; beef, lamb, pork, poultry, and seafood are more common in 21st century Australia.

Australia is home to the macadamia nut, which is seen throughout Australian food. Macadamia Nut Dukkah is an Australian spin on an ancient Egyptian dish, dukkah, a blend of ground herbs and nuts.

Australia is also home to Vegemite, a widely popular product. Vegemite is a processed food that was developed in 1922 by Australia-based Fred Walker and Company. The company wanted to create an extract that would compete with a similar British product called Marmite. A Walker Company scientist came up with a recipe for an extract made from brewer's yeast, which was mixed with vegetables and salt to make a thick paste, which could be spread on bread or

Australia

crackers. A competition was held to name the product, and Vegemite was the winner. Vegemite is a good source of vitamin B, but it is also one of the highest-sodium products available. In 2011, My First Vegemite, a new product containing about 50 percent less salt, was released for children.

Grated Carrot, Apple, and Raisin Salad

Ingredients
1 head of lettuce
1 medium carrot, grated
1 medium red apple, chopped fine
¼ cup raisins
1 tablespoon coconut, flaked
Juice of a lemon

Directions
1. Carefully remove several firm leaves from the head of lettuce and arrange in a bowl.
2. Mix the remaining ingredients in another bowl.
3. Mound mixture in the lettuce "cup." Serve with cottage cheese, chicken, or lean cold meat.

Serves 6.

ANZAC Biscuits

Ingredients
1 cup (2 sticks) margarine or butter
2 tablespoons corn syrup
4 tablespoons water
1 teaspoon baking soda
2 cups oatmeal
2 cups sugar
1 cup white flour
1 cup whole wheat flour

Directions
1. Preheat oven to 325°F.

A popular Australia treat is the ANZAC biscuit. ANZAC is short for Australia and New Zealand Army Corps. © JANET FAYE HASTINGS/SHUTTERSTOCK.COM.

2. Combine oatmeal, sugar, white flour, and whole-wheat flour in a bowl.
3. Melt margarine (or butter) and add corn syrup and water in a small pan over heat.
4. Add the baking soda to pan and stir until fizzy.
5. Pour contents of the pan into the bowl with dry ingredients and stir well.
6. Shape dough into balls and flatten with a fork on a tray.
7. Bake for about 15 minutes or until golden brown.

Makes about 4 dozen biscuits.

A typical breakfast may consist of fruit, toast with Vegemite (a salty yeast spread), fried eggs and bacon, and juice. Pikelets are eaten as the Australian version of the American pancake.

Australia

Lunch may be an apple or a salad (such as Grated Carrot, Apple, and Raisin Salad), a sandwich filled with tuna or deli meats, and an ANZAC biscuit for a treat. (ANZAC is the acronym for Australia and New Zealand Army Corps. No one knows for sure, but many people think these biscuits were first prepared for troops—and for Australian and New Zealand families—around 1915 during World War I.)

Pikelets

Ingredients
1 cup flour
Dash of salt
¼ teaspoon baking soda
1 egg
¾ cup milk
2 tablespoons sugar
¼ teaspoon vanilla extract
2 teaspoons butter (melted)

Directions
1. In a large bowl, mix flour, salt, and baking soda.
2. Add milk, egg, sugar, vanilla, and melted butter. Mix until smooth.
3. Pour ¼ cup of batter onto a greased, heated pan. Cook until bubbles appear.
4. Flip the pikelet over with a spatula; continue to cook until golden brown.
5. Remove from pan and let cool.

Makes around 20 pikelets.

Australian Meat Pie

Ingredients
1½ pounds ground beef
1 cup beef broth
1 onion, chopped
1 teaspoon salt
2 tablespoons flour

Meat pie, with dozens of recipe variations, is considered the Australian national dish. It is frequently served topped with ketchup. © ROBYN MACKENZIE/SHUTTERSTOCK.COM.

½ teaspoon pepper
1 tablespoon Worcestershire sauce
1 package of pie crust
Egg yolk for glaze
Ketchup for serving

Directions
1. Combine ground beef, broth, onion, salt, flour, pepper, and Worcestershire sauce in a pan.
2. Heat until boiling. Lower heat, cover, and simmer for about one hour, until thickened.
3. Allow to cool before filling pie shells.
4. Preheat oven to 350°F.
5. Roll out pie crust according to package directions and line a pie pan with dough.
6. Carefully fill the pie shell with the meat mixture. Top with crust and pinch the edges together to seal.
7. Cut several slits in the top to allow steam to escape during baking.
8. Beat the egg yolk with about a teaspoon of water. Brush the tops of the pies with the egg mixture.
9. Bake for about 40 minutes, or until the pie crust is golden brown.
10. Serve with ketchup, if desired.

Serves 8 to 10.

Australia

Lamingtons

Ingredients
½ cup butter, softened
1 teaspoon baking powder
¾ cup sugar
½ teaspoon baking soda
1 teaspoon vanilla extract
4 eggs
2 cups flour
½ cup milk
Pinch of salt

Icing:
4 cups confectioners' sugar
5 tablespoons unsweetened cocoa powder
2 teaspoons butter
½ cup milk
Shredded coconut

Directions
1. Preheat oven to 350°F.
2. Lightly grease an 8-inch square cake pan.
3. Mix together butter, sugar, vanilla, and eggs.
4. Mix together flour, baking powder, baking soda, and salt.
5. Add ½ the flour mixture to the butter mixture and stir well to combine.
6. Add the milk, stirring well
7. Add remaining ½ of the flour mixture and stir gently to form a thick batter.
8. Pour mixture into the greased cake pan and bake for about 45 minutes.
9. Let cool and store overnight in a sealed container, covered.
10. *Make icing:* Measure confectioners' sugar and cocoa into a large mixing bowl.
11. Heat milk and 2 teaspoons butter until the butter is melted. Add the milk gradually to the sugar mixture, stirring constantly. The icing should be fluid but not too runny.
12. Cut the cooled cake into 2-inch squares, and put the coconut into a shallow baking dish. Have ready a cooling rack set over a sheet of waxed paper to catch icing drips.
13. Holding a cake square with two forks, dip it into the icing, and then roll in the coconut. Transfer to rack to dry. Repeat until all cake squares are coated.

Serves 16.

A Biscuit for a Treat?

Australians, like the British, call cookies "biscuits." They often use the nickname "bickies" or "bikkies" especially when offering a biscuit to a child (or even when offering a treat to a pet). Every household has a biscuit tin, a decorative round tin with a lid, to keep the supply of biscuits handy.

Dinnertime often brings leg of lamb or barbecued prawns (shrimp), roasted vegetables, a salad, and a custard or tart for dessert. Damper, a simple homemade bread, and billy tea, named for the pot in which it is heated, both remain staples for any meal.

Meat pie is considered the Australian national dish. An Official Great Aussie Meat Pie Competition has been held each September since 1990. Almost 260 million pies are consumed every year, or about 12 per person as of 2010. Meat pies are popular with men, who eat almost twice as many meat pies as women. The most common type of meat pie is filled with chopped steak (ground beef). Other ingredients, such as onions, potatoes, or mushrooms may also be added.

A well-loved bakery treat is the lamington, a coconut-covered rectangular single serving of cake. No one knows the precise history of the cake, but the earliest known recipe was published around 1902. Groups such as Boy Scouts and Girl Scouts, sports teams, and church youth groups, often make dozens of the cakes to sell to raise funds. Volunteers for these groups work together in a kind of assembly line, dipping blocks of sponge cake into chocolate icing and then rolling them in dried flaked coconut. July 21 has been designated as National Lamington Day to recognize this popular sweet treat.

4 Food for Religious and Holiday Celebrations

Most Australians spend holidays with family, participating in special events and preparing a festive meal. Since the temperatures are mild, meals are often consumed outdoors at a picnic or on the beach. Because Australia is in the Southern Hemisphere, the seasons are the opposite of those in North America and Europe. Christmas falls in the middle of summer, when most school children are on their summer vacation. A typical Christmas menu may include a variety of hot and cold meats, seafood, pasta, salads, and many types of desserts. Mince pies, fruitcake, shortbread, and plum pudding are also popular after-dinner treats. Christmas puddings may contain a small favor baked inside. It is said that the person who finds the favor will be blessed with good luck.

Easter is also widely celebrated in Australia. A traditional menu consists of roast lamb, beef, or chicken with roasted vegetables such as potatoes, carrots, peas, or broccoli. Seafood, lasagna, and salads are also favorites. Pavlova, an elegant dessert made of egg whites and sugar and garnished with fruit, is a popular Easter dessert. Most children prefer candy, and chocolate eggs are Easter favorites. Treats are often shaped like an Easter bilby, an endangered Australian mammal that resembles the North American Easter bunny.

Christmas Shortbread

Ingredients
2 cups flour
1⅛ cups butter, cubed
⅓ cup sugar
2 tablespoons rice flour (optional)

Directions
1. Preheat oven to 325°F.
2. Grease two cookie sheets.
3. Mix flour, sugar, and rice flour in a bowl.
4. Add the butter by rubbing in with fingertips until all the butter and flour are combined and the mixture resembles coarse cornmeal.
5. Press mixture together to form a dough ball.
6. Place dough on a lightly floured surface.
7. Knead gently.
8. Divide dough in half, placing one rounded ½-inch thick piece on each cookie sheet.
9. Gently mark out eight equal portions on each piece, radiating from the center.
10. Prick dough with a fork.
11. Bake for 30 to 35 minutes.
12. Allow the shortbread to cool; store in an airtight container.

5 Mealtime Customs

Australians traditionally spent hours in the kitchen preparing meals for family and friends. The introduction of microwave cooking helped to speed the cooking process for busy Australian families, and also helped keep their kitchens cooler. In the early 2000s, about 80 percent of all households owned a microwave oven.

Australia

Pavlova

Ingredients
4 egg whites
1 teaspoon cornstarch (corn flour)
Pinch of salt
1 teaspoon vinegar or lemon juice
½ teaspoon vanilla
¾ cup castor sugar (finer than regular sugar, but regular sugar may be substituted)
Whipping cream or whipped topping
Strawberries and kiwi for topping (other fruits or berries may be substituted)

Directions
1. Preheat oven to 250°F.
2. Cover a cookie sheet with cooking parchment.
3. In a very clean and dry bowl, use an electric mixer to beat egg whites until soft peaks form.
4. Slowly add sugar, sprinkling it into the bowl a little at a time. Continue to add sugar and beat the mixture until all but 1 teaspoon of sugar has been added.
5. Sprinkle in a pinch of salt, then slowly add the vinegar and vanilla, a few drops at a time. Finally, beat in the cornstarch.
6. Continue beating until the mixture stands in stiff peaks.
7. Place mixture onto the center of the paper on tray, and spread it into a circle about 8 or 9 inches in diameter (20 to 22 centimeters).
8. Make a slight indentation in the center.
9. Place the cookie sheet on the center rack in the oven and bake for 1 hour. Do not open the oven door while the pavlova is baking.
10. Leave pavlova in the oven to cool.
11. When completely cool, peel off the paper and place the pavlova on a serving plate.
12. Whip the heavy whipping cream with the teaspoon of sugar.
13. Spread the pavlova with whipped cream and sliced fruit (kiwi and strawberries are traditional).

Slice and serve.

Quick No-Cook Mini-Pavlova

While not authentic, this recipe will produce a dessert that resembles traditional pavlova.

Ingredients
6 meringue shells
Whipped topping
Strawberries and kiwi, sliced

Directions
1. Place meringue shells on a serving tray.
2. Fill each with a generous dollop of whipped topping.
3. Cover with sliced strawberries and kiwi.

Serves 6.

Australians eat three meals each day and enjoy an afternoon break for "tea and biscuits." Breakfast is normally eaten between 7 a.m. and 10 a.m. Lunch is increasingly being bought on the go as fast food. Australians' afternoon "tea and biscuits," served around 4 p.m., is usually composed of tea (or other beverage) accompanied by biscuits (cookies), small sandwiches, scones, or cakes. For school children, afternoon tea is the after-school snack. Dinner, the largest meal of the day, is served around 6 p.m. and is traditionally eaten European style, with the fork in the left hand and the tines pointing down, and the knife in the right.

Children normally enjoy snacks during the day, such as fruit, a beverage, or a small sandwich. Milo, similar to instant hot chocolate mix, is often used as an ingredient in snacks or drunk alone. Lamingtons, Chocolate Crackles (similar to crispy rice cereal treats in North America), ANZAC biscuits, or just a simple fruit salad, are also popular among children.

Australia

Pavlova is often served with strawberries and kiwis on top. © ANDESIGN101/SHUTTERSTOCK.COM.

Chocolate Crackles

Ingredients
4 cups crispy rice cereal
1 cup vegetable shortening or margarine
1 cup confectioners' sugar, sifted
3 tablespoons cocoa

Directions
1. Melt the shortening in a large saucepan over low heat or in a microwave oven.
2. Add crispy rice cereal, confectioners' sugar, and cocoa to the saucepan.
3. Spoon mixture into paper cupcake holders.
4. Chill for 12 to 24 hours in the refrigerator.

Makes 24 treats.

Restaurants offer a wide variety of cuisines for those who prefer to eat out. They often offer seafood and meats that are not normally prepared at home, such as stingray and emu (similar to the ostrich). Cafés offer lunch and afternoon tea and serve as meeting places. Such places also offer a variety of beverages. Coffee is growing in popularity, although tea is preferred in the afternoon and on Sundays, a traditional day for visiting with family and friends.

6 Politics, Economics, and Nutrition

Beginning in the 1980s, Australian adults (like adults in many developed countries) began to

Australia

The iconic Australian spread, Vegemite, is shown on toast.
© BRETT MULCAHY/SHUTTERSTOCK.COM.

Toast with Vegemite

Ingredients
4 slices of bread
Vegemite (available at some supermarkets)

Directions
1. Toast 4 slices of bread.
2. Spread with Vegemite spread.
3. Cut toast into triangles and serve with milk or juice as a snack. May be eaten as a light breakfast or after-school snack.

---

improve their eating habits. Meat, a source of saturated fat, is being consumed less. Chicken and seafood are eaten more frequently. Fruits, vegetables, and grains are also consumed more often. There is, however, also an increase in the purchase and consumption outside of the home of foods and beverages that are generally higher in fat.

Approximately 61 percent of the Australian population were overweight or obese in 2008. Around 5 percent of Australian children from the ages of 5 to 17 were overweight or obese.

Promoting healthy eating habits among children is an important issue in Australia. The government has allocated funding for community projects, mostly for the disadvantaged. Fresh and nutritious foods are often unavailable for children in rural and remote areas. Indigenous (native) groups, such as the Aborigines, frequently live in these disadvantaged areas.

Food is readily available to the population of Australia. In fact, Australia is one of the most food secure nations. It ranks fourth in the world (after Brazil, Argentina, and the Netherlands) as a net exporter of agricultural products. Australia exports 60–70 percent of its agricultural products. Australia's farmers feed the country's 22 million people plus about 50–60 million in other countries.

7 Further Study

BOOKS

Evans, Pete. *My Grill: Outdoor Cooking Australian Style*. San Francisco: Welcon Owen, 2011.

Germaine, Elizabeth. *Cooking the Australian Way*. Minneapolis: Lerner Publications, 2004.

Newman, Graeme, and Betsy Newman. *Good Food from Australia: A Down Under Cookbook*. New York: Hippocrene Books, 1997.

Pascoe, Elise. *Australia the Beautiful Cookbook*. San Francisco: Collins Publishers, 1995.

Saunders, Alan. *Australian Food*. Berkeley, CA: Ten Speed Press, 1999.

Sheen, Barbara. *Foods of Australia*. Detroit: KidHaven Press, 2010.

Symons, Michael. *One Continuous Picnic: A Gastronomic History of Australia*. 2nd ed. Carlton, Victoria, Australia: Melbourne University Press, 2007.

Zanger, Mark H. *The American Ethnic Cookbook for Students*. Phoenix, AZ: Oryx Press, 2001.

WEB SITES

Aussie Cooking. http://www.aussiecooking.com.au/ (accessed on February 2, 2012).

Australian Food News. http://www.ausfoodnews.com.au/ (accessed on February 2, 2012).

Australian Institute of Health and Welfare. http://www.aihw.gov.au/ (accessed on February 2, 2012).

Department of Agriculture, Fisheries, and Forestry. http://www.daff.gov.au/ (accessed on February 2, 2012).

Global Gourmet: Australia. http://www.globalgourmet.com/destinations/australia/ (accessed on February 2, 2012).

Government of Australia Department of Agriculture and Food. http://www.agric.wa.gov.au/ (accessed on February 2, 2012).

Nutrition Australia. http://www.nutritionaustralia.org/ (accessed on February 2, 2012).

Whats4Eats: Australia Recipes and Cuisine. http://www.whats4eats.com/pacific/australia-cuisine/ (accessed on February 2, 2012).

Australia: Aborigines and Bush Tucker

- Damper (European Style) 36
- Damper (Aboriginal Style) 36
- Macadamia and Fruit Snack 37
- Billy Tea 38
- Macadamia Nut Cookies...............38
- Plum Ice Cream 39
- Bush Tomato Relish.......................40

1 Geographic Setting and Environment

Aborigines (ah-bow-RIH-jeh-neez) are people who have lived in Australia for approximately 40,000 to 60,000 years. The word comes from the Latin words—*ab* and *origine*—which mean "from the beginning." Historically, the Aborigines were hunters and gatherers, and a small percentage were still living this traditional lifestyle as of the early 21st century. Gathering plants or hunting animals usually depends on the climate. Central Australia is fairly dry and plants are sparsely scattered over the land. Aborigines rely on hunting animals and eating seeds and roots of plants for survival. In northeastern Australia, tropical trees offer a variety of fruits, vegetables, and nuts, including the popular macadamia nut. Those living along the coast who follow the traditional Aboriginal lifestyle have access to seafood.

Most Aborigines are known to be skilled at growing things and most use the land efficiently. Historically, they discovered that ashes from a fire acted as a natural fertilizer, providing nutrients for new plants to grow. Despite their agricultural skill, some groups living in the dry Australian desert regions have suffered from a lack of food and have been forced to move elsewhere.

The Australian government reported in 2011 that 32 percent of Aboriginal children and youth were living in Australia's major cities, with the state of New South Wales having the highest number. About 44 percent lived in smaller towns in Australia, and 24 percent lived in remote, sparsely populated areas of the country.

2 History and Food

Before the arrival of Europeans in the late 1700s, the Aborigines were successful hunters and gatherers. They lived off the land by understanding plants, animals, and natural resources. Aborigines continue to believe that they have a special relationship with the land.

The Europeans brought a new, unfamiliar way of life to the Aborigines. The European

35

Australia: Aborigines and Bush Tucker

Damper (European Style)

Ingredients

2½ cups self-rising flour
1 teaspoon salt
1 teaspoon butter, softened
1 teaspoon sugar
1 cup milk (or ½ cup powdered milk and 1 cup water)

Directions

1. Preheat oven to 350°F.
2. Grease and lightly flour a baking sheet.
3. Mix flour, salt, sugar, and butter together in a bowl.
4. Add milk and mix well. Knead the dough for about 5 minutes.
5. Shape into a flat circle and place on the baking sheet.
6. Bake for about 30 minutes. (Traditionally, balls of dough might be placed on rocks at the edge of a campfire to cook. Alternatively, wads of dough might be wrapped around the tip of a stick and held over an open fire to cook.)

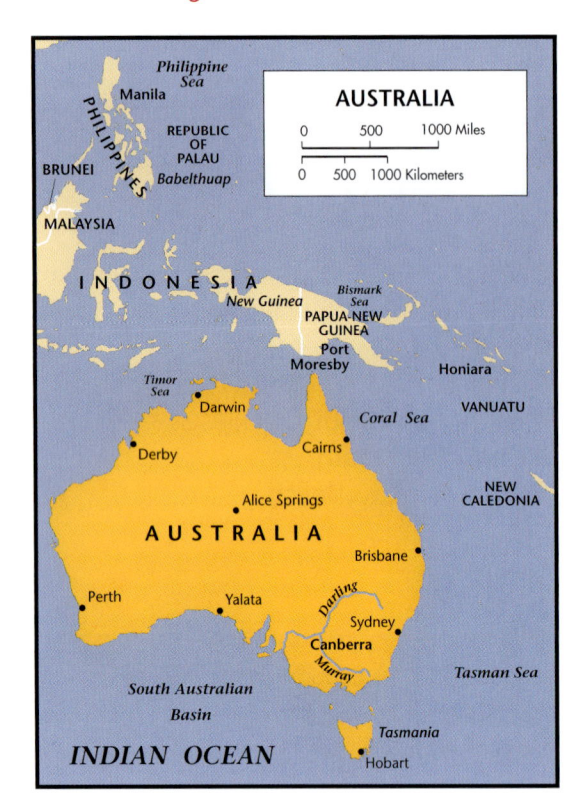

colonists established permanent homes, prepared food in pots and pans, and traded goods outside of Australia. Some Europeans adopted customs from the Aborigines, such as food-gathering techniques, but most continued to live by European customs.

Along with a different way of life, the Europeans carried new diseases, often infecting the Aborigines, who had no resistance to foreign illnesses. Thousands of Aborigines died and their population decreased. Many who survived were forced to abandon their land and move to areas that were governed by the European settlers. This limited their ability to live a traditional lifestyle. It became difficult to grow, gather, hunt, and prepare traditional foods.

Damper (Aboriginal Style)

Ingredients

2 cups flour (not self-rising)
Pinch of salt
1 cup water (or enough to make a stiff dough)

Directions

1. Preheat oven to 350°F.
2. Mix flour and salt together. Add water slowly until a stiff dough is formed.
3. Pat the dough into a round shape on a greased baking sheet. Bake for one hour.
4. To serve, break off pieces. Discard crust if too hard, and eat the soft center. (Traditionally, the Aborigines would bake the dough in the ashes of the fire. The crust, dirty with ashes, would be torn away.)

③ Foods of the Aborigines

The Aborigines ate simple, balanced diets prior to the arrival of the Europeans in the late 1700s. Their diets contained meat and fish, as well as fruits, vegetables, and nuts. Honey was a popular sweetener, gathered from the hives of native bees found among the rocky crevices or in muddy riverbanks. Aborigines used many different ways to find the beehives. According to legend, an Aborigine hunter would catch a bee and carefully attach something, such as a tiny fragment of a feather or a blade of grass, to it. This would help the tracker see the bee, and it would also slow its flight slightly. The hunter would follow the bee back to its hive.

Native plants and animals that the Aborigines ate became known as bush tucker (or bushfoods). Bush is the term Australians use for natural territory or wilderness, and tucker is another name for food. Bushfoods—native and wild foods—became a national industry in Australia in the early 1980s. There were bushfood restaurants and growers and packagers of the popular native Australian foods. This industry expanded well beyond the early bushfood industry—macadamia plantations—of the late 1800s.

Bush tucker varies depending on the region, climate, and season. Kangaroo, emu, and possum are available all year round and are popular meat choices among the Aborigines. Other meats, such as lizards, frogs, and turtles, are most often enjoyed during the summer. Seafood is also a common meal, particularly in communities along the seacoast. In the mountains of New South Wales, the Aborigines may consume moths, which are rich in fat.

A woman in Australia prepares damper dough. © LONELY PLANET IMAGES/ALAMY.

The deserts of central Australia are home to witchety grubs (larvae) found in the roots of acacia bushes. The larvae, which are high in calories, protein, and fat, were once staples in the Aboriginal diet. Other insects in the traditional Aboriginal diet are bees, ants, and termites.

Macadamia and Fruit Snack

Ingredients

1 jar macadamia nuts
1 package dried fruit (may be cranberries, raisins, cherries, or apples)

Directions

1. Combine nuts and dried fruit in a bowl.
2. To serve, shake a small amount from the bowl into the person's cupped hands, or use a cup or ladle to scoop servings out of the bowl.

Australia: Aborigines and Bush Tucker

Billy Tea

Ingredients

Billy pot (pot with handle, available at camping stores)
Water
Handful (2 or 3 tablespoons) of loose tea leaves
Small fire was traditionally the heat source. (Stove burner may be substituted.)
Clean stick for stirring (wooden spoon or chopstick may be substituted)
Drinking mug
Sugar or honey (optional)
Milk (optional)

Directions

1. Fill billy pot three-fourths full with water.
2. Place the pot on a burner and heat the water to a boil. (The traditional method is to hang the pot over an open fire.)
3. When the water is boiling, add the tea leaves.
4. Remove the pot from the fire or stove.
5. Stir leaves and water with stick (or wooden spoon).
6. Let the mixture stand (steep) for a few minutes, allowing the tea leaves to settle to the bottom of the pot. (Traditionally, someone would swing the pot by its handle in a wide circle over his or her head, using centrifugal force to settle the tea leaves. A safer method is to use the stick to tamp (push down) the leaves to the bottom of the pot.)
7. Pour the tea slowly into the drinking mug.
8. Add sugar (or honey). Adding milk is a variation preferred by Australians of European descent.

Native edible plants include yams, onions, spinach, tomatoes, berries, and grass seed. Roots of some other native plants are also harvested to eat. Seeds and flowers of the acacia were ground to make a kind of flour that could be mixed with water to make a simple cake. Plums were used to make sweet treats.

Macadamia nuts from native trees were gathered by the Aborigines when they lived solely in outlying areas of Australia. © REGIEN PAASSEN/SHUTTERSTOCK.COM.

Macadamia Nut Cookies

Ingredients

½ cup butter or margarine, softened
½ cup shortening
½ teaspoon baking soda
2½ cups powdered sugar
2½ cups flour
¼ teaspoon salt
2 eggs
1 cup macadamia nuts, chopped and roasted

Directions

1. Preheat oven to 350°F.
2. Combine baking soda, powdered sugar, flour, and salt in a bowl.
3. In a separate bowl, mix the butter, shortening, and eggs until smooth.
4. Combine and mix together all ingredients into one bowl. Add nuts.
5. Drop teaspoons of dough about 2 inches apart on an ungreased cookie sheet.
6. Bake for 10 to 12 minutes.

Makes 3 to 4 dozen cookies.

Plum Ice Cream

Ingredients

8 cups vanilla ice cream
8 plums
⅓ cup water

Directions

1. Let ice cream thaw.
2. Cut the plums into eighths, removing the pits.
3. Place plums in medium saucepan with water and cook until soft (around 8 minutes).
4. Puree the plums in a blender or food processor until smooth.
5. In a large bowl, mix together thawed ice cream and plum mixture.
6. Place in freezer for 2 to 3 hours, or until frozen.

Serves 10.

The bush tomato, similar to the familiar garden tomato grown in the West, was a popular food for Aborigines living in central Australia. The fruit could be eaten fresh, but it was also dried and ground into a paste. The paste was rolled into balls and stored for use during the seasons when fresh food was not available. Bush tomato chutney and relish are popular recipes. Because bush tomatoes are not easy to find outside of Australia, fresh tomatoes or sun-dried tomatoes may be substituted. The taste will be a little more tart (acidic) and not quite as strong.

Probably the most widely recognized bush tucker recipe is damper, a simple type of bread made of water and flour. Although the Aborigines originally baked this bread, it was the Europeans that gave it the name damper.

Billy tea, named for the "billy" (pot) with a handle that is used for cooking over an open fire, is also popular. The billy is used to boil water for tea. Billy tea is now enjoyed by all Australians, both Aborigines and Europeans alike. When a sweet drink is desired, the water is sweetened with either honey or nectar collected from flowers. Some people also enjoy billy tea prepared according to the European custom of adding milk and sugar to the brewed tea, just before it is drunk.

4 Food for Religious and Holiday Celebrations

Australia's national Journey of Healing Day, better known as Sorry Day, is a significant modern national holiday for the Aborigines. In the 1970s, the Australian government recognized that forcing the European lifestyle upon the Aboriginal people was wrong. It declared May 26 as Journey of Healing Day. On this day, all citizens celebrate Aboriginal culture and customs. The celebration includes parades, public speakers, and other festivities. Aborigines often use this day to show off some of their best native cuisine.

Beginning in the 1990s, one week in July was designated NAIDOC week. (NAIDOC is the acronym for National Aborigines and Islanders Day Observance Committee. It also became the name of a week of activities designed to celebrate Aborigine culture.) The Australian government supports the activities and has a goal to support the preservation of Aboriginal culture. In 2008, the government surveyed the Aborigine population about their participation in cultural activities. The survey reported that 65 percent of Aborigine children and youth had been involved in cultural events during the past year. Aboriginal children living in rural areas were the most likely to participate in cultural events. About 80 percent of children in remote areas, compared to 61 percent of those living

Australia: Aborigines and Bush Tucker

in cities, had participated in cultural activities. Cultural activities could include participating in NAIDOC Week activities, festivals, or fishing and hunting with elders.

Bush Tomato Relish

Dried ground bush tomatoes are available through specialty stores.

Ingredients
3 fresh tomatoes
1 onion
Olive oil
1 clove garlic, pressed through a garlic press
1 tablespoon dried ground bush tomatoes (or 1 tablespoon chopped sun-dried tomatoes)
Salt and pepper

Directions
1. Chop tomatoes and onion.
2. Heat oil in a frying pan and add the chopped onion. Cook until softened and gold in color.
3. Add chopped tomatoes and garlic.
4. Cook until the mixture is soft.
5. Stir in ground bush tomatoes (or sun-dried tomatoes). Add salt and pepper to taste.
6. Serve on top of toasted bread or crackers.

Serves 4 to 6.

For Aborigines, food is closely associated with spirituality. They believe that everything living, including humans, was created by great spiritual beings. A key part of their spirituality is the mysterious spiritual world, which they call The Dreaming. Dreaming stories recount the belief that the great spirits live on in nature and through rituals. The Aborigines believe that the spirits do not want them to eat certain foods.

Customs of hunting, gathering, preparation, and cooking evolved through these spiritual beliefs. Each person feels a connection between himself or herself and a particular plant or animal. This special plant or animal is known as the person's totem (unique personal symbol). Many people do not kill or eat their totems, except during special ceremonies.

Bush tomatoes grow in rural areas of Australia, known as the 'bush.' They are picked, dried, and ground to be sold as a seasoning. © EPD PHOTOS.

5 Mealtime Customs

Historically, Aboriginal males were responsible for hunting most animals, including birds, various seafood, and kangaroo. Larger animals, such as the kangaroo that is more challenging to catch, were often hunted by groups of hunters. Men used spears, harpoons, nets, traps, clubs, and even boomerangs for hunting wild creatures.

In Aboriginal communities, women tended to be responsible for the gathering of plants, shellfish, and insects. These gender roles continue today in traditional Aboriginal families.

Even when plants are plentiful, the Aborigines are careful not to waste. They use all parts of the plants, including seeds, roots, stems, leaves, and fruits. However, many plants require special preparation. Some are poisonous, others are tough, covered with prickly foliage, and most require washing, pounding, or grinding before they can be boiled in water.

Food preparation methods differ among regional groups, often depending upon climate. Food has often been cooked in the smoldering ashes remaining after a fire. Alternatively, food may be placed directly on top of glowing coals, boiled in water, or steamed in an oven-like pit in the ground. By the 21st century, more and more Aborigines were using modern products (such as aluminum foil) for traditional cooking techniques such as steaming. The billy (pot) introduced by Europeans is widely used by Aborigines to make cooking easier.

Historically, Aborigine children had to begin caring for themselves at an early age. Most were given their first small spear before age four or five. Sons would follow their fathers to watch how they hunted and made tools. Daughters would learn how to gather foods and prepare meals from their mothers. Some Aboriginal families continue to follow the occupations of their parents.

6 Politics, Economics, and Nutrition

At the beginning of the 21st century, nearly 400,000 Aborigines lived in Australia. Many of them are poor. Low incomes and living in isolated areas make it difficult for them to purchase food. Because of the cost to ship food to isolated areas, food sometimes costs almost twice as much in an outlying region than in densely populated urban areas. The long shipping distance may also cause fresh fruits and vegetables to spoil. As a result, rural community stores

Boomerang

The Aborigines use a type of boomerang that is different from the modern "returning boomerang" that is popular in modern-day Australia. When an Aborigine hunter throws a "non-returning boomerang," he uses a spinning motion. The boomerang hits the target with more force than a stick or rock. Many Aborigines also use the boomerang to scrape animal hides (and for other scraping tasks) and to start fires. Children use them as toys.

often carry convenience foods and pre-packaged processed foods. Such foods are often higher in fat, sugar, and salt. These foods may last longer on shelves, but sometimes lack nutrients that are needed for a healthy life.

With the majority of income being spent on purchasing food, less money is available for Aborigines to spend on utilities, such as electricity, gas and water for cooking, and refrigeration for storage. Convenience foods that do not require much preparation are favored over healthier foods. As a result, Aboriginal children and adults have a higher rate of health-related problems than other Australians. Poorer diets lead to higher rates of obesity, diabetes, and heart disease. In 2008, the Australian government reported that more than half (57 percent) of Aborigines aged 15 years and over were overweight or obese.

The Australian census, completed in 2006, showed that the dropout rate for Aborigine students was declining. Between 2001 and 2006, the proportion of Aborigines age 15 years and over who had completed 12 years of school increased from 20 percent to 23 percent. About

Australia: Aborigines and Bush Tucker

Shown here is a selection of bush tucker foods in central Australia. Included are seeds, nuts, and various plants. © DAVO BLAIR/ALAMY.

31 percent of Aborigine children living in cities in 2007 stayed in school until 12th grade, compared to 14 percent in remote parts of the country.

7 Further Study

BOOKS

Australian Aborigines. Chicago: World Book, 2009.

Clarke, Philip A. *Aboriginal People and Their Plants*. Dural, NSW, Australia: Rosenberg, 2007.

Isaacs, Jennifer. *Bush Food: Aboriginal Food and Herbal Medicine*. Sydney, Australia: Lansdowne, 1996.

Marshall, Diana. *Aboriginal Australians*. New York: Weigl Publishers, 2004.

Webb, Lois Sinaiko, and Lindsay Grace Roten. *Holidays of the World Cookbook for Students*. Santa Barbara, CA: Greenwood, 2011.

WEB SITES

Aboriginal Culture. "Aboriginal Bush Foods: Insect, Animal, and Plant Foods." http://www.aboriginalculture.com.au/bushfoods.shtml (accessed on February 1, 2012).

Australian Bureau of Statistics: Aboriginal and Torres Strait Islanders. http://www.abs.gov.au/websitedbs/c311215.nsf/web/Aboriginal+and+Torres+Strait+Islander+Peoples (accessed on February 1, 2012).

Bush Tucker Plants (Australian Native Food Plants). http://www.teachers.ash.org.au/bushtucker/ (accessed on February 1, 2012).

The Epicentre: Destinations Bush Tucker. http://www.theepicentre.com/Australia/aufood2.html (accessed on February 1, 2012).

Indigenous Australia: Aboriginal Bush Tucker. http://www.indigenousaustralia.info/food.html (accessed February 2, 2012).

NAIDOC. http://www.naidoc.org.au/ (accessed February 2, 2012).

Use of Insects by Australian Aborigines, Cultural Entomology Digest 1. http://www.insects.org/ced1/aust_abor.html (accessed February 2, 2012).

Brazil

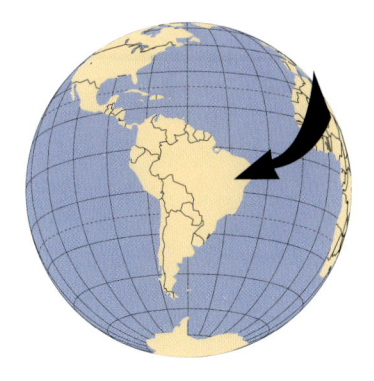

- Ambrosia 46
- Orange Salad 46
- Polenta (Fried Corn Mush) 47
- Feijoada (Meat Stew) 48
- Pineapple-Orange Drink 48
- Pepper-Scented Rice 49
- Corn Cake 49
- Banana Frita (Fried Bananas) 50
- Pudim (Thick Custard) 50
- Pão de Queijo 51
- Quejadinhas 51
- Bolinho de Chuva 52

❶ Geographic Setting and Environment

Brazil is the largest country in South America, and the fifth-largest country in the world. It lies on the East Coast of South America. Because Brazil lies in the Southern Hemisphere, the seasons are reversed from those in North America: the winter months are May through August, and the warmest summer month is January. The mighty Amazon River, the world's second-longest river after the Nile in Egypt, flows across northern Brazil. The area around the Amazon River is known as one of the world's largest rain forests.

About one-fourth of all the world's known plants are found in Brazil. In the latter part of the 1900s, logging and other commercial industries were damaging the rain forest of Brazil. Dozens of animal and plant species became extinct in Brazil during the 1900s. The destruction of the rain forest environment has slowed a little, however. Brazil's soil was once thought to be not fertile enough for agriculture. However, since the 1960s, agriculture has grown dramatically in the country.

As of 2011, Brazil ranked as one of the top exporters of agricultural products in the world. Brazil has increased its beef exports, which are now 10 times what they were in 2000. Brazil ranks number one in the world in poultry and sugar cane exports. Brazil supplies one-third of the world's soybean exports. It is also one of the world's top producers of cocoa.

❷ History and Food

Brazil is a large country that is made up of many different cultures. Each region has a different food specialty. The Portuguese arrived in Brazil in 1500 and brought their tastes and styles of cooking with them. They brought sugar,

Brazil

citrus fruits, and many sweets that are still used for desserts and holidays. The Brazilian "sweet tooth" was developed through the influence of the Europeans. Brazilians use many eggs, fruits, spices (such as cinnamon and cloves), and sugar to make sweet treats, such as ambrosia. They also use savory (not sweet) seasonings such as parsley and garlic. Other nationalities that settled in Brazil were Japanese, Arabs, and Germans. More than one million Italians had migrated to Brazil by 1880. Each immigrant group brought along its own style of cooking.

Long before the Europeans arrived, however, the Tupí-Guaraní and other indigenous (native) groups lived in Brazil. They planted manioc (a root vegetable like a potato), from which Brazilians learned to make tapioca and *farofa*, toasted ground manioc, which is similar to fine breadcrumbs. It is toasted in oil and butter and sprinkled over rice, beans, meat, and fish. Farofa is still used as the Brazilians' basic "flour" to make cookies, biscuits, and bread.

Ambrosia

Ingredients
4 cups milk
2 cups sugar
9 large egg yolks
1 tablespoon lemon juice
4 whole cloves

Directions
1. Place the milk in a large saucepan and bring to a boil over medium-high heat.
2. Remove it from the heat, and add the sugar and the egg yolks, one at a time, mixing well with a wire whisk after each addition. Add the cloves and the lemon juice.
3. Cook over medium heat for about an hour, stirring occasionally, until the mixture becomes golden and grainy.
4. Chill and serve cold.

Serves 8.

Orange Salad

Ingredients
5 oranges
1 teaspoon sugar
Salt and pepper

Directions
1. Peel the oranges and remove the inner core.
2. Cut the oranges into thin slices. Arrange the slices on a plate.
3. Sprinkle them with sugar, salt, and pepper.
4. Serve, or cover with plastic wrap and refrigerate until ready to eat.

❸ Foods of the Brazilians

Rice, black beans, and manioc (a root vegetable like a potato) are the main foods for many Brazilians. The national dish is *feijoada*, a thick stew of black beans and pieces of pork and other meats. It is usually served with orange salad, white rice, farofa (toasted ground manioc), and *couve* (kale), a dark green leafy vegetable that is diced and cooked until slightly crispy.

Almost every kind of fruit grows in Brazil, including apples, oranges, peaches, strawberries, bananas, papayas, mangoes, and avocados. Fruits, vegetables, meat, and flowers are sold at *feiras* (street markets). These outside markets are set up on streets, which are closed to vehicle traffic. The markets use a new location every day. Vendors sell fruit that is ready to eat and offer beautiful displays of produce to please every shopper.

Churrasco, chunks of beef cooked on a metal skewer over hot coals, is another favorite. Sometimes the beef is soaked in a mixture of vinegar, lemon juice, and garlic before cooking. This "Brazilian barbecue" is served with rice, potato salad, and polenta (fried corn mush). Gauchos (cowboys) living in the region of Rio Grande do Sul especially enjoy churrasco. After the gauchos eat their meal, they drink maté (an herbal tea drunk in many parts of South America). The tea leaves are placed inside a hollowed-out gourd, and then boiling water is poured over them. Gauchos slowly sip the maté through a metal straw, called a *bombilla*, with a strainer on the lower tip of it. The gourd and straw are carried, hanging from the belt.

Another popular beverage is guaraná, made from a small red fruit that is high in caffeine and grows in the Amazon River area. It is a refreshing soft drink, unique to Brazil and with a taste some describe as similar to creme soda. People in the Amazon River area also chew the guaraná seeds, or make a drink by dissolving a powder made from the seeds in water. Powdered guaraná is available in the United States in some health food stores, or in markets specializing in foods from South America.

Polenta (Fried Corn Mush)

Ingredients
3¼ cups water
¾ teaspoon salt
1 cup cornmeal

Directions
1. Stir ingredients in a saucepan over medium-high heat until they come to a slow boil.
2. Reduce heat to low, cover and cook for 15 minutes. Stir frequently.
3. Spread the polenta in a bread pan.
4. Wait until it is completely cool, then cut into 2-inch wide slices.
5. Fry them in a skillet over medium heat in 2 tablespoons of butter, 10 minutes on each side until crunchy.

4 Food for Religious and Holiday Celebrations

Although Brazil has no national religion, the Portuguese who arrived in Brazil in 1500 brought their Roman Catholic religion with them. About 68 percent of Brazilians considered themselves Roman Catholic in 2010. Those who do not follow the Roman Catholic religion still enjoy the world-renowned Brazilian Carnaval (Carnival) tradition. Carnaval in Brazil is the largest celebration of the holiday in the world. During Carnaval, colorful parades are held on the streets, and children and adults dress in costumes. There is dancing and celebrating in the streets all day and all night. People eat and drink continuously during Carnaval, enjoying spice dishes, such as pepper-scented rice and feijoada,

Brazil

and sweets. Carnaval is a week-long party that ends on Ash Wednesday, the beginning of the 40-day religious period of Lent before the Christian celebration of Easter. During Lent, it is a Roman Catholic tradition not to eat meat.

Feijoada (Meat Stew)

Ingredients

3 strips of raw bacon
2 onions
3 cloves garlic (or 1 teaspoon garlic powder)
1 pound smoked sausage
1 pound boneless beef (any cut of meat)
1 can (14-ounce) stewed tomatoes
1 cup hot water
1 tablespoon yellow mustard
4 cups canned black beans
Salt and pepper

Directions

1. Cut the bacon strips into big pieces. Fry them in a large pot over medium-high heat for about 3 minutes, stirring often.
2. Turn the heat down to medium.
3. Cut the onion in half. Peel off the skin and outer layer. Chop both halves into small pieces.
4. Peel the cloves of garlic. Chop them into small pieces.
5. Add the onions and garlic to the bacon in the pot. Stir until the onions are soft, about 3 minutes.
6. Cut the sausage and beef into 1-inch pieces. Add them to the onions and garlic.
7. Cook until the meat is brown on all sides.
8. Add the stewed tomatoes (with juice), hot water, yellow mustard, and some salt and pepper. Turn the heat down to simmer. Cover the pot.
9. Cook for about 45 minutes, stirring often. If it looks too thick, add more water, ¼ cup at a time. Add the black beans (with liquid).
10. Cover the pot and cook for 10 more minutes.

Serves 10 to 12.

Here, the cook has assembled many of the raw ingredients for feijoada. © VINICIUS TUPINAMBA/SHUTTERSTOCK.COM.

Pineapple-Orange Drink

Ingredients

2 tablespoons crushed ice
2 tablespoons sparkling water or seltzer water
½ cup orange juice
½ cup pineapple juice

Directions

1. Pour the crushed ice and water into a large drinking glass.
2. Add the orange juice and the pineapple juice. Stir and drink.

This drink can also be made quickly in a blender.
Serves 1 or 2.

Brazil

Pepper-Scented Rice

Ingredients
1 tablespoon vegetable oil
1 small onion, finely diced
1 garlic clove, minced
1 cup long-grain rice
1 chili pepper
2 cups hot water
½ teaspoon of salt

Directions
1. Pour the vegetable oil into a large saucepan and heat for a few seconds. Add the onion, garlic, and rice.
2. Fry gently, stirring for about 4 minutes.
3. Add the chili pepper, hot water, and salt. Stir well and bring to a boil.
4. Simmer for 15 to 20 minutes, until the rice is soft and the water has been absorbed.
5. Remove the chili pepper and serve.

Serves 4.

Maté, an herbal tea-like beverage, is enjoyed in many parts of South America. The cup, made from a hollowed-out gourd, and metal **bombilla** *(straw) are carried by gauchos, hanging from their belts.* © VESVES/SHUTTERSTOCK.COM.

Corn Cake

Ingredients
1 can (11-ounce) corn, drained
7 tablespoons softened butter
1 cup whole wheat flour
3 eggs, beaten
1 can (14-ounce) coconut milk
1 tablespoon baking powder
2 cups granulated sugar

Directions
1. Preheat oven to 350°F.
2. Place all of the dry ingredients into a bowl and mix; slowly add coconut milk, eggs, butter, and corn; mix until smooth.
3. Pour the mixture into a large greased loaf pan.
4. Bake for about 50 minutes.
5. To test if the cake is done, stick a toothpick into the center; the cake is done when the toothpick comes out clean.
6. Remove the cake from the pan by turning it over onto a wire rack to cool.
7. Slice and serve.

Serves 12.

Festivas Juninas (June Festivals) are held in honor of Roman Catholic saints—St. Anthony, St. Peter, and St. John. Brazilians believe St. John protects the corn and green bean harvests, giving them plenty of food in the upcoming year. They celebrate St. John's Day with a harvest festival.

Junior Worldmark Encyclopedia of Foods and Recipes of the World, 2nd Edition

Brazil

During the Festivas Juninas, corn is popular in many forms, such as corn-on-the-cob and popcorn, and corn-based dishes such as corn puddings, polenta, and corn cake.

Banana Frita (Fried Bananas)

Ingredients

6 small bananas, peeled
1 large egg, beaten
1 cup fine bread crumbs
½ cup (1 stick) unsalted butter
Salt, to taste

Directions

1. In a mixing bowl, gently toss the bananas with egg to moisten, then lightly roll the bananas in the bread crumbs.
2. In a large skillet, melt the butter over medium heat.
3. When the foam goes away, add the bananas and fry on all sides until golden.
4. Season with salt and serve hot.

Serve 6.

Brazil is the world's largest producer of coffee. It produces about one-third of all the coffee in the world. Brazilians use coffee in many unique ways in cooking. For example, on Christmas Day, Brazilians prepare a turkey basted with a rich dark coffee with cream and sugar. The traditional stuffing contains farofa, pork sausage, onions, celery, and seasonings. Side dishes for this meal are mashed white sweet potatoes, banana frita (fried bananas), and green beans. Dessert is an assortment of fruit *doces* (sweetened fruits, preserved through slow cooking), star fruit, and slices of mango.

Pudim (Thick Custard)

Ingredients

1 pound sugar
½ tablespoon butter or margarine
½ cup water
6 egg yolks, beaten
1 cup shredded coconut

Directions

1. Preheat oven to 350°F.
2. Grease the cups of a 12-cup muffin tin and sprinkle a bit of sugar into each cup.
3. In a saucepan, combine sugar and water. Bring to a boil, stirring until mixture forms a thin syrup.
4. Add butter and remove from heat and allow to cool.
5. When syrup is cool, add the egg yolks and coconut and mix well.
6. Pour mixture into sections of the muffin tin.
7. Place tin in a larger pan filled with 1 inch of hot water.
8. Bake for 30 to 40 minutes.
9. To test if they are done, stick a toothpick into the center; the custard is done when the toothpick comes out clean.
10. When the custards are cool, turn the tin over onto a large platter.

Serve in bowls. Serves 12.

5 Mealtime Customs

Because Brazil is the world's largest producer of coffee, a typical *pequeno almoço* (breakfast) consists of a cup of *café come leite* (a hot milk and coffee mixture) and a piece of French bread. Many Brazilian children also drink a coffee and milk mixture for breakfast.

Lunch, usually the biggest meal of the day, consists of rice, beans, salad, meat, or other dishes, depending on where the family lives

Pão de Queijo

Ingredients

1 egg
⅓ cup olive oil
⅔ cup milk
1½ cups flour
½ cup grated cheese (any kind)
1 teaspoon of salt
1 mini muffin tin

Directions

1. Preheat oven to 400°F.
2. Blend all ingredients together until mixture is smooth.
3. Grease a mini muffin tin and fill cups until about three-quarters full.
4. Bake in the oven for 15 to 20 minutes, until bread is puffy and light brown.
5. Let cool and serve.

Makes 16 small puffs.

Many casual restaurants in cities serve food buffet style and charge by weight. Customers choose their foods and then the plate is weighed. Waiters serve only beverages.

Most Brazilians do not eat while walking or doing other things. It is considered rude to eat while on public transportation or in a public place that is not a restaurant or café.

Some Brazilians like to take a midmorning and midafternoon café, which includes coffee, hot milk, and cookies. *Pastels* and *empadas*, little fried or baked pastries filled with any combination of shrimp, meats, and cheeses, are a favorite

Pão de queijo is a favorite snack among Brazilians. It is best served warm, right out of the oven. © EPD PHOTOS.

Quejadinhas (Coconut and Cheese Snacks)

Ingredients

1 cup tightly packed fresh grated coconut
1 can (8-ounce) sweetened condensed milk
2 tablespoons freshly grated Parmesan cheese
2 large egg yolks

Directions

1. Preheat the oven to 450°F.
2. Place all of the ingredients in a medium-size bowl and mix well.
3. Place paper cups into the cups of a muffin tin. Drop the mixture by the spoonful into the paper cups.
4. Place the muffin tin in a larger pan that has been filled with about 1 inch of water and cook for about 35 minutes.
5. These will keep well if they are stored in a tightly closed cookie tin.

snack. These can be purchased from street vendors (Brazilian "fast food") or made at home. Pão de Queijo is a popular cheese bread sold by vendors, but it can also be made at home.

In the late evening, most Brazilians eat a light supper. Children enjoy desserts such as

Brazil

pudim or churros, fried dough rolled in sugar and filled with caramel, chocolate, or sweetened condensed milk. *Bolinho de Chuva* (raindrop doughnuts) are a Brazilian treat, named for their small, round shape. The Portuguese brought oranges and other citrus fruits to Brazil in 1500, and they are used in several dishes and juices. Students may enjoy a fruity drink, such as pineapple-orange drink, as an after-school snack.

Children may take *quejadinhas* (coconut and cheese snacks) to school as part of their lunch. These treats do not need to be heated and, if stored correctly, they stay fresh for several days.

Bolinho de Chuva

Note: This recipe involves hot oil and requires adult supervision.

Ingredients
1 cup flour
½ cup cornstarch
2 teaspoons baking powder
½ cup milk
2 eggs
4 tablespoons granulated sugar
Pinch of salt
Canola oil
Sugar with cinnamon for topping

Directions
1. In a large bowl, mix eggs, sugar, and salt.
2. Add in flour, cornstarch, baking powder, and milk. Mix until batter is smooth.
3. Heat canola oil in a pot until it reaches around 325°F to 350°F (use a candy thermometer to measure the temperature).
4. Place a tablespoon of batter into the pan. Fry for about 3 to 4 minutes until golden brown, flipping one time to even the browning.
5. Remove donuts from oil and place on a paper towel.

Brazil is famous for its coffee, which is enjoyed by young and old alike. © GROCAP/SHUTTERSTOCK.COM.

6. Sprinkle with powdered sugar and cinnamon.
7. Repeat the process until the batter is gone.

Makes 25 doughnut balls.

⑥ Politics, Economics, and Nutrition

Agriculture in Brazil is thriving. The government supports both small and large farms and operates two separate ministries related to farming—the Ministry for Commercial Agriculture and the Ministry for Family Farms. Small farms are mostly operated by families and serve the needs of Brazilians. The large farms are mostly

Many types of fruit grow in Brazil, including bananas. The fruit is used in many Brazilian recipes. Here, a large shipment of bananas arrives at a market in Manaus. © GUENTERMANAUS/SHUTTERSTOCK.COM.

commercial enterprises and most of their crops are exported. The government provides subsidies to family farms to increase productivity. Family farms cultivate about one-fourth of the country's total farmland, but employ about three-fourths of farm workers.

About 6 percent of the population of Brazil is classified as undernourished by the World Bank. This means they do not receive adequate nutrition in their diet. Of children under the age of five, about 2 percent are underweight, and about 7 percent are stunted (short for their age).

Child poverty is one of the country's most serious concerns, according to the government of Brazil. About one-third of all Brazilian children live in poverty. Thousands of children spend their days on the streets of Brazil's cities; many abuse drugs and resort to crime and prostitution to get money to live. Many shopkeepers consider these street children a nuisance and ask police to keep the children away from their stores. International observers consider the child poverty in Brazil to be a human rights issue, but many Brazilians see such children as a threat to security in the cities.

In 2003 Brazil created its Zero Hunger Programme, which includes several different initiatives to fight hunger. Through this program, the government provides tokens to people who need food assistance. These tokens can be used to buy the food from small family farms. In addition, the Zero Hunger Programme set up a national school food program to feed nutritious meals to impoverished children who attend school.

Brazil also started the program Bolsa Família in 2003, which pays small sums to impoverished families in exchange for keeping their children in school and having periodic health checks for their children. The program makes it easier for families to keep their children healthy with the health checks and money for food. Plus, it also keeps children off the streets and in school.

The World Bank estimates the program helped 50 million impoverished Brazilians in 2010 and raised 20 million Brazilians out of poverty between 2003 and 2009. It also has made inroads in addressing the income inequality of the country and is a model that has been followed by other countries across the globe.

In 2006, a law creating a National Food and Nutritional Security System was enacted. Expansion of the Bolsa Família, called Brazil without Misery, was implemented in 2012. Though millions of Brazilians still live in poverty, these programs have served to decrease levels of hunger and malnutrition.

7 Further Study

BOOKS

Behnke, Alison. *Cooking the Brazilian Way*. Minneapolis: Lerner Publications, 2004.

Locricchio, Matthew. *The Cooking of Brazil*. New York: Benchmark Books, 2005.

Schwartz, Leticia Moreinos. *The Brazilian Kitchen*. London: Kyle Books, 2010.

Sheen, Barbara. *Foods of Brazil*. Detroit: KidHaven Press, 2008.

Zanger, Mark H. *The American Ethnic Cookbook for Students*. Phoenix, AZ: Oryx Press, 2001.

WEB SITES

Celebrate Brazil: Brazil Food. http://www.celebratebrazil.com/brazil-food.html (accessed January 23, 2012).

Cook Brazil. http://www.cookbrazil.com (accessed January 23, 2012).

Global Destinations: Brazil. http://globalgourmet.com/destinations/brazil/ (accessed January 23, 2012).

Recipe Source: Brazilian Recipes. http://recipesource.com/ethnic/americas/brazil/ (accessed January 23, 2012).

Brazil: Afro-Brazilians

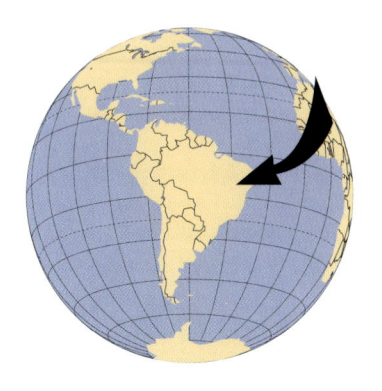

- Quiabo (Okra) 57
- Carurú 57
- Basic Rice 57
- Cocada 58
- Moqueca (Spicy Fish Stew) 58
- Moqueca aos Ovos (Egg Stew) 59
- Quindins (Coconut Macaroons) 59
- Brazilian Black Beans 60
- Angu de Milho (Cornmeal Dish) ... 60
- Empanadas (Little Baked Pies) 61
- Acaçá (Rice Flour Pudding) 63
- Olho de Sogra 63

1 Geographic Setting and Environment

The majority of Afro-Brazilians live in the nine states of the country's northeastern section—home to nearly one-third of all Brazilians. Most Afro-Brazilians live near the coastal regions where there is an abundance of rainfall.

The northeast states have three distinct areas. The flat coastal strip has rich soil that is suitable for the cultivation of sugarcane. Many plantations are found in this area. Vast hills and mountain ranges begin just miles from the fertile coastline. Highland shrubs and cacti grow here in large numbers. Lastly, the semi-arid interior covers nearly three-quarters of the northeast's area. However, this topographic region is sparsely population. Few Afro-Brazilians live in the interior; most of the population there is of Portuguese or Indian descent.

Brazil holds about one-third of the world's rain forests. Since the 1990s, deforestation has been occurring at a rapid rate, although it has slowed a little. Forests are cleared to make way for cattle pastures, for other agricultural purposes, for logging, and for development projects.

2 History and Food

The Portuguese claimed the rights to the territory that makes up modern-day Brazil in 1500, and in 1532, they began bringing African slaves to Brazil. The Africans introduced the Brazilians to new cooking styles and tastes, such as cooking food in *dendê* (palm oil), using okra as a thickener and a vegetable, and using the banana in different dishes. Africans also introduced a wide variety of chili peppers and ginger to season food. This practice has continued to be part of Brazilian cooking.

Another cooking technique that Africans brought to Brazil was the use of dried smoked fish and shrimp. One of the oldest African dishes

Brazil: Afro-Brazilians

or other gifts to the Orixás. As of 2011, there were more than 800 Umbanda churches in Rio de Janeiro, Brazil's capital. Another religion that traces some of its roots and beliefs to Africa is Candomblé. Followers of these religions suffer discrimination, since some Brazilians think that they are a form of witchcraft.

❸ Foods of the Afro-Brazilians

Most of the descendents of the African slaves, who were brought to Brazil by the Portuguese in the 1500s, live in the state of Bahia. Although Afro-Brazilian cuisine can be seen throughout Brazil, it is especially noticed in Bahia, where the people have kept the culture, food, and Candomblé religion (a mix of Roman Catholic and African religions) alive. The Afro-Brazilian cuisine features *malagueta* (chili peppers), dendê, seafood, coconut milk, bananas, and okra. Dendê adds a bright orange color to dishes.

Vatapá, popular in Bahia, is a creamy dish containing fish, shrimp, ground peanuts, coconut milk, dendê, and bread. It is usually served over rice. Another favorite dish is *moqueca,* a stew made with fish, shrimp, crab, or a mixture of seafood in a dendê oil and coconut milk sauce. Moqueca is usually served over white rice.

Afro-Brazilian cuisine is known for its sweets and desserts, probably because of the influence of the Portuguese colonists who brought their love of sugar with them from Europe. The African slaves added their own style to the existing recipes. The women of the state of Bahia, the heart of Afro-Brazilian culture, make delicious sweets. One favorite is *cocada,* a coconut candy boiled in sugar water with ginger or lemon. *Quindins* (coconut macaroons) are another favorite sweet. Quindins are often served for dessert.

in Brazil, *carurú*, dates back to the 1600s. It is a spicy stew made with smoked fish or shrimp, *quiabo* (okra), onions, dendê, and peppers. In the 21st century, the African influence on ingredients and cooking techniques still thrives, especially in the northeastern state of Bahia.

Salvador, a city in the northeast state of Bahia, has the largest number of Afro-Brazilians, about 1.9 million. The majority of Afro-Brazilians live in urban areas, often in favelas (slums), where there is no formal ownership of property.

About 400,000 Afro-Brazilians traditionally practiced a unique religion known as Umbanda. Gods known as Orixás are depicted as descended from Africa. The supreme being is known as Oxala. Many of the deities are also associated with Jesus, St. Barbara, and the Virgin Mary of Christianity. Many Brazilians are aware of the Orixás. Some even join in the practice of dressing in white on New Year's Day to leave gifts for Iemanja, the Umbanda ocean goddess. Practitioners of Umbanda offer food, flowers,

Quiabo (Okra)

Ingredients
2 cups water
1 pound small okra pods, topped and tailed
½ teaspoon butter

Directions
1. Place the water in a large saucepan and bring to a boil over medium heat.
2. Trim the tops and stem ends from the okra.
3. Place the okra in the water and cook for 3 to 5 minutes.
4. Remove from heat, drain, and serve hot with butter.

Serves 4.

Carurú

The tops and pointy tips (tails) of okra may be trimmed using clean scissors or a knife. © ANDREASNIKOLAS/SHUTTERSTOCK.COM.

Note: This recipe involves hot oil and requires adult supervision.

Ingredients
2 pounds okra
1 large onion
2 cloves garlic
1 tablespoon grated ginger
1 pound dried small shrimp (found in Asian markets)
3½ cups chopped cashews
¾ cup palm oil
Juice of one lime
½ cup water

Directions
1. Chop onion and okra into small pieces.
2. Grind dried shrimp in food processor.
3. Heat oil in large saucepan.
4. Fry onion and garlic until soft.
5. Add ginger and okra. Cook until okra is soft, stirring occasionally.
6. Add ground shrimp and chopped cashews. Cook for an additional 5 minutes.
7. Add water and lime juice. Cook about 15 additional minutes, adding water if mixture is dry.

Serves 4 to 6.

Basic Rice

Ingredients
3½ cups water
1½ cups long-grain rice
1 teaspoon salt
1 tablespoon butter

Directions
1. Bring the water to a boil in a saucepan over medium heat.
2. Stir in the rice, salt, and butter.
3. Cover and reduce the heat to low.
4. Simmer for about 20 minutes.
5. Remove the saucepan from the heat, and let it sit for about 5 minutes.

Serves 4 to 6.

Brazil: Afro-Brazilians

Cocada

Ingredients

- 5½ cups sweetened shredded coconut
- ½ cup sweetened condensed milk

Directions

1. Preheat oven to 350°F.
2. Grease an 8x8-inch glass baking dish.
3. Mix the coconut and condensed milk in a bowl.
4. Press the mixture into the baking dish.
5. Bake for about 20 minutes, until the coconut is evenly browned.
6. Let cool and cut into squares.

Makes 16 squares.

4 Food for Religious and Holiday Celebrations

The African slaves transported to Brazil by the Portuguese brought their religion with them. The religion of the modern-day Afro-Brazilians, Candomblé, is a blend of the Roman Catholicism of the Portuguese and African religions.

Throughout the year, people who follow Candomblé worship Orixás, African gods and goddesses. Orixás are similar to Catholic saints. Each has a distinct name and a favorite food. People who follow the Candomblé religion eat meals made from the saint's favorite food on the day that saint is celebrated.

Iemanja, the goddess of the ocean, is honored on February 2 of each year, and her favorite food is watermelon. Fishermen believe she protects them when they are out at sea, and that she will send large schools of fish for them to catch.

Moqueca (Spicy Fish and Coconut Milk Stew)

Ingredients

- 1 tablespoon vegetable or olive oil
- 2 to 4 cloves garlic, peeled
- 1 onion, finely chopped
- 2 cups coconut milk
- 2 tablespoons tomato paste
- 1 teaspoon fresh cilantro (stems removed), chopped
- 1 pound shrimp, shelled and deveined
- 2 tablespoons white vinegar
- 2 limes
- 2 tablespoons dendê oil (palm oil), optional
- Salt
- Pepper
- White rice (prepared separately)

Directions

1. Place the shrimp in a bowl.
2. In another small bowl, combine the juice of one lime, vinegar, and salt. Pour over shrimp and marinate in the refrigerator for at least 30 minutes.
3. Add 1 tablespoon vegetable or olive oil to a large saucepan and heat over medium heat. Add garlic cloves and cook until golden brown.
4. Add onion and cook, stirring often with a wooden spoon, for about 5 minutes until the onions are softened.
5. Pour shrimp and marinade into pan.
6. Add cilantro, tomato paste, and pepper to taste.
7. Stir in coconut milk and bring the stew to a boil.
8. Lower heat and simmer 10 minutes until shrimp is cooked through.
9. Stir in dendê oil and cook for 5 minutes more. (This step may be omitted.)
10. Serve over white rice.

Serves 6.

Brazil: Afro-Brazilians

Moqueca aos Ovos (Spicy Egg Stew)

Ingredients
12 eggs
3 tablespoons olive oil
2 cloves garlic, minced
3 onions, thinly sliced
2 teaspoons fresh cilantro, minced
White rice (prepared separately)

Directions
1. Break the eggs into a bowl and beat gently.
2. Heat the oil in a large skillet over medium heat and cook the garlic, onion, and cilantro, stirring, until they are lightly browned.
3. Pour the eggs into the skillet, stir, and cook for a few seconds.
4. Reduce the heat to low. Continue to cook, stirring occasionally, about 5 minutes.
5. Season and serve hot over white rice.

Serves 4 to 6.

Quindins (Coconut Macaroons)

Ingredients
¾ cup sugar
1 tablespoon softened butter
1 cup tightly packed grated coconut
5 egg yolks
1 egg white, beaten into stiff peaks

Directions
1. Preheat the oven to 350°F.
2. In a medium-size bowl, mix the sugar, butter, and coconut together.
3. Beat in the egg yolks one at a time, stirring well.
4. In another bowl and using an electric mixer, beat the egg white until it is very stiff and peaks remain on the surface when the beaters are lifted from the whites.
5. Fold (stir very carefully) the beaten egg white into the egg yolk mixture.

Cocada is a sweet treat made from coconut, which is sweetened with condensed milk and baked into bars. © EPD PHOTOS.

6. Grease the molds of a 12-muffin tin with butter and divide the mixture into the molds.
7. Place the muffin tin in a larger baking pan filled with 1 inch of water.
8. Bake for 35 minutes, or until the quindins are golden.
9. Let them cool and remove from the tin.

Serves 12.

Oxalá (Jesus Christ), father of all Orixás, is honored at the Bonfim festival, held each year on the third Thursday in January. Since black beans are thought to be Oxalá's favorite food, many dishes for the festival are made with them.

Festivas Juninas (June Festivals) are held in honor of certain Orixás (the Catholic names for them are St. Anthony, St. Peter, and St. John). Corn, prepared in different ways (including puddings and cakes), is eaten at all of the June Festivals. One popular cornmeal dish, similar to polenta, is *angu de milho*.

⑤ Mealtime Customs

The heart of Afro-Brazilian culture, practiced by descendants of the African slaves brought to

Junior Worldmark Encyclopedia of Foods and Recipes of the World, 2nd Edition **59**

Brazil: Afro-Brazilians

Brazil by the Portuguese, is in the state of Bahia in northeastern Brazil. A large percentage of the people living in these regions are poor. Afro-Brazilians usually eat foods that come from their surroundings, such as fruit and seafood. Other foods are bought at large produce markets in towns or from farms.

Breakfast includes papayas, mangoes, pineapples, warm tapioca with milk and cinnamon, and coffee. Favorite snacks are empanadas (small meat pies) and *pastels*, little pastries filled with meat or fish and olives and cheese.

Brazilian Black Beans

Ingredients

4 strips raw bacon
1 onion
2 cloves garlic
1 cup water
3 cans (14 ounces each) black beans, drained and rinsed
Salt and pepper

Directions

1. Cut the bacon strips into large pieces and fry them in a large pan over medium to high heat, stirring often.
2. Cut the onion in half and peel off the skin and outer layer. Chop both halves into large pieces.
3. Peel the cloves of garlic and chop into small pieces.
4. Add the onion and garlic to bacon, and cook until they are golden brown (about 3 minutes).
5. Add the water and black beans. Turn the heat to low. Cover and simmer for 20 minutes, until thick. If the beans look too thick, stir in more water, ¼ cup at a time. Season with salt and pepper to taste and serve.

Serves 6 to 8.

Angu de Milho (Cornmeal Dish)

Ingredients

3 cups cold water
2 teaspoons salt
¾ cup cornmeal
4 teaspoons butter

Directions

1. Place half of the water (1½ cups) in a medium-size saucepan.
2. Add the salt and bring to a boil over medium heat.
3. Slowly mix the cornmeal into the remaining 1½ cups of water.
4. Gradually pour the cornmeal mixture into the boiling water, stirring constantly.
5. Add the butter and continue to stir continuously while it thickens until it can hold its shape.
6. Pour into a well-buttered 6-cup mold or casserole.
7. Let it cool before removing it from the mold.

Serves 4 to 6.

Along with other foods, street vendors (the equivalent of "fast food") sell the popular snack *acaçá* (steamed rice-flour pudding). It is prepared, wrapped in banana leaves, and steamed. In homes, acaçá is often eaten as a side dish with seafood meals.

A popular dinner is *vatapá*, a creamy dish of fish, shrimp, ground peanuts, coconut milk, dendê oil, and bread, typically served over white rice. *Ximxim de galinha* (chicken with peanuts and cashews) is another well-known dish. Sorbet, or passion fruit-, mango-, lime-, or burnt coconut-flavored ice, is a favorite dessert. Another popular dessert, which has been made for many years, is *olho de sogra* (mother-in-law eyes). These are actually prunes stuffed with coconut, but they look like eyes.

Empanadas (Little Baked Pies)

Ingredients

Dough:

2 cups flour
½ teaspoon salt
5 tablespoons unsalted butter
1 egg
1 tablespoon water

Egg wash:

1 tablespoon water
1 egg yolk

Filling:

1 tablespoon olive oil
1 onion, grated
1 tomato, peeled, seeded, and chopped
¼ cup canned chicken stock
⅛ teaspoon ground nutmeg
1 cup raw shrimp or cooked and shredded chicken
½ cup pitted green or black olives, chopped
1 tablespoon parsley
Salt and pepper, to taste

Directions

Dough:

1. In a bowl, combine flour, salt, and butter.
2. Add the egg and 1 tablespoon of water and mix until smooth. The dough should form a large ball.
3. Cover and set aside.

Egg wash:

1. Beat the egg yolk with 1 tablespoon of water to brush the tops of the empanadas.
2. Set the egg wash aside.

Filling:

1. For the filling, heat the oil over medium heat in a medium skillet.
2. Add the onion and cook for 1 minute.
3. Add the tomato, stock, nutmeg, shrimp or chicken, olives, parsley, and salt and pepper.
4. Simmer and cook for 2 minutes.
5. Remove from the heat.

Empanadas:

1. Preheat oven to 375°F.
2. On a lightly floured board, roll out the dough to ⅛-inch thickness. (Work with half the dough at a time if necessary.)
3. Using a large round cookie cutter or rim of a large glass, cut out circles in dough.
4. Place a heaping tablespoon of the filling onto a circle of dough.
5. Fold in half and press the edges together with fingers or by pressing with the back of a fork.
6. Poke a hole in the top using a toothpick.
7. Brush the tops of the empanadas with the egg wash, and place them on a baking sheet.
8. Bake for 20 minutes, or until golden brown.

Serves 6 to 8.

6 Politics, Economics, and Nutrition

Living conditions for Afro-Brazilians are often poor, with an overwhelming number living in favelas, or slums. Apparent discrimination against Afro-Brazilians keeps many uneducated, illiterate (unable to read), and living in poverty. According to the World Bank, those living in the impoverished areas of Brazil's northeastern states earn about one-tenth of the national average (annual per capita income in 2010 was $10,800). About 6 percent of the population of Brazil is classified as undernourished by the World Bank. This means they do not receive adequate nutrition in their diet.

Brazil: Afro-Brazilians

Many Afro-Brazilians celebrate Iemanja, the goddess of the ocean, on February 2 each year. She is said to protect fishermen at sea and bring large schools of fish their way. © VINICIUS TUPINAMBA / SHUTTERSTOCK.COM.

To address this problem, several programs were set up beginning in the first decade of the 21st century. In 2002 the government of Brazil passed legislation that set quotas for government hiring and university admissions in an effort to improve opportunities for Afro-Brazilians. In 2003 Brazil created its Zero Hunger Program. Many Afro-Brazilians cannot afford the fresh and nutritious foods available to other Brazilians. Through the Zero Hunger Program, several different initiatives to remedy this situation have been put in place. The government provides tokens to people who need food assistance. Many city dwellers and Afro-Brazilians receive these tokens, which can be used to buy food. In addition, school lunch programs have been set up to feed nutritious meals to children in school.

The Brazilian government considers child poverty one of the country's most serious problems. It estimates that about one-third of the children in Brazil live in poverty. In addition, half of the poorest Brazilians are less than 19 years old. Of the Brazilians living in extreme poverty, about 71 percent are Afro-Brazilian. Many impoverished children spend their days on the streets of Brazil's cities. International observers consider the child poverty in Brazil to be a human rights issue, but many Brazilians see the children as a threat to security in the cities.

Acaçá
(Steamed Rice Flour Pudding)

Ingredients

2 tablespoons olive oil
1⅓ cups canned unsweetened coconut milk
1 cup milk
1½ cups rice flour (available at Latin American and specialty food stores)
⅓ cup heavy cream
Salt and pepper, to taste

Directions

1. In a large saucepan, mix together the olive oil, coconut milk, milk, and salt and pepper.
2. Bring to a boil over high heat.
3. Reduce the heat to medium and whisk in the rice flour a little at a time, stirring constantly until mixture is smooth and thick (about 8 minutes).
4. Gradually add the cream, mix, and pour into a lightly oiled 8x8-inch shallow oven-proof pan.
5. Let it cool for a few minutes.
6. Cut into small squares and serve.

Serves 8 to 12.

Olho de Sogra
(Mother-in-Law Eyes)

Ingredients

1 cup water
1¼ cup sugar
1 cup coconut, grated
2 large egg yolks
½ teaspoon vanilla extract
1 pound pitted prunes
Whole cloves, for garnish

The sweet treats, Olho de Sogra (Mother-in-law Eyes), may be enjoyed anytime. Some people may prefer not to eat the whole clove in the center. © EPD PHOTOS.

Directions

1. Place 1 cup each of the sugar, water, and coconut in a medium-size saucepan and cook over low heat until mixture thickens, about 15 minutes.
2. Remove from heat and let cool.
3. Whip egg yolks until lemon-colored, and add them to the coconut mixture.
4. Add the vanilla and return mixture to stove.
5. Cook and stir over low heat for about 5 minutes.
6. Remove from heat and cool again.
7. Slice the prunes open lengthwise.
8. Stuff the inside of the prunes with the mixture.
9. Place a piece of clove in the center of the mixture.
10. Roll the prunes in the remaining sugar.
11. Serve them on a platter or in individual paper baking cups.

Serves 8 to 12.

To combat extreme poverty, the government of Brazil also started the program Bolsa Família in 2003, which pays small sums to impoverished families in exchange for keeping their children in school and having periodic health checks for their children. The program makes it easier for families to keep their children healthy through improved diet, vaccinations, and nutrition monitoring, and it gives an incentive to keep children off the streets. The World Bank estimates the program raised 20 million out of poverty between 2003 and 2009, and about 12.7 million families (50 million people) were receiving such assistance in 2010. In 2006, a National Food and Nutritional Security System was enacted into law, and in 2012, an expansion of Bolsa Família, Brazil without Misery, was enacted. The program aims to eliminate extreme poverty in four years. This combination of programs has caused steep, noticeable drops in child mortality and malnutrition in less than a decade, though much work remains to be done.

7 Further Study

BOOKS

Fleetwood, Jenni. *South American Food and Cooking*. London, UK: Southwater, 2005.

Idone, Christopher. *Brazil: A Cook's Tour*. New York: Clarkson N. Potter, 1995.

Living in Bahia. London: Taschen, 2008.

Merrell, Floyd. *Capoeira and Candomble*. Princeton, NJ: Markus Wiener Publishers, 2005.

Robinson, Alex. *Bahia: The Heart of Brazil's Northeast*. Chalfont St. Peter: Bradt Travel Guides, 2010.

Sheen, Barbara. *Foods of Brazil*. Detroit: KidHaven Press, 2008.

WEB SITES

Alden, Alexandra. "The Museum of Bahian Cuisine." *Rio Times*. http://riotimesonline.com/brazil-news/rio-travel/the-museum-of-bahian-cuisine/ (accessed on January 23, 2012).

Global Gourmet. http://www.globalgourmet.com/destinations/brazil/guarana.html (accessed on January 23, 2012).

Whats4Eats. http://www.whats4eats.com/south-america/brazil-cuisine/ (accessed on January 23, 2012).

Cameroon

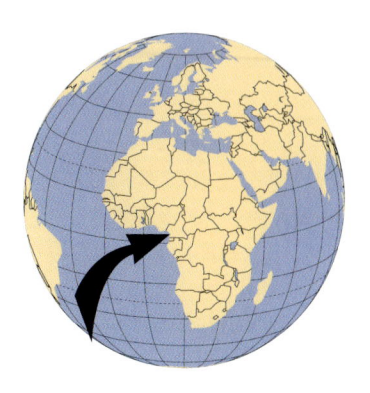

- Safou a la Sauce Tomate 67
- Traditional Fufu.............................68
- Easy Fufu 68
- Koki 68
- Ndolé (Bitterleaf Stew) 70
- Banana and Pineapple Salad 70
- Boiled Cassava 70
- Coconut Rice 71

1 Geographic Setting and Environment

Situated in West Africa, Cameroon, shaped like an elongated triangle, contains an area of 183,568 square miles (475,440 square kilometers). Comparatively, the area occupied by Cameroon is slightly larger than the state of California. Cameroon is rich in natural resources. In 2008, its exports included crude oil, timber, and aluminum products. The country also grows coffee, tea, bananas, rubber, palms (for palm oil), pineapples, and cotton for export.

There are four geographical regions: the western lowlands, which extend along the Gulf of Guinea coast; the northwestern highlands, which consist of forested volcanic mountains, including Mount Cameroon, the nation's only active volcano and the highest peak in West Africa; the central region, which extends eastward to the border with the Central African Republic; and the northern region, which is essentially a vast tropical plain that slopes down to the Chad Basin.

The southern and northern regions of the country are two distinct climatic areas. In the south there are two dry seasons, December to February, and July to September. The northern part of the country has a more comfortable climate.

2 History and Food

Many staples of the Cameroonian diet came from the explorers from Europe. The Portuguese arrived in Cameroon in 1472 and brought with them such foods as hot peppers, maize (corn), cassava (a root vegetable), and tomatoes.

Other Europeans settled on the Cameroon coast in the mid-1800s. The British arrived first, followed by the French and Germans. The French influence is reflected in the presence of some foods, such as omelets and French bread, as well as in the preparation of some dishes. For the most part, Cameroonian cooking has maintained traditional methods for preparing traditional foods.

Cameroon

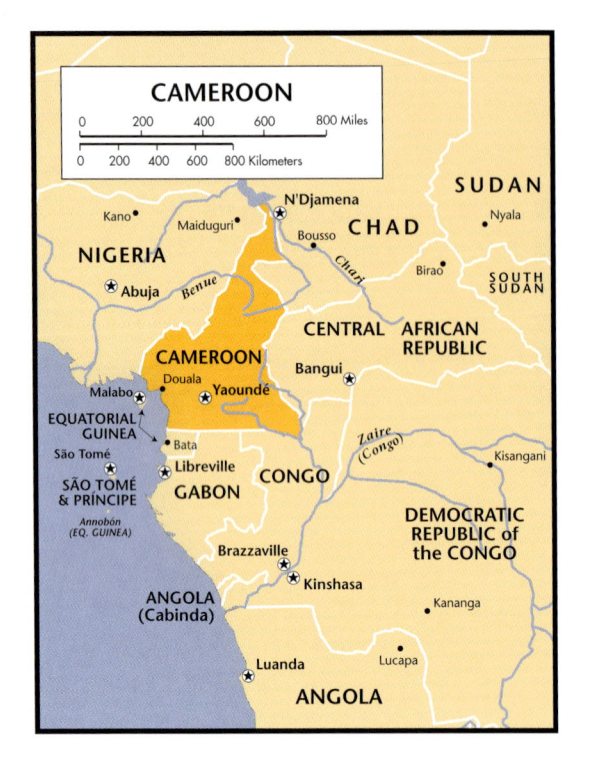

Foreign restaurants can be found in the larger towns and cities of Cameroon. Restaurants in the coastal city of Douala feature seafood from the waters of the Gulf of Guinea. Inland, restaurants in the capital city, Yaoundé, offer a variety of cuisines, including Chinese, French, Italian, Russian, and traditional Cameroonian food. In the smaller cities, street vendors and restaurants serve more traditional favorites than foreign dishes.

3 Foods of the Cameroonians

The staple foods eaten by the people of Cameroon vary from region to region, depending on climate, and what is grown locally. In general, the Cameroonian diet is characterized by bland, starchy foods that are eaten with spicy (often very hot) sauces. Meat on skewers, fried and roasted fish, curries, and peppery soups are common dishes. A favorite dish from the southern part of the country, *ndolé*, has become popular everywhere in the country, and it is considered the national dish.

Staple foods eaten in the north are corn, millet, and peanuts. In the south, people eat more root vegetables, such as yams and cassava, as well as plantains (similar to bananas). In both north and south regions, the starchy foods are cooked, then pounded with a pestle (a hand-held tool, usually wooden) until they form a sticky mass called *fufu* (or foofoo), which is then formed into balls and dipped into tasty sauces.

Cassava, plantains, and other ingredients may be found in the produce section of larger grocery stores outside of Africa, as well as in Asian and African specialty stores.

The sauces in Cameroon are made of ingredients such as cassava leaves, okra, and tomatoes. The food most typical in the southern region of Cameroon, ndolé, is made of boiled, shredded bitterleaf (a type of green), peanuts, and melon seeds. It is seasoned with spices and hot oil, and it can be cooked with fish or meat.

Bobolo, made of fermented cassava shaped into a loaf, is popular in both the south and central regions. *Koki* is a popular bean-based dish. Traditionally, the koki is wrapped in banana leaves, but aluminum foil is now widely used in place of the leaves.

Fresh fruit is plentiful in Cameroon. The native mangoes are especially enjoyed. Other fruits grown locally and sold in village marketplaces include oranges, papayas, bananas, pineapples, coconuts, grapefruit, and limes. Coconut is a popular ingredient used to flavor dishes such as coconut rice.

Fried prunes are simmered in a savory tomato sauce and served over rice for a filling, casual family dinner. © EPD PHOTOS.

Safou a la Sauce Tomate (Prunes in Tomato Sauce)

Ingredients
- 12 prunes
- 1 cup water
- 2 cups tomato sauce
- 2 tablespoons peanut oil
- 2 cups cooked rice

Directions
1. Rinse the prunes, cut them in half, and remove the pits.
2. In a saucepan, simmer the prunes with water until soft, about 4 minutes. Drain.
3. In a frying pan, heat the peanut oil over medium heat and fry the prunes, about 2 minutes.
4. Measure the tomato sauce into a medium saucepan, then add the fried prunes.
5. Cook over medium heat for 5 minutes. Serve over rice.

Serves 4 to 6.

❹ Food for Religious and Holiday Celebrations

During the month-long observance of the holiday of Ramadan, Cameroon's Muslims, like many Muslims elsewhere, fast from dawn to dusk. (About 20 percent of the population is Muslim.) This means they are forbidden to eat or drink during the day. The evening meal during Ramadan may include a rich soup.

In most areas, a *fete des mouton* festival (also known elsewhere as Eid al-Adha) is celebrated two months after Ramadan. The festival is held to remember the willingness of Abraham to obey God's command that he sacrifice his own son. This celebration lasts for several days, during which it is customary for people to slaughter and roast a sheep and then visit their friends and neighbors, giving them gifts of meat.

Cameroon

Traditional Fufu

Ingredients
2 to 4 pounds (4 to 8 large) white or yellow yams (not sweet potatoes

Directions
1. Scrub the yams. Place them in a large pot and cover them with water.
2. Bring the water to a boil and cook for 20 to 30 minutes, until the yams are soft. (The skins will be easy to cut through with a fork or knife.)
3. Drain yams into a colander, and run cold water over them to cool them.
4. Peel the yams and return them to the pot.
5. Using a potato masher or wooden spoon, mash and beat the cooked yams for 10 to 15 minutes until completely smooth. (A helper can hold the pot steady while the yams are being beaten.)
6. Shape the fufu into balls and serve with stew, sauce, or gravy.

Serves 8 to 10.

Easy Fufu

This is a good recipe to make with a friend, so you can share the job of stirring the stiff mixture and holding the pot steady. Neither the ingredients nor the process is authentic, but the results are similar in texture to the fufu prepared from cassava.

Ingredients
2½ cups instant flour mix (such as Jiffy Mix or Bisquick)
2½ cups instant mashed potato flakes
1 cup tapioca (made from cassava)
6 cups water

Directions
1. Bring the water to a boil in a large pot.
2. Mix the instant flour mix, instant potato flakes, and tapioca together. Add the mixture to the boiling water, about 2 cups at a time. The mixture should be thicker and stiffer than mashed potatoes.
3. Stir constantly for 10 to 15 minutes while the mixture continues to boil. (The mixture will become very thick and difficult to stir, but it is important that it be stirred continuously.)
4. Let the mixture cool. Form the fufu into balls.
5. Serve with a spicy stew or soup.

Serves 8 to 10.

Koki

Note: This recipe involves hot oil and requires adult supervision.

Ingredients
2 15-ounce cans black-eyed peas, rinsed and drained
1 sweet pepper
1 cup palm oil
Salt
Aluminum foil

Directions
1. Chop pepper into small pieces.
2. Place rinsed black-eyed peas into a bowl and crush them with a wooden spoon until they form a thick paste. Stir in a little water to make paste smooth.
3. Heat the oil in a pan. When warm, add half the oil to the bean paste.
4. Fry chopped pepper in the remaining oil.
5. Add fried peppers to the bean paste.
6. Wrap servings of the mixture in aluminum foil. Use about 1 cup of bean paste per aluminum wrap.
7. Place wrapped bean packets into a large pot or stovetop steamer.
8. Boil or steam for one to three hours, depending on the size of the packets. Finished koki will be cooked to the center.
9. Serve hot or cold.

Serves 8 to 10.

Cameroon

Fresh fruit is plentiful in Cameroon and available from vendors at various outdoor markets. © SETH LAZAR/ALAMY.

Most Cameroonians, even those who are not Christian, celebrate Christmas. (About 40 percent of the population is Christian.) It is a time for visiting friends and family, and for exchanging gifts. Holidays and events, such as saying goodbye to someone going abroad, weddings, and even funerals, are marked by feasts and meals at which friends and neighbors gather to eat local favorite dishes. It is traditional to slaughter and cook a sheep or goat on important occasions. Chicken dishes are also popular holiday fare.

5 Mealtime Customs

At mealtime, damp towels may be passed out to diners (before and after the meal), to wash their hands. Cameroonians eat out of communal bowls. Using their right hands, they dip three fingers into the starchy food—often fufu or a millet dish—and then into the stews or sauces of the meal. It is customary for the men to serve themselves first, while the women wait patiently. The children eat what is left after the adults have finished.

People of Cameroon eat three meals a day. A variety of foods, including fruit, porridge, and boiled plantains, may be eaten for breakfast. Eggs and boiled cassava are also popular choices. Lunch and dinner are likely to feature a starchy dish such as fufu, boiled cassava, rice, or millet, generally served with a vegetable soup or a hearty stew.

Cameroon

Ndolé (Bitterleaf Stew)

Ingredients

2 cups dried bitterleaf (a type of green common to Cameroon; may substitute spinach, kale, collards, or turnip greens)
½ pound cooked shrimp (or 1 cup dried shrimp, if available)
1 cup natural-style peanut butter
1 large onion, chopped
2 cups water
2 tablespoons fresh ginger, grated
2 cloves garlic, crushed
6 tomatoes, chopped
2 to 3 tablespoons vegetable oil
Salt and pepper to taste

Directions

1. If using bitterleaf, soak the bitterleaf overnight; drain in the morning and press out the excess water.
2. If using kale, collards, or turnip greens, wash the greens, chop them, and cook them in a pot of boiling water for 5 minutes.
3. If using spinach, wash the leaves and chop the spinach.
4. Heat 2 tablespoons of oil in a large pot and add the onions, garlic, and ginger. Sauté for 3 minutes.
5. Add the chopped tomatoes, reduce heat, and simmer for about 3 minutes.
6. Add the greens and simmer, stirring frequently, about 5 minutes. (If using spinach, do not add it yet.)
7. Add the peanut butter. Stir to combine well, cover the pot, and continue simmering until the greens are tender (about 15 minutes). If mixture seems too dry, add water, ½ cup at a time.
8. Cut shrimp into small pieces.
9. Cook for 10 more minutes, then add the spinach.
10. Serve with rice or boiled plantains and fufu.

Serves 6 to 8.

Banana and Pineapple Salad

Ingredients

2 firm, ripe bananas, peeled and sliced
2 firm, ripe tomatoes, sliced
1 small pineapple, peeled and sliced
1 avocado, peeled, pitted, and sliced
1 tablespoon roasted peanuts, chopped
1 can coconut milk

Directions

1. Boil the coconut milk until it thickens.
2. Set it aside to cool.
3. Pile the bananas, tomatoes, pineapple, and avocado alternately in layers in individual glass dishes.
4. Top with chopped peanuts and the thickened coconut milk.
5. Serve cold.

Serves 4 to 6.

Boiled Cassava

Ingredients

2 cassava
Water
1 teaspoon salt

Directions

1. Wash the cassava, then peel off the thin white and brown skins.
2. Cut the cassava into 3- to 4-inch long pieces.
3. Cut each piece in two and remove the midrib.
4. Place the cassava into a pot with enough water to cover the cassava half way. Add salt.
5. Boil until the cassava is soft, but not falling apart.
6. Drain and serve hot with fish or meat stew.

Serves 2 to 4.

Cameroon

Carrots, pepper, thyme, allspice, lemon zest, and rice are added to simmering coconut milk. The finished dish, Coconut Rice, is a colorful mixture of rice, vegetables, and spices. © EPD PHOTOS.

Coconut Rice

Ingredients

1 cup long grain rice
2½ cups coconut milk
1 onion
2 carrots
Grated zest from 1 lemon
1 yellow pepper
1 teaspoon allspice
1 teaspoon thyme
2 tablespoons olive oil

Directions

1. Chop onion, carrots, and pepper into small pieces.
2. Heat the oil in a large pan and fry the onion until soft and translucent.
3. Pour in the coconut milk and bring to a boil.
4. Stir in the carrots, pepper, thyme, allspice, lemon zest, and the rice.
5. Bring to a simmer and then cook over low heat until rice has absorbed almost all the liquid.
6. Cover the pot and then steam until rice is fully cooked.

Serves 4.

Many dishes feature fresh fruits grown in the country. Coconut milk and peanuts are two other common ingredients that appear in recipes for soups, sauces, and other dishes.

Meal preparation is very time consuming. Preparation of fufu, for example, can take days. The cassava or yams must be boiled and pounded into a pulpy mass. The preparation of fufu from powdered starch or rice is less complicated, but still requires much stirring. Cooking in the villages generally takes place over wood or charcoal fires, with iron pots and wooden spoons. In towns, canisters of propane may be used to power gas stoves. Even at the beginning of the 21st century, electricity is seldom available for cooking use except in the largest cities.

6 Politics, Economics, and Nutrition

The United Nations classifies Cameroon as a low-income, food deficit country (LIFDC). The Cameroonian government has tried unsuccessfully to improve nutrition and health care. About 40 percent of the population lives in

Cameroon

A vendor in Douala, Cameroon, grills up some barbecued meat and some fresh plantains for customers. © PETER TREANOR/ALAMY.

poverty, earning just $1 per day. Half of those living in poverty live in rural areas. In 2005, the country's local leaders signed an agreement to improve food security in their communities. They also agreed to take action to improve the way food is distributed.

This agreement wasn't enough. In 2006, it was estimated that almost 17 percent of children under five were malnourished. Lack of nutrition was reported as a leading cause of death in children in Cameroon in 2009, especially in the north of the country. In 2011, the government began a program to improve the supply of rice. Working with the International Fund for Agricultural Development (IFAD), the government was to provide farmers with better rice seed. Farmers also receive training in how to avoid crop losses. IFAD also helps farmers learn to be better at selling their rice. The IFAD project helps farmers grow onions, which have commercial value and can help the farmers earn more money.

Cameroon also has a shortage of doctors and medical supplies. The overall life expectancy is just about 54 years. Less than half the children receive immunization against common diseases such as tuberculosis, polio, and measles.

In 2008, about 74 percent of the total population had access to safe drinking water. In rural areas, only 51 percent had safe water, while 92 percent of those living in cities did.

Tetanus is a major cause of death among mothers and newborns, especially in the northern regions. In 2010, the United Nations began a campaign in northwest Cameroon to provide tetanus vaccinations to eliminate maternal neonatal tetanus in Cameroon.

Families spend about one-third of their income on food—mostly on plantains, cassava, corn, millet, and small amounts of meat. Peanuts, called groundnuts, are an important source of protein.

7 Further Study

BOOKS

Cusick, Heidi Haughy. *Soul and Spice*. San Francisco: Chronicle Books, 1995.

Heine, Peter. *Food Culture in the Near East, Middle East, and North Africa*. Westport, CT: Greenwood, Press, 2004.

McCann, James. *Stirring the Pot: A History of African Cuisine*. Athens: Ohio University Press, 2009.

Montgomery, Bertha Vining, and Constance Nabwire. *Cooking the West African Way*. Minneapolis: Lerner Publications, 2002.

Sheehan, Sean. *Cameroon*. 2nd ed. New York: Marshall Cavendish Benchmark, 2011.

WEB SITES

African Cooking and Recipes. http://www.africancooking.org/ (accessed on January 23, 2012).

CeltNet Cameroonian Recipes. http://www.celtnet.org.uk/recipes/cameroon.php (accessed on January 23, 2012).

Friends of Cameroon: Cooking. http://www.friendsofcameroon.org/cooking (accessed on January 23, 2012).

U.S. Peace Corps: Cameroon. http://www.peacecorps.gov/index.cfm?shell=learn.wherepc.africa&cntry=Cameroon (accessed on February 2, 2012).

UNICEF: Cameroon. http://www.unicef.org/infobycountry/cameroon.html (accessed on February 2, 2012).

Canada

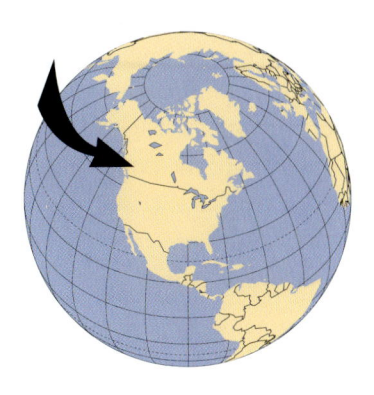

- Yorkshire Pudding 77
- Sautéed Fiddleheads 77
- Canadian Bacon 78
- Sweet Corn Pancakes 78
- Canada Day Cake 79
- Cock-a-Leekie Soup 80
- Nanaimo Bars 81
- Fish and Brewis 82
- Maple Syrup Upside-Down Cake 82
- Maple Sundae 82

1 Geographic Setting and Environment

Canada is the world's second-largest country (after Russia) and is the largest country in North America. The eastern provinces, known as the Maritimes, are separated from the rest of the country by low mountain ranges. Newfoundland and Prince Edward Island are island provinces in the Atlantic Ocean.

Along the border with the United States in the center of Canada is a fertile plain bounded by the Saint Lawrence River, Lake Ontario, and the Hudson Bay. Also along the U.S. border farther to the west are farms and ranches. Extending through western Alberta to the Pacific Ocean is the northern portion of the Rocky Mountain range. Mount Logan, at 19,524 feet (5,915 meters) the highest peak in Canada, is near the Alaska border. The climate varies across the vast Canadian territory. The West Coast gets about 60–120 inches (150–300 centimeters) of rain each year; the center part of the country gets less that 20 inches (50 centimeters), and the Maritime provinces, 45–60 inches (115–150 centimeters). In British Columbia, there are 252 rainy days each year, but in the center of the country, there are just 100.

Statistics Canada reported that the 2010 population was about 34 million, up from 30 million in 2001. Nearly 80 percent of Canadians live in communities with a population of 10,000 or more. More than half of the population is concentrated in four broad regions: southern Ontario; Montréal and the surrounding region; southern British Columbia and southern Vancouver Island; and the region stretching between Calgary and Edmonton in the western province of Alberta.

Commercial agriculture is one of the top five sectors of the economy. Major crops for export include wheat, other grains, and seeds for making oils. Other agricultural products include dairy products, fish, and fruits and vegetables.

Canada

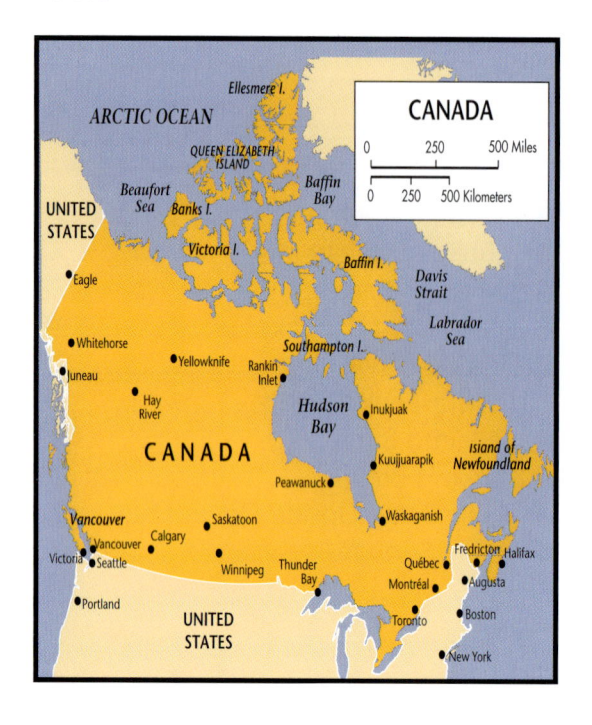

② History and Food

France and England battled over who would colonize the territory of Canada in the late 1400s. The English explorer John Cabot (active 1471–1498) arrived in Newfoundland in 1497. About 40 years later, in 1534, Jacques Cartier (1491–1557) began his exploration of Canada on behalf of France. By the early 1600s, there were permanent French colonies, and in 1663, New France was established as a territory of France. French fur traders competed with the traders of the Hudson's Bay Company, run by British merchants. Wars in North America, known as the French and Indian Wars, were waged in the 1700s. The Treaty of Paris in 1763 ended the armed fighting and established British rule over all of the territory formerly called New France.

In 1846 conflict over the western portion of the United States–Canada border was resolved, and the border was set at 49°north latitude. This border has been undisputed ever since.

Food and other customs in Canada still carry hints of the colonial influences of Great Britain and France. Canadians speak English, although both French and English are official languages, reflecting the influence of French settlers. In Quebec, the official language by law is French and 80 percent of the population speaks French as their first language. (English is spoken in Quebec as well.) But there are other regional differences in food and customs, too.

Food in the provinces of Eastern Canada shows signs of British heritage, except in Quebec where the influence is French. In the provinces of Western Canada, the cuisine reflects the explorers and settlers, who, like their southern neighbors in the United States, made simple, hearty meals from available ingredients. In northern Canada—Northwest, Yukon, and Nunavut territories—the diet is limited by the short growing season, dominated by preserved food ingredients, and influenced by the native Inuit diet. Along the West Coast in British Columbia, immigrants from Asian nations influenced food and cultural practices. In Vancouver in the west and Toronto in the east (and in many places elsewhere in Canada), Lunar New Year celebrations were inspired by the citizens of Asian heritage living there, but are enjoyed by many other Canadians as well.

③ Foods of the Canadians

The favorite foods of Canadians vary slightly from region to region, and are strongly influenced by their family heritage, especially in relation to holiday celebrations. Along the Atlantic coast, seafood and dishes derived from British traditions (except in Quebec) are common. Yorkshire pudding, adapted from the British recipe, is a favorite among Canadians. In Quebec, favorite foods come from the area's French heritage.

Yorkshire Pudding

Ingredients
1 cup flour
1 pinch salt
1 pinch pepper
2 eggs
1¼ cup milk
Vegetable oil

Directions
1. Preheat oven to 425°F
2. In a large bowl whisk together flour, salt and pepper, eggs and milk until batter is smooth.
3. Refrigerate batter for about 30 minutes.
4. Place a pea-sized drop of vegetable oil into each cup in a 6-muffin tin and heat in the oven until oil is smoking.
5. Pour batter into muffin tin cups until they are about three-quarters full.
6. Cook for about 25 minutes, until golden brown.
7. Remove and serve hot.

Makes 6 pudding cups.

Sautéed Fiddleheads

Ingredients
1 bunch fiddleheads
1 tablespoon butter
1 tablespoon olive oil

Directions
1. Trim the fiddleheads so that the stem end is about 2 inches long. Rub the dry brown flakes off the fiddleheads and rinse well.

These fiddleheads have been cleaned and are ready for cooking.
© KML/SHUTTERSTOCK.COM.

2. Fill a saucepan with cool water and plunge the fiddleheads into the water to rinse off any grit.
3. Remove the fiddleheads from the pan, change the water, and repeat the soaking. Rinse the fiddleheads under running water to remove any remaining grit.
4. Rinse and dry the saucepan. Measure oil and butter into it and heat until the butter is melted.
5. Add the fiddleheads and sauté, stirring with a wooden spoon, for about 5 minutes. Fiddleheads will be bright green and crispy.

Serves 8 to 10.

Throughout Canada, maple syrup and maple products are popular, reflecting the significance of the maple tree, whose leaf adorns the flag of Canada. Many families enjoy a visit in early spring to a maple sugar "shack," the special rustic building where sap from maple trees is boiled in a large open pan to make maple syrup.

Later in the spring, many people in Eastern Canada visit a wooded area to harvest fiddleheads, so named because they look like the coiled end of a violin ("fiddle"). Fiddleheads are the tasty new sprouts of woodland ferns, picked before they develop into large lacy fronds. They

Canada

are a fragile spring specialty, usually available for just a few weeks in the spring. Grocery stores in Canada may stock frozen fiddleheads alongside other frozen vegetables.

Western Canadians enjoy the products of the large ranches and farms in that part of the country. Barbecued food, beef, and corn dishes, such as sweet corn pancakes, are popular. Berries, such as blueberries and saskatoon berries, are popular accompaniments to pancakes and waffles. These fruits are often made into syrups, jams, and preserves.

Although Canada is known for some for its beers (such as Molson and Labatt), nonalcoholic beverages that are favorites in Canada are spruce beer (made from spruce trees, a specialty of eastern Canada), and apple and cherry ciders.

Canadian Bacon with Maple Glaze

Ingredients

½ cup cider vinegar
¾ cup maple syrup
1 tablespoon brown sugar
1 pound (approximately) Canadian bacon

Directions

1. Preheat oven to 300°F (150°C).
2. Combine vinegar, maple syrup, and brown sugar in a bowl. Set aside.
3. Slice Canadian bacon about ½-inch thick. Arrange the slices in a casserole or baking dish, and spoon the syrup mixture over the slices.
4. Bake for 30 minutes. Serve hot or at room temperature. (To serve as a snack, cut slices into bite-sized pieces and serve with toothpicks.)

Serves 6 for lunch or dinner, or up to 20 as a snack.

④ Food for Religious and Holiday Celebrations

Canadian Thanksgiving is celebrated on the second Monday in October. A typical menu for Thanksgiving is similar to that served in the country's neighbor to the south, the United States.

Sweet Corn Pancakes

Ingredients

6 eggs, separated (Note: To separate eggs, crack the egg and allow just the white to fall into the bowl, holding the yolk in one of the shell halves. Transfer the yolk back and forth between the two shell halves, being careful not to break it, until all the white has dripped into the bowl. Put the yolk into a separate bowl.)
¼ cup half-and-half
1 tablespoon sour cream
⅓ cup flour
1 teaspoon baking soda
1 teaspoon baking powder
½ cup corn (may be fresh or frozen corn kernels)
Vegetable oil to grease the pan

Directions

1. Beat the egg whites until they hold soft peaks when the beaters are lifted up.
2. In another bowl, combine the egg yolks, half-and-half, and sour cream.
3. Gradually add the dry ingredients to the egg yolk mixture. Add the beaten egg whites, using a gentle stirring motion to combine them with the yolk mixture.
4. Add the corn and stir gently. Pour a small amount of oil into a non-stick pan and heat it over medium heat. Drop batter, about 1 tablespoonful at a time, into the pan for each pancake and cook until golden brown on each side.

Serves 4 to 6.

Canadian bacon is a popular meat in Canada. In grocery stores, it often comes with a layer of peameal around it. © MICHAEL C. GRAY/SHUTTERSTOCK.COM.

Canada Day Cake

Ingredients
1 white or yellow cake mix
1 container white frosting
1 quart strawberries
Picture of Canadian flag

Directions
1. Prepare cake according to package directions. Bake in a 9-inch by 13-inch cake pan. Allow cake to cool.
2. Frost cake with white frosting. Using a knife or spatula, make surface of frosting as smooth as possible. (It may help to dip the knife or spatula into a glass of water.)
3. Slice the strawberries, and arrange in rows at the left and right edges of the cake to represent the stripes at the edges of Canada's maple leaf flag.
4. Referring to the picture of the flag, arrange the sliced strawberries in the center of the cake to represent the Maple Leaf.

Serves 24.

Burns Day is celebrated January 25 to commemorate the birthday of poet Robert Burns (1759–1796). It is especially significant for people of Scottish descent worldwide, and Scottish-Canadians are no exception. On Burns Day, the menu includes such Scottish favorites as haggis,

Canada

> ### Typical Thanksgiving Menu
>
> Beet Soup
>
> Roast Turkey with Corn Bread Stuffing
>
> Cranapple Relish
>
> Brussel Sprouts
>
> Mashed Potatoes
>
> Burnished Squash Wedges
>
> Pumpkin Pie

cock-a-leekie soup (chicken-based leek soup), and Dundee cake (a rich fruitcake).

Cock-a-Leekie Soup

Ingredients

2 tablespoons vegetable oil
2 cups sliced leeks
2 boneless, skinless chicken breasts, cubed
6 cups chicken stock
¾ cup long grain rice
1 strip lemon peel
1 bay leaf
1 teaspoon salt
¼ teaspoon pepper

Directions

1. Heat oil over medium heat in a large pan. Add sliced leeks and cook until softened.
2. Add chicken to mixture and cook on medium-high until meat is cooked all the way through.
3. Add the chicken stock, rice, lemon peel, and bay leaf, bringing the mixture to a boil.
4. On low heat, simmer the mixture for 20 minutes until rice is tender.
5. Discard lemon peel and bay leaf.
6. Add salt and pepper and serve warm.

Serves 4.

On Canada Day (July 1), Canadians celebrate their independence from the United Kingdom with picnics and fireworks (similar to the Fourth of July in the United States). It became a national holiday in 1982. Dishes served are typical casual dining fare, such as hamburgers and hot dogs, and table settings feature the patriotic color scheme of Canada's red and white maple leaf flag.

A common treat served across Canada is the Nanaimo bar. It is believed that Nanaimo bars, a sweet bar cookie made in layers, originated in the 1950s in the Vancouver area, when a recipe was published in the *Vancouver Sun* newspaper. (The city of Nanaimo is located west of Vancouver on Vancouver Island.) Since then, many variations on the original recipe have been developed. The recipe appears more complicated than it is because of the three separate layers.

5 Mealtime Customs

Most Canadians eat three meals each day, with breakfast featuring cold cereal, pastries, fruit juices, and hot beverages such as coffee, tea, or hot chocolate. At around noon, Canadians may enjoy a sandwich or soup; students may carry a ham and cheese sandwich, chips or pretzels, and fruit to eat at noon during the school lunch break.

For dinner, depending on where they live, Canadians may have seafood (West Coast or Maritime East Coast provinces), beef (western Canada, especially Alberta), or chicken or pork. Many Canadians enjoy gravy, serving it frequently with potatoes prepared in many different ways. A traditional Newfoundland dish, "fish and brewis," features salt cod and a "hard bread" called brewis. Both ingredients may be stored through the long winter months. Desserts featuring maple syrup, such as Maple Syrup Upside-Down Cake or a simple maple sundae, are popular treats.

Nanaimo Bars

Nanaimo Bars have three layers.

Ingredients

Bottom layer:
½ cup butter
¼ cup sugar
⅓ cup unsweetened cocoa
1 egg
1 teaspoon vanilla
2 cups crushed graham crackers (packaged graham cracker crumbs may be used)
1 cup shredded coconut
½ cup chopped walnuts

Middle layer:
¼ cup butter
2 cups confectioners' sugar
2 tablespoons vanilla custard powder (available in Canada, but not in the United States; instant vanilla pudding powder may be substituted)
3 tablespoons milk

Top layer:
4 ounces semisweet chocolate
1 tablespoon butter

Directions
1. *Make bottom layer:* Grease a 9-inch square cake pan.
2. Combine ½ cup butter, sugar, cocoa, egg, and vanilla in a heavy sauce pan. Heat over low heat, stirring constantly, until mixture thickens.
3. Add graham crackers crumbs, coconut, and chopped walnuts, stirring to combine. Press the mixture in the greased pan.
4. *Make middle layer:* Beat together ¼ cup butter, confectioners' sugar, vanilla custard or pudding powder, and milk, until the mixture is creamy.

The Nanaimo Bar, with its three sweet layers, is a popular treat in Canada. © SIMONE VAN DEN BERG/SHUTTERSTOCK.COM.

5. Spread over graham cracker base in cake pan. Refrigerate bars until firm, at least 1 hour.
6. *Make top layer:* Melt semi-sweet chocolate and 1 tablespoon butter. Drizzle over chilled bars. Return to refrigerator to chill until firm (at least 1 hour).
7. Cut into squares and serve.

Serves 16.

6 Politics, Economics, and Nutrition

Agriculture contributes to both the national and provincial economies. Only about 5 percent of Canada's land is considered arable (able to grow crops). As of 2011, agriculture contributed about 2.2 percent to the country's gross domestic product (GDP), though agribusiness (which includes things such as food and tobacco processing and food and beverage industries) contributed about 8 percent to the GDP. The trend is toward larger farms, with many small farmers dependent on non-farm income. Canadian farms produce grains such as wheat, barley, corn, and oats. Canada ranks as one of the world's top grain exporters. Canadian farmers and ranchers also raise livestock for export, especially in Alberta, Saskatchewan, and Manitoba.

Canada

Fish and Brewis

Ingredients
2 pounds salt cod
6 loaves hard bread, called brewis (not readily available in the United States)
1 cup salt pork

Directions
1. Place salt cod in a saucepan, cover with water, and allow to soak overnight. Place brewis in another saucepan, cover with water, and allow this to soak overnight also.
2. *Make fish:* Drain salt cod and return to saucepan. Refill saucepan with fresh water, heat to simmering, and cook, covered, for 20 minutes. Drain, flake the fish into serving-sized pieces, and arrange with brewis on a serving platter.
3. *Make brewis (hard bread):* Do not drain hard bread. Heat over medium-low heat until water simmers. Simmer, covered, for about 15 minutes. Drain and place cooked brewis on a serving platter with fish. Place the platter, loosely covered, in the oven on the lowest setting to keep warm.
4. *Make scrunchions:* Dice the salt pork into small cubes and sauté them in a skillet until golden brown.
5. Serve the fish and brewis, topped with scrunchions.

Serves 6 to 8.

Maple Syrup Upside-Down Cake

Ingredients
1 cup maple syrup
1 tablespoon butter, softened
3 tablespoons sugar
1 egg
1 cup flour
2 teaspoons baking powder
Pinch of salt
¼ teaspoon cinnamon or nutmeg
½ cup milk
¼ cup chopped walnuts (optional)
Vanilla ice cream or whipped topping as accompaniment (optional)

Directions
1. Preheat oven to 350°F (175°C).
2. Measure butter, sugar, and egg into a bowl, and beat with a wooden spoon or electric mixer until creamy.
3. Mix flour, baking powder, salt, and cinnamon (or nutmeg) together. Add the dry ingredients and the milk, a little at a time and alternating between the two, to the creamed butter mixture. Stir until well blended.
4. Measure syrup into a small saucepan. Heat the syrup until it boils, and pour it into a generously buttered 8-inch square baking pan. If using chopped walnuts, add them to the hot syrup.
5. Scoop up the dough in four large balls and drop them into the hot maple syrup. Using two forks, stretch the edges of the dough balls until the dough forms one large mass. Bake at 350°F (175°C) for 30 minutes.
6. Serve warm, with ice cream or whipping cream (if desired).

Serves 16.

Maple Sundae

Ingredients
3 tablespoons pure maple syrup
Vanilla ice cream
Chopped nuts (optional)
Whipped topping (optional)

Directions
1. Spoon vanilla ice cream into bowls.
2. Drizzle about 3 tablespoons of maple syrup over the ice cream.
3. Top with chopped nuts and whipped topping (if desired), and serve immediately.

Serves 1.

Canada is known for its maple syrup and maple candies. In fact, the maple leaf is even on the Canadian flag. © FABIO BERNARDI/SHUTTERSTOCK.COM.

At the World Food Summit in 1996, Canada and 186 other nations pledged to cut the number of undernourished people in the world by half by 2015. Most Canadians (more than 90 percent) have enough food. However, almost 8 percent of the population does not receive adequate nutrition.

7 Further Study

BOOKS

Duncan, Dorothy. *Nothing More Comforting: Canada's Heritage Food.* Toronto: Dundurn Press, 2003.

McCourt, Jeff. *Flavours of Prince Edward Island.* North Vancouver, BC: Whitecap, 2010.

Menzel, Peter. *What I Eat: Around the World in 80 Diets.* Berkeley, CA: Material World Books, Ten Speed Press, 2010.

Roy, Suman. *From Pemmican to Poutine: A Journey through Canada's Culinary History.* Toronto: Key Publishing House, 2010.

Stewart, Anita. *Great Canadian Cuisine: The Contemporary Flavours of Canadian Pacific Hotels.* Vancouver, BC: Douglas & McIntyre, 1999.

WEB SITES

AllRecipes.com: Canadian Recipes. http://allrecipes.com/Recipes/world-cuisine/canada/main.aspx (accessed on January 25, 2012).

Canada: Agriculture Facts. http://www.fas.usda.gov/remote/canada/index.htm (accessed on January 25, 2012).

Canada

Food.com: Canadian Beginner Cook Recipes. http://www.food.com/Recipes/canadian-beginner-cook (accessed on January 25, 2012).

Whats4Eats: Canada Recipes and Cuisine. http://www.whats4eats.com/north-america/canada-cuisine (accessed on January 25, 2012).

Canada: Aboriginals

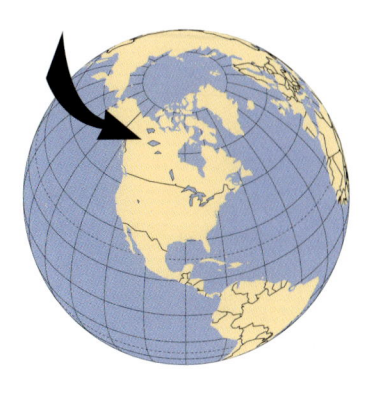

- Pemmican Cakes............................86
- Saskatoon Berry Snack 87
- Soapberry Ice Cream......................87
- Squash Soup 88
- Three Sisters Soup.........................89
- Bannock...90
- Bannock on a Stick........................90
- Wild Rice Cakes 91
- Man-O-Min (Ojibwa Wild Rice)......92

1 Geographic Setting and Environment

The phrases "native Canadians" or "Aboriginal Canadians" describe the descendants of the people who were living in what is modern-day Canada before European colonists, explorers, and traders arrived in the 1600s. In fact, the name Canada comes from Kanata, an Iroquois word that means village.

Giving labels to these Aboriginal groups is complicated by emotional and historical issues. Aboriginals inhabited all regions of Canada and the United States. Dozens of tribal groups, lived, hunted, fished, and foraged (gathered native plants) all across North America. The provinces of modern-day Canada obviously did not exist when the Europeans arrived on the east coast of Canada.

The three principal Aboriginal groups in Canada are North American Indian (also known as First Nation), Métis, and Inuit. Statistics Canada reported that, in the 2006 census, 1,172,790 people identified themselves as Aboriginal, up from 976,305 in 2001 and 799,010 in 1996. Of those, in 2006 there were nearly 700,000 North American Indians, 390,000 Métis, and just over 50,000 Inuit.

The Métis, who were descended from North American Indian women and European fur traders, established their own communities and spoke a unique language. In the 21st century, the Métis were the fastest-growing of the Aboriginal groups. The Métis population grew by about 33.3 percent between 2001 and 2006. The Métis homeland includes the three Prairie Provinces (Manitoba, Saskatchewan, and Alberta) and parts of Ontario, British Columbia, and the Northwest Territories. It extends into the northern part of the United States.

The Inuit inhabit the northernmost parts of Canada. On April 1, 1999, Nunavut (pronounced NOON-ah-voot) became Canada's newest territory, created from about half the land that made up the Northwest Territories. The majority of the population of Nunavut are Inuit.

Canada: Aboriginals

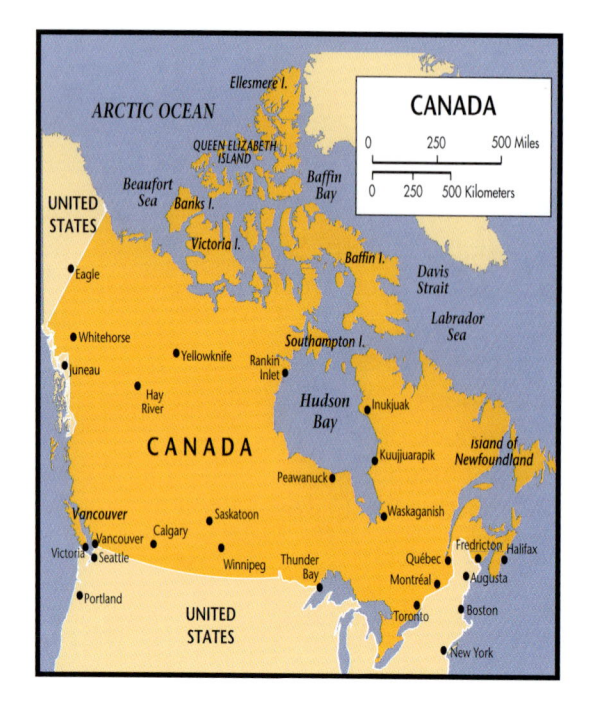

2 History and Food

North American Indians (or First Nations people) are members of the approximately 50 recognized "First Nations" or tribal groups in Canada, and they inhabit all parts of Canada. The Métis are descendants of the intermarriages that occurred between the men employed by the early European fur trading companies (Hudson's Bay Company and Northwest Fur Company) and native Canadian women.

The Inuit are the descendants of the Thule people who migrated from the Canadian Arctic some 700 to 800 years ago. They have inhabited the territory of modern Canada for thousands of years. They were historically hunters and fishers. Because of the harsh climate of their northern homelands, the Inuit diet included very few fresh vegetables or fruits. In the short summers, they would gather berries, both for eating fresh and for drying to eat during the long, cold winter. They would also gather seeds and nuts to store to supplement the winter diet. Grains such as corn, wheat, and wild rice were harvested and dried. Grains would sometimes be ground to produce flour, or mixed with water and cooked.

Pemmican is a nutritious, high calorie food that can be prepared in quantities and stored. The French and British explorers, trappers, and traders bought large quantities of pemmican from the Aboriginals, and even learned to make pemmican. Pemmican would be sealed inside an animal skin or stomach cavity to preserve it. Europeans carried these pemmican stores on long fur-trading expeditions.

Pemmican Cakes

Ingredients

- 1 package beef jerky
- 1 cup dried berries, such as dried blueberries, cranberries, or cherries
- 1 cup chopped nuts or sunflower seeds
- ¼ cup beef suet or vegetable shortening
- Honey to taste (1 to 3 teaspoons)
- 12-cup muffin tin

Directions

1. Line muffin cups with paper liners (or grease cups well).
2. Grind or chop beef jerky into confetti-size pieces to make about 1 cup. Melt suet or shortening in a saucepan.
3. Remove from heat, stir in beef jerky, dried berries, and seeds. Stir in honey.
4. Spoon about ¼ cup of the pemmican mixture into each muffin cup. Press down firmly to make a cake, smoothing the top.
5. Refrigerate until well set.

Serves 12.

Canada: Aboriginals

Saskatoon berries have been a favorite snack among Canadian Aboriginals for many years. © SCOTT PROKOP/SHUTTERSTOCK.COM.

❸ Foods of Aboriginal Canadians

The traditional diet of Aboriginal people was made up of the animals and plants found on the land and in the sea around them. Seal, whale, buffalo, caribou, walrus, polar bear, arctic hare (rabbit), all kinds of fish and many species of bird were hunted or fished. Raw blubber (fat) was enjoyed or mixed with meat or berries. Every part of the animal was consumed or used to make clothing or shelter. Because the foods were eaten raw or with minimal processing, the Aboriginal people were generally well nourished.

Saskatoon Berry Snack

Saskatoon berries, similar to blueberries, have been picked and eaten in the wild by Aboriginal Canadians for centuries. In the late 20th century, commercial fruit growers began planting crops of these tasty berries to sell to grocery stores.

Ingredients

1 pint Saskatoon berries (may substitute blueberries, raspberries, strawberries, or other fresh berries)

or

1 package dried berries (blueberries, cranberries, or other berries)

Directions

1. If using fresh berries, rinse them under running water.
2. Divide berries into several waxed paper bags or plastic storage bags. Carry these along for snacks during the day or to share with a friend.

Serves 8 to 10.

Soapberry Ice Cream

Soapberries are used to make an untraditional ice-cream-like dessert enjoyed by Aboriginal Canadians.

Ingredients

1 cup soapberries
¼ cup water
4 tablespoons brown sugar

Directions

1. Whip together ingredients in a bowl until they form a thick foam.
2. Chill and serve.

Serves 2 to 3.

Junior Worldmark Encyclopedia of Foods and Recipes of the World, 2nd Edition

Canada: Aboriginals

Modern-day First Nations, Métis, and Inuit people have added processed foods and convenience foods to their traditional diet. As such, they are experiencing the health problems that come from consumption of foods rich in sugar and additives (such as tooth decay and obesity).

Their traditional diet was nutritious and high in calories, but the calories were needed to help keep their bodies warm through the long, frigid winters. During the short summers, Aboriginals (mainly the women) would plant small gardens and gather wild berries and seeds.

Corn, beans, and squash were common vegetables grown in the small gardens of Manitoba and Alberta. These vegetables were often simmered to make soups or stews, such as Squash Soup and Three Sister Soup (the "sisters" are corn, beans, and squash).

Snacks were often enjoyed right on the trail—a few berries or dried seeds plucked from the wild plants. Some were eaten right on the spot, and some may have been carried home to share or save for another day.

Aboriginal peoples who lived on the prairies of western Canada consumed buffalo (and used buffalo skins for clothing and shelter). In central Canada, Ojibwa people would gather wild rice from the waters of Ontario and Manitoba, allowing it to dry and then roasting it. The fur traders, who came into contact with Aboriginal peoples all across Canada, introduced a bread similar to the Scottish scone. It became known as bannock. Bannock may be baked (Aboriginal people would lay it on hot rocks near a campfire) or twisted onto a stick and cooked over hot coals.

Squash Soup

Ingredients

6 cups seeded, 2-inch wide chunks butternut squash (about 2 large squash)
¼ cup melted butter
1 tablespoon salt
2 teaspoons pepper
3 cups chicken or vegetable stock
4 tablespoons honey
1 teaspoon minced ginger
½ cup heavy cream
¼ teaspoon nutmeg

Directions

1. Preheat oven to 400°F (205°C).
2. Brush squash cubes with butter, salt, and pepper.
3. Roast the squash for 30 to 35 minutes, until soft.
4. Mash squash until consistency is mixable.
5. In a pot, simmer stock, honey, ginger, and squash.
6. Stir in the heavy cream.
7. Serve as soup, season with salt, pepper, and nutmeg.

Serves 6.

Aboriginal peoples living in the region of modern-day British Columbia enjoyed foods such as salmon cooked over an open fire, a popular modern-day delicacy.

4 Food for Religious and Holiday Celebrations

The traditional feasts held by Aboriginal peoples usually revolved around a harvest, or seasonal excess of food. For example, if there was a large salmon catch, a feast would be held. When a youth killed his first seal or caribou, a celebration feast might be held.

Canada: Aboriginals

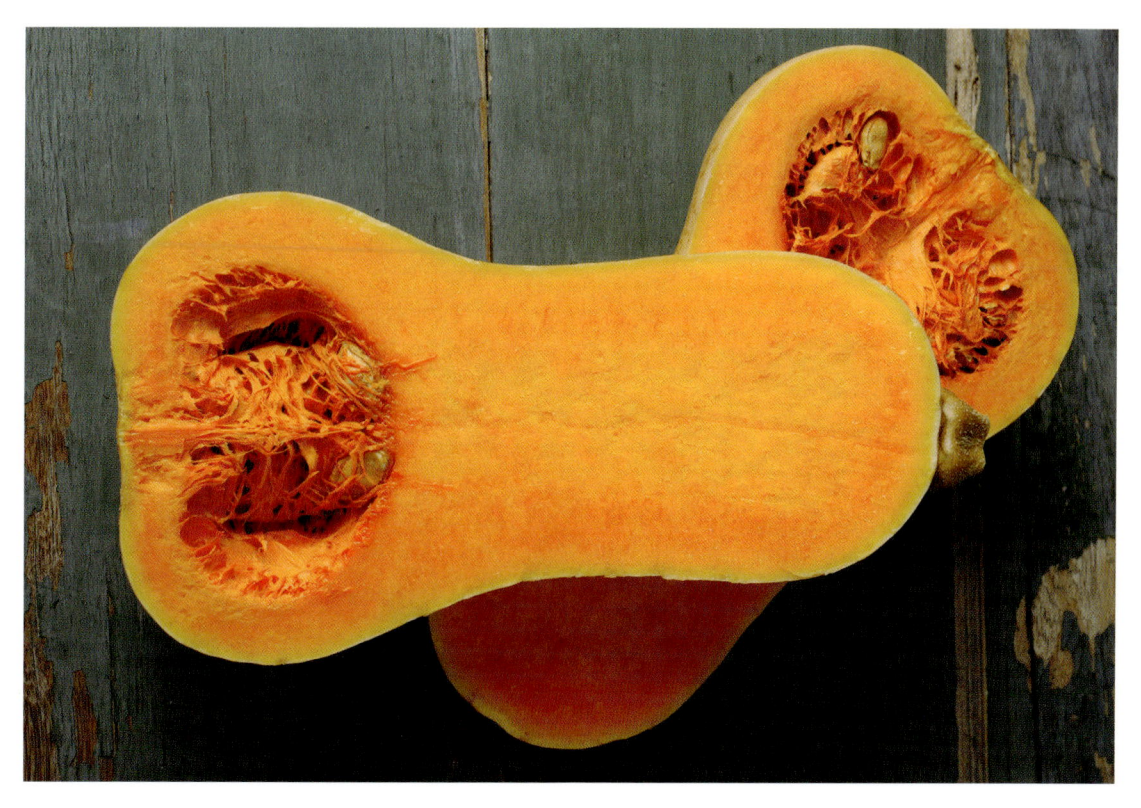

The seeds and stringy fibers must be scooped out of a butternut squash half. Butternut squash is a main ingredient in squash soup and Three Sisters Soup. © PHLOEN/SHUTTERSTOCK.COM.

Three Sisters Soup

Ingredients
3 cans chicken broth
2 cups frozen corn, thawed
1 cup green beans or yellow wax beans, washed and ends trimmed off
1½ cups of butternut squash (or pumpkin)
2 bay leaves
Salt and pepper to taste
Optional spices: ½ teaspoon red pepper flakes or 1 teaspoon each fresh (or ½ teaspoon each dried) parsley, basil, and oregano

Directions
1. Pour the chicken broth into a large saucepan or kettle. Heat until the broth begins to boil.
2. Add the corn, beans, squash, and bay leaves.
3. Lower heat and simmer for 45 minutes.
4. Add optional spices if desired and simmer 15 more minutes.
5. Remove the bay leaves and transfer the soup in batches to the blender to puree if desired. Serve with bannock (bread).

Serves 8 to 10.

In western Canada, Aboriginal peoples held ceremonial parties called potlatches to celebrate the birth of a child, a young woman reaching puberty, or the marriage of a son. Modern-day potlatches are held to celebrate and preserve Aboriginal culture.

Bannock

Bannock may be baked in the oven or over a charcoal or open fire (recipe for Bannock on a Stick follows).

Ingredients

4 cups all-purpose flour
1 tablespoon sugar
2 tablespoons baking powder
½ teaspoon salt
2 cups milk (or water)

Directions

1. Combine flour, baking powder, sugar, and salt in a large mixing bowl.
2. Measure the milk (or water) and add it to the flour mixture, stirring with a fork to combine. A dough should form. If the mixture seems too dry and crumbly, add more liquid, one tablespoon at a time.
3. Turn the dough out onto a surface lightly coated with flour. Knead for about 3 minutes. (To knead, press down the dough, turn it clockwise, fold it in half, and press it down. Repeat.)
4. Preheat oven to 350°F (175°C).
5. Pat the dough into a circle about ¾-inch thick. Transfer the dough to a well-greased cookie sheet. Prick the surface of the dough all over with a fork.
6. Bake about 20 to 30 minutes, or until golden brown.

In 1996 an annual National Aboriginal Day was proclaimed, to be celebrated on June 21 each year. There is no specific menu associated with the celebration of this holiday, but many traditional foods, such as salmon, wild rice, and even buffalo, are enjoyed during the festivities staged by many of the Aboriginal groups.

Bannock on a Stick

Directions

1. Prepare bannock dough (see preceding recipe). Have ready several sticks, 3- to 4-feet in length.
2. Divide the dough into balls slightly larger than golf balls. Shape each ball into a rope about 8 inches long by rolling it between the hands.
3. Wrap each dough rope around a stick. Hole the dough over a bed of red hot coals (charcoal, wood, or gas grill flame set at medium.) Turn the stick frequently to bake the dough evenly.

Serves 10 to 12.

5 Mealtime Customs

Aboriginal peoples are hospitable and always have stews or teas simmering and available to serve to guests. Historically, cooking utensils were fashioned from natural materials and cooking was done over an open fire. Food preservation methods included smoking, drying, and encasing in melted animal fat or whale blubber.

6 Politics, Economics, and Nutrition

The Canadian government's Indian Affairs and Northern Development department changed its name in May 2011 to the Aboriginal Affairs and Northern Development Canada (AANDC) department. It continues its work to address the concerns of the Aboriginal peoples of Canada. Addressing historic wrongs and developing modern-day programs is challenging, and representatives of the government and the First Nations, Métis, and Inuit peoples are striving to communicate and design goals to meet the needs of all Canadians.

Bannock is sometimes wrapped around a stick and cooked over hot coals. © PETER CARROLL/ALAMY.

Wild Rice Cakes

Ingredients

1 cup wild rice
4 cups water
1 teaspoon salt
¼ cup cornmeal
1–2 tablespoons bacon drippings (or butter)

Directions

1. Rinse the wild rice in a sieve under cold running water and drain.
2. Measure the 4 cups of water into a saucepan and add rice and the salt. Heat until the water boils, reduce heat, and simmer for about 30 minutes. The rice should be tender but not soft.
3. Add the cornmeal slowly, stirring constantly with a wooden spoon and cook for 3 or 4 minutes. Remove from the heat.
4. Melt bacon drippings (or butter) in a skillet.
5. Shape the rice mixture into pattie-like cakes about 1½ inches in diameter.
6. Sauté the patties until they are brown on one side (about 5 minutes). Carefully turn the cakes over to brown the other side. Drain on paper towels.

Serves 12; may be served hot or at room temperature.

The substitution of packaged and fast foods for the nutrient-rich traditional Aboriginal diet has contributed to health problems among

Canada: Aboriginals

Aboriginal children. Another concern is environmental contamination that might also contaminate traditional foods, such as seafood. The AANDC works to keep Aboriginal people informed about the safety of their food supply.

Man-O-Min (Ojibwa Wild Rice)

Ingredients
1 cup wild rice
4 cups water
1 teaspoon salt

Directions
1. Wash the wild rice in a colander or bowl, changing the water two or three times.
2. Measure water into a large saucepan; add salt. Heat the water to boiling.
3. Slowly add the rinsed rice to the boiling water. Lower heat to medium and simmer the rice, undisturbed, for about 40 minutes. (Do not stir the rice.)
4. The rice grains will swell to four times their original size.
5. Serve hot or at room temperature.

Serves 12.

Wild rice doubles in size when cooked. Wild rice has a nutty flavor and is denser than white rice in texture. © ANNA HOYCHUK/SHUTTERSTOCK.COM.

Aboriginal people in Canada are not as healthy as a group as the total population of Canada. Programs to improve the health of Inuit and Métis have been effective. Since the late 1980s, infant death rates and the death rate from circulatory disease have decreased. Communicable diseases are being brought under control. To identify other health problems, the AANDC planned a 2012 survey of all Aboriginal people, with results scheduled to be released that fall.

Another area being studied is the rate of suicide among Aboriginal teenagers. According to Health Canada, the suicide rate among Inuit and First Nations youth is much higher than the rate for non-Aboriginal adolescents overall. Health Canada has programs to help First Nations and Inuit people who struggle with problems of substance abuse and alcohol abuse.

7 Further Study

BOOKS

Alexander, Cherry. *Inuit*. New York: PowerKids Press, 2010.

Andrew, George. *A Feast for All Seasons: Traditional Native People's Cuisine*. Vancouver, BC, Canada: Arsenal Pulp Press, 2010.

Bennett, John. *Uqalurait: An Oral History of Nunavut*. Montreal: McGill-Queen's University Press, 2004.

Jackson, John C. *Children of the Fur Trade: Forgotten Métis of the Pacific Northwest*. Corvallis: Oregon State University Press, 2007.

Kent, Deborah. *The Inuit*. Berkeley Heights, NJ: Enslow Elementary, 2005.

Kuiper, Kathleen. *Indigenous Peoples of the Arctic, Subarctic, and Northwest Coast*. New York: Rosen Educational Publishing, 2011.

Lutz, Norma Jean. *Nunavut*. Philadelphia: Chelsea House, 2000.

Menzel, Peter. *What I Eat: Around the World in 80 Diets*. Berkeley, CA: Material World Books, Ten Speed Press, 2010.

Morris, Neil. *Living in the Arctic*. Chicago: Raintree, 2008.

Mstokosho, Mathieu. *Caribou Hunter*. Vancouver, BC: Greystone Books, 2006.

Santella, Andrew. *The Inuit*. New York: Children's Press, 2001.

WEB SITES

Aboriginal Canada Portal: Food and Recipes. http://www.aboriginalcanada.gc.ca/acp/site.nsf/eng/ao35296.html (accessed on February 5, 2012).

Centre for Indigenous Peoples' Nutrition and Environment, McGill University. http://www.mcgill.ca/cine/ (accessed on February 5, 2012).

Heath Canada: Statistical Profile on the Health of First Nations in Canada. http://www.hc-sc.gc.ca/fniah-spnia/intro-eng.php (accessed on February 5, 2012).

Mark's Daily Applie: How to Make Pemmican. http://www.marksdailyapple.com/how-to-make-pemmican/ (accessed on February 5, 2011).

Métis Nation. http://www.metisnation.ca/ (accessed February 5, 2012).

National Aboriginal Day. http://www.ainc-inac.gc.ca/ach/ev/nad/index-eng.asp (accessed on February 5, 2012.

Canada: French Canadians

- French-Canadian Creton (Pate).....96
- Doughboys (Dumplings)...............97
- French-Canadian Pea Soup...........97
- Butter Tarts.....................................98
- Tourtière (Meat Pie).......................98
- Pudding au Chomeur.....................99
- Tarte au Sucre (Sugar Pie).............99
- Pizza-ghetti..................................100
- Crêpes de la Chandeleur.............100
- Ragoût de Boulettes....................101
- St. Catherine's Taffy....................102
- Quebec Poutine...........................103

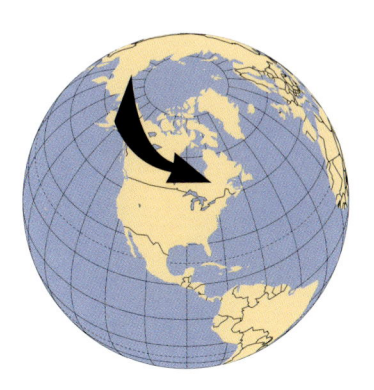

1 Geographic Setting and Environment

People who speak French as their first or second language number more than 9.5 million in Canada. Most (about 7 million) live in the province of Quebec, where French is the only official language and is spoken by more than 80 percent of the population. The majority of the remaining 2.5 million live in the three northeastern provinces, known as the Maritime Provinces, of New Brunswick, Prince Edward Island, and Nova Scotia.

An estimated 22 percent of Canadians speak French as their first language. In Ontario, 1.4 million people speak French. In New Brunswick, both English and French are official languages. With more than 300,000 French speakers, New Brunswick is Canada's only officially bilingual province. There are 96,000 French speakers in Nova Scotia.

Quebec is bordered on the north by the Hudson Strait, on the east by Labrador, on the southeast by the Gulf of St. Lawrence, on the south by New Brunswick and the U.S. region of New England, and on the west and northwest by Ontario, James Bay, and Hudson Bay. It is the largest of Canada's provinces. The highest peak in Quebec is Mont d'Iberville (5,321 feet/1,622 meters), located in the Torngat Mountains in the northeast corner of the province. About half of the province is covered in forest.

2 History and Food

French Canadians make up about one-third of Canada's total population. In the province of Quebec, about 80 percent of the population

Canada: French Canadians

French-Canadian Creton (Spicy Pork Pate)

Creton may be served as an appetizer before a festive meal or as a picnic snack.

Ingredients
1 pound ground pork
2 onions, chopped
2 cloves garlic, minced
1 teaspoon (or more) cinnamon
1 teaspoon (or more) cloves
1 cup dry bread crumbs

Directions
1. Combine the pork, onions, and garlic in a saucepan and cook over medium-low heat. Cook, stirring frequently with a wooden spoon, for about 30 minutes.
2. Add the cinnamon and cloves and continue simmering for about 20 to 30 minutes more. (For a spicier mixture, more cinnamon or cloves may be added.)
3. Add bread crumbs and simmer for about 15 more minutes.
4. Place a colander in the sink and pour the creton mixture into it to drain off excess liquid. (Rinse the sink thoroughly because the liquid may contain grease from the meat.)
5. Place the cooked creton in several small containers (such as empty margarine tubs or small bowls), packing the mixture down tightly.
6. Refrigerate. Serve cold as a spread for French bread or crackers.

❸ Foods of the French Canadians

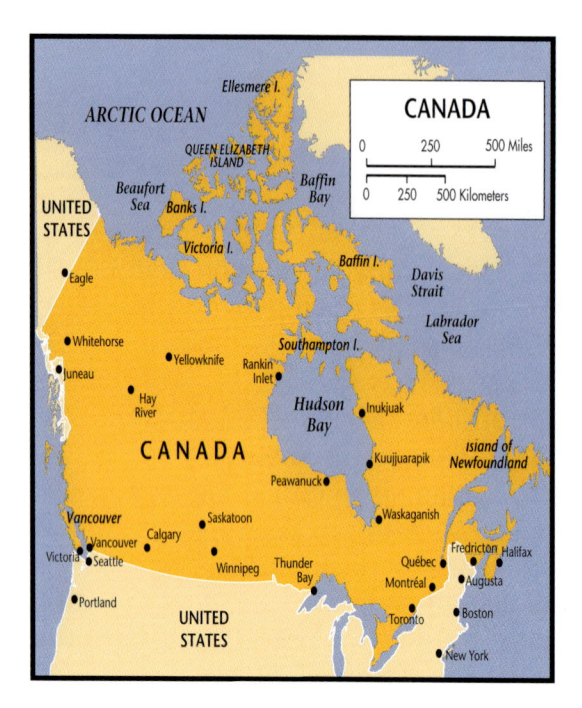

identify themselves as French Canadian, but in other provinces and territories, only 10–14 percent of the population claims French Canadian heritage. French Canadians who live in the Maritime Provinces are often referred to as Acadians.

Since the 1960s, interest in preserving French Canadian culture and traditions has grown. French Canadians share many common cultural practices. Most are Roman Catholic; most enjoy food, art, and music; and many participate in activities that began with their French ancestors.

In 1968, French was added as a second official language in Canada. In 1974, French was recognized as the only official language of Quebec. In 2002, New Brunswick added French as a second official language.

Probably the best-known French Canadian dish is pea soup. It is enjoyed all over Canada, and it is the traditional lunch (called dinner) on Saturday in Newfoundland, when it is usually served with dumplings, called doughboys, floating in it. However, it was a common meal served on Fridays. Until the 1960s and 1970s, Roman Catholics followed a church guideline and did not eat meat on Fridays.

4 Food for Religious and Holiday Celebrations

French Canadians celebrate holidays related to the Roman Catholic Church, especially Easter and Christmas. On Christmas Eve, families traditionally attend a religious service called a Mass (many attend Midnight Mass), followed by a festive holiday meal. One of the traditional dishes is a spicy meat pie called a *tourtière*, made on Christmas Eve using ground pork.

Doughboys (Dumplings)

These dumplings may be cooked in the pot of pea soup before serving.

Ingredients
- 1½ cups flour
- ¼ cup butter
- 3 tablespoon baking powder
- 1 teaspoon salt
- ½ to ¾ cup water or milk

Directions
1. Using a fork or two knives, blend butter into flour, baking powder, and salt.
2. Gradually add the liquid until a soft dough forms.
3. Drop the dough by large spoonfuls into simmering soup, usually pea soup. Cover the pot tightly and simmer for about 15 minutes.
4. Serve bowls of soup with one doughboy floating in each bowl.

Makes 8 to 10 servings.

French-Canadian Pea Soup

Ingredients
- 10 cups water
- 2 cups dried yellow peas
- 1 small onion, chopped
- 1 carrot, chopped
- 1 stalk celery, chopped
- 1 potato, cut into bite-sized chunks
- ½ cup diced ham or 2 to 3 slices cooked bacon, crumbled

Directions
1. Measure peas into a colander and rinse well, picking out any discolored peas or pebbles.
2. Measure the water into a saucepan and heat over high heat until the water begins to boil. Add the rinsed peas to the boiling water.
3. Lower heat immediately, and simmer peas until they are very soft (about 1 to 1½ hours). Add remaining ingredients and salt to taste and simmer for about 30 minutes longer, until vegetables are tender.
4. Make doughboys (if desired; see recipe), or serve immediately.

Serves 8 to 10.

Quebec has a number of unique snack and fast foods. A popular dish found in fast food and casual restaurants in Quebec is pizza-ghetti. Though the dish is a mix between pizza and spaghetti, which both originated in Italy, the combination is almost exclusively found in Quebec.

On February 2, French Canadian Roman Catholics celebrate the Fête de la Chandeleur (Candlemas), honoring the day in the church calendar when Mary took the baby Jesus to the temple. On this day, French Canadians eat crêpes (thin pancakes). A traditional French Canadian proverb says *"Manger des crêpes à la chandeleur*

Canada: French Canadians

apporte un an de bonheur" (Eating crêpes on Candlemas brings a year of happiness).

Butter Tarts

Ingredients

Pastry for double crust pie
¾ cup raisins
1 egg, slightly beaten
½ cup brown sugar
1 teaspoon vanilla
½ cup maple syrup
¼ teaspoon salt
¼ cup shortening

Directions

1. Preheat oven to 425°F (220°C).
2. Roll pastry out on a lightly floured surface. Cut into rounds with 4-inch round cutter. Fit the pastry into medium-sized muffin cups.
3. Put raisins into pastry shells, dividing evenly.
4. Measure all the other ingredients into a bowl and mix well to make the filling.
5. Fill each tart about two-thirds full with filling mixture, covering the raisins. Place muffin tin on bottom shelf of oven, and bake tarts for 12 to 15 minutes or until the filling is set.
6. Place tin on a wire rack; allow tarts to cool. Remove from pan and serve.

Serves 12.

Butter tarts are popular both for a snack or for dessert. Although they are most common in Quebec, they can be purchased elsewhere in Canada. © SALLY SCOTT/SHUTTERSTOCK.COM.

Tourtière (Meat Pie)

Ingredients

2 tablespoons vegetable oil
1½ pounds ground meat (traditionally pork for Christmas Eve)
1 onion, chopped
½ teaspoon allspice
½ teaspoon ground cloves
½ teaspoon ground cinnamon
1 tablespoon Worcestershire sauce
2 potatoes, grated
Salt and pepper to taste
Pastry for double crust pie (may use prepackaged pie crust)

Directions

1. Preheat oven to 375°F (190°C).
2. Prepare pastry (may use frozen or prepackaged pie crust).
3. Fit crust into pie plate and set aside.
4. Measure oil into a large skillet. Heat over medium heat for about 1 minute. Add onions and meat.
5. Cook until meat has lost all of its pink color. Add allspice, cloves, cinnamon, Worcestershire sauce, and grated potatoes. Mix well, using a wooden spoon. Let simmer 5 minutes.
6. Fill pastry shell and cover with a second crust.
7. Bake 30 minutes (until crust is golden). Serve hot. May be topped with ketchup or chili sauce.

Serves 6 to 8.

Pudding au Chomeur (Poor Man's Pudding)

This is an upside-down cake with caramel base.

Ingredients

For pudding (cake):
½ cup milk
3 tablespoons butter, melted
2 teaspoons vanilla
¾ cup flour
1½ teaspoons baking powder
½ teaspoon salt
2 eggs
¾ cup sugar

For caramel sauce:
1½ cups brown sugar
½ cup chopped nuts (optional)
2 tablespoons butter
Vanilla ice cream as an accompaniment (optional)

Directions

Make pudding (cake):
1. Preheat oven to 350°F (175°C).
2. Combine ½ cup milk, melted butter, and vanilla in small bowl.
3. Stir together flour, baking powder, and salt in medium bowl.
4. Using electric mixer, beat eggs and ¾ cup sugar in large bowl until thick and fluffy, about 3 minutes.
5. Add about one-third of the flour mixture to the egg mixture and stir to combine.
6. Next add about ½ of the milk mixture and stir to combine. Continue adding flour and milk, beating well after each addition. Set batter aside.

Make caramel sauce:
1. Combine brown sugar and butter in a small saucepan and cook over low heat until butter melts and sugar dissolves completely.
2. Stir in nuts, if using.
3. Pour sauce into an 8-inch-diameter ceramic soufflé dish.
4. Spoon cake batter over brown sugar mixture in soufflé dish. Bake until tester inserted into center of cake comes out clean and syrup is bubbling at edges, about 40 minutes.
5. Serve hot with vanilla ice cream.

Makes 6 to 8 servings.

Tarte au Sucre (Sugar Pie)

Ingredients

Pastry for 9-inch pie, or frozen pie crust
2 cups brown sugar, firmly packed in the measuring cup
2 tablespoons flour
Salt
2 eggs
1 egg yolk (discard egg white or reserve for other use)
1 cup milk
1 teaspoon vanilla

Directions

1. Roll out pastry and fit into 9-inch pie plate. Trim and flute edges.
2. In bowl, blend sugar, flour, and salt.
3. In separate bowl using an electric mixer, beat eggs and yolk until frothy; beat in milk and vanilla.
4. Stir egg mixture into sugar mixture until smooth. Pour into prepared pie shell.
5. Bake in 400°F (205°C) oven for 10 minutes; reduce to 350°F (175°C) and bake for about 35 minutes or until crust is golden brown and filling is set.
6. Allow to cool on rack.

Serves 6 to 8.

Canada: French Canadians

Pizza-ghetti

Ingredients

1 small cheese pizza
A serving of spaghetti and tomato sauce

Directions

1. Preheat oven to 400°F (205°C).
2. Cut the pizza in half and place both halves on a cookie sheet.
3. Place the spaghetti with sauce between the two pizza halves.
4. Heat for about 15 minutes and serve. Eat with utensils.
5. Note: Pizza-ghetti may also be heated in a microwave oven. Prepare the dish on a glass or paper plate and heat for 2 minutes on high and test. Heat for 30 seconds more until the pizza-ghetti is warm and ready to eat.

Serves 1 to 2.

Pizza-ghetti is served in fast food restaurants around Quebec. Pizza-ghetti is made by cutting the pizza in half and placing a serving of spaghetti in the middle. © EPD PHOTOS.

Crêpes de la Chandeleur (Candlemas Pancakes)

Ingredients

1 cup flour
½ teaspoon baking powder
½ teaspoon baking soda
½ teaspoon salt
2 eggs
¾ cup milk
Vegetable oil

Directions

1. Break eggs into a large mixing bowl and beat with a wire whisk.
2. Measure flour, baking powder, baking soda, and salt into another bowl and stir to combine. Add gradually to egg mixture.
3. Add milk gradually, continuing to stir with the wire whisk. The batter should be smooth, with no lumps.
4. Pour oil into an 8-inch skillet to cover the bottom. Heat the oil over medium-high heat.
5. Using a soup ladle, carefully pour a ladleful (about ¼ cup) of the batter into the hot oil. Tilt the pan carefully to spread the batter into a large, thin crêpe that covers the bottom of the skillet.
6. Cook until the crêpe is golden brown on the bottom (about 3 to 4 minutes).
7. Carefully flip the crêpe over to cook the other side. Remove crêpe from the pan and blot it on a paper towel to remove excess oil.
8. Serve with maple syrup.

Serves 8 to 10.

November 25 marks the celebration of St. Catherine's Day, a day on which girls celebrate the patron saint of unmarried women. Young women make St. Catherine's Taffy in celebration.

Canada: French Canadians

Ragoût de Boulettes (Spicy Meatballs)

Ingredients

- ¾ cup flour
- ¾ cup onion, chopped
- 1 tablespoon olive oil
- 2 pounds ground pork (or combination of 1 pound ground pork and 1 pound ground beef or veal)
- ½ teaspoon cinnamon
- ½ teaspoon nutmeg
- ½ teaspoon ground cloves
- 1 teaspoon salt
- ¼ teaspoon pepper
- 3 cans beef broth (about 6 cups)

Directions

1. *Make browned flour:* Measure the flour into a large skillet and heat over low heat. Stir frequently until flour is slightly browned. Set aside.
2. Measure oil into a skillet and heat over medium-high heat. Add chopped onions and cook, stirring frequently, until onions are translucent.
3. In a large mixing bowl, combine cooked onions, ground meat, and seasonings. With very clean hands, combine meat and seasonings thoroughly.
4. Shape meat mixture into meatballs about 1½ inches in diameter.
5. Pour broth into a large saucepan and heat to boiling. Drop meatballs into boiling stock, lower heat, and simmer about 1½ hours. (Cover pan with the lid slightly offset to allow some steam to escape.)
6. Sprinkle in the browned flour, a little at a time, stirring with a wooden spoon, until gravy thickens.

Serves 8 to 10.

In Quebec, June 24, La Fête nationale du Québec (Quebec National Day) is celebrated. It became an official holiday in 1977. The holiday, which historically was St. John the Baptist Day, is also observed by French Canadians elsewhere in Canada, too. No special foods are associated with this holiday, but a typical menu might include tourtière, creton, or other French-Canadian favorites.

5 Mealtime Customs

French Canadians may eat a pastry, such as a croissant, for breakfast, accompanied by coffee or tea. For those with time for a heartier breakfast, the meal may consist of eggs with Canadian bacon or sausage accompanied by toast and coffee. Lunch may be a ham and cheese sandwich made on crusty French-style or whole grain bread. Pea soup, served at home and in restaurants, is a favorite hearty weekend meal. Dinner may be *ragoût de boulettes* (spicy meatballs) or another meat dish, accompanied by potatoes, usually with gravy. Traditionally, polite diners never put their elbows on the table until the meal is finished. Men may rest their forearms on the table, but women typically just hold their wrists against the table's edge while dining.

In Quebec, street vendors and restaurants sell a quick snack called *poutine*, which is French fries smothered in gravy. The fries are often served with melted cheddar cheese curds. Although it is not considered a traditional French Canadian food, poutine is a very common and popular snack or accompaniment to a casual meal everywhere in Quebec.

6 Politics, Economics, and Nutrition

A major concern of French Canadians is the preservation of their French language and culture, since English is the dominant language in the rest of Canada and in their influential southern

Canada: French Canadians

St. Catherine's Taffy is made by boiling a mixture of molasses and other ingredients. A candy thermometer, shown here, helps determine when the taffy is ready to be pulled. After cooling slightly, the mixture must be pulled and folded until the final light color and firm taffy texture is reached. The mixture is sticky, so it is important to coat one's clean hands with shortening. © EPD PHOTOS.

neighbor, the United States. A movement to separate the French-speaking province of Quebec from the rest of the country became a national issue in the 1970s; in 1980, voters defeated a proposal that would have granted Quebec its independence from Canada. Canadian voters went to the polls in 1995 and again the proposal was defeated, but by a very narrow margin. Many French-Canadian separatists continue the campaign.

Canadians in general receive adequate nutrition in their diets, and the health care system is funded by the government, covering about 75 percent of health care costs for Canadian families. However, in 2001, a government study revealed that about half of French-speakers outside Quebec did not access French-language health services. For many French speakers, health care services were three to seven times more likely to be available in English. As a result, the Consultative Committee for French-Speaking Minority Communities (CCFSMC) began a program to raise awareness and improve access to health care information in French for all French speakers.

St. Catherine's Taffy

Ingredients

½ cup molasses
½ cup corn syrup
1 cup brown sugar
1 cup white sugar
¼ cup butter
1 tablespoon white vinegar
¼ teaspoon cream of tartar
⅛ teaspoon baking soda

Directions

1. Combine molasses, corn syrup, brown and white sugars, vinegar, cream of tartar, and one-half of the butter in a pot. Bring to a boil over low heat.
2. Stir for 5 to 10 minutes until mixture forms a ball when dropped into a small bowl of cold water.
3. Mix in the baking soda.
4. Pour into buttered dishes and let taffy cool slightly.
5. Pull taffy in half, then in half again until pale golden, and almost white. If it sticks to your hands, put a little butter on them.
6. Pull taffy a last time and twist into small pieces. Cut with clean, cooking scissors.
7. Let cool and serve.

Quebec Poutine

Ingredients

1 bag frozen French fries
8 ounces shredded cheddar cheese
1 jar beef or onion gravy (or packet of gravy mix)

Directions

1. Prepare French fries in the oven according to the instructions on the package.
2. While the French fries are cooking, pour the gravy into a saucepan and heat it to just bubbling.
3. Remove the French fries from the oven, scatter shredded cheddar cheese over them, and return them to the oven for one minute, just long enough to melt the cheese.
4. Transfer the cheese-covered French fries to individual plates or bowls, and drizzle with the gravy.

Serves 8 to 10.

Further Study

BOOKS

Barer-Stein, Thelma. *You Eat What You Are: People, Culture, and Food Traditions.* 2nd ed. Toronto: Firefly Books, 1999.

Claman, Marcy. *Rise & Dine Canada: Savory Secrets from Canada's Bed & Breakfast Inns.* 2nd ed. Montreal, Quebec: Callawind Publications, 1999.

McCourt, Jeff. *Flavours of Prince Edward Island.* North Vancouver, BC: Whitecap, 2010.

Menzel, Peter. *What I Eat: Around the World in 80 Diets.* Berkeley, CA: Material World Books, Ten Speed Press, 2010.

Roy, Suman. *From Pemmican to Poutine: A Journey through Canada's Culinary History.* Toronto: Key Publishing House, 2010.

Stewart, Anita, and Robert Wigington. *The Flavors of Canada: A Celebration of the Finest Regional Foods.* Vancouver, BC: Raincoast Books, 2006.

Poutine, French fries with gravy, is a favorite snack for Canadians living in or visiting Quebec. © PAUL BINET/ SHUTTERSTOCK.COM.

Tritenbach, Paul. *Traveling Taste Buds: Delectable Dishes from All Over the U.S. and Canada.* Bishop, CA: Excellence Press, 2000.

WEB SITES

AllRecipes.com: Canadian Recipes. http://allrecipes.com/Recipes/world-cuisine/canada/main.aspx (accessed on February 3, 2012).

Bonjour Quebec. http://www.bonjourquebec.com/ (accessed February 3, 2012).

Food.com: Quebec Recipes. http://www.food.com/recipes/quebec (accessed on February 3, 2012).

Canada: French Canadians

What's Cookin? French Canadian Recipes. http://www.whats-cooking.ca/french-canadian-recipes/ (accessed on February 3, 2012).

Whats4Eats: Canada Recipes and Cuisine. http://www.whats4eats.com/north-america/canada-cuisine (accessed on February 3, 2012).

Chile

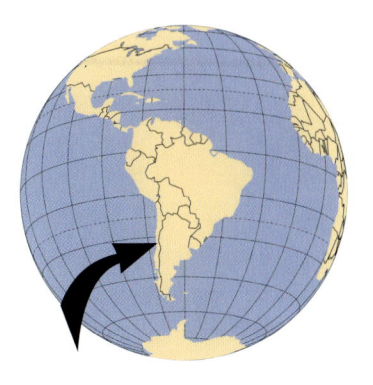

- Ensalada Campesina 106
- Pastel de Choclo 107
- Té con Leche (Tea with Milk) 108
- Ensalada Chilena (Salad) 108
- Tomaticán (Stew) 109
- Cola de Mono (Eggnog) 110
- Torta de Cumpleaños (Cake).......111
- Chancho en Piedra......................111
- Ponche (Berry Punch) 112
- Arroz con Leche (Rice Pudding) ..112
- Barros Jarpa 113
- Cajeya de Almendra....................114

1 Geographic Setting and Environment

Chile is located along the southwestern coast of South America. Chile is 2,653 miles (4,270 kilometers) long, but it averages just 109 miles (175 kilometers) wide. The country has the rugged Andes Mountains in the east and another lower mountain range along the coast of the Pacific Ocean. Between the two mountain ranges lies a fertile valley where Chile's agricultural activity is centered.

Around the main cities—especially in Santiago, the capital, and in Rancagua—there is air and water pollution. The government has tried many different programs to reduce pollution. When air pollution levels are high, cars are banned from the central part of the cities.

Also, Chileans are no longer allowed to burn wood for heat. The measures have reduced the number of air pollution emergencies from about 100 pollution alerts per year in the 1990s to about 20 in first decade of the 2000s.

Chile's main environmental problem is deforestation (clearing of forestland by cutting down all the trees), which leads to soil erosion. About 70 to 80 percent of Chile's forests have been cleared to make way for other uses of the land.

Agricultural output improved from the 1990s into the early 2010s. Exports of fresh fruit, especially grapes, pears, lemons, and peaches, expanded during this period. The country hoped to become one of the top 10 food exporters in the world by 2015.

Chile has a long coastline, giving the country access to the rich food resources of the Pacific Ocean. Chileans include many kinds of seafood in their diets as a result.

105

Chile

21st century. Popular dishes include *humitas* (corn that is pureed and cooked in corn husks) and *pastel de choclo* (a corn and meat pie).

In 1848, many German immigrants came to Chile, bringing rich pastries and cakes with them. Italian and Arab immigrants also settled in Chile, along with immigrants from other countries in Europe. Each group brought its style of cooking to Chile. The Italians brought ices and flavored them with the different Chilean fruits. The Arab immigrants brought their use of certain spices and herbs, and the combination of sweet and salty tastes.

Ensalada Campesina

Ingredients

2 cups canned chickpeas (also called garbanzo beans), drained
2 medium-sized red onions, chopped
2 cups Monterey jack or cheddar cheese, shredded
⅓ cup olive oil
3 tablespoons lemon juice
3 tablespoons chopped cilantro or parsley
Salt and pepper
4 to 6 large lettuce leaves

Directions

1. Combine chickpeas, onions, and cheese in a large bowl.
2. Mix oil, lemon juice, cilantro or parsley, salt, and pepper.
3. Mix oil and chickpea mixtures together.
4. Refrigerate for at least 20 minutes.
5. Arrange lettuce leaves on individual plates and top with a serving of salad.

Serves 4 to 6.

2 History and Food

The Spanish came to Chile in 1541 and they brought grapes, olives, walnuts, chestnuts, rice, wheat, citrus fruits, sugar, garlic, and spices. They also brought chicken, beef, sheep, pigs, rabbits, milk, cheeses, and sausages.

Long before the Spanish came to Chile, the native Amerindians used corn in many of their dishes. The combination of the Spanish and Amerindians' foods formed popular corn-based dishes that are still part of the typical diet in the

Pastel de Choclo
(Corn and Meat Pie)

Ingredients

- 4 cups frozen corn
- 8 leaves fresh basil, finely chopped (or 1 teaspoon dried, crumbled)
- 1 teaspoon salt
- 3 tablespoons butter
- 1 cup milk
- 4 large onions, chopped
- 3 tablespoons oil
- 1 pound ground beef
- Salt and pepper, to taste
- 1 teaspoon ground cumin
- 1 cup black olives
- 1 cup raisins
- 2 pieces of cooked chicken breast, cut into cubes or strips
- 2 tablespoons confectioners' sugar

Directions

1. Preheat oven to 400°F.
2. Heat the corn, basil, salt, and butter in a large pot.
3. Slowly add the milk, stirring constantly until the mixture thickens.
4. Cook over low heat for 5 minutes.
5. Set aside while the meat filling is prepared.
6. Fry the onions in oil until they are soft.
7. Add the ground beef and stir to brown.
8. Drain grease from pan.
9. Add salt, pepper, and ground cumin.
10. Use an oven-proof dish to prepare the pie. Spread the onion and ground beef mixture on the bottom of the dish, then arrange the olives and raisins on top.
11. Place chicken pieces over the top.
12. Cover the filling with the corn mixture, then sprinkle on the confectioners' sugar.
13. Bake in the oven for 30 to 35 minutes until the crust is golden brown.
14. Serve hot.

Makes 4 to 6 servings.

Corn husks wrap humitas, *a favorite snack in Chile. Inside is a paste of grated corn seasoned with onions, herbs, salt, and pepper.* © EPD PHOTOS.

Between 1880 and 1900, British immigrants brought tea to Chile. Teatime—inviting friends over for tea and coffee—continues to be enjoyed in modern Chile.

Chileans serve *té con leche* (tea with milk). Small sandwiches and pastries are popular to serve with tea or coffee.

During the 20th century, more European cooking styles, especially French, were introduced to Chile. In addition, the colorful logos marking fast food chains became common in cities of all sizes.

Chile

Té con Leche (Tea with Milk)

Ingredients

2 teabags
2 cups water
2 cups boiling milk
Sugar, to taste

Directions

1. Heat 2 cups of water to boiling.
2. In a saucepan, heat the milk just to boiling, and remove from heat.
3. Place tea bags into 2 separate cups.
4. Pour the water into cups, filling one-third of cup.
5. Let the tea steep (soak) for 5 minutes, then remove bag.
6. Fill the rest of the cup with the hot milk.
7. Add sugar to taste.

Recipe may be doubled or tripled to serve more guests.

Serves 2.

By the 21st century, the streets of major cities like Santiago were lined with restaurants offering foods from all over the world, such as Asian, Middle Eastern, Indian, and others.

❸ Foods of the Chileans

Chile has a wide variety of foods, including seafood, beef, fresh fruit, and vegetables. A traditional Chilean meal is *pastel de choclo*, a "pie" made with corn, vegetables, chicken, and beef. This dish is usually served with *ensalada chilena* (Chilean salad). *Ensalada Campesina*, translated as "peasant's salad," is an easy dish made with chickpeas.

Empanadas, little pies usually stuffed with beef, olives, and onions, are another favorite. A popular dish is *bistec a lo pobre* (poor man's steak), which is steak topped with two fried eggs and served with fried onions and French fries. Despite the name, poor Chileans cannot afford to eat this meal because beef is very expensive; this dish is actually eaten by wealthier people. *Tomaticán* (tomato and corn stew) is often served as a side dish with meat, chicken, or fish.

Ensalada Chilena (Chilean Salad)

Ingredients

4 cups onions, finely sliced
4 cups peeled tomatoes (may be canned and drained well), finely sliced
3 tablespoons oil
Lemon juice, to taste
½ cup fresh cilantro leaves, chopped
Salt and pepper, to taste

Directions

1. Place the sliced onions in a bowl.
2. Cover with cold water and let set for 1 hour, then drain the water.
3. Mix onions with the tomatoes on a large platter.
4. Season with salt and pepper.
5. Pour oil and lemon juice on mixture.
6. Mix and serve with chopped cilantro sprinkled on top.

Serves 4.

❹ Food for Religious and Holiday Celebrations

About 70 percent of Chileans are Roman Catholic, the religion that the Spaniards brought with them when they came to Chile in 1541. For Christmas, which occurs during the summertime in the Southern Hemisphere, families decorate Christmas trees, and on Christmas Eve they gather to eat a late meal. After the families eat, they open presents. Children enjoy *pan de*

Chile

Ensalada Chilena is a simple salad made from the freshest ingredients. It is a favorite among Chileans. © EPD PHOTOS.

pascua, a Christmas cake made with fruits and nuts that comes from the German influence in Chile. During the holiday season, family and friends drink *cola de mono* (Chilean eggnog).

Tomaticán (Tomato and Corn Stew)

Ingredients

1 large onion, peeled and finely chopped
3 cloves garlic, peeled and chopped
2 tablespoons olive oil
3 large plum tomatoes, peeled and diced
1 cup fresh or frozen corn kernels
1 pinch fresh parsley, chopped
Salt, to taste

Directions

1. In a large saucepan, cook the onion and garlic in hot oil.
2. Add the tomatoes and cook, covered, for 5 minutes.
3. Add the corn and cook for another 3 minutes.
4. Add salt to taste, sprinkle parsley on top.
5. Serve hot.

Serves 4.

Chileans also drink eggnog on New Year's Eve, celebrated on December 31. This is a favorite holiday. At midnight, Chileans hug and kiss each other, saying (in Spanish), "Good luck and may all your wishes come true." Some believe they will have good luck if they eat *lentejas* (lentils) at midnight.

Chile

Cola de Mono (Chilean Eggnog)

Ingredients
1 gallon milk
1 cup sugar
1 vanilla bean
1 cup whole coffee beans (or ½ cup instant coffee)
6 egg yolks

Directions
1. Bring the milk to a boil with the sugar, vanilla, and coffee.
2. Let it simmer slowly, stirring occasionally, until the milk turns a light brown.
3. Remove from the heat, strain, and return to low heat.
4. Add a couple of tablespoons of the hot milk to the egg yolks to dilute and warm them.
5. Stir the yolks back into the mixture and cook for about 3 to 5 minutes.
6. Let it cool completely before drinking.

Serves 8 to 12.

Because many Chileans are Roman Catholic, days named after saints are important holidays. Children often celebrate the saint's day with the same name as theirs. October 4 is St. Francis of Assisi's day. Girls named Francisca and boys named Francisco celebrate this saint's day with a party and cake, as if it were their birthday. They also celebrate their own real birthdays. At both celebrations, *torta de cumpleaños* (birthday cake) is served.

5 Mealtime Customs

Most Chileans eat four meals each day: breakfast, lunch, tea, and dinner. Mealtimes are an important part of family life. Families almost always eat together at home, only going to a restaurant on a special occasion.

A selection of vegetables is shown at a produce market in Santiago, Chile. © TOMAS SKOPAL/SHUTTERSTOCK.COM.

Mothers prepare a light breakfast of toast and milk for their children. Lunch is the biggest meal of the day. Many people take two hours for lunch, sometime between noon and 3 p.m. It is not uncommon for businesses to close for almost three hours so people can go home and eat lunch with their families and take a siesta (nap).

Most people serve two main dishes for lunch. The first dish might be a salad with seafood. The other dish might be *cazuela de ave*, a thick stew of chicken, potatoes, rice, green peppers, and, occasionally, onions. *Chancho en Piedra* (Chili and Tomato Spread) is often served with bread as an accompaniment to meals, or may be eaten by students as a snack.

Torta de Cumpleaños (Birthday Cake)

Ingredients
1 box yellow cake mix (prepare the cake according to the package, using 2 round pans, 10-inch each)
1 cup grape jelly (another flavor may be substituted)
2 cups pastry cream (vanilla frosting may be substituted)

Pastry cream:
2 cups whole milk
1 tablespoon vanilla extract
5 egg yolks
1 cup sugar
½ cup flour
1 tablespoon butter, melted

Directions

Pastry cream:
1. Simmer the milk in a saucepan for 5 minutes and cover.
2. In a large mixing bowl, beat the egg yolks with the sugar until the mixture is light yellow.
3. Stir in flour, and pour the hot milk over the egg mixture, beating continuously with a whisk.
4. Pour the mixture back into saucepan and bring to a slow simmer, stirring constantly.
5. Lower the heat and cook for 2 minutes, stirring quickly.
6. Remove from heat.
7. Add vanilla extract, and pour the cream into a bowl and spread melted butter over it.
8. Cover until ready to use.

Assemble the cake:
1. Once the cake is cool, remove from the pans.
2. In Chile, each layer would be sliced horizontally into two separate layers, so that the cake has 4 layers in all. This is an optional step; the cake will taste almost the same with just two layers.
3. Place one layer of cake on a plate, spread some pastry cream or frosting on it and follow with a layer of jelly. If using more than two layers, alternate jelly and pastry cream or frosting between layers of cake.
4. Cover the top and sides of the cake with the remaining cream.
5. Let the cake sit overnight before eating.

Serves 8 to 12.

Chancho en Piedra (Chili and Tomato Spread)

Ingredients
4 garlic cloves, peeled and mashed
1 small jar chopped green chilies
1 small can chopped tomatoes, drained
1 tablespoon olive oil
Salt, to taste (preferably kosher-style)

Directions
1. Combine garlic and chilies in a glass bowl, and "smash" together, using a wooden spoon. (Traditional Chileans would use a marble mortar and pestle to grind the ingredients together.)
2. Add salt.
3. Gradually add the tomatoes, mixing them well.
4. Stir in the oil.
5. Pour mixture into a small serving bowl.

Spread on slices of crusty bread or toast.

At around 5 p.m., many people enjoy afternoon tea, called *las onces*. Light sandwiches and pastries are served, with tea and coffee. Sandwiches, such as avocado or cucumber on thin bread, are a popular snack. Children may also take sandwiches to school for lunch. One popular ham and melted cheese sandwich is called *Barros Jarpa*, named after a Chilean who ate large amounts of these sandwiches.

Chile

Ponche (Berry Punch)

Ingredients
1½ quarts cranberry juice
½ teaspoon cinnamon powder
½ teaspoon nutmeg
6 whole cloves
1 lemon peel (wash lemon well before peeling)
1 orange peel (wash orange well before peeling)

Directions
1. In a pot, simmer the cranberry juice with the cinnamon, nutmeg, cloves, and the lemon and orange peels for 15 minutes.
2. Let it cool and throw away the cloves and fruit peels.
3. Pour into glasses and serve.

Serves 4.

Dinner is rarely served before 9 p.m. and most restaurants don't open until 8 p.m. Dinner is a lighter meal, but people will linger at the table, enjoying conversation.

Restaurants range from snack bars to expensive restaurants. A favorite Chilean "fast food" meal is a *completo*, which is similar to a hot dog. The completo is typically accompanied with mustard, avocado, tomatoes, and mayonnaise. *Ponche* (Chilean punch) is a traditional and popular beverage.

Chileans enjoy entertaining friends for teatime (or las onces), a tradition from the British immigrants who came to Chile in the late 1800s. Dinner is usually one main dish. For dessert, Chileans eat fresh fruit, ice cream, or other desserts such as *cajeya de almendra* (almond cakes) or *arroz con leche* (rice pudding).

Arroz con Leche (Rice Pudding)

Ingredients
1 cup rice
2 cups water
1 cup whole milk
2 large eggs
½ cup sugar
1 teaspoon vanilla extract
1 teaspoon grated lemon peel (thoroughly washed)
1 teaspoon butter, for greasing the pan
1 cup heavy cream
Cinnamon to sprinkle on top

Directions
1. Preheat oven to 350°F.
2. Put the rice and water in a medium-size saucepan and bring to a boil over medium-high heat. Reduce to low heat and cover the pan.
3. Cook the rice for about 20 minutes, or until tender.
4. In a medium bowl, stir the milk, eggs, sugar, vanilla extract, and lemon peel until blended.
5. Add the rice and stir gently until all ingredients are well mixed.
6. Butter a 9-inch pie pan and spoon the mixture into it. Bake for 25 minutes.
7. Remove pudding from the oven, stir it, and cool for 15 minutes.
8. While the pudding cools, beat the heavy cream in a large bowl until it forms soft peaks.
9. Fold the rice pudding into the whipped cream.
10. Serve in a dish, warm or chilled, and sprinkle with cinnamon.

Serves 4.

6 Politics, Economics, and Nutrition

The United Nations ranks the countries of the world using the Human Development Index (HDI), which considers the health, education,

Arroz con Leche (rice pudding) may be served warm or chilled. A sprinkle of cinnamon adds just a hint of spice to complement the lemon peel in the pudding. © PATTY ORLY/SHUTTERSTOCK.COM.

and income of each country's population. Chile's HDI rank has improved steadily. The country ranks 44 out of 187 countries. Chile ranks above average when compared to other countries in its region, which is Latin America and the Caribbean.

Barros Jarpa (Ham and Cheese Sandwich)

Ingredients
1 tablespoon olive oil
4 slices sandwich bread
2 slices cooked ham
2 slices Monterey Jack cheese

Directions
1. Heat the oil in a pan.
2. Place one slice each of ham and cheese on a slice of bread and place the other slice of bread on top.
3. Toast the sandwich in the pan on both sides until the cheese melts.
4. Serve.

Serves 2.

According to a report by the World Bank, about 5 percent of the total population is undernourished (does not receive adequate nutrition in their daily diet). Most children receive adequate nutrition, however. Less than 1 percent of children under age five in Chile in 2008 were malnourished (did not get enough food). Obesity was considered a problem for the population as a whole. More than 9 percent of children under age five were overweight in 2008. The National Health Ministry reported in 2010 that almost 22 percent of first-grade students and 25 percent of all adults were obese.

Cajeya de Almendra

Ingredients
2 cups sugar
5 egg whites
1 cup water
¾ cup chopped almonds
Small muffin tin

Directions
1. Preheat oven to 350°F.
2. Cook the sugar and water together in a pot until the mixture is somewhat thick.
3. Beat egg whites until stiff and add sugar and water mixture, beating constantly.
4. Add the chopped nuts.
5. Pour batter into small muffin tin lined with cups. Bake for 12 to 15 minutes.
6. Let cakes cool and serve with fruit.

Makes about 24 cakes.

Almost everyone (95 percent) has access to safe drinking water. The National System of Health Services (Sistema Nacional de Servicios de Salud or SNSS) is Chile's national health system. It employed about 40 percent of the country's doctors. The SNSS operates 27 regional offices to serve all the people of the country.

7 Further Study

BOOKS

Essentials of Latin Cooking. Birmingham, AL: Oxmoor, 2010.

Fleetwood, Jenni. *South American Food and Cooking*. London, UK: Southwater, 2005.

Joelson, Daniel. *Tasting Chile*. New York: Hippocrene Books, 2004.

McCarthy, Carolyn, Jean Bernard Carillet, and Kevin Raub. *Chile and Easter Island*. Oakland, CA: Lonely Planet Publications, 2009.

McNair, Sylvia. *Chile*. New York: Children's Press, 2000.

Sheen, Barbara. *Foods of Chile*. Detroit: KidHaven Press, 2011.

Van Waerebeek-Gonzalez, Ruth. *The Chilean Kitchen: Authentic, Homestyle Foods, Regional Wines, and Culinary Traditions of Chile*. New York: HPBooks, 1999.

WEB SITES

Chile Guide: Food and Drink. http://www.contactchile.cl/en/chile-food-drink.php (accessed on February 5, 2012).

Global Gourmet. http://www.prochile.us/flavors/chile-global-gourmet (accessed on February 5, 2012).

South America: Typical Chilean Food. http://www.southamerica.cl/Chile/Food.htm (accessed on February 5, 2012).

Whats4Eats: Chile. http://www.whats4eats.com/south-america/chile-cuisine/ (accessed on February 5, 2012).

China

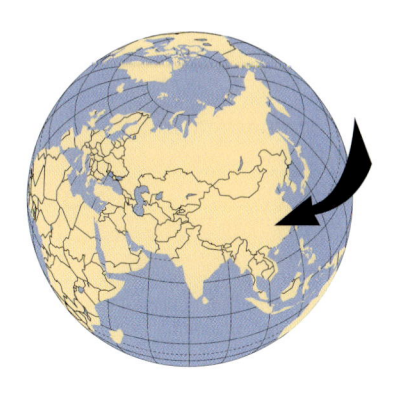

- Jasmine Bubble Tea 116
- Egg Drop Soup 117
- Wonton Soup 119
- Sweet and Sour Pork 119
- Baat Bo Fon (Rice Pudding) 120
- Fried Rice 120
- Chinese Mooncakes 121
- Birthday Noodles with Sauce 122
- Fu Yung Don (Egg Fu Yung) 123
- Fried Wonton 124
- Almond Cookies 125
- Spiced Chicken 126

1 Geographic Setting and Environment

The official name of China is the People's Republic of China. China is one of the world's largest countries. The land elevation increases from east to west. Eastern China is made up of lowlands. The middle and western sections of the country are mountainous. The largest river in China is the Yangtze, which travels almost 4,000 miles (6,400 kilometers).

China's climate is varied. In the northeast and northwest, crops are harvested once a year. In northern China and in the some areas around the Yangtze River, crops may be harvested twice a year. In the south, crops may be harvested three times a year.

China is the most populous country in the world, with a 2011 population of 1.34 billion. About 53 percent of the population lives outside of the cities. Since around the late 1990s, there has been a strong migration to the cities by rural Chinese seeking work. About 200 million rural laborers and their families have moved to cities on China's east coast to find work. More than 60 Chinese cities have populations over 750,000. Both Shanghai and Beijing have populations around 20 million people. (To compare to U.S. cities: New York City has about 19.7 million people, Los Angeles has about 15 million, and Chicago has about 7 million.)

Even though many people have moved to cities, there are still many millions of Chinese who live and work in rural areas. China joined the World Trade Organization (WTO) in 2001. Since then, the Chinese government has been trying to help farmers improve production by creating cooperative farms. There were more than 150,000 farmer cooperatives as of 2011, with more than 38.7 million members. China ranked fourth in the world in terms of agriculture exports that year.

115

China

farther from their homes, cooking methods and foods were shared among the different regions within China.

In the 21st century, many Chinese people have enough money to buy food and they are demanding better food. This is especially true in cities, where Chinese people are adding more meat and richer foods to their diets.

Jasmine Bubble Tea

Ingredients

1 cup sugar
1 cup large tapioca pearls
6 jasmine tea bags (or jasmine and green tea)
½ cup sweetened condensed milk

Directions

1. Boil sugar and one cup of water in a small pot. Once it reaches a boil, remove and let cool.
2. In a large pot, boil eight cups of water.
3. Add tapioca pearls and return water to a boil, stirring occasionally for 15 minutes. Let pearls sit for another 15 minutes.
4. Drain tapioca pearls and put them in a container with the sugar water mixture. Refrigerate.
5. Pour four cups boiling water over the teabags and let steep for 20 minutes. Remove bags and refrigerate tea.
6. Once tea is chilled, put ½ cup tapioca pearls in the bottom of a glass.
7. In a pitcher, mix tea and sweetened condensed milk.
8. Pour tea mixture over the pearls. Serve with an extra wide straw.

Serves 4

❷ History and Food

Throughout its history, China's growing population has been difficult to feed. By the year 1000, China's population reached 100 million. In 1980, China became the first country to reach one billion in population. By 2011, with a population of 1.34 billion, China hosts one-fifth of the world's population.

Through history, the Chinese constantly had to adapt new eating habits because of the scarcity of food. Meat was scarce, so dishes were created using small amounts of meat mixed with rice or noodles, both of which were more plentiful. Vegetables were added, and stir-frying, the most common method of cooking, became a way to conserve fuel by cooking food quickly.

Regional differences in cuisine became noticeable in the 1200s when invaders from neighboring Mongolia swept into China. Cooking styles and customs began to be exchanged between the two countries. As people traveled

❸ Foods of the Chinese

Food in China varies by region. There are four main regional types of Chinese cooking. The cooking of Canton province in the south is called Cantonese cooking. It features rice and lightly seasoned stir-fried dishes. Because many Chinese immigrants to America came from this region, it is the type of Chinese cooking that is most widely known in the United States. Typical Cantonese dishes are wonton soup, egg rolls, and sweet and sour pork.

Egg Drop Soup

Ingredients
1 egg, room temperature
1 can chicken stock (about 2 cups)
½ teaspoon salt
½ teaspoon sugar
1 teaspoon soy sauce
Large scallions cut into tiny circles (green parts only)

Directions
1. Remove the egg from the refrigerator and allow it to come to room temperature.
2. Beat the egg lightly in a bowl.
3. Put the stock in a saucepan or wok and bring to a boil.
4. Lower heat to the lowest setting.
5. Hold the bowl with the beaten egg above the pan with the simmering broth.
6. Slowly and carefully pour the egg into the broth in a very thin stream.
7. Hold a fork in your other hand, and trace circles on the surface of the broth, drawing out long filmy threads of egg on the surface of the broth.
8. Simmer for about 1 minute, and then remove the saucepan from heat and cover for 45 seconds.
9. The egg should be set in tender flakes.
10. Add salt, sugar, and soy sauce, and sprinkle the scallions on top.
11. Stir the mixture two or three times.
12. Transfer to individual soup bowls and serve.

Serves 2.

A Chinese farmer is shown planting rice in the countryside.
© LIN, CHUN-TSO/SHUTTERSTOCK.COM.

The Mandarin cuisine of Mandarin province in northern China features dishes made with wheat flour, such as noodles, dumplings, and thin pancakes. The best known dish from this region is Peking duck, a dish made up of roast duck and strips of crispy duck skin wrapped in thin pancakes. (Peking was the name of Beijing, the capital of China, until after the Cultural Revolution of the late 1960s. This traditional recipe is still known in the United States, and in restaurants in China that cater to tourists, as "Peking duck.")

Shanghai cooking, from China's east coast, emphasizes seafood and strong-flavored sauces. The cuisine of the Szechuan province in inland China is known for its hot and spicy dishes made

China

To make wontons, a spoonful of pork filling is placed on the wonton skin (upper left); two edges of the pastry are then moistened with water (upper right); and the skin is then folded in half (lower left). Finally, the filled wonton skin is gently pinched into a half-moon shape. © EPD PHOTOS.

with hot peppers, garlic, onions, and leeks. This type of cooking became popular in the United States in the 1990s.

The Chinese eat many foods that are unfamiliar to North Americans. Shark fins, seaweed, frogs, snakes, and even dog and cat meat are eaten. However, the Chinese follow the spiritual teaching of balance signified by yin ("cool") and yang ("hot"). This philosophy encourages the Chinese to find a balance in their lives, including in the foods they eat. While preparing meals, the Chinese may strive to balance the color, texture, or types of food they choose to eat.

Rice is China's staple food. The Chinese word for rice is "fan," which also means "meal." Rice may be served with any meal, and it is eaten several times a day. Scallions, bean sprouts, cabbage, and gingerroot are other traditional foods. Soybean curd, called tofu, is an important source of protein for the Chinese. Although the Chinese generally do not eat a lot of meat, pork and chicken are the most commonly eaten meats. Vegetables play a central role in Chinese cooking, too.

Tea, the beverage offered at most meals, is China's national beverage. The most popular types of tea—green, black, and oolong—are commonly drunk plain, without milk or sugar added. Teacups have no handles or saucers. Bubble tea, made with tapioca pearls, offers a fun, sweet twist to traditional tea.

Wonton Soup

Ingredients
½ pound pork or beef, ground
1 tablespoon scallions, finely chopped
1 egg, beaten
1 teaspoon salt
1 tablespoon soy sauce
1 tablespoon sugar
1 teaspoon sesame oil (optional)
1 tablespoon water
2 packages wonton skins
3 cans (15 ounces each) chicken or other broth (about 6 cups)

Directions
1. Mix ground pork (or beef), scallions, egg, salt, soy sauce, sugar, sesame oil, and water in a bowl.
2. Place 1 teaspoon of meat mixture in the center of a wonton skin.
3. Moisten the edges of wonton skin with water and fold it to form a triangle. Press the edges together to seal.
4. Fill and fold the rest of the wonton skins.
5. Bring a large pot of water to a boil to cook the wontons.
6. In another pot, heat the broth. (Wontons will be cooked first in the boiling water and then added to the broth.)
7. Add a few wontons at a time to the boiling water, giving them room to float freely. Cook over medium heat 8 to 10 minutes.
8. Add the cooked wontons to hot broth. Use about 3 dozen wontons for 6 cups of broth.

Recipe makes 48 wontons.

Sweet and Sour Pork

Note: This recipe involves hot oil and requires adult supervision.

Ingredients
½ cup flour
½ teaspoon salt
½ teaspoon black pepper
1 pound lean pork loin, cut into bite-size pieces
3 tablespoons peanut or vegetable oil
2 green peppers cut in large pieces
1 onion, sliced
1 carrot, sliced
½ cup pineapple chunks
½ cup pineapple juice
¼ cup white vinegar
2 tablespoons soy sauce
¼ cup brown sugar
2 tablespoons cornstarch
A few drops red food coloring (traditional, but optional)
Boiled rice, warm

Directions
1. Prepare rice according to package and keep warm.
2. Mix flour, salt, and pepper in a large plastic bag with a locking seal.
3. Add the pork pieces to the bag and seal.
4. Shake the bag well to coat each piece.
5. Remove the pork and throw the bag away.
6. Heat the oil in a large frying pan.
7. Cook the pork pieces on all sides until brown.
8. Lower the heat and cook for 20 minutes.
9. Add the peppers, onion, and carrot, and cook for 5 minutes.
10. Stir in pineapple, pineapple juice, vinegar, soy sauce, brown sugar, cornstarch, and food coloring.
11. Cook until the mixture is hot.
12. Serve over cooked rice.

Serves 4 to 5.

China

Sweet and sour pork is a popular dish among the Chinese and is also served at many restaurants in the United States. © JOSH RESNICK/SHUTTERSTOCK.COM.

Baat Bo Fon (Rice Pudding)

Ingredients
¾ cup rice
1½ cups water
Pinch of salt
4 cups milk
½ cup sugar
½ teaspoon vanilla extract
Sliced almonds, whipped cream, cinnamon

Directions
1. Combine the rice, water, and salt in a large pot.
2. Heat until almost boiling, stirring often.
3. Lower the heat, cover pot, and simmer for 15 minutes, or until most of the water has been absorbed.
4. Stir in the milk and sugar.
5. Cook uncovered for 30 to 40 minutes, or until mixture is thick and creamy, stirring often.
6. Stir in vanilla.
7. Serve topped with sliced almonds, whipped cream, or a sprinkle of cinnamon.

Serves 6.

Fried Rice

Note: This recipe involves hot oil and requires adult supervision.

Ingredients
3 tablespoons peanut oil
4 cups boiled rice, cold
1 teaspoon salt
½ teaspoon black pepper
½ green, red, or yellow pepper, chopped
½ cup mushrooms, sliced
¼ cup water chestnuts, sliced
½ cup bean sprouts
¼ cup scallions, chopped
3 eggs, beaten
½ cup parsley, chopped

Directions
1. Cook rice according to instructions on package.
2. Allow to cool.
3. Heat the oil in a wok or skillet over high heat.
4. Add rice and fry until hot, stirring constantly.
5. Stir in salt and pepper.
6. Add the green pepper, mushrooms, water chestnuts, bean sprouts, and scallions, stirring often.
7. Push the mixture to the sides of the wok or skillet, making an empty space in the center of the rice mixture.
8. Pour beaten eggs into the empty space.
9. Let the eggs cook halfway through.
10. Blend the eggs with the rest of the rice mixture.
11. Heat until the eggs are fully cooked.
12. Remove the pan from heat.
13. Sprinkle the chopped parsley over each serving.

Serves 4 to 6.

4 Food for Religious and Holiday Celebrations

Although day-to-day cooking in China is quite simple, elaborate meals are served on holidays and festivals. A typical holiday meal might consist of steamed dumplings, suckling pig (or a spicy chicken dish), and a selection of desserts. Unlike in the United States, desserts are generally reserved for special occasions only. Most ordinary meals end with soup.

The most important festival of the year is the Chinese New Year, which is set according to the phase of the moon, and falls in January or February. Oysters are believed to bring good fortune and have become a traditional food for dinners celebrating the New Year. Oranges and tangerines (for a sweet life), fish (symbolizing prosperity), and duck are also eaten. Dumplings are commonly eaten in the north. *Neen gow,* New Year's Cake, is the most common dessert. Each slice of the cake is dipped in egg and pan-fried. A special rice flour makes the cake slightly chewy.

Chinese Mooncakes

Ingredients
¼ cup sugar
2 egg yolks
¼ cup salted butter
1 cup flour
1 cup strawberry jam

Directions
1. Mix together 1 of the yolks, sugar, and butter.
2. Slowly mix in flour until the mixture becomes a dough.
3. Refrigerate dough for 30 minutes.
4. Roll the dough into half-cup sized balls.
5. Make a hole in the middle of the balls. Fill with a teaspoon of jam.
6. Brush the other egg yolk over the balls.
7. Bake for about 20 minutes, until golden brown.

Makes 24 cakes.

Peking Duck Holiday Feast Menu
Peking duck

Mandarin pancakes

Fish in wine sauce

Seaweed

Chinese celery cabbage in cream sauce

Pickled cabbage Peking style

Buddha Jumps Over the Wall Feast Menu
Buddha Jumps Over the Wall (feast dish with as many as 30 main ingredients; takes up to 2 days to prepare)

Snow pea shoots with steamed mushrooms

Choi sum with yunnan ham

Mustard green stems in sweet mustard sauce

Another important holiday is the Mid-Autumn Festival in September. To celebrate this festival, which occurs during the full moon, the Chinese eat heavy, round pastries called mooncakes. They are filled with a sweet paste and sometimes have an egg yolk in their center. Other foods eaten at this time are rice balls and a special cake called *yue bing.*

After a baby is one year old, the Chinese typically only celebrate birthdays every 10 years, starting with the 10th birthday. The Chinese eat noodles on their birthdays. They believe that eating long noodles will lead to a long life. Another traditional birthday food is steamed buns in the shape of peaches, a fruit that also represents long life.

China

Birthday Noodles with Peanut Sauce

Ingredients

2 tablespoons peanut butter or sesame paste, smooth
¼ cup hot water
3 tablespoons soy sauce
1 teaspoon honey
4 cups Chinese-style noodles or spaghetti, cooked
2 scallions cut in ½-inch pieces (optional)
Bean sprouts (optional)
Chopped peanuts (optional)

Directions

1. Cook noodles according to package instructions and drain.
2. In a large bowl, use a fork to stir the peanut butter or sesame paste with the water until it is creamy.
3. Stir in the soy sauce and honey. Add the noodles to the peanut butter mixture and mix well.
4. Refrigerate the mixture until ready to serve.
5. Serve the noodles cold, topped with scallions, sprouts, or chopped peanuts.

Suggestion: Eat with chopsticks.

Serves 4.

Birthday Party Menu

Noodles with peanut sauce

Honey-glazed chicken wings

Steamed buns

Almond cookies

5 Mealtime Customs

Togetherness and cooperation is reflected in China's mealtime customs. A dish is never served to just one person, either at home or in a restaurant. Each person has his or her own plate, but everyone at the table shares food. Instead of a knife and fork, the Chinese eat with chopsticks, a pair of wooden sticks held in one hand. Food is cut into bite-size pieces while it is being prepared, so none of it has to be cut at the table. It is considered good manners to hold a bowl of rice up to your mouth with one hand. Chopsticks, held in the other hand, are used to help scoop the rice into the person's mouth. Drinking soup directly from the bowl is also an acceptable custom. It is rude, however, to leave chopsticks sticking straight up in a bowl of rice.

A typical family dinner consists of rice or noodles, soup, and three or four hot dishes. At a formal dinner, there will also be several cold appetizers.

A well-known type of Chinese snack is called dim sum ("touch of heart"). These are bite-size foods served with tea in mid-morning, afternoon, or at night. Typical dim sum are filled dumplings, shrimp balls, and spring rolls (also called "egg rolls" in the United States). Wontons, which can be boiled in soup, are also served fried as dim sum.

6 Politics, Economics, and Nutrition

The rapidly growing population in China has been difficult to feed throughout history. About 10 percent of the total population in China is undernourished according a report issued by the World Bank. This problem is most significant in rural areas. People living in inland areas are more likely to be poor and to have a diet lacking in adequate nutrition. About 12 percent of children under age five are underweight.

Mooncakes are often stamped with a design. These mooncakes, made in a Chinese bakery, feature various designs. © FOTOHUNTER/SHUTTERSTOCK.COM.

Fu Yung Don (Egg Fu Yung)

Note: This recipe involves hot oil and requires adult supervision.

Ingredients
8 large eggs at room temperature
1 cup peanut oil (used in varying amounts)
¼ teaspoon salt
Pinch of pepper, preferable freshly ground
¼ cup scallion, finely sliced (green part only)
½ pound cooked shrimp, each shrimp cut in half

Directions
1. In a large bowl, beat eggs with 1½ tablespoons of peanut oil until bubbles start to form.
2. Add the shrimp to the beaten eggs and gently stir.
3. Mix in the salt, pepper, and scallions, reserving a few scallions for garnish.
4. Heat 2 tablespoons of peanut oil in a wok or large skillet over high heat for about 20 seconds.
5. Tip the skillet or wok back and forth carefully to coat it thoroughly with oil.
6. Stir the eggs briefly once again, and pour the mixture into the hot skillet or wok.
7. Cook the eggs, stirring gently with a wooden spoon until scrambled, about 3 minutes.
8. Turn off the heat and transfer the eggs to a heated platter and serve.
9. Sprinkle with scallions.

Serves 4 to 6.

China

Many people enjoy dipping fried wonton in plum sauce. © WOLFMASTER13/SHUTTERSTOCK.COM.

Fried Wonton

Note: This recipe involves hot oil and requires adult supervision.

Ingredients
24 wontons
Vegetable oil for frying

Directions
1. Prepare wontons according to recipe for Wonton Soup (or purchase packaged wontons).
2. Fry in hot oil until golden brown and crispy.
3. Drain the wontons on a paper towel and serve hot with sweet and sour sauce, plum sauce, or red rice wine vinegar.

Water pollution is a problem in China, but most Chinese people have access to safe drinking water.

China's agricultural regions can sometimes be subjected to floods and droughts. In 2009, northern China experienced a severe drought. This had a major impact on the region's winter wheat crops as well as the availability of water for people and livestock. In 2011, another drought threatened the area's wheat production. As a result, the country maintains a large wheat reserve. However, shortages of wheat as the result of drought or floods can drive up wheat prices.

Another food-related concern in China in the early 21st century is that of food safety.

China

Almond cookies are often served with a whole almond in the center. © TOBIK/SHUTTERSTOCK.COM.

Various products have been found to be unsafe for consumption. For example, in 2008, milk from more than 20 Chinese dairies was found to contain melamine, an industrial chemical. The melamine was added to boost the protein content of the milk. The tainted milk killed at least six infants and caused kidney stones, kidney failure, urinary tract problems, and other health problems in several hundred thousand others. Melamine was also discovered in animal feed. Different problems with tainted milk surfaced in 2011.

Almond Cookies

Ingredients
2½ cups flour
1 cup sugar
1 teaspoon baking soda
½ teaspoon salt
1 cup vegetable shortening
2 eggs, beaten
1 tablespoon almond extract
About 48 whole almonds, unsalted

Directions
1. Preheat oven to 325°F. Grease cookie sheets.
2. Mix flour, sugar, baking soda, and salt in a bowl.
3. With a fork, slowly add shortening, a little at a time, to the flour mixture.
4. Add the beaten eggs and almond extract.
5. Shape the dough into balls the size of a large cherry.
6. Place the dough onto the cookie sheets and press an almond into the center of each cookie.
7. Bake for 25 minutes.

Makes about 4 dozen cookies.

Spiced Chicken

Ingredients
- 3 pounds chicken pieces (may be chicken wings, boneless breasts cut into strips, or drumsticks)
- ¼ cup soy sauce
- 2 cloves garlic, crushed
- 1 teaspoon pepper
- ¼ cup sugar
- 2 tablespoons vegetable oil
- Several lettuce leaves

Directions
1. Rinse the chicken in cool water and pat dry with paper towels.
2. Mix the soy sauce, garlic, pepper, sugar, and oil in a bowl.
3. Thoroughly coat the chicken pieces with this mixture, reserving a little mixture in the bowl. Refrigerate the reserved soy sauce mixture.
4. Let the chicken stand (marinate) for 2 to 4 hours in the refrigerator.
5. Preheat oven to 350°F.
6. Place chicken into a lightly oiled baking pan. Bake for about 40 minutes.
7. Every 10 minutes during roasting, turn the chicken and use the basting brush to brush on the remaining soy sauce mixture. When the chicken is tender, remove from oven.
8. Arrange pieces on a bed of lettuce on a serving platter and serve warm or at room temperature.

Serves 6.

7 Further Study

BOOKS

Bhumichitr, Vatcharin. *The Big Book of Noodles*. Lanham, MD: Kyle Books, 2011.

Horn, Ken. *Complete Chinese Cookbook*. Toronto: Firefly Books Ltd., 2011.

Liao, Yan. *Food and Festivals of China*. Philadelphia: Mason Crest Publishers, 2011.

Low, Bee Yini. *Easy Chinese Recipes*. Rutland, VT: Tuttle Publishing, 2011.

Yan, Martin. *Chinese Cooking for Dummies*. Foster City, CA: IDG Books, 2000.

WEB SITES

Allrecipes.com: Chinese Food. http://allrecipes.com/Recipes/world-cuisine/asia/china/main.aspx (accessed on February 5, 2012).

Asia Foods. http://www.asiafoods.com (accessed February 5, 2012).

Chinese Food. http://chinesefood.about.com (accessed February 6, 2012)

Global Gourmet China: 2000 Years of Cooking. http://www.globalgourmet.com/destinations/china/ (accessed on February 5, 2012).

Whats4Eats: Chinese Recipes and the Cooking of China. http://www.whats4eats.com/east-asia/china-cuisine/ (accessed on February 5, 2012).

Côte d'Ivoire

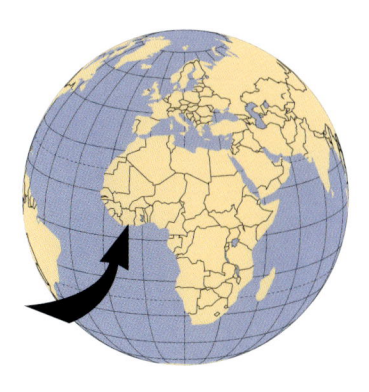

- Aloko (Fried Bananas) 128
- Sauce Pimente 128
- Pineapple Salad 129
- Cornmeal Cookies 129
- Fufu 130
- Melon Fingers with Lime 131
- Kedjenou 132
- Baked Yams 132
- Chilled Avocado Soup 134
- Calalou (Vegetable Stew) 134
- Avocado with Dressing 135
- Arachid Sauce 135

1 Geographic Setting and Environment

The Republic of Côte d'Ivoire (which means "ivory coast" in French) lies on the south coast of the western bulge of Africa. It has an area of 124,502 square miles (322,460 square kilometers). Comparatively, the area occupied by Côte d'Ivoire is slightly larger than the state of New Mexico. The greater part of Côte d'Ivoire is a vast plateau, tilted gently toward the Atlantic Ocean. The Guinea Highlands (in the northwest, from Man to Odienné) have peaks higher than 3,280 feet (1,000 meters).

The greatest annual rainfall, 78 inches (198 centimeters), is along the coast and in the southwest. The coastal region has a long dry season from December to mid-May, followed by heavy rains from mid-May to mid-July, a short dry season from mid-July to October, and lighter rains in October and November. Farther north, there is only one wet and one dry season, with rainfall heaviest in summer.

Many Ivoirians are employed in agriculture and related fields. More than two-thirds of the labor force work in these areas. The nation is among the largest producers of cocoa, which it exports to various countries around the world. Other crops that are important to the nation's economy include palm oil and coffee.

2 History and Food

Thousands of years prior to the arrival of the Europeans in the 1460s, independent tribes occupied present-day Côte d'Ivoire. They survived mostly on gathered seeds and fruits and hunted animals. Foods and eating habits were most likely influenced by outsiders who used the land as a trade route from as early as the 700s. Little, however, is known about the early inhabitants.

Côte d'Ivoire

Aloko (Fried Bananas)

Note: This recipe involves hot oil and requires adult supervision.

Ingredients

5 bananas
Oil

Directions

1. Cut the bananas lengthwise, then into little pieces.
2. Pour about 4 inches of oil into a saucepan and heat until boiling.
3. Place one-half of the sliced bananas into the oil.
4. Fry both sides until reddish-brown, then very carefully remove.
5. Fry the other one-half, then remove.
6. Serve immediately alone, or with grilled fish.

Serves 4 to 6.

Sauce Pimente

Ingredients

2 large tomatoes
1 onion
Garlic, crushed
¼ cup hot peppers, diced
1 eggplant, peeled and cut into small pieces
1 cup chicken broth
Oil

Directions

1. Chop onions and tomatoes into small pieces.
2. Sauté onions in oil. Add tomatoes and garlic.
3. Add chicken broth, eggplant, and hot peppers.
4. Boil until the mixture is a thicker consistency and most of the liquid has evaporated.
5. Serve over aloko (fried bananas) or as a sauce on bread or meats.

Serves 4 to 6

By the late 1400s, the Portuguese began to show a significant interest in Côte d'Ivoire. They were interested in spreading Christianity, purchasing slaves, and discovering new trade routes.

The Portuguese soon established several trading centers along the country's coast, but poor coastal harbors helped to spare the country from the buildup of a large slave trade. However, the Europeans desperately sought the country's supply of ivory (from the tusks of elephants) and gold, so trading and exploitation of these goods continued.

The country's nickname, the Ivory Coast (Côte d'Ivoire), originated because of the area's well-known supply of ivory. In return for the gold and ivory, the Portuguese brought European weapons and cassava, now a daily food staple, to the Ivoirians.

Côte d'Ivoire

Pineapple Salad

Ingredients
1 cup canned, crushed pineapple
1 teaspoon cardamom
¼ teaspoon cloves
2 cups whipped cream

Directions
1. In a bowl, mix pineapple, cardamom, and cloves.
2. Fold the pineapple mixture into the whipped topping.
3. Chill for at least an hour and serve cold.

Serves 4

Pineapple Salad is considered a sweet delicacy in Côte d'Ivoire.
© EPD PHOTOS.

By the mid-1800s, French merchants discovered that large amounts of ivory and gold originated from Côte d'Ivoire. In exchange for money and the promise of French protection, Côte d'Ivoire gave France permission to take control of the country's coastal trade routes. With the hopes of planting profitable cash crops (crops grown to make money), the French began planting coffee, cocoa, and palm oil (an essential ingredient for preparing African food) along the coast. Eventually one-third of the cocoa, coffee, and banana plantations belonged to the French.

As a result of France's push toward a strong economy based on cash crops, Côte d'Ivoire continued to mass-produce several crops after gaining its independence from France in 1960. Côte d'Ivoire is the world's leading producer of cocoa, and it is among the largest producers of coffee in the world (behind Brazil and Colombia and a few others). Côte d'Ivoire also became Africa's leading exporter of pineapples and palm oil. However, many of the country's rainforests have been destroyed in order to plant more cocoa (and other cash crops). Corn, rice, millet, and yams have also thrived, but mostly as crops eaten by the people of Côte d'Ivoire.

Cornmeal Cookies

Ingredients
¾ cup margarine
¾ cup sugar
1 egg
1¼ cups flour
½ cup cornmeal
1 teaspoon baking powder
¼ teaspoon salt
1 teaspoon vanilla

Directions
1. Preheat oven to 350°F.
2. In a mixing bowl, beat margarine and sugar together until light and fluffy.
3. Add the egg and vanilla and beat well.
4. In a separate bowl, combine the flour, cornmeal, salt, and baking powder.
5. Slowly add the dry ingredients to the margarine mixture and mix well.
6. Drop dough in spoonfuls onto a greased cookie sheet and bake for 15 minutes.

Makes 3 dozen.

Côte d'Ivoire

Fufu (Boiled Cassava and Plantains)

Ingredients
- 2½ cups cassava (also called manioc or yucca); do not use the very center of the cassava
- 5 plantains; do not use the very center of the plantains

Directions
1. Prepare the cassava and plantains by peeling them, slicing them lengthwise, and removing the woody core. Then cut the cassava and plantains into chunks and place in a large saucepan. Cover with water.
2. Heat the water to boiling and then lower heat to simmer. Simmer the cassava and plantains until tender (about 20 minutes). Drain.
3. Return the pan to low heat and pound, mash, and stir the mixture, using a wooden spoon or potato masher. Add a sprinkling of water to keep the mixture from sticking. Continue pounding and mashing for 15 minutes, until the mixture is smooth.
4. Form into balls and serve.

Makes 3 fufu balls.

Cassava is an important staple food for the Ivorians, especially in rural areas. © JAKUB PAVLINEC/SHUTTERSTOCK.COM.

Cassava is fairly easy to grow in Côte d'Ivoire. Many people in rural Côte d'Ivoire get more than half their daily calories from cassava. In the 2010s, farmers were experimenting with using cassava to feed chickens. However, cassava is an important food in the human diet, so it may be considered too valuable to be used to feed chickens.

❸ Foods of the Ivoirians

Côte d'Ivoire's roughly 60 ethnic groups bring diversity to the country's cuisine. Each group has developed a diet that is suitable to its lifestyle. The Agni and Abron groups survive by farming cocoa and coffee. The Senufo peoples live in the country's northern savanna (treeless plain). They cultivate rice, yams, peanuts, and millet (a type of grain). Rice with a peppery peanut sauce is often enjoyed by the Senufo people. The Dioula of the far northwest depend on their cultivation of rice, millet, and peanuts to survive, while the Kulango people of the north, who are mostly farmers, grow yams, corn, peanuts, and watermelons. Those living near the coast enjoy a wide variety of seafood.

Despite varying diets and food customs, the people of Côte d'Ivoire generally rely on grains and tubers (root vegetables) to sustain their diet. Yams, plantains (similar to bananas), rice, millet, corn, and peanuts (known as groundnuts in Africa) are staple foods throughout the country. At least one of these is typically an ingredient in most dishes. The national dish is *fufu* (FOO-fue), plantains, cassava, or yams pounded into a sticky dough and served with a seasoned meat (often chicken) and vegetable sauce called *kedjenou* (KED-gen-ooh). As with most meals, it is typically eaten with the hands, rather than utensils. Kedjenou is most often prepared from peanuts, eggplant, okra, or tomatoes. *Attiéké*

(AT-tee-eck-ee) is a popular side dish. Similar to the tiny pasta grains of couscous, it is a porridge made from grated cassava.

For those who can afford meat, chicken and fish are favorites among Ivoirians. Most of the population, however, enjoys an abundance of vegetables and grains accompanied by various sauces. Several spicy dishes, particularly soups and stews, have hot peppers to enrich their flavors. Fresh fruits are the typical dessert, often accompanied by *bangui* (BAN-kee), a local white palm wine or ginger beer. Children are fond of soft drinks such as Youki Soda, a slightly sweeter version of tonic water.

Often the best place to sample the country's local cuisine is at an outdoor market, a street vendor's stall or cart, or a *maquis*, a restaurant unique to Côte d'Ivoire. These reasonably priced outdoor restaurants are scattered throughout the country and have grown in popularity. To be considered a maquis, the restaurant must sell braised food (food that has been cooked over a low fire). The popular meats of chicken and fish are the most commonly braised food and are usually served with onions and tomatoes. Rice, fufu, attiéké, and kedjenou are also sold.

4 Food for Religious and Holiday Celebrations

Côte d'Ivoire's population is largely split between Muslims (39 percent) and Christians (33 percent). Around 12 percent of the population practices traditional African religions. They honor their ancestors and believe in the spirits of nature. Although Ivoirians are split between Islam and Christianity, 70 percent of migrant workers (foreign workers) are Muslim, while only 20 percent are Christian.

Eid al-Fitr Menu

Chilled avocado soup

Kedjenou

Fufu

Rice

Boiled yams

Fresh melon

Melon Fingers with Lime

Melon Fingers make a delicious and refreshing dessert.

Ingredients
1 large honeydew, chilled
1 lime

Directions
1. Cut the melon into eighths, or sections, about 1-inch wide and remove the seeds.
2. Next, make cuts cross-wise about ¾-inch wide across each melon slice.
3. Arrange the slices on a large serving plate.
4. Section the lime and place a slice of lime in the center of each melon slice.

Serves 8.

Probably the most anticipated time of the year for Muslims (believers of Islam) is Ramadan, a month-long observance in which food and drink are not consumed between sunrise and sunset. Eid al-Fitr, the feast that ends this fasting month, lasts two to ten days. The feast may include a variety of seasoned meats with sauce, rice, yams or eggplant, salads, and soups or stews. Eid al-Adha (the feast of the sacrifice) starts on the

Côte d'Ivoire

10th day of the last month of the Islamic calendar. After prayers, the head of each household typically sacrifices (kills) a sheep, camel, or an ox. It is often eaten that evening for dinner and is shared with those who could not afford to purchase an animal to sacrifice.

Kedjenou (Seasoned Meat and Vegetable Sauce)

Ingredients

2 chickens, cut into pieces
3 large onions, chopped
6 tomatoes, peeled and diced
1 piece ginger root, peeled
1 clove of garlic, crushed
1 bay leaf
Salt, to taste
Hot red pepper, to taste
Rice as an accompaniment

Directions

1. Place the chicken, onions, tomatoes, ginger, garlic and bay leaf in a heavy pot with a lid.
2. Season with the salt and pepper.
3. Cover tightly, so that steam does not escape.
4. Put the pot on medium to high heat.
5. When the ingredients start to simmer, turn the heat down to medium to low.
6. Remove the pot from the heat. Holding the pot with potholders and without removing the lid, carefully shake the pot well to stir up the contents so that the mixture cooks evenly.
7. Repeat this procedure every 5 minutes for 35 to 40 minutes. Remove bay leaf.
8. Place the contents of the pot on a warm platter and serve with rice.

Serves 8.

Baked Yams

Ingredients

5 cups yam pieces, boiled until soft
1 egg, beaten
1 tablespoon butter, room temperature
Salt, to taste
1 egg yolk, beaten
Nutmeg and cinnamon, for dusting

Directions

1. Mash the soft yam pieces in a mixing bowl.
2. Gradually add the beaten egg, butter, and salt, mixing well to make sure that all ingredients are blended.
3. Spoon the mashed yam into an ovenproof casserole dish and spread the top with the beaten egg yolk.
4. Place it in the oven for 15 minutes, or until golden brown.
5. Sprinkle the top with nutmeg and cinnamon.

Serve hot. Makes 4 to 6 servings.

Christians, both Protestant and Roman Catholic, observe such holidays as Good Friday, Easter, and Christmas. Similar to the custom of Muslims on their special days, many Christians gather with family and friends on Christian holidays to enjoy a meal together. Cities are often decorated with bright lights and decorations, and people gather in the streets to sell fruits and other items. Réveillon, the Christmas Eve dinner served after midnight mass, is often considered the most important meal of the year. A Yule log is traditionally eaten as a special dessert.

The people of Côte d'Ivoire also celebrate secular (nonreligious) holidays such as National Day (December 7), commemorating the country's independence, and New Year's Day (January 1). At the beginning of harvest time, yam festivals take place to honor the spirits who

A woman prepares deep fried dough balls at a street market in Côte d'Ivoire. © TOMMY TRENCHARD/ALAMY.

people believe protect their crops each year. To celebrate, the Kulango people exchange gifts, eat a meal of mashed yams and soup, and participate in dances and song. Some villagers celebrate the harvest of other important crops, including rice.

5 Mealtime Customs

Some of the country's tastiest food can be found in people's homes. The Ivoirians are generous, hospitable people who enjoy inviting others to join them for a meal.

Ivoirians believe that those who are blessed enough to be able to prepare a meal should share their good fortune with others.

In a typical village, people eat together in a common area. They believe eating not only gives the body nourishment, but also unites people with community spirit.

Women and girls eat as one group, men as another, and young boys as a third group. Most villagers eat on a large mat placed on the ground. With their right hand (the left is considered unclean), villagers will scoop up their food from large bowls placed in the center of the mat for everyone to share.

To scoop up the food, villagers most often roll rice into a tight ball. The rice ball is then used to scoop up meat and sauce.

Côte d'Ivoire

Chilled Avocado Soup

Ingredients
2 ripe avocados, peeled and pitted
4 cups cold chicken or vegetable stock (two 14-ounce cans)
2 tablespoons lime juice
1 tablespoon plain yogurt
2 dashes Tabasco sauce, or to taste
Salt and pepper
4 paper-thin lime slices, for garnish

Directions
1. Add the avocado flesh to a blender and puree.
2. Add the stock and continue blending until smooth.
3. Blend in the lime juice, yogurt, Tabasco sauce, and salt and pepper.
4. Refrigerate for at least 1 hour.
5. When ready to serve, spoon into bowls and top each with a thin slice of lime.

Serves 4.

Avocados are a common ingredient in Ivorian cooking. Ripe avocados will be dark green in color and firm on the outside; they will give slightly when squeezed. The creamy flesh inside should be lighter green in color. © FRANCESCO83/SHUTTERSTOCK.COM.

Calalou (Vegetable Stew)

Ingredients
Cooking oil
2 to 3 pounds meat (beef, poultry, or fish), cut into bite-sized pieces
2 pounds greens (traditionally cassava leaves, taro leaves, sorrel leaves; substitute mustard greens or spinach), stems removed and cleaned (note that taro greens must be boiled for a short time, then rinsed)
2 tomatoes, peeled and chopped
1 cup dried shrimp
Garlic, minced (optional)
Salt, pepper, or cayenne pepper, to taste
1 onion, finely chopped
Rice as an accompaniment

Directions
1. Heat the oil in a large pot.
2. Fry the meat and onion until the meat is browned.
3. Add all the remaining ingredients and enough water to partially cover them.
4. Cover, reduce heat, and simmer on a very low heat for 2 or more hours.
5. Serve with rice.

Serves 6 to 8.

The eldest villagers eat first. They do this in order to detect any contaminated or sour food. If bad food is suspected, the elder members will stop the younger members, including children, from eating from the bowl.

Once everyone has begun eating, there are some rules that are followed. It is considered rude and selfish to reach across the table for food. Villagers want to make certain that everyone receives similar amounts of food.

Coughing, sneezing, and talking during the meal is discouraged. If a person needs to cough or sneeze, it is customary to get up and walk away from the mat before doing so.

After the meal is over, a bowl of water is passed around to cleanse the hands. Talking amongst the villagers will typically resume as the diners relax to digest their meal.

6 Politics, Economics, and Nutrition

About 14 percent of the population of Côte d'Ivoire is classified as undernourished by the World Bank. This means they do not receive adequate nutrition in their diet. This represents an improvement in the availability of food. In 1990, more than half the population was classified as undernourished.

In 2011, of children under the age of five, about 17 percent were underweight and 40 percent were stunted (short for their age).

Avocado with Groundnut Dressing

Ingredients
2 ripe avocados (should feel soft when ripe)
1 tablespoon lemon juice
2 tablespoons peanuts, shelled
½ teaspoon paprika
½ teaspoon cinnamon
Cayenne, to taste
Salt, to taste

Directions
1. Peel the avocados and cut out the pit.
2. Cut the avocados into cubes.
3. Sprinkle with lemon juice and set aside.
4. Grind the peanuts roughly with a rolling pin or in a grinder for a few seconds.
5. Mix the peanuts and spices well and sprinkle over avocados.
6. Refrigerate until ready to serve.

Serves 4.

Arachid Sauce

Ingredients
2 tablespoons peanut butter
Water
4 pimentos (a type of pepper)
20 cherry tomatoes, mashed
Meat (beef, chicken, or fish)
Pinch of salt
1 tablespoon oil
½ small onion

Directions
1. Place the peanut butter in a pot and add 4 tablespoons water.
2. Mix well until it is sauce-like and add 1 cup water.
3. Bring the sauce to a boil and add 2 more cups of water over a 25-minute period.
4. Add the pimentos.
5. Take 12 cherry tomatoes, remove the seeds, and mash.
6. Add the tomato mash and another 4 cups of water to the sauce and continue to boil.
7. After 50 minutes of boiling, add 2½ more cups of water, then let it boil again gently for 20 minutes.
8. Add precooked meat of choice and a pinch of salt and keep boiling for an addition 35 minutes.
9. Add the remaining cherry tomatoes, prepared as before, the oil, and the mashed onion.
10. Cook for at least 15 more minutes.

Serves 4 to 6.

A U.S. government-funded research study in 2010 found that a significant number of children were working on the cocoa farms in Côte d'Ivoire, most without pay and many not enrolled in school.

In 2012, the number of these child laborers was estimated to be between 600,000 and 800,000. Many child workers are exposed to harsh chemicals and pesticides, which can lead to health problems, including respiratory trouble. The government of Côte d'Ivoire was working to address the issue.

Political unrest in the country following a disputed 2010 presidential election led to a spike in food insecurity (not having enough food). It also impacted living conditions. Some people found it difficult to gain access to health care, among other issues.

7 Further Study

McCann, James. *Stirring the Pot: A History of African Cuisine*. Athens: Ohio University Press, 2009.

Montgomery, Bertha Vining. *Cooking the West African Way*. Minneapolis: Lerner Publications, 2002.

Sheehan, Patricia, and Jacqueline Ong. *Côte d'Ivoire*. New York: Marshall Cavendish Benchmark, 2010.

Weber, Valerie. *I Come from Ivory Coast*. Milwaukee: Weekly Reader Early Learning Library, 2007.

WEB SITES

Whats4Eats: Ivory Coast, Côte d'Ivoire: Cuisine and Recipes. http://www.whats4eats.com/africa/ivory-coast-cuisine (accessed February 6, 2012)

World Food Programme: Côte d'Ivoire. http://www.wfp.org/countries/c%C3%B4te-divoire (accessed February 6, 2012)

Cuba

- Moors and Christians 139
- Tuna in Sauce 139
- Fried Plantains 140
- Flan (Baked Custard) 140
- Yucca (Cassava) 141
- Ensalada Cubana Tipica (Salad) ... 141
- Helado de Mango (Sherbet) 142
- Piña Asada 143
- Aceitunas Alinadas (Olives) 143
- Arroz con Leche (Rice Pudding) .. 143
- Crème de Vie (Cuban Eggnog) ... 144
- Pastelitos 144
- Cubano 146

1 Geographic Setting and Environment

The Republic of Cuba consists of one large island and several small ones situated on the northern rim of the Caribbean Sea, about 100 miles (160 kilometers) south of Florida. With an area of 42,803 square miles (110,860 square kilometers), Cuba is the largest country in the Caribbean. The area occupied by Cuba is slightly smaller than the state of Pennsylvania.

Cuba's coastline is marked by bays, reefs, keys, and islets. Along the southern coast are long stretches of lowlands and swamps. Slightly more than half the island consists of flat or rolling terrain, and the remainder is hilly or mountainous. Eastern Cuba is dominated by the Sierra Maestra mountains, whose highest peak is Pico Real del Turquino. Central Cuba contains the Trinidad (Escambray) Mountains, and the Sierra de los Órganos is located in the west. The largest river is the Cauto.

Except in the mountains, the climate of Cuba is semitropical or temperate.

About 20 percent of the country's people live in Havana, the capital and largest city. During the 1990s, there were food and fuel shortages in Havana. The government encouraged people living in the city to start gardening. Government-owned research gardens were created. Urban farming employed about 25,000 people, who tended gardens throughout the city. Some were very small and others were larger plots, cultivated by groups of farmers. The fuel shortages did not affect the selling of the vegetables that these gardens produced because they did not have to be trucked long distances.

Cuba continued to grow more crops in the early 2000s and 2010s. The country received $20 million in aid through the UN Development

Cuba

and vegetables. They also grew sugar cane, a major Cuban crop. African slaves were unable to bring any items along with them on their journey to Cuba. They were, however, able to introduce their African culture.

The slaves developed a taste for fruits and vegetables such as maize (corn), okra, and cassava. In time, Spanish and African cultures joined together to create several popular dishes, including *arroz congri* (rice and beans, often known as Moors and Christians) and *tostones* (pieces of lightly fried fruit, similar to the banana).

Cuban cuisine, however, drastically changed after the Cuban Revolution in 1959. Fidel Castro (1926–) overthrew the government. Cubans who opposed him began to flee the island, including chefs and restaurant owners. As a result, food shortages became frequent, and food that was still available was of poor quality.

In 2008, Fidel Castro transferred power to his brother Raúl (1931–). Trade restrictions imposed on Cuba remained, so living conditions and shortages of food were still a problem. Several hurricanes swept over Cuba, damaging farmland, in the early 2000s.

Raúl Castro announced that helping the country's farmers recover would be a top priority of his government. Among the programs, which were begun before Raúl Castro took power, was one to reintroduce the use of oxen and other animals to replace tractors on Cuban farms. Another was to sell produce close to where it is grown, to cut down on transportation costs. As a result the Cuban Ministry of Agriculture reported that in 2003 farmers used one-half the diesel fuel they had used in 1989.

Programme to support the goal of expanding the number of and types of crops grown. The program also helps improve the skills of Cuban farmers.

2 History of Food

Christopher Columbus (1451–1506) discovered the island of Cuba on October 28, 1492, claiming it in honor of Spain. As colonies were established, the Spanish began mistreating and exploiting the indigenous inhabitants of the island until they were nearly extinct. The colonists resorted to importing black slaves from Africa to operate mines and plantations. As a result, both Spanish and African cultures formed the foundation of Cuban cuisine.

Spanish colonists brought with them citrus fruits, such as oranges and lemons, as well as rice

Moors and Christians (Black Beans and Rice)

Ingredients
1 pound black beans, dried (or 2 cups canned black beans)
1 large onion, diced
3 garlic cloves, crushed
3 teaspoons cumin, ground
½ cup green pepper, chopped
Olive oil, for frying
2 cups chicken broth
3 tablespoons tomato paste
1 cup long-grain white rice
Salt and pepper, to taste

Directions
1. If you are using canned beans, drain the water from them and set them aside.
2. If using dry beans, cover them with water. Bring to a boil, remove from heat, and let stand 1 hour. Drain the beans.
3. Use a large, covered cooking pot and sauté the onion, garlic, and green pepper in the olive oil until tender.
4. Add the tomato paste, black beans, cumin, and chicken broth.
5. Add rice, cover and cook over low heat, stirring occasionally until rice is fully cooked (about 30 minutes).
6. Add salt and pepper to taste.

Serves 4 to 6.

A favorite dish all year round is Moors and Christians made from black beans and rice. The name refers to the African (black beans) and Spanish Christian (white rice) roots of Cuban culture and cooking. © EPD PHOTOS.

❸ Foods of the Cubans

Although Spain and Africa contributed most to Cuban cuisine, the French, Arabic, Chinese, and Portuguese cultures were also influential. Traditional Cuban dishes generally lack seasonings and sauces. Black beans, stews, and meats are the most popular foods. Root vegetables are most often flavored with *mojo*, a combination of olive oil, lemon juice, onions, garlic, and cumin.

Tuna in Sauce

Ingredients
2 cans tuna, in oil
1 medium onion, chopped
1 medium green peppers, chopped
3 cloves of garlic, mashed
1 small can tomato sauce
1 teaspoon Tabasco sauce
Rice

Directions
1. Mix all ingredients in a saucepan and cook over medium heat, stirring constantly for about 10 minutes.
2. Cover, lower heat and simmer for 20 minutes.
3. Serve over white rice.

Serves 4.

Cuba

Fried Plantains

Note: This recipe uses hot oil and requires adult supervision. The peels of the firm, ripe plantains called for in this recipe are black and yellow, not completely black.

Ingredients
4 firm, ripe plantains
Vegetable oil for frying

Directions
1. With a small, sharp knife, cut ends from each plantain. Slice through the peel and remove it.
2. Cut the fruit into thin slices, about ⅛-inch thick.
3. In a large, deep skillet, heat oil (about ¼-inch deep) and fry 12 to 15 plantain slices at a time for 2 to 3 minutes, or until golden, turning them over once.
4. Use a slotted spoon or spatula to remove cooked slices and place them on paper towels to drain. Season the slices with salt. Plantain slices should be slightly crisp on the outside but soft on the inside.
5. The slices are best served immediately; however, they may be made 1 day ahead, cooled completely, and kept in an air-tight container.
6. Reheat plantain slices on a rack in a shallow baking pan in a preheated 350°F oven for 5 minutes, or until heated through.

Serves 8.

Middle- and upper-class Cubans, including tourists, usually consume a wider variety of foods, if available. The most common meals include those made with pork, chicken, rice, beans, tomatoes, and lettuce. Hot spices are rarely used in Cuban cooking. Fried (*pollo frito*) or grilled (*pollo asado*) chicken and grilled pork chops are typically eaten. Beef and seafood are rarely prepared, with the exception of lobster. Rabbit (*conejo*), when available, is also eaten.

Flan (Baked Custard)

Ingredients

Caramel Coating:
½ cup sugar
1 tablespoon butter
2 tablespoons water

Flan:
1 (14-ounce) can sweetened condensed milk
½ cup milk
½ cup water
4 egg yolks, beaten
1 teaspoon vanilla extract

Directions

Caramel Coating:
1. Measure sugar, butter, and water into a saucepan and cook over medium heat, stirring until bubbly and caramel brown. Be careful not to burn the mixture.
2. Pour into a warm baking dish, reserving a small amount to drizzle on top of finished flan. Roll dish to coat the sides completely with the caramel.

Flan:
1. Preheat oven to 350°F.
2. Mix all flan ingredients and pour into a 2-quart baking dish that has been lined with a caramel coating (directions above).
3. Place pan in a larger pan that contains water. Bake 55 to 65 minutes, or until pudding is soft set.
4. Chill. Drizzle caramel on top when serving.

Other common dishes in Cuba are *ajiaco* (a typical meat, garlic, and vegetable stew); *fufú* (boiled green bananas mashed into a paste), which is often eaten alongside meat; empanadas *de carne* (meat-filled pies or pancakes); and *piccadillo* (a snack of spiced beef, onion, and tomato). Ham and cheese is a common stuffing for fish and steaks, or it is eaten alone. The best place to find the freshest fruits and vegetables on the island is at a farmers market. Popular desserts include *helado* (ice cream), flan (a baked custard), *chu* (bite-sized puff pastries filled with meringue), *churrizo* (deep-fried doughnut rings), and *galletas* (sweet biscuits). *Piña asada* (Cuban grilled pineapple) can be made into a tasty dessert, or left as a fruit snack.

Constant food shortages in the 1980s and 1990s made finding certain foods nearly impossible. After the break-up of the Soviet Union in 1991, Cuba, a Communist country, lost the support of a valuable trading partner. The government broke up the large state-run farms. Smaller cooperatives now farm in Cuba, and the country has better control over its own food supply.

Yucca (Cassava)

Ingredients

4 to 6 yucca (cassavas), peeled and halved
1 teaspoon salt
4 cloves garlic, minced
Juice of 1 lemon
½ cup olive oil

Directions

1. Scrape the peel from the yucca, and cut the yucca into pieces. Boil the yucca in salted water until tender (about 25 minutes).
2. Drain the yucca and add garlic and lemon juice.
3. Heat olive oil in a pan until bubbling, then pour over yucca. Mix well and serve.

Serves 4.

Ensalada Cubana Tipica (Cuban Salad)

Ingredients

Salad:
2 ripe red tomatoes
1 head of iceberg lettuce
Radishes, sliced thin
1 white onion

Dressing:
½ cup olive oil
2 tablespoons white vinegar
2 tablespoons fresh lemon juice
2 cloves garlic
1 teaspoon salt
¼ teaspoon pepper

Directions

1. Cut the tomatoes into wedges.
2. Cut the onion in thin slices.
3. Break up the lettuce by hand.
4. Toss all the ingredients together with the radishes. Place all the vegetables in the refrigerator to chill.
5. In a separate bowl, mash the garlic with the salt and pepper.
6. Add the olive oil, vinegar, and lemon juice to the crushed garlic. Whisk together thoroughly.
7. Just before serving, gradually add the dressing, a little at a time, while you toss the salad with a large salad fork.
8. Add just enough dressing to cover the salad. Add more dressing, to taste.

❹ Food for Religious and Holiday Celebrations

Cuba is officially an atheist country (denies the existence of God or a higher being). However, it is estimated that about half of all Cubans are believers of a particular faith.

Cuba

Helado de Mango (Tropical Mango Sherbet)

Ingredients

1 cup water
½ cup sugar
Dash of salt
2 mangoes, peeled and sliced
½ cup light cream
¼ cup lemon juice
2 egg whites
¼ cup sugar

Directions

1. In a saucepan, make syrup by combining the water, ½ cup of sugar, and dash of salt. Cook for 5 minutes on medium heat. Remove from heat and allow to cool.
2. In blender, combine mangoes and cream and blend until smooth and creamy. (If you do not own a blender, you can mash the mangoes with a fork and stir in the cream).
3. Stir in cooled syrup and lemon juice. Pour the mixture into one 6-cup or two 3-cup shallow pans and freeze until mixture is partially frozen (slushy).
4. Separate egg whites from eggs one at a time. Discard the yolks, or reserve for use in another recipe.
5. Beat egg whites to soft foamy peaks and gradually add the remaining ¼ cup sugar.
6. Place frozen mixture into a chilled mixing bowl, breaking partially frozen mixture into chunks. Beat until smooth.
7. Carefully mix in the beaten egg whites. Return mixture to freezing container and freeze until firm.

Serves 6 to 8.

There are three general faiths that religious Cubans tend to follow: Afro-Cuban religions (saint worship), Judaism, and Christianity. For Christians, celebrating Christmas during the second half of the 20th century was often difficult. For years the government, ruled by Fidel Castro, did not encourage the celebration of a Christian holiday. However, the holiday of Christmas has been making a comeback since the end of the 1990s. Those who celebrate Christmas prepare a large meal on Christmas Eve.

A typical Christmas menu in Cuba might include *aceitunas alinadas* (marinated olives), ham spread, or ham croquettes (a ham-filled fried cake) for appetizers. Cuban salad, black beans, mashed plantains fufu, Cuban bread, Spanish potatoes, white rice, yucca with garlic, and roasted pig may be a typical dinner. For dessert, rice pudding, mango bars, coconut flan, rum cake, Three Milks Cake, or Cuban Christmas cookies may be served. To accompany their meal, Cubans might drink Cuban eggnog, Spanish sparkling hard apple cider, or a Cuban rum and mint drink.

Some Cuban public holidays are January 1 (triumph of the Revolution in 1959); April 4 (Children's Day); May 1 (Labor Day); and December 25 (Christmas Day). During these days, grocery stores are usually closed and people often head for the island's warm beaches to celebrate, often packing food for the trip. On New Year's Eve, a small feast is prepared. At the stroke of midnight, 12 grapes are often eaten (in memory of each month) and cider is served.

5 Mealtime Customs

A typical Cuban breakfast, normally served between 7 and 10 a.m., may include a tostada (grilled Cuban bread) and *café con leche* (espresso coffee with warm milk). The tostada is often

Piña Asada

Ingredients
1 pineapple
½ cup brown sugar
¼ cup water
3 tablespoons melted butter

Directions
1. Cut the pineapple into rings.
2. Mix brown sugar, water, and melted butter in a bowl.
3. Dip each ring into the mixture, making sure both sides are coated.
4. Place slices on grill (or in a hot pan) for about 2 to 5 minutes for each side.
5. Remove from grill when slices start to brown. Let cool and serve alone or with vanilla ice cream and cinnamon.

Makes 4 to 6 rings.

Aceitunas Alinadas (Marinated Olives)

Ingredients
2 cups green Spanish olives, drained (unpitted olives are traditional, but pitted olives may be used)
¼ cup olive oil
¼ cup red wine vinegar
¼ teaspoon ground pepper
3 cloves garlic, mashed
Freshly ground black pepper, to taste
Peel of 1 lemon (wash lemon before peeling)
Juice of 1 lemon
½ teaspoon cumin

Directions
1. Mix all the ingredients together in a glass bowl.

This typical Cuban dinner consists of roast pork, black beans and rice, and fried sweet plantains. © LISA F. YOUNG/SHUTTERSTOCK.COM.

2. Cover and refrigerate for a minimum of two days.
3. Serve at room temperature. (The olives will keep in the refrigerator for several weeks.)

Arroz con Leche (Rice Pudding)

Ingredients
½ cup rice
1 cup sugar
1½ cups water
1 quart milk
¼ teaspoon salt
1 lemon rind (wash lemon peel thoroughly)
1 teaspoon vanilla
1 cinnamon stick
Ground cinnamon

Directions
1. Boil the rice with water, lemon rind, and cinnamon stick in a pot until soft, stirring occasionally.
2. Reduce heat to low.
3. Add milk, salt, vanilla, and sugar.
4. Cook over medium heat, stirring occasionally until thick (about 1 hour).
5. Sprinkle with cinnamon and serve.

Serves 8.

Cuba

Crème de Vie (Cuban Eggnog)

Ingredients
1 cup water
2 cups sugar
1 can evaporated milk
1 can condensed milk
8 egg yolks, beaten
1 teaspoon vanilla extract

Directions
1. Before you begin, have a large bowl ready to fill with ice at the end of the cooking time.
2. Separate the egg yolks from the egg whites, and place the egg yolks into a small bowl. (The egg whites may be discarded or saved for another use.) Beat the egg yolks until they are well combined.
3. Next, combine the water and sugar in a saucepan. Heat to boiling and allow to simmer until the mixture becomes syrupy.
4. Let cool.
5. In another saucepan, heat the evaporated and condensed milk and vanilla over low heat; do not let the mixture boil. (If it starts to boil, take the pan off the heat right away.)
6. Add a little of the hot milk to the egg yolks to warm them.
7. Then very gradually add the egg yolks to the hot milk mixture.
8. Heat for about 5 minutes, stirring constantly with a wire whisk.
9. Remove pan from heat and put pan into large bowl filled with ice to chill the mixture.
10. While the mixture is cooling, add the sugar and water mixture and stir to combine.
11. Strain the mixture through a coffee filter or a sieve lined with cheesecloth.
12. Pour into a pitcher or bottle, cover, and refrigerate until ready to serve. (Note: In Cuba, the egg yolks are added to cold milk and are not heated. Heating the yolk mixture thoroughly is recommended, because uncooked egg yolks may contain bacteria that could cause food poisoning.)

Pastelitos

Note: This recipe calls for puff pastry, which is available in the frozen food section of the grocery store. Follow the directions on the package for defrosting the puff pastry before beginning to make the recipe.

Ingredients
½ cup water
½ cup sugar
2 sheets puff pastry (see note above)
1 egg
½ cup cream cheese
2 tablespoons sugar
1 teaspoon vanilla extract
Jelly

Directions
1. Bring water and sugar to a boil in a small pot, cooking until sugar dissolves.
2. Preheat oven to 400°F.
3. Whisk the egg. Place ½ whipped egg into bowl and mix with a tablespoon of water.
4. Beat the other ½ whipped egg with cream cheese, 2 tablespoons sugar, and vanilla, until smooth.
5. Cut each sheet of puff pastry into 9 squares.
6. Cover 9 of the squares with the cream cheese filling. Top with a spoonful of jelly.
7. Cover the squares with the remaining 9 squares. Seal the edges with a fork and brush with the egg and water mixture.
8. Place on cookie sheet and bake for 12 minutes.
9. After 12 minutes, take the pastries out of the oven and brush them with the sugar water mixture.
10. Bake for an additional 3 to 5 minutes or until golden brown.

Makes 9 pastries.

Lunch often consists of empanadas (Cuban sandwiches containing chicken or another meat, topped with pickles and mustard) or Cubanos

Cuba

Cream cheese and guava jelly are the traditional filling for pastelitos. Here, layers of puff pastry are cut into squares (upper left); filling is spooned onto the puff pastry (upper right); the filling is covered by another layer of puff pastry and the edges are then sealed with a fork (lower left). The baked pastelitos (lower right) will be flaky and delicate. © EPD PHOTOS.

(toasted sandwiches on Cuban bread). *Pan con bistec*, a thin slice of steak on Cuban bread with lettuce, tomatoes, and fried potato sticks, is also popular. Other dishes might include black beans and rice, pollo con arroz (chicken and rice), or roast pork or beef.

Finger foods are popular snacks eaten throughout the day. *Pastelitos*, small, flaky turnovers (in various shapes) filled with meat, cheese, or fruit (such as guava), are also common snacks. Because many Cubans are meat eaters, meat, chicken, or fish will normally be the main dish at dinner. It is almost always served with white rice, black beans, and fried plantains. A small salad of sliced tomatoes and lettuce may also be served.

Fast food establishments exist in Cuba, though popular U.S. chains do not. Many street vendors sell sandwiches and pizza. One of Cuba's fast-food chains is called El Rápido. It opened in 1995 and serves chicken, pizza, and hamburgers, among other menu items. *Burgui*, another chain, has restaurants throughout major Cuban cities.

Fresh fruit is also available as a snack from street vendors. Also, fresh produce markets, called *agromercados*, dot the city streets.

Junior Worldmark Encyclopedia of Foods and Recipes of the World, 2nd Edition

Cuba

Cuban sandwiches are specifically made on Cuban bread, which is similar to French or Italian bread. To make a Cubano sandwich, layer mustard, pickles, cheese, ham, and pork onto the bread. © REDAV/SHUTTERSTOCK.COM.

Cubano

Ingredients

1 loaf Cuban bread (can be bought at a store or substituted with French bread)
1 pound cooked ham, sliced
1 pound roasted pork, sliced
½ pound Swiss cheese, sliced
Mayonnaise and mustard
Sliced dill pickles

Directions

1. Cut the loaf of bread in half, lengthwise. Then cut it into quarters.
2. Make the sandwich with mayo, mustard, layers of ham, pork, cheese, and pickles.
3. Coat the surface of a pan or griddle with nonstick spray.
4. Place sandwiches on the pan for about 2 to 5 minutes for each side, pressing each side down to flatten.
5. Make sure all the cheese is melted and the bread is golden brown. Slice diagonally and serve.

Makes 4 sandwiches.

Many Cuban restaurants are government-owned. They have a reputation for providing slow service and bland meals. Privately owned restaurants, called *paladares*, normally serve a better meal, but are under strict government guidelines. Paladares are not allowed to sell shrimp or lobster, and they are only allowed to serve up to 12 people at one table. However, most paladares serve these dishes anyway. Government-owned restaurants often try to disguise themselves as being privately owned to attract more customers. In Cuban restaurants, it is common to have several menu items unavailable due to shortages of food. Some of the highest quality food on the island is often found at expensive hotels that mostly serve tourists.

6 Politics, Economics, and Nutrition

About 5 percent of the population of Cuba is classified as undernourished by the World Bank. This means they do not receive adequate nutrition in their diet. About 3 percent of children under the age of five were considered to have a low birth weight while 7 percent of children under five were stunted (short for their height). These statistics are among the lowest found in developing countries. Cuba was also making good progress in eliminating childhood obesity. During the 1980s, childhood obesity increased. By the 1990s and early 2000s, government programs encouraged healthier eating. Childhood obesity has been at around 5 percent since 1998.

Despite some undernourishment, Cubans are in relatively good health. Cuba has a national health care system, which provides services to all citizens. Safe water was available to nearly all (94 percent) in 2008. Almost all doctors work for rural medical services after graduation, allowing rural Cubans to have nearly equal health care services as those who live in Cuba's larger cities. Having access to doctors and various health care services may help to reduce the cases of malnourishment in children.

7 Further Study

BOOKS

Baker, Christopher P. *Moon Handbooks: Cuba*. 5th edition. Emeryville, CA: Avalon Travel Publishing, 2010.

Behnke, Alison. *Cooking the Cuban Way*. Minneapolis: Lerner Publications, 2004.

Castro, Lourdes. *Latin Grilling*. Berkeley, CA: Ten Speed Press, 2011.

Cortina, Martha Abreu. *Authentic Cuban Cuisine*. Gretna, LA: Pelican Publishing, 2011.

Perez, Papi. *Food with Attitude: Cooking the Cuban-Rican Way*. River Forest, IL: Wicker Park Press Limited, 2011.

Rabade Roque, Raquel. *The Cuban Kitchen*. New York: Alfred A. Knopf, 2011.

Sainsbury, Brendan. *Lonely Planet: Cuba*, 5th ed. Oakland, CA: Lonely Planet Publications, 2009.

Zanger, Mark H. *The American Ethnic Cookbook for Students*. Phoenix, AZ: Oryx Press, 2001.

WEB SITES

AllRecipes.com: Cuban Recipes. http://allrecipes.com/recipes/world-cuisine/latin-america/caribbean/cuba/main.aspx (accessed February 8, 2012).

Food.com: Cuban Recipes. http://www.food.com/recipes/cuban (accessed February 8, 2012).

Taste of Cuba. http://www.tasteofcuba.com/ (accessed February 8, 2012).

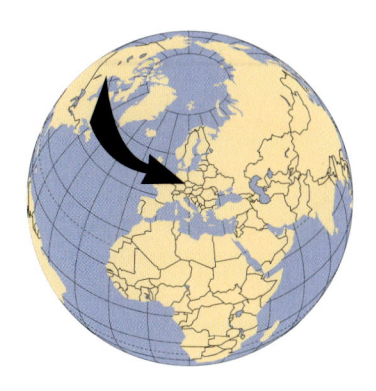

Czech Republic

- Sour Cream Cucumber Salad 151
- Houbova Polevka Myslivecka......151
- Strawberry Cookie Bars..............151
- Knedlíky (Czech Dumplings) 152
- Topinky S Vejci (Eggs on Toast) ...152
- Fazolovy Gulás...........................154
- Kure Na Paprice 155
- Moravske Vano ni Kukyse 156
- Mala Sousta Se Syre...................157

1 Geographic Setting and Environment

The Czech Republic is located in the middle of Eastern Europe. It borders Poland to the northeast, Germany to the north and northwest, Austria to the south, and Slovakia to the southeast. The country was formally known as Czechoslovakia. It decided to end its union with Slovakia on January 1, 1993.

The land of the Czech Republic is made up of two regions. Rolling hills, plains, and plateaus make up the western region, known as Bohemia. The eastern region, known as Moravia, is very hilly. Czech summers are relatively cool, with temperatures averaging 66°F (19°C). Winters are cold, cloudy, and humid, with temperatures typically around 30°F (-1°C).

Czech farmers raise crops, such as grains (wheat, rye, oats, corn, and barley), hops, potatoes, sugar beets, fruit; livestock (hogs and cattle); and poultry to supply food for the Czech people. They also provide products such as grain, milk, livestock, sugar, and malt for export. At one time, most of the farmland was owned by the government. As of 2011, most farms were owned by individuals.

2 History and Food

Czech cuisine was influenced historically by the surrounding regions that dominated the country. In 1273, Count Rudolph (1218–1291), King of Germany, founded the Hapsburg dynasty. Eventually the dynasty controlled most of Europe, including the region of the present-day Czech Republic. The Germans brought with them roast goose, sauerkraut, and dumplings, which have since become Czech staple dishes.

In 1526, Ferdinand I (1503–1564) began his reign as King of Bohemia (a western region in the Czech Republic) and the Hapsburg rule of Central Europe grew. From Vienna, the capital city of Austria, schnitzels (breaded and fried chicken or pork patties) were introduced to the Czechs.

Czech Republic

are popular in soups, such as *houbova polevka myslivecka* (Hunter's mushroom soup).

Seafood is not widely available because the country is not located near any large bodies of water. However, the landscape of the Czech Republic is dotted with thousands of ponds. Fish have been farmed in these ponds for hundreds of years. In southern Bohemia, there are nearly 500 ponds used for fish farming. Fish, especially carp and trout, are raised in ponds and human-made channels. The fish farms help preserve the environment. In fact, UNESCO has declared that the Trebon region in South Bohemia is a biosphere reserve and protected landscape area because of the marshes found there.

Czechs eat a wide variety of meats, from pork, beef, *ryba* (fish), and chicken, to duck, hare (similar to a rabbit), and venison (deer meat). The meats are commonly served with *knedlíky* (dumplings), *brambory* (potatoes), or *re* (rice), and are covered in a thick sauce. Dumplings are a popular side dish, and they are even stuffed with fruit as a dessert. The sauces are thick, like gravy, and are commonly made with wine. Sometimes fruit (such as cherries or berries of some sort), mushrooms, or onions are added for more flavor. Other common flavorings in Czech dishes are caraway seeds, bacon, and salt.

One of the most popular dishes is called *vepro-knedlo-zelo,* which is roast pork served with *zeli* (sauerkraut) and knedlíky (dumplings), made by boiling (or steaming) a mixture of flour, eggs, milk, and either dried bread crumbs or potatoes. Another popular dish is *kure na paprice*, chicken made with a spicy paprika sauce. Sliced dumplings are used to mop up gulás (goulash) for a filling lunch or dinner. A Czech specialty is *svíčková na smetane*, roast beef and bread

Other culinary influences come from Hungary and Eastern Europe, whose people used present-day Czech Republic as a crossroad to other European countries. Hungary introduced *gulás* (goulash) to the Czechs, a meat-based dish served with dumplings, and Eastern Europe offered such flavorings as sour cream, vinegar, and pickles.

❸ Foods of the Czechs

Czech cuisine is considered heavy and very filling, with meals centered on meats and starches. This is because Czech winters are long and cold, which does not allow for a variety of fresh vegetables. In fact, if salads are available, they typically are limited to two vegetables, such as tomato and cucumber. *Houby* (mushrooms) are the exception, which flourish in local forests and dumplings in a sour cream sauce, with lemon and lingonberries (similar to cranberries).

Sour Cream Cucumber Salad

Ingredients
3 medium cucumbers
½ teaspoon salt
½ teaspoon pepper
¼ cup sour cream
Lemon juice

Directions
1. Peel cucumbers and cut into thin slices.
2. Combine sour cream with salt, pepper, and lemon juice.
3. Mix in the cucumber.
4. Chill for 20 minutes and serve cold.

Serves 6.

Houbova Polevka Myslivecka (Hunter's Mushroom Soup)

Ingredients
¾ pound mushrooms, sliced
1 onion, chopped
1 tablespoon vegetable oil
2 strips bacon, cut into small pieces
¼ cup flour
5 cups water
1 chicken or beef bouillon cube
¼ cup heavy whipping cream
¾ cup cooking wine (or substitute water)
Salt and pepper, to taste

Directions
1. In a large pot, heat oil over medium heat.
2. Add the bacon pieces and fry until crispy.
3. Add the mushrooms and onion and fry until tender, about 4 minutes.
4. Add the flour and stir until the flour begins to brown.
5. Add the water and bring to a boil, then add the bouillon cube.
6. Stir until dissolved.
7. Reduce heat to medium and simmer about 20 minutes, stirring occasionally.
8. Add cream, salt, pepper, and cooking wine (or water).
9. Simmer for an additional 15 minutes.

Makes 4 servings.

Strawberry Cookie Bars

Ingredients
1 cup butter, softened
1 cup white sugar
2 egg yolks
1 teaspoon vanilla extract
⅛ teaspoon ground cardamom
¼ teaspoon allspice
2 cups flour
½ cup strawberry jam
1 cup chopped pecans

Directions
1. Grease an 8x8 inch pan and preheat the oven to 325°F.
2. Cream together butter, sugar, egg yolks, and vanilla.
3. Mix together cardamom, allspice, and flour.
4. Gradually add flour and mix until batter is combined.
5. Spread half of the mixture in the bottom of the pan.
6. Layer strawberry jam and nuts on top.
7. Cover the jam and nuts with the second half of the butter mixture.
8. Bake at 325°F for about 50 minutes or until brown.
9. Let cool, then cut into bars.

Makes about 16 squares.

Czech Republic

Knedlíky
(Czech Dumplings)

Ingredients
1 egg, beaten
½ cup milk
1 cup flour
⅛ teaspoon baking powder
1 teaspoon salt
4 to 5 slices white bread, cut into cubes

Directions
1. In a mixing bowl, combine beaten egg, milk, flour, baking powder, and salt until smooth.
2. Add bread cubes in batter and mix well.
3. Make 2 small balls from the dough.
4. Fill a large pot about half full with water and bring to a boil.
5. Drop the dough balls into the pot of boiling water and cook 10 minutes, then roll knedlíky over and cook an additional 10 minutes.
6. Remove immediately from the water and cut in half to release steam.
7. Serve with roast pork, sauerkraut, or *kure na paprice* (see recipe later in this entry).

Makes 4 servings.

Topinky S Vejci
(Eggs on Toast)

Ingredients
½ cup goat cheese or cheddar cheese, grated
3 eggs
Salt, to taste
8 slices bread
2 tablespoons vegetable oil
Paprika, to taste

Directions
1. In a mixing bowl, beat the eggs.
2. Add the grated cheese and salt.
3. Arrange the bread slices on a cookie sheet.
4. Cover the bread slices evenly with the egg and cheese mixture.
5. In a frying pan, heat the oil on medium heat.
6. With a pancake turner or spatula, pick up the bread slices one at a time and flip them down, into the oil.
7. Fry the bread about 2 minutes, or until the eggs are cooked. Be careful not to burn.
8. When ready to serve, sprinkle with paprika. Serve immediately.

Serves 8.

④ Food for Religious and Holiday Celebrations

In the 2011 Census, about 10.5 percent of the Czech Republic population listed themselves as Roman Catholic. A small number listed other Christian denominations, and 6.7 percent described themselves as believers who didn't attend church.

Nearly half of the 10.5 million Czechs surveyed did not affiliate themselves with any religion. However, two of the biggest religious holidays are Christmas and Easter, and these are widely celebrated.

Christmas Eve is celebrated on December 24 with a large dinner. According to one of the many Czech Christmas customs and traditions, a bowl of garlic is placed under the dinner table to provide protection to a family.

There is an old superstition that if anyone leaves the dinner table early, they will die the following year. As a result, everything is prepared and placed on the table before anyone sits down so no one needs to get up before the meal is finished.

The traditional Christmas Eve meal is usually served around 6 p.m. and might include potato salad, soups, cookies, a fruit bread called

Czechs serve **knedlíky**, *or dumplings, with a variety of foods. Here, they have been sliced to help mop up a plate of beef goulash.*
© TRISTANBM/SHUTTERSTOCK.COM.

vánocka, koláce (a type of pastry), and carp. Czechs go fishing for carp before Christmas Eve and usually keep the fish alive in the bathtub until it is ready to be prepared. Most Czechs also exchange gifts on Christmas Eve. Children believe that the newborn infant Jesus helps deliver Christmas gifts.

The food that is prepared for Easter dinner is usually taken to Mass on Easter Sunday, where it is placed on the altar and blessed by the priests. The blessed food is then taken home to be eaten.

A traditional Easter dinner may include baked ham or lamb; *polevka z jarnich bylin-velikonocni* (Easter soup), made of different herbs and egg; and a loaf of sweet bread called *mazanec,* made with raisins and almonds.

5 Mealtime Customs

A typical *snídane* (breakfast) in a Czech home is hearty–bread with butter, cheese, eggs, ham or sausage, jam or yogurt, and coffee or tea. For a quick breakfast, a Bohemian koláce (pastry) topped with poppy seeds, cottage cheese, or plum jam may be bought at a bakery.

Obed (lunch) is the main meal of the day for Czechs, where dinner may be no more than a cold plate of meats or cheese, such as *mala sousta se syre* ("small cheese bites"), and condiments. Obed is eaten between 11 a.m. and 1 p.m. Popular dishes may include gulás (goulash), *svícková,* roast beef in a creamy sauce topped with lemon and lingonberries (similar to cranberries),

Czech Republic

A vendor in a Czech market sells a variety of fruits and vegetables. © DANIEL KORZENIEWSKI/SHUTTERSTOCK.COM.

smazen syr (fried cheese), or *smázené zampiony* (fried mushrooms).

Fazolovy Gulás S Hovezim Masem (Bean Goulash with Beef)

Ingredients

1½ cups canned kidney beans
½ cup shortening
¾ pound beef, sliced
Salt and pepper, to taste
⅓ cup flour
2 tablespoons tomato sauce
½ cup onion, chopped
½ teaspoon paprika
2 cups water

Directions

1. Heat beans in a large saucepan over medium heat until cooked through, about 3 minutes.
2. Add salt to taste.
3. Add the water and bring to a boil, then reduce heat to medium.
4. In a frying pan, heat the shortening over medium heat until it melts.
5. Add the beef and onion. Fry for about 4 minutes. Season with pepper.
6. Dust mixture with the flour and brown it.
7. Add a little water from the beans to the meat and onion mixture to make a paste.
8. Add this mixture to the saucepan of beans. Add tomato sauce and paprika.
9. Simmer for about 20 minutes on low heat.
10. Serve with bread.

Serves 4 to 6.

Czech Republic

Kure Na Paprice (Chicken Paprikas), a favorite Czech dish, is typically served with **knedlíky** *(dumplings).* © EPD PHOTOS.

Kure Na Paprice (Chicken Paprikas)

Ingredients

2 pounds boneless, skinless chicken, cut into chunks
4 teaspoons paprika
1 tablespoon butter
1 tablespoon olive oil
½ cup onion, chopped
1 cup chicken broth
¼ cup sour cream
Salt and pepper, to taste

Directions

1. Season chicken with 1 teaspoon paprika, salt and pepper.
2. Heat olive oil in skillet over medium to high heat and sauté chicken on both sides until thoroughly cooked. Set aside.
3. Add butter to skillet. Sauté onion until softened, about 3 to 4 minutes.
4. Add remaining 3 teaspoons paprika and stir.
5. Add chicken broth to mixture and boil until sauce is thickened, about 8 minutes.
6. Place chicken back in skillet. Turn heat down to low and add sour cream, mixing to blend thoroughly. Season with salt and pepper to taste.
7. Serve with knedlíky (dumplings; see recipe earlier in this entry).

Makes 6 to 8 servings.

Travelers may stop at a street stand and buy a *párek* (hotdog), *klobása* (spicy sausage), or *hamburgery*, which are not like Western hamburgers. A hamburgery is ground pork (not beef) with sauerkraut, mustard, and ketchup on

Czech Republic

Gingerbread cookies are enjoyed by many Czechs during the Christmas season. © VIKTOR1/SHUTTERSTOCK.COM.

children have resulted in a low infant mortality rate (number of infant deaths) of about 3.7 per 1,000 live births in 2011.

School children are provided with medical attention, including X rays and annual examinations. Children up to one year old are immunized for a number of diseases, including tetanus and measles.

Moravske Vano ni Kukyse (Moravian Christmas Cookies)

Moravia is an eastern region in the Czech Republic.

Ingredients

- ⅓ cup molasses
- 3 tablespoons shortening
- 2 tablespoons brown sugar
- ½ teaspoon each cinnamon, ground ginger, baking soda, and salt
- 1¼ cup flour, more if needed

Directions

1. In a large mixing bowl, combine molasses, shortening, brown sugar, cinnamon, ginger, baking soda, and salt.
2. Add flour, a little at a time, to form dough.
3. Cover with plastic wrap or foil and refrigerate for at least 4 hours.
4. Preheat oven to 375°F.
5. Divide dough into 4 balls; keep the balls covered with a damp towel.
6. On a lightly floured surface, roll each ball, one at a time, to about ⅛-inch thick (very thin).
7. Cut into desired shapes using cookie cutters or the rim of a glass and place on greased cookie sheet.
8. Bake about 6 minutes, until lightly browned.

Makes about 24 cookies.

a bun. Stands also sell Middle Eastern specialties such as falafel (deep-fried chickpea balls) and shawarma (grilled, skewered meat). Open-faced sandwiches called *oblozené chlebícky* are also popular, which are commonly made with cold meat, eggs, cheese, or mayonnaise-based salads, such as ham and pea, or potato. Sandwiches may be eaten with soups, such as *rajska* (tomato and rice), *polevka jatrovymi knedlícky* (soup with liver dumplings), or *polevka z hlavkoveho zeli s parkem* (cabbage soup with frankfurters).

6 Politics, Economics, and Nutrition

The Czechs have very few nutritional problems. Free assistance and care provided to women and

Mala Sousta Se Syre (Small Cheese Bites)

Ingredients

1 cucumber, thickly sliced

1¼ cups goat cheese or cheddar cheese, thickly sliced

2 tangerines, peeled and sectioned, or 8 grapes

Directions

1. Place a slice of cheese on each slice of cucumber.
2. Pin a piece of tangerine or grape on top with a toothpick.

Serves 4.

As high-calorie fast food and drinks are added to the Czech diet, healthcare professionals have become concerned about childhood obesity. In 2009, the government began offering training in childhood obesity prevention to pediatricians.

7 Further Study

BOOKS

Atkinson, Brett, and Lisa Dunford. *Lonely Planet: Czech & Slovak Republics*. 6th edition. Oakland, CA: Lonely Planet, 2010.

Chamberlain, Lesley. *Cooking around the World: German, Austrian, Czech, and Hungarian*. London: Lorenz, 2005.

Salfellner, Harald. *Best Czech Recipes*. Prague: Vitalis, 2005.

Trnka, Peter. *The Best of Czech Cooking*. New York: Hippocrene Books, 2008.

WEB SITES

CzechUnderScope: Czech Sweets Recipes. http://czechunderscope.com/culture/czech-sweets/czech-sweets-recipes/lng/en/ (accessed February 8, 2012).

My Czech Republic: Czech Food and Drink. http://www.myczechrepublic.com/czech_culture/czech_cuisine.html (accessed February 8, 2012).

Prague.net: Traditional Czech Food. http://www.prague.net/traditional-czech-food (accessed February 8, 2012).

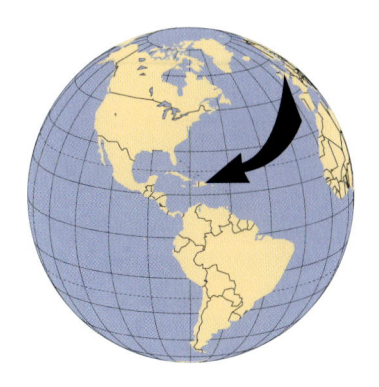

Dominican Republic

- Pan de Maiz 160
- Paleta de Coco 161
- Mangú 161
- Guavas in Syrup 162
- Sancocho 164
- Rainbow Rice 164
- Tostones 166
- Habichuelas con Dulce 166
- Jengibre (Ginger Tea) 166
- Jalalo 167
- Morir Soñando 167

❶ Geographic Setting and Environment

The Dominican Republic covers the eastern two-thirds of the Caribbean island of Hispaniola. The Atlantic Ocean lies on its northern coast. The Caribbean Sea lies along its southern coast. The country's western border is with Haiti, which covers the western one-third of Hispaniola.

The Dominican Republic has a total area of about 18,815 square miles (48,730 square kilometers). The Cordillera Central mountain range runs from east to west throughout the center of the country. Wide valleys lie north and south of the mountains. Pico Duarte, at 10,417 feet (3,175 meters) elevation, is the highest point in the Caribbean region. Lago Enriquillo, at 151 feet below sea level (-46 meters), is the lowest point in the region. It is a saltwater lake.

The climate is semitropical, with warmer temperatures along the coast and much cooler temperatures in the mountains. The rainy season is from June to November, with the dry season from December to May. Tropical hurricanes occur every few years and can cause great damage.

The soils are rich in the northern and southern valleys, where farmers grown sugarcane, coffee, tobacco, and cacao for export. Other crops include rice, tomatoes, vegetables, bananas, other tropical fruits, root crops, and sorghum. In 2011, agriculture made up about 7.3 percent of the nation's gross domestic product (GDP). Tourism has been growing in importance since the 1990s.

❷ History and Food

The Taínos, a group of indigenous people of the Dominican Republic, are now extinct. Still, they left a large impression on the food culture of the country. The Taínos, whose name means "friendly people," contributed sweet potatoes, peanuts, guava, and pineapple to the Dominican diet. They also contributed tobacco to the

Dominican Republic

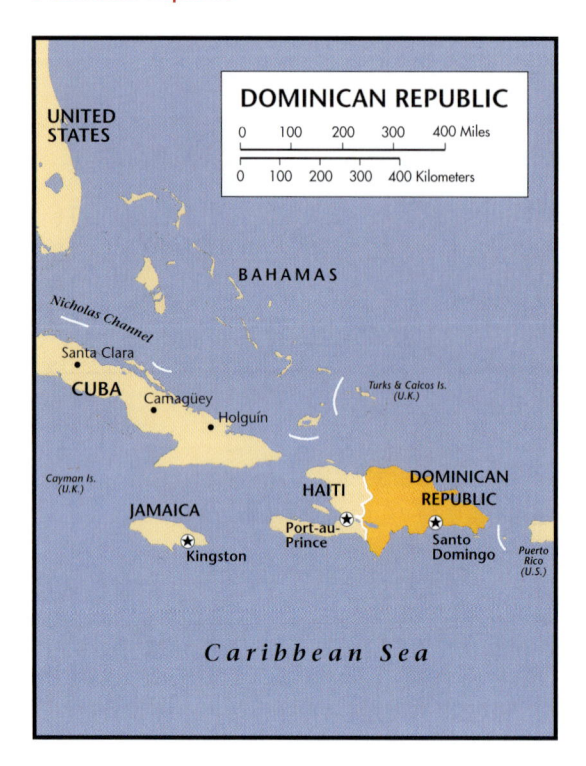

Dominican lifestyle. These contributions continue to influence the daily diet of Dominicans.

In 1492, Christopher Columbus (1451–1506) landed on the island of Hispaniola, which today includes two countries: Haiti and the Dominican Republic. Although Columbus claimed the entire island for Spain, by 1700 the French had taken control of Haiti on the western half of the island. The eastern half of the island, then known as Santo Domingo, remained under Spanish rule.

Columbus and his fellow European explorers and colonists introduced the growing of sugar cane from Spain's Canary Islands to what is now the Dominican Republic in around 1493. The first sugar mill in the Americas was established on Hispanola in the early 1500s. Soon after, the Europeans began transporting slaves from Africa to work on the sugar plantations. Sugar production became an important economic activity.

Pan de Maiz

Ingredients
- 1 cup butter (2 sticks), softened
- 3 cups of evaporated milk
- 3 eggs
- 1 cup cornmeal
- 1 cup flour
- 1 cup sugar
- 1 teaspoon baking powder
- ½ teaspoon salt
- ¼ cup raisins
- ½ teaspoon cinnamon
- ½ teaspoon nutmeg
- ½ teaspoon cloves

Directions
1. Preheat oven to 400°F.
2. Stir together cornmeal, evaporated milk, and eggs in a bowl and set aside.
3. In another bowl, stir together flour, sugar, baking powder, and salt.
4. Add softened butter to the mixture.
5. Stir in cinnamon, nutmeg, cloves, and raisins.
6. Slowly add cornmeal and milk mixture, mixing to combine.
7. Pour into a greased pan, 9 by 13 inches.
8. Bake until golden brown, 25 to 30 minutes.
9. Let cool, cut into squares, and serve with chocolate or tea.

Makes 16 squares.

The Dominicans declared independence from Spain in 1821 but shortly after fell under Haiti's rule. They remained under the control of Haiti until 1844. In 1861, fearing the threat of invasion, the Dominican government agreed to return to Spanish rule, which would come with military protection.

Dominican Republic

Paleta de Coco

Ingredients
2 cups coconut milk
¼ cup powdered sugar
¼ cup shredded coconut

Directions
1. Mix ingredients together and pour into popsicle molds or 3 ounce cups.
2. Freeze for two hours.
3. When half frozen, insert popsicle sticks.
4. Continue to freeze until set.

Serves 8.

Dominicans may enjoy pan de maiz *(cornmeal bread) as a sweet snack or as a dessert.* © EPD PHOTOS/CLARA GONZALEZ/DOMINICANCOOKING.COM.

Mangú

Ingredients
4 unripe plantains
4 tablespoons of butter
1 tablespoon of oil
1 red onion, thinly sliced
1 tablespoon of vinegar
1 cup of cold water
Salt

Directions
1. Peel the plantains and cut into 8 pieces.
2. Boil plantains in salted water until tender. Allow to cool slightly.
3. Meanwhile, heat 1 tablespoon of oil in a pan. Sauté onions, sprinkle with salt and vinegar to preserve their color, until softened slightly.
4. Drain plantains and mash them with a fork.
5. Mix mashed plantains with butter. Add cold water slowly, up to 1 cup, until a smooth mixture forms.
6. Serve topped with onions.

Serves 4.

Most Dominican people did not want to be ruled by Spain. As a result, the War of Restoration began. The war ended in 1865, and the Spanish troops were expelled.

When the War of Restoration ended, the country became an independent nation. Although the country has been through a series of dictators and periods of political unrest including civil war, it has remained independent.

Exporting agricultural products, such as sugar, coffee, and tobacco, was important to the economy until the 1990s and early 2000s. Most sugar mills and cane fields were concentrated in the southeast coastal plains.

Since the 1990s, tourism, telecommunications, and other service industries have become more important. The economy is one of the fastest growing in the region.

Everywhere in the Dominican Republic, sweet treats are enjoyed. Sugary syrups and toppings add to the natural sweetness of the local fruits. Fruits such as guava and pineapple are used to make popular snacks and desserts.

Dominican Republic

Guavas in Syrup

Ingredients

8 large fresh guavas
½ cup of sugar
2 cinnamon sticks
6 whole cloves
2 cups water
1 teaspoon vanilla extract

Directions

1. Peel the guavas and slice them in half.
2. Scoop out and save the seeds.
3. Combine the seeds, sugar, cinnamon sticks, and cloves in 2 cups of water. Simmer over medium heat for about 20 minutes.
4. Pour mixture through a sieve and discard seeds and spices.
5. Return liquid to pan and add guava slices and vanilla.
6. Simmer gently until guavas are tender.
7. Chill well before serving.

Serves 4 to 6.

❸ Foods of the Dominicans

Dominican food shows the influence of many cultures—from Spain, the indigenous Taíno culture, Africa, Italy, China, and the Middle East. Vegetables grow in the valleys of the central highlands. One vegetable crop that is unique to the Dominican Republic is the root vegetable, yautía, sometimes called Creole celery root. It is an ingredient in many recipes including mangú, a dish that is almost always part of the morning meal. Mangú is a puree made from mashed plantains and yautía (or yucca [cassava root] can be substituted).

A typical Dominican breakfast might consist of mangú with onion on top, two fried eggs, fried cheese, and salami. Breakfast might also include tropical fruits, including bananas, mangos, papaya, passion fruit, pineapple, and guava.

Lunch is the most important meal in the Dominican culture. Most Dominicans return home to eat a meal known as La Bandera Dominicana (the Dominican Flag). This meal is typically made up of stewed beans, white rice, meat, and perhaps some green salad and steamed vegetables. However, there are many variations: The stewed beans may be made from white, red, or black beans; the meat may include beef, pork, chicken, or goat. Steamed vegetables and salad usually accompany La Bandera Dominicana. Tayota, called chayote elsewhere, are small, green squash that resemble pears. Tayota are among the vegetables commonly served.

Salso criolla (Creole sauce) is typically added to seafood and some meats. The sauce is made with chopped onions, red and green peppers, and tomatoes. Although some peppers and spices are used, Dominican dishes are not generally hot or spicy.

Street foods are often sold during lunchtime and are popular among Dominicans. Empanadas, fried pastries stuffed with meat fillings, are a popular snack.

Chocolate drinks are popular in the Dominican Republic. Hot chocolate and sweet coffee often accompany or follow a meal. Ginger and lemongrass teas are also enjoyed.

The Dominican diet differs in different parts of the country. The northeast Samana peninsula region is famous for dishes made with coconut, due to the abundance of coconut palm trees there. *Paleta de coco* (coconut ice pops) are a favorite treat on hot summer days.

In the west, goat meat seasoned with oregano is used in popular recipes such as *chivo picante guisado* (spicy goat stew). Along the

Dominican Republic

To make guavas in light syrup, whole guavas (upper left) are peeled and sliced in half (upper right). The seeds are simmered with spices (lower right) to make a lightly spiced syrup. The guavas halves are then simmered in the syrup until soft. © EPD PHOTOS/ CLARA GONZALEZ/DOMINICANCOOKING.COM.

southern Caribbean coast, the cuisine reflects the history of Arab and European settlements established in the 1800s. Workers from Africa, who were imported to work at the sugar plantations and refineries, added their touch to local food traditions.

Dominican Republic

Sancocho

Ingredients

2 pounds beef stew meat
1½ pounds boneless chicken breasts and thighs, cut into pieces
2 lemons
1 celery stalk, chopped
½ teaspoon coriander
½ teaspoon oregano
1 or 2 cloves garlic, mashed
½ teaspoon thyme
2 teaspoons vinegar
½ capers
2 cubes of beef stock
½ pound yam, cut into 1-inch pieces
½ pound of cassava, cut into 1-inch pieces
2 large onions, chopped
2 large green bell peppers, cut into bite-sized pieces
3 unripe plantains, peeled
2 teaspoons Tabasco sauce
Vegetable oil
Water
Cooked white rice for serving.

Directions

1. Cut the lemons in half. Rub the beef and chicken all over with lemon.
2. Marinate the beef with celery, coriander, oregano, garlic, thyme, vinegar, capers, and pinch of salt in a bowl in the refrigerator for one hour.
3. Heat some oil in a large pot and add the beef pieces. Turn the pieces with tongs until they are browned on all sides.
4. Lower heat, cover loosely, and continue cooking for about 15 minutes.
5. Add beef stock and water (up to 4 cups) so that the ingredients are covered by about 1 inch of liquid. Bring the mixture to a boil.
6. Peel the cassava and cut into 1-inch pieces. Peel the yams and cut into 1-inch pieces.
7. Add cassava and yam pieces to the pot. Add more water if necessary. Simmer for 10 minutes.
8. Cut two plantains into 1-inch pieces and add to the pot.
9. Add the remaining ingredients: Tabasco sauce, onions, and green bell peppers. Add more water if necessary to cover ingredients.
10. Simmer, stirring frequently, until vegetables are tender, about 20 minutes.
11. Grate the third plantain and add it to the pot. Simmer for 10 more minutes.
12. Serve with white rice.

Serves 6 to 10.

Rainbow Rice

Ingredients

1 cup uncooked rice
1 sweet red pepper
1 green pepper
1 cup sweet corn
1 onion
1 teaspoon parsley, chopped
3 tablespoons butter
Salt and pepper
2 cups water

Directions

1. In medium saucepan, bring 2 cups water to a boil.
2. Add rice, cover, and simmer for about 20 minutes.
3. While rice is cooking, chop up peppers into small pieces.
4. In a separate pan, sauté green and red peppers, corn, and onion in butter.
5. Mix together rice and pepper mixture. Add salt and pepper to taste.
6. Top with chopped parsley and serve.

Serves 4.

Dominican Republic

To make sancocho (clockwise from top left), marinate the beef in a bowl; brown the meats and then simmer them in a pot for about 15 minutes; peel the plantains (shown) and the yams; after cutting the plantains and yams into 1-inch pieces, add them to the pot. © EPD PHOTOS/CLARA GONZALEZ/DOMINICANCOOKING.COM.

④ Food for Religious and Holiday Celebrations

Sancocho, a Dominican stew, is a traditional dish that is served for special occasions. Sancocho comes in many different variations. It is prepared to take advantage of the different seasonal foods available. The popular *sancocho de siete carnes* (stew with seven meats) is typically made with goat meat, pork sausage, beef bones, pork, chicken, pork ribs, and bones from smoked ham. Dominicans hold *aguinaldos* (informal community evening celebrations) around Christmas. The celebrations involve caroling singers, who stop at homes in the neighborhood, where they are given *jengibre*, a warm ginger tea. They may also be treated to a *bocadita* (a small share of the family's dinner).

Families often serve roast pig (*lechón asado*) as part of their Christmas celebration. This may be accompanied by a side dish known as *moro de guandules* (rice and pigeon peas). Pigeon peas are tropical green peas with a nutty flavor.

Dominican Republic

Tostones

Note: This recipe involves hot oil and requires adult supervision.

Ingredients
2 unripe plantains
½ cup oil
4 teaspoons of cold water
½ teaspoons of minced garlic
Salt

Directions
1. Cut plantains into 1-inch slices.
2. Heat oil and fry plantain slices until golden.
3. Remove the plantains from the pan and flatten them, using a spoon or the bottom of a glass.
4. Return flattened slices to the pan, and fry again for about 30 seconds on each side.
5. Remove from the pan and drain on a paper-towel lined plate.
6. Mix water, garlic, and a small amount of salt. Sprinkle over plantains and serve.

Serves 4.

One of the most popular street foods are empanadas (shown above). © ANALIA VALERIA URANI/SHUTTERSTOCK.COM.

Habichuelas con Dulce

Ingredients
1 can kidney beans, drained
2 cups water
3 cups evaporated milk
1 cup coconut milk
1 cup sweetened condensed milk
½ cup of sugar
2 cinnamon sticks
¼ cup raisins
1 large sweet potato (batatas), cut into small cubes
8 to 10 whole cloves
½ teaspoon salt
2 tablespoons butter

Directions
1. Put drained beans, water, coconut milk, and evaporated milk into a pot. Heat until the mixture begins to boil.
2. Lower heat to medium and add the condensed milk, sugar, cinnamon sticks, raisins, and cubed sweet potato. Continue to cook, stirring constantly, for about 10 minutes.
3. Add the cloves, salt, and butter. Continue to cook, stirring constantly, until the beans are the consistency of a thick soup. They will thicken some more when chilled.
4. The beans may be served warm or cold. Typically, a few small cookies are floated on top.

Serves 4 to 6.

Jengibre (Ginger Tea)

Ingredients
5 cups of water
8 cinnamon sticks
½ cup of fresh gingerroot, sliced
Sugar

Directions
1. Boil water in pot with cinnamon sticks.
2. Add sliced gingerroot and boil for 5 minutes.
3. Remove from heat and strain into cups.
4. Add sugar to taste.

Serves 4.

Jalalo

Ingredients

2 cups shredded coconut
1 cup honey

Directions

1. Mix together coconut and honey in a pot and heat until golden brown.
2. Allow the mixture to cool. With very clean hands, form the mixture into 12 small balls. Press them onto a cookie sheet.
3. Let the balls cool completely, until they are firm.

Makes 12 balls.

Morir Soñando

Ingredients

2 cups orange juice
2 cups chopped or shaved ice
1½ cups evaporated milk
¼ cup sugar

Directions

1. Combine all ingredients and beat until foamy. If using a blender or food processor to mix the ingredients, use less ice.
2. Serve cold.

Serves 4.

Independence Day is celebrated on February 27 to commemorate the Dominican Republic's independence from Haiti. It is an important holiday in the Dominican Republic. The day is marked with celebration, dancing, and lots of food. *Pan de maiz* (cornmeal bread) may be served, either with sancocho, as a sweet snack, or as a dessert. *Tostones* (twice-fried plantains) are also a popular side dish to accompany the meal.

For Ash Wednesday, the first day of the 40-day period (Lent) preceding the Christian holiday of Easter, most homes prepare a large pot of *habichuelas con dulce* (sweet beans). This dish is also served on Good Friday, the Friday before Easter. Habichuelas con dulce is a kind of pudding made of kidney beans, condensed milk, coconut, spices, and raisins.

❺ Mealtime Customs

The popular dish La Bandara (Dominican Republic flag) is often served at lunch, the most important meal of the day in the country. The dish is named after the Dominican Republic flag because it holds such an important status within the culture. All types of people from every class sit down around noon to enjoy this meal.

Because lunch is the staple meal, dinner is light. Dinner may consist of a sandwich followed by hot chocolate or juice. *Morir soñando* (literally, to die dreaming) is a mixture of juice with sweet milk.

Sweet desserts are sometimes served after dinner.

❻ Politics, Economics, and Nutrition

Adequate nutrition is one of the leading concerns in the Dominican Republic. International organizations, such as UNICEF and the World Health Organization (WHO), estimate that 4 to 7 percent of children under age five are moderately or severely underweight. Malnutrition (not enough nutritious food) widely varies by region. Children living in large cities, such as Santo Domingo and Santiago, are more likely to experience inadequate nutrition. The

Dominican Republic

Health Protection Agency, based in the United Kingdom, estimates that 20 to 40 percent of children under six were anemic, which means they do not have enough healthy red blood cells. This is likely due to poor nutrition. The infant mortality rate was about 22 deaths per 1,000 live births in 2011.

Diseases are common in the Dominican Republic, including cholera, which is caused by bacteria in food and water. Due to frequent outbreaks, regular inspections of food and water conditions must be done to insure proper sanitation. In 2008, about 86 percent of the population had access to clean drinking water.

7 Further Study

BOOKS

Essentials of Latin Cooking. Birmingham, AL: Oxmoor, 2010.

Gonzalez, Clara, and Ilana Benady. *Traditional Dominican Cookery*. Santo Domingo, DR: Lunch Club Press, 2007.

Rogers Seavey, Lura. *Dominican Republic*. New York: Children's Press, 2009.

Temple, Bob. *Dominican Republic*. Broomall, PA: Mason Crest, 2008.

Vanderhoof, Ann. *The Spice Necklace*. Boston: Houghton Mifflin Harcourt, 2010.

Zanger, Mark H. *The American Ethnic Cookbook for Students*. Phoenix, AZ: Oryx Press, 2001.

WEB SITES

Aunt Clara's Kitchen Dominican Cooking. http://www.dominicancooking.com/ (accessed February 8, 2012).

Embassy of the Dominican Republic in the United States: The Dominican Republic Kids Corner. http://www.domrep.org/kids.html (accessed February 8, 2012).

Egypt

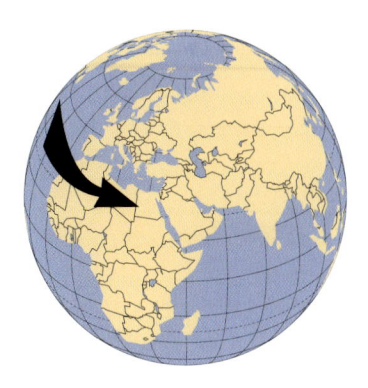

- Ful Mudammas 170
- Shai (Mint Tea) 171
- Koushari 172
- Hummus 173
- Belila 173
- Bamia (Sweet and Sour Okra) 174
- Lemon and Garlic Potato Salad ... 174
- Gebna Makleyah 175
- Lettuce Salad 176
- 'Irea (Cinnamon Beverage) 176
- Khoshaf 176
- Spinach with Garlic 177

1 Geographic Setting and Environment

The Arab Republic of Egypt is located in the northeastern region of the African continent, bordering both the Mediterranean and Red Seas. The climate is arid and dry and most of the country receives less than 1 inch (2.5 centimeters) of rainfall each year. The Mediterranean may offer Egypt's northern coastline up to 8 inches (20 centimeters) of rainfall each year, while keeping year-round temperatures cooler than the inland deserts. The widespread lack of rainfall makes it extremely difficult to grow crops. Egypt has no forests and only 2.9 percent of the land is arable (land that can be farmed).

The well-known Nile River, the longest river in the world, runs north and south through eastern Egypt and empties into the Mediterranean Sea. The Nile River Valley, which includes the capital city of Cairo, is the most fertile land in Egypt. Approximately 95 percent of the country's population lives along the Nile River. However, overcrowding in this region is threatening Egypt's wildlife and endangering the Nile's water supply.

In 2011, the country experienced unrest as protesters took to the streets to demand the end of the nearly 30-year authoritarian rule of Egyptian President Hosni Mubarak. When the revolution began in late January, demonstrators sought a change in government to address problems such as poverty, food insecurity (not having enough food), rising food prices, unemployment, and corruption. Ultimately, Mubarak was driven from office after 18 days of protest.

2 History and Food

Thousands of years ago, ancient Egyptians left evidence of their love for food. Well-preserved wall paintings and carvings have been discovered on tombs and temples, depicting large feasts and

Egypt

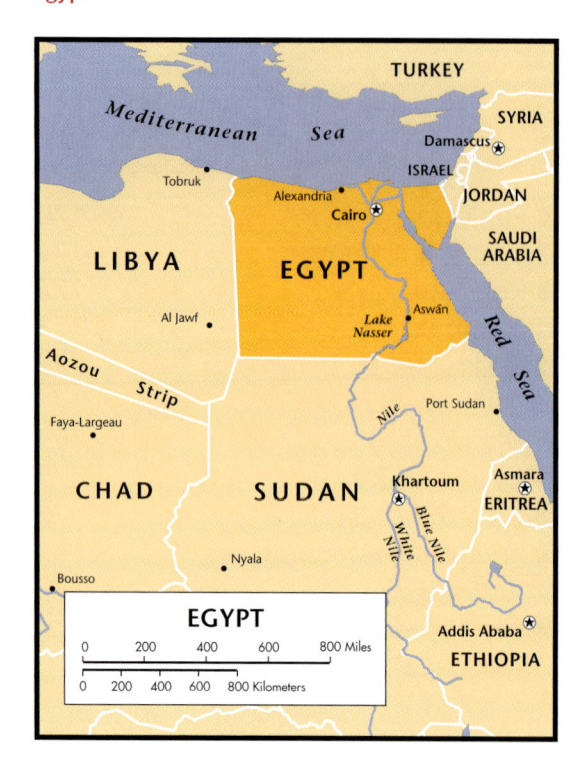

a variety of foods. Many of these ancient foods are still eaten in Egyptian households today. Peas, beans, cucumbers, dates, figs, and grapes were popular fruits and vegetables in ancient times. Wheat and barley, ancient staple crops, were used to make bread and beer. Fish and poultry were also popular. Dried fish was prepared by cleaning the fish, coating the pieces with salt, and placing them the sun to dry. *Fasieekh* (salted, dried fish) remains a popular meal in Egypt.

The unique Egyptian cuisine has been influenced throughout history, particularly by its neighbors from the Middle East. Persians (modern-day Iranians), Greeks, Arabs, Romans (modern-day Italians), and Ottomans (modern-day Turks) first influenced Egyptian cuisine thousands of years ago. More recently, the foods of other Arabic people in the Middle East such as the Lebanese, Palestinians, Syrians, as well as some foods from Europe, have impacted the Egyptian diet. However, Egyptian cuisine maintains its uniqueness. After thousands of years, rice and bread remain staple foods, and *molokhiyya* (a spinach-like vegetable) and *ful mudammas* (cooked, creamy fava beans), a national dish, are nearly as popular as they were long ago.

Ful Mudammas (Broad Beans in Sauce)

Ingredients

2 cans (15-ounces each) cooked fava beans
6 cloves garlic, or to taste
1 teaspoon salt, or to taste
1 tablespoon lemon juice, freshly squeezed
¼ cup olive oil
1½ tablespoons parsley, minced
Garnish, such as radishes, hard-boiled eggs, chopped scallions, pita bread (toasted and cut into wedges)

Directions

1. Press the garlic cloves through a garlic press into a medium-sized bowl.
2. Mash the garlic and salt together.
3. Next, add the lemon juice, olive oil, and parsley to the garlic mixture and combine thoroughly.
4. Drain the beans well, rinse, and put beans into a large pot over low heat.
5. Add garlic mixture and stir with a wooden spoon to combine thoroughly.
6. Serve warm with the garnishes arranged on a platter.
7. Each person is served a plateful of ful mudammas and adds the garnishes of his or her choice.

Serves 4 to 6.

③ Foods of the Egyptians

Egypt has a variety of national dishes. *Ful* (pronounced "fool," fava bean paste), tahini (sesame paste), *koushari* (lentils, macaroni, rice, and chickpeas), *aish baladi* (a pita-like bread), *kofta* (spicy, minced lamb), and kebab (grilled lamb pieces) are the most popular. Hummus is a popular snack, often served with pita or vegetables.

Aish, the Arabic name for bread, means "life." It accompanies most meals and is served in various forms. The most common bread is pita, usually made with whole wheat (or sometimes white) flour. Long, skinny French-style loaves of bread are also widely eaten throughout the country. Traditional Egyptian cheeses, as well as feta imported from neighboring Greece, are frequently served alongside bread at meals.

Despite the country's dry climate and shortage of arable land (land that can be farmed), Egypt grows a variety of fresh fruits. *Mohz* (bananas), *balah* (dates), *burtu'aan* (oranges), *battiikh* (melons), *khukh* (peaches), *berkuk* (plums), and *'anub* (grapes) are commonly grown.

Cinnamon and other spices are shown for sale at an outdoor market in Cairo, Egypt. © DMYTRO KOSTENKO/SHUTTERSTOCK.COM.

Shai (Mint Tea)

Ingredients
1 package mint tea (loose or in tea bags)
Sugar
4 to 6 cups water (depending on how many people are being served)

Directions
1. Bring water to a boil.
2. If using loose tea, measure 1 teaspoon of tea leaves into a teapot for each person being served.
3. Otherwise, place one tea bag per person into the teapot.
4. Pour boiling water over tea.
5. Allow to steep (soak) for about 3 minutes.
6. Pour tea into cups. (In Egypt, small glass tumblers are used.)
7. If loose tea is used, allow the tea leaves to settle to the bottom of the pot and pour carefully to avoid disturbing them.
8. Add 4 or 5 teaspoons of sugar to each cup.

Serves 4 to 6.

Shai can be enjoyed with a piece of baklava purchased from a bakery.

Ful (creamy bean paste made from fava beans), one of the country's several national dishes, is a typical breakfast meal. It is often served in a spicy sauce, topped with an egg. Lunch, normally served between 2 p.m. and 4

Egypt

p.m., usually includes meat or fish, rice, bread, and seasonal vegetables. Salad (*mezza*, or *mezze* if more than one is served), topped with typical Middle Eastern fare such as olives, cheese, and nuts, may also be eaten. Meat (usually lamb, chicken, fish, rabbit, or pigeon), vegetables, and bread make up a typical dinner in Egypt.

Koushari (Lentils, Macaroni, Rice, and Chickpeas)

Koushari, a vegetarian dish, combines lentils, chick peas, macaroni, and rice in a tomato sauce subtly flavored with onions and garlic. It is usually accompanied by pita bread.
© EPD PHOTOS.

Ingredients
1 cup lentils
1 teaspoon salt
1 cup elbow macaroni
1 cup rice
1 can (15-ounces) chickpeas (also called ceci)
2 tablespoons olive oil

Sauce:
1 cup canned tomato puree
¼ cup olive oil
2 onions
1 garlic clove, or to taste

Directions

1. *Prepare lentils:* Place the lentils in a sieve and rinse thoroughly. Place them in a large saucepan with 3 cups of water and 1 teaspoon salt.
2. Heat until the water begins to boil. Lower the heat and simmer for about 1 hour until lentils are tender. Drain and set the lentils aside.
3. *Prepare the macaroni:* Fill the same saucepan with water (add salt if desired). Heat until the water begins to boil.
4. Add the macaroni and boil about 12 to 15 minutes, until macaroni is tender. Drain and set the macaroni aside. (It is okay to combine the macaroni and lentils.)
5. *Prepare the rice:* Heat the 2 tablespoons of olive oil in the same saucepan. Add the rice and cook for 2 or 3 minutes, thoroughly coating the rice with oil.
6. Add 2 cups of water and heat until the water begins to boil. Cover the saucepan and simmer until the rice is tender, about 15 minutes.
7. Remove from heat and allow to cool for about 5 minutes.
8. *Assemble koushari:* Drain chickpeas and rinse. Add chickpeas, lentils, and macaroni to cooked rice and toss very gently with a fork.
9. *Make sauce:* Peel the onions and cut them in half lengthwise. Slice each half crosswise into thin slices.
10. Heat ¼ cup olive oil in a skillet. Add onions and cook, stirring often with a wooden spoon, until onions are golden brown.
11. Add garlic clove and cook 1 or 2 more minutes. Stir in tomato puree and heat until bubbly.
12. Now pour the sauce over the lentil mixture and heat over very low heat for about 5 minutes, until completely warm.
13. Serve with pita bread.

Serves 4 to 6.

Tea and a dessert, such as baklava (honey pastry), *basbousa* (cream-filled cake), or *konafa* (cooked batter stuffed with nuts), are familiar after-dinner treats. Belila is a warm wheat dessert served like cereal with milk.

Tea and coffee are widely consumed. Egypt's numerous coffee and teahouses brew very strong coffee and tea (often mint tea), usually offering both full of sugar. Coffeehouses are typically filled with men who gather to play dominoes or backgammon. Coffee is served *saada* or "bitter" (no sugar) or *ziyada* or "very sweet." Egyptians also enjoy a drink called *sahleb*, made from wheat, milk, and chopped nuts.

Hummus

Ingredients
1 (15 ounce) can garbanzo beans
1 clove garlic, crushed
2 teaspoons ground cumin
½ teaspoon salt
1 tablespoon olive oil
Pita chips or vegetables, for serving

Directions
1. Drain liquid from garbanzo beans can into small bowl, set aside.
2. Blend beans, garlic, cumin, salt, and olive oil on low speed.
3. Add extra liquid from garbanzo beans until the mixture has a spreadable consistency.
4. Serve with pita chips or vegetables.

Serves about 4.

4 Food for Religious and Holiday Celebrations

Approximately 90 percent of Egyptians are Muslims, which means they practice the religion of Islam. The most important time of the year for Muslims is a month-long holiday called Ramadan. During the month of Ramadan (the ninth month on the Islamic calendar), Muslims fast (do not eat or drink) from sunrise to sunset. They think about people around the world who do not have enough food. Muslim families will often come together to prepare hearty meals, including a variety of sweets, after sunset. Muslims end Ramadan with a three-day celebration called Eid al-Fitr.

Hummus can be served with plain pita, pita chips, or vegetables. It may also be served alongside grilled chicken, fish, or eggplant. © ROBYN MACKENZIE/SHUTTERSTOCK.COM.

Belila

Ingredients
1 cup whole wheat grains, sold as wheat berries
A pinch of salt
1⅔ cup milk
1 tablespoon sugar
½ cup chopped almonds

Directions
1. Soak wheat overnight in water.
2. The next day, bring wheat to a boil in pan with water and salt. Simmer for 35 minutes.
3. Drain the wheat and set aside.
4. Boil milk and sugar. Add in wheat and let simmer for a few minutes.
5. Mix in chopped almonds.
6. Serve warm with warm milk. Sprinkle with additional sugar if desired.

Serves 4.

Egypt

Bamia (Sweet and Sour Okra)

Ingredients
1 pound small okra pods
2 tablespoons olive oil
1 tablespoon honey
Salt and freshly ground black pepper, to taste
1 tablespoon lemon juice, freshly squeezed
½ cup water

Directions
1. Wash the okra and pat it dry with paper towels.
2. Discard any blemished or hard pods.
3. Heat the olive oil in a heavy saucepan and sauté the okra in the oil for 3 to 5 minutes, turning each pod once.
4. Add the honey, salt, pepper, lemon juice, and water. Cover, lower the heat and simmer for 15 minutes, adding more water if necessary.
5. Serve hot.

Serves 4 to 6.

Lemon and Garlic Potato Salad

Ingredients
2 pounds of red potatoes, scrubbed but with skin left on
½ cup parsley, chopped
4 garlic cloves, minced
Juice of 1½ lemons
1 tablespoon vegetable oil
Salt and pepper, to taste

Directions
1. Boil potatoes until tender (½ hour to 1 hour, or until a fork can easily pierce the skin) and let cool.
2. Add parsley, garlic cloves, lemon juice, oil, and salt and pepper; mix well.
3. Chill and serve.

Serves 4.

Food played an important role in ancient Egypt. These hieroglyphics, found in the Temple of Ramses II in Abydos, feature food, including bread. © BASPHOTO/SHUTTERSTOCK.COM.

Eid al-Adha, a three-day long "great feast," is another important holiday for Muslims. In recognition of the biblical story of Abraham's near sacrifice of his son, Isaac, families will sacrifice (kill) a sheep or a lamb. The animal is slaughtered and cooked whole on a spit over an open fire, and some of the meat is usually given to poorer families. These animals are also sacrificed on other important occasions, such as births, deaths, or marriages.

Throughout the year, various *moulids* may take place. A moulid is a day (or as long as a week) celebrating the birthday of a local saint or holy person. Several events take place during this time. Food stands decorating the town's streets are usually set up near the holy person's tomb. Moulids are held in Cairo, the capital of Egypt, every year. The largest moulid, Moulid el Nabit, commemorates the birthday of the Islamic prophet Muhammad and takes place in Cairo in early August.

Just under 10 percent of Egypt's population are Christians, whose most important holiday is Easter, falling in either March or April. It is common for families to come together to share a hearty meal, much as Christians worldwide do. Egyptian Christians observe the Orthodox calendar, which places Christmas on January 7 each year.

5 Mealtime Customs

Dining customs vary throughout the country and between different religions. When eating with Muslims (who make up approximately 90 percent of Egypt's population), there are some general guidelines one should follow. The left hand is considered unclean and should not be used for eating. Feet should always been tucked under the table. Alcoholic beverages and pork should not be requested.

When invited to be a guest in an Egyptian household, it is polite for guests to bring a small gift to the host, such as flowers or chocolate, to show their appreciation for the meal. Before dinner, drinks (usually nonalcoholic) are frequently served. This is a time for socializing and becoming acquainted. *Mezze* (salads and dips) would also be served at this time.

Gebna Makleyah (Oven-Fried Cheese)

Ingredients

1 cup firm feta cheese, crumbled, or traditional Egyptian cheese such as labna or gebna
1 tablespoon flour
1 egg
Salt and freshly ground black pepper, to taste
Olive oil
Lemon wedges and pita bread cut into triangles, for serving

Directions

1. Preheat oven to 400°F.
2. Place the cheese, flour, egg, salt, and pepper in a bowl and mix well with very clean hands.
3. Roll the mixture into 1-inch balls.
4. If the mixture seems too loose to hold the ball shape, add a little more flour.
5. If the mixture seems too dry, add a bit of lemon juice, vinegar, or water.
6. Pour 2 or 3 tablespoons of olive oil onto a cookie sheet to grease.
7. Arrange the cheese balls on the cookie sheet, rolling them around to coat thoroughly with the oil.
8. Bake 5 minutes.
9. Wearing an oven mitt, open the oven door and gently shake the cookie sheet to prevent the cheese balls from sticking and to turn them.
10. Bake 5 more minutes, until golden brown.
11. Remove with a spatula and drain on absorbent paper.
12. Serve warm with lemon wedges and triangles of pita bread.

Serves 4 to 6.

When dinner is ready, usually between 9 p.m. and 10 p.m., guests seat themselves and food is placed in the middle of the table. Bread will almost always accompany meals. Dinner may include vegetables, rice dishes, soups, and

Egypt

meat dishes. Following dinner, guests will move into another room and enjoy coffee or mint tea. Guests should always compliment the cook.

The majority of Egyptians cannot afford a large meal. Their diet includes vegetables, lentils, and beans. Meat, which is more costly, is eaten on special occasions. Most middle-class families eat a similar diet, but add more expensive ingredients when they can afford it. All social classes, however, enjoy purchasing quick light snacks at Egyptian cafés or from street vendors. Traditional teahouses will serve tea in tall glasses (rather than teacups). Cafés normally offer strong, sweet Turkish coffee. Street vendors sell a variety of inexpensive foods, including ful (fava beans) and koushari (a macaroni, rice, and lentil dish) as a lunchtime favorite. Vendors also sell a variety of *asiir* (fresh-squeezed juices) made from fruits like bananas, guavas, mangos, pomegranates, and strawberries. Vendors also make a sweet juice from other items, such as sugarcane and even hibiscus flowers.

Lettuce Salad

Ingredients

1 small head of lettuce, shredded
¾ cup orange juice
¼ cup dried hibiscus flowers or dried cranberries (optional)
Pinch of salt
1½ teaspoons pepper, or to taste

Directions

1. Toss lettuce with orange juice.
2. Season with a pinch of salt and pepper.
3. Scatter optional dried hibiscus flowers or dried cranberries over the salad.

Makes 6 to 8 servings.

'Irea (Cinnamon Beverage)

Ingredients

2 cinnamon sticks
2 teaspoons sugar, or to taste
1 cup cold water
Mixed nuts

Directions

1. Place the cinnamon and sugar in a small saucepan with the cold water and bring to a boil, stirring occasionally.
2. Lower the heat and allow the mixture to simmer for 10 minutes, or until it is brownish.
3. Remove the cinnamon sticks and pour the drink into a cup.
4. Serve with mixed nuts sprinkled into the cup.

Makes 1 cup.

Khoshaf

Ingredients

1 cup dried prunes
1 cup dried apricots
1 cup dried small figs, halved
1½ cups raisins
1 cup sugar, or to taste
2½ cups boiling water

Directions

1. Place all the fruits in a bowl and mix together gently.
2. Sprinkle the sugar on top of the dried fruits.
3. Carefully pour the boiling water into the bowl, cover, and allow to cool to room temperature.
4. Refrigerate for several hours, or overnight if possible. Khoshaf is best when allowed to marinate overnight or for several hours before serving.)

Serves 4.

Egypt

A floating restaurant makes its way down the Nile River in Egypt. © BEST4PHOTO/SHUTTERSTOCK.COM.

Spinach with Garlic

Ingredients
- 1 medium onion, chopped
- 1 tablespoon vegetable oil
- 2 garlic cloves, chopped
- 1 can (15-ounce) tomato sauce
- 10 ounces frozen spinach, thawed
- ½ cup water
- 2 cups cooked rice

Directions
1. Heat oil in a large skillet.
2. Add onions and cook, stirring with a wooden spoon, until onions are softened.
3. Add the garlic and continue to cook for 2 minutes.
4. Add the tomato sauce and bring to a boil.
5. Simmer for 10 minutes on low heat.
6. Add the spinach and water, then heat to a boil again.
7. Cover and simmer on low heat for 15 minutes.
8. Serve warm over cooked rice.

Serves 4.

6 Politics, Economics, and Nutrition

In 2011, agriculture made up approximately 14.4 percent of Egypt's economy, while employing about one-third of all Egyptians. However, Egypt's agriculture also contributed to the slowing of economic growth. A shortage of arable

Egypt

land (land that can be farmed) has become a serious problem. The lack of farmable land has caused Egyptian farmers to move to other countries.

Irrigation necessary to grow its major crops, such as sugarcane, barley, wheat, corn, cotton, and rice, is also a growing problem. Egypt imports most of the wheat it needs to provide food for the population.

The Nile River is Egypt's main water source for both drinking and irrigation, and overuse could risk the country's delicate water supply. More than 2,000 years ago, Greek historian Herodotus wrote: "Egypt is the gift of the Nile." Without the Nile River, Egypt would be virtually dry. It would be impossible to grow crops.

In 2008, about 22 percent of the population lived below the poverty line, on less than $1 per day. The UN World Food Programme reported in 2009 that about 50 percent of Egyptians do not get adequate nutrition. The typical diet lacks nutrition and protein.

The Egyptian government's reports confirm that this is a growing problem. Results of Egypt's 2008 government health survey were published in 2009. The report showed that there was a 6 percent increase since 2000 in undernourishment in children under age five. About 29 percent of children younger than five were considered malnourished.

The government has tried to address this problem. Since 1963, the government has worked with the World Food Programme to supply fortified date bars to schools with large numbers of undernourished children. The government has also distributed flour and cooking oil containing vitamins.

This solution is not enough. Grain prices went up in 2007 and 2008 and the price of bread in Egypt rose 37 percent. Even though the government was distributing bread, it did nothing at that time to increase food supplies. Food prices increased almost 20 percent before President Hosni Mubarak was ousted in 2011. The instability of the government following Mubarak's departure has disrupted the economy and contributed to food insecurity.

7 Further Study

BOOKS

Abdennour, Samia. *Egyptian Cooking: And Other Middle Eastern Recipes.* New York: American University in Cairo Press, 2005.

Gifford, Clive. *Food and Cooking in Ancient Egypt.* New York: PowerKids Press, 2010.

Sheen, Barbara. *Foods of Egypt.* Detroit: KidHaven Press, 2010.

Webb, Lois Sinaiko, and Lindsay Grace Roten. *Holidays of the World Cookbook for Students.* Santa Barbara, CA: Greenwood, 2011.

Zanger, Mark H. *The American Ethnic Cookbook for Students.* Phoenix, AZ: Oryx Press, 2001.

WEB SITES

Global Gourmet. http://www.globalgourmet.com/food/kgk/1199/kgk111399.html#axzz1nUGVRKl (accessed February 8, 2012).

Tour Egypt: Recipes for Food and Cuisine in Egypt. http://touregypt.net/recipes/ (accessed February 8, 2012).

Whats4Eats: Egypt Recipes and Cuisine. http://www.whats4eats.com/middle-east/egypt-cuisine (accessed February 8, 2012).

El Salvador

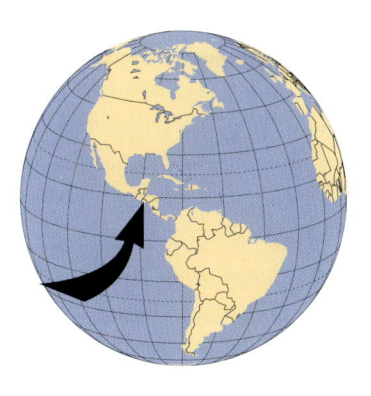

- Fried Plantains 180
- Pupusas 181
- Casamiento 182
- Riguas 182
- Horchata 185
- Fried Yucca with Curtido 185
- Leche Poleada 186

1 Geographic Setting and Environment

El Salvador is the smallest country in Central America. With a 2011 population estimated at 6 million, it is also the most densely populated country in the region. In addition to its coastline along the Pacific Ocean, it shares borders with Guatemala and Honduras. The climate is warm along the coastal plains. In the mountains in the northern parts of the country, the climate is cooler. El Salvador has a wet season from May to October. During that time, there is a risk for flooding and landslides. During the dry season, there is the risk of drought.

A number of small rivers flow through El Salvador. The largest, the Lempa River, originates in Guatemala. It flows southward through El Salvador before emptying into the Pacific Ocean. There are several hydroelectric dams along the river.

Two other important bodies of water, Lake Ilopango and Lake Coatepeque, are volcanic crater lakes. Both active and dormant volcanoes exist throughout the country. Earthquakes are a constant threat. Two major earthquakes occurred in 2001, killing over 1,000 people. Small earthquakes are fairly common and have occurred in most years since then, including in 2010 and 2011.

El Salvador farmers produce coffee, cotton, maize (corn), and sugarcane. Palm and coconut trees are found throughout the country. Fruits, such as melons and mango, grow along the Pacific coast where the climate is warm. In the 21st century, Salvadoran farms began to grow such crops as jalapeno peppers, okra, pineapple, and flowers, mostly for export. Cattle raising is also an important activity.

Along the coast there are beautiful beaches, great places for surfing, and the seafood is plentiful. Salvadorans of all walks of life enjoy dishes that include shrimp, crab, and other fish caught in coastal waters.

El Salvador

periods of unrest followed. From 1980 to 1992, the country suffered through a violent civil war and thousands of people left the country. Thousands of those who remained in the country were killed during the conflict.

The years of civil war destroyed much of El Salvador's agriculture. After the end of the civil war, agriculture slowly recovered. Today, the country grows coffee and sugarcane, among other crops, for export.

Like the cuisine in many other countries in Central America, Salvadoran cuisine mixes foods of the Spanish colonists and the indigenous people who preceded them. The Maya, Lenca, and Pipil all lived in parts of present-day El Salvador, and their most important crop was maize (corn). Other staples of the indigenous diet included beans, plantains, yucca root, cacao, sugarcane, and various spices. Europeans introduced domesticated animals, including cattle and pigs.

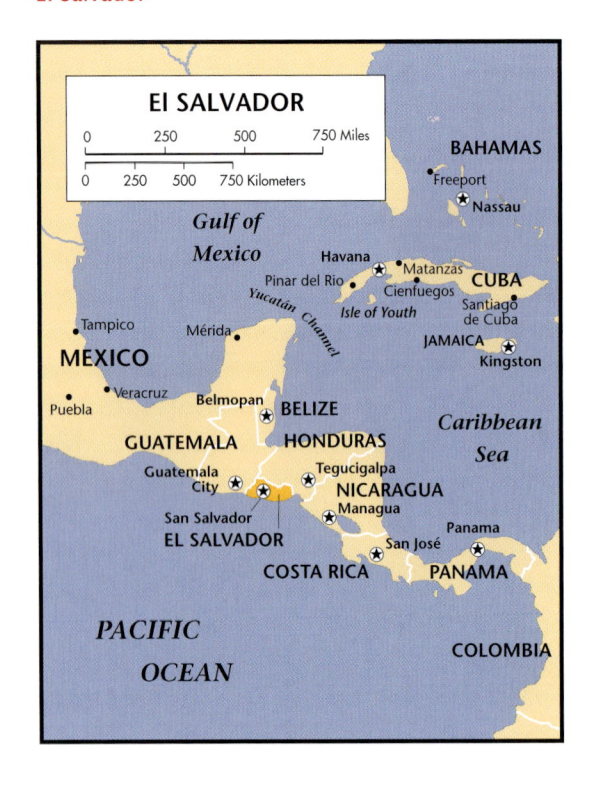

❷ History and Food

Spanish explorers visited and settled in the area of El Salvador in the 16th century. The village of San Salvador, which grew into the modern capital city, was established in 1525. Charles I (1500–1558), king of Spain, gave the village its name in 1546. The country lived under Spanish control until the early 1800s. Around that time, people began to wish for independence. On November 5, 1811, a Roman Catholic priest, Jose Matias Delgado (1767–1832), issued a call for the people to fight for freedom. In 1821, 10 years later, El Salvador (and its neighbors in Central America) declared independence.

El Salvador joined with its neighbors to form the Provinces of Central America. This lasted from 1823 to 1838, when El Salvador became an independent republic. Many revolutions and

Fried Plantains

Note: This recipe involves hot oil and requires adult supervision.

Ingredients
2 ripe plantains, peeled and sliced lengthwise
Vegetable oil for pan frying

Directions
1. Heat oil in large pan over medium to medium-high heat. (Oil should reach about halfway up the sides of the plantains).
2. Lay the plantains in the pan. Once the bottom side has browned, gently flip the plantains using tongs, a spatula, or a combination of the two.
3. Once the other side has browned and the plantains are tender, remove from the pan and place on paper towels to drain the excess oil.

Serves 4 to 6.

El Salvador

Pupusas with Curtido and Salsa Roja

Note: This recipe involves hot oil and requires adult supervision.

Ingredients

Curtido:
1 medium cabbage, shredded
1 carrot, halved lengthwise and sliced thinly
½ onion, sliced thinly
1 tablespoon oregano
Salt
4 cups cider vinegar
4 cups water

Salsa Roja:
2 teaspoons oil
¼ cup of onion, minced
1 garlic clove, minced
1 can (14-ounces) tomato puree

Pupusas:
2 cups masa harina (corn flour)
1 cup water
½ cup queso fresco, or other melting cheese, crumbled. Note: An acceptable substitute is made by combining equal parts of dry-curd cottage cheese and feta cheese.
½ cup canned pinto beans, drained and mashed into a paste
1 cup oil for frying (less if using a griddle)

Directions

For Curtido:
1. Combine cabbage, carrot, onion, oregano, and salt in a large sealable container.
2. Add vinegar and water, and stir to combine.
3. Let sit overnight before serving. Will keep for up to a month in the refrigerator.

For Salsa Roja:
1. Sauté onion in oil in a small saucepan over medium heat until softened, 2 to 4 minutes.
2. Add minced garlic and cook until fragrant, about 15 seconds.

Plantains are often consumed in El Salvador. They are cooked to create either a side dish or a snack. © VLADIMIR MELNIK/ SHUTTERSTOCK.COM.

3. Add tomato puree and stir together.
4. Simmer for 5 to 10 minutes. Season to taste with salt and pepper.
5. Can be made ahead and refrigerated.

For Pupusas:
1. Mix masa harina and water. Knead into uniform dough. Let dough rest for 5 to 10 minutes.
2. Combine cheese and beans in a small bowl.
3. Lightly oil hands before working with dough. Divide dough into 20 to 25 balls and cover with a damp cloth.
4. Working with one dough ball at a time, gently flatten into a disk about ¼-inch thick by patting the dough ball between your hands.
5. Add one tablespoon of cheese and bean filling to the middle of the disk.
6. Pinch the edges of the dough together around the filling, and then gently pat the filled dough ball back into a fat disk. Try to avoid tears in the dough as the filling will leak out during cooking.
7. Heat a greased griddle (or large, non-stick pan to which the 1 cup of oil has been added) over medium heat.
8. Place pupusas on a griddle or in a hot, flat-bottomed frying pan, cooking each side until spotted brown.
9. Top pupusas with curtido and salsa. Serve hot.

Serves 4 to 10.

El Salvador

Casamiento

Ingredients

2 cups drained, rinsed canned red beans
1 medium onion, chopped
1 green pepper, chopped
1 garlic clove, chopped
1 cup chicken broth
1½ cups uncooked white rice
1 tablespoon vegetable oil
Salt and pepper
Sour cream for topping (optional)

Directions

1. Heat the vegetable oil in a skillet and add the chopped onion and garlic. Cook until the onion is softened, but not browned.
2. Add the green peppers and cook for about 5 minutes.
3. Add the uncooked rice to the pan, stirring frequently until rice is translucent, 2 to 3 minutes.
4. Add one cup beans to the rice, stirring carefully to avoid smashing the beans. Stir in the chicken broth.
5. Add the remaining cup of beans, cover, and cook over low heat until the rice is cooked through and liquid in the pan has been absorbed.
6. Season with salt and pepper.
7. Spoon onto plates and serve. Top with sour cream if desired.

Serves 4 to 6.

Fish and seafood caught in coastal waters have been part of the diet in El Salvador for decades. Typical dishes enjoyed by Salvadorans for lunch or as a starter for dinner may be crab legs or *sopa mariscada* (seafood soup), a favorite of Salvadors from all parts of society.

Fried plantains, a typical dish enjoyed everywhere in El Salvador, may be served as a side dish or a snack.

Riguas

Ingredients

15 corn on the cob (or 1 bag of frozen corn kernels, thawed)
Salt
½ cup (1 stick) butter
Plantain or banana leaves (frozen banana leaves are sold in specialty markets)
Sour cream (optional)

Directions

1. Cut the corn off the cob, if using fresh corn.
2. Place the corn kernels, about 2 cups at a time, into a blender and process. Add salt and enough butter (about 1 tablespoon) to make a thick batter-like mixture. Repeat until all the corn has been processed.
3. Cut leaves into rectangles, about 8 inches by 10 inches.
4. Place a leaf on a cutting board. Top one half of the leaf with 2 to 3 tablespoons of the mixture. Fold the leaf over the mixture. Press down to seal.
5. Carefully transfer the leaf to a hot skillet. Fry, turning every 5 minutes, for about 15 minutes. The mixture will begin to pull away from the leaf.
6. Once the corn mixture is fully cooked, separate from the leaf and place directly on the skillet and fry, turning once, until golden brown.
7. Serve hot with sour cream or cheese.

Serves 6 to 8.

❸ Foods of the Salvadorans

Pupusas are the most well-known of Salvadoran foods. They are thick corn or rice tortillas stuffed with a combination of cheese and beans. Some also include pork or *loroco*, a local flower bud. Pupusas are served with *curtido*, a mixture of shredded cabbage, onions, and carrots pickled in vinegar, and a light tomato sauce. The three since the Salvadoran civil war (1980–92). Tens of thousands of Salvadorans emigrated from El Salvador to the United States during the conflict, and over 2.5 million now live in the United States. They took their cuisine along with them. Pupuserias, food stands that prepare pupusas, are found everywhere in El Salvador. They are also found in communities in other parts of the world where Salvadorans resettled. As of 2011, Los Angeles County was home to more than 350,000 Salvadorans. This is the largest concentration of Salvadorans outside of El Salvador.

Coffee has long been a Salvadoran export, and it is also a favorite beverage, especially among adults. However, hot chocolate is also very popular. Chocolate, as Salvadorans refer to it, is made by dissolving a solid block of chocolate with sugar and cinnamon in water. It is not as sweet as hot chocolate in the United States. Salvadoran chocolate is more like a rich tea.

Many Salvadoran dishes, such as *riguas*, feature corn as a principal ingredient.

A cook at a restaurant in El Salvador smiles as she makes pupusas. © RJ LERICH/SHUTTERSTOCK.COM.

4 Food for Religious and Holiday Celebrations

On September 15, Salvadorans celebrate Independence Day, marking the day in 1821 when the Central American Independence Act was signed and the country gained independence from Spain. Schools and government offices are closed, and people participate in parades, which last all day. Bands made up of school children begin practicing at school months before the celebration. It is common for the president to give a speech, and the day typically ends with a fireworks display.

Salvadorans prepare *hojuelas* (deep-fried pastries drizzled with honey), tamales, and

elements are piled on top of one another and eaten by hand. Pupusas may be served at any meal and are served quite often as a snack between meals.

Although pupusas may be eaten throughout the day, the typical Salvadoran breakfast is a hearty combination of eggs, fried plantains, and *casamiento*, a mixture of rice and beans. Plantains are readily available to Salvadorans; many who live in more rural parts of the country have their own plantain trees.

Salvadoran foods, especially pupusas, have become more available in the United States

El Salvador

Agricultural workers in El Salvador begin preparing a field for planting food crops. © DBIMAGES/ALAMY.

pumpkin cooked in brown sugar for All Saint's Day. Celebrated on November 1, it is a day of remembrance for the deceased when Salvadorans return to the graves of loved ones to place flowers.

Around the Christian holiday of Easter, Salvadorans also prepare *coyoles*, preserves in heavy syrup, and *torrejas*, a Central American version of French toast.

The Feast of the Indians is a holiday that honors the Virgin of Guadalupe, considered the patron saint of all of Latin America. It is celebrated on December 12. On this day, children dress in costumes of the indigenous (native) people of El Salvador, and participate in a procession led by a representation of the Virgin. Latin Americans believe that the Virgin of Guadalupe appeared in 1531 to Juan Diego, an Aztec of Mexico, who converted to Roman Catholicism. In 2002, Diego was canonized by the Roman Catholic Church, becoming the first indigenous Central American to be made a saint.

Each town and city in El Salvador celebrates the holiday of its patron saint. The Fiesta de San Salvador is celebrated in the capital during the first week of August each year. Very early in the morning festivities begin with mariachi bands serenading people. The day is filled with parades, sporting events, and day-long feasting on pupusas and other traditional foods.

El Salvador

Horchata

Ingredients
½ cup morro seeds (pumpkin seeds may be substituted)
1 teaspoon cinnamon
1 teaspoon nutmeg
1 teaspoon coriander
1 teaspoon ground allspice
1 cup rice
½ cup sugar
1 cup milk or water

Directions
1. Toast the rice in a dry skillet over low heat. Remove rice and place in blender.
2. Add seeds and spices to the skillet and toast over low heat until golden. Add to rice in the blender.
3. Process the rice, seeds, and spices in the blender until the mixture forms a fine powder.
4. Pour mixture into a bowl and cover with warm water. Refrigerate at least 8 hours.
5. Pour the mixture into the blender and process until smooth.
6. Strain the mixture through a sieve lined with two layers of cheesecloth. This is optional.
7. Add the sugar and milk or water, stirring until the sugar is completely dissolved. Taste and add more sugar if desired.
8. Pour into glasses filled with ice and serve.

Serves 4 to 6.

Fried Yucca with Curtido

Ingredients
1 medium yucca (also known as cassava)
4 cups water
1 teaspoon salt
2 garlic cloves
Pepescas (small salty fish) or pork rinds
¼ head of cabbage (or about 2 cups packaged shredded cabbage)
1 carrot, chopped
1 green pepper, chopped
1 onion, sliced
½ cup vinegar
¼ teaspoon oregano
Salsa (optional)
Oil

Directions
1. Cut the yucca into large pieces, place them in a pan, and cover with water.
2. Add salt and garlic and heat to boiling. Simmer until the yucca pieces are soft.
3. Drain, cut the yucca into 2-inch pieces.
4. Heat about 2 tablespoons of oil in a frying pan and fry yucca pieces until golden brown.
5. Fry the pepescas or pork rinds over low heat.
6. To make the curtido, bring a pot of water to boiling and add chopped cabbage, carrots, onions, and green peppers. Boil for about 5 minutes, until crisp-tender.
7. Drain in a colander and add to a large bowl. Add vinegar and oregano.
8. To serve, place some fried yucca on a plate, top with the curtido (cabbage slaw), and fried pork rinds. Add a spoonful of salsa, if desired.

Serves 4.

Christmas in El Salvador is a joyous time. Most families attend a Roman Catholic Mass on Christmas Eve, and then return home for a large family feast of roast turkey or chicken, rice, and a variety of side dishes and salads. For children, fruit juices and *horchata* are typical beverages to accompany the Christmas dinner. Horchata is a milky beverage made with grains, seeds, or nuts served in Mexico and elsewhere in Latin America, but the El Salvador recipe is unique. Salvadoran horchata may be flavored with nutmeg, coriander, and allspice. Many Salvadoran recipes call for the seeds of morro, a green, hard-shelled fruit similar to a coconut. Morro seeds are not readily available in North America, so

El Salvador

pumpkin seeds may be substituted. Powdered horchata mix may be found in some Hispanic markets.

Leche Poleada

Ingredients

¼ cup cornstarch
1 quart milk
3 egg yolks
1 cup of sugar (can be adjusted for taste)
1 cinnamon stick
1 tablespoon vanilla
Cinnamon for garnish

Directions

1. Put cornstarch, milk, egg yolks, and sugar in a blender. Blend thoroughly.
2. Pour mixture into a pan over low heat, adding the cinnamon stick and vanilla. Stir constantly with a wooden spoon until the mixture begins to thicken.
3. Remove from heat and allow mixture to cool. Pour into serving glasses and dust with cinnamon.

Serves 4.

5 Mealtime Customs

El almuerzo (lunch) is the main Salvadoran meal. Many businesses close during this time. Independent restaurants and casual eateries are found everywhere in cities and small towns. Most serve traditional Salvadoran foods, although the popularity of American-style fast food is growing. *Pollo encebollado*, translated as "onion chicken," is a popular home-style dish that may be served at lunchtime. *Licuados* (fruit drinks) are available from roadside vendors, often served in a small plastic bag wrapped tightly around a plastic straw. For dessert, Salvadorans might eat *leche poleada*, similar to custard.

Around Easter, Salvadorans prepare a Central American version of French toast, **torrejas.** © TOPSELLER/SHUTTERSTOCK.COM.

6 Politics, Economics, and Nutrition

El Salvador experienced a brutal civil war from 1980 to 1992. Rural areas were the hardest hit, causing extensive damage to agriculture. Since the end of the war, El Salvador has pursued free-market policies in an effort to attract foreign investment. The economy continues to have major disparities between the wealthy and the poor, an inequality that has persisted since colonialism. Remittances, money sent to El Salvador from the 3 million Salvadorans working abroad, totaled roughly $3.6 billion in 2010. These remittances were received by one-third of the population in 2011.

The UN World Food Programme estimates that roughly 16 percent of rural families are unable to meet basic food needs and almost 20 percent of children under the age of five face chronic undernutrition. In the most rural areas, up to 50 percent of children are undernourished.

Rising food prices have caused greater poverty throughout the nation.

From 1998 to 2011, the country experienced several natural disasters, including Hurricane Mitch (1998), two earthquakes, Tropical Storm Stan (2005), Hurricane Ida (2009), and floods (2011). Such disasters drive more people into poverty, especially those who live in rural areas. Poverty affects about one-third of the total population, and international agencies provide food and other types of aid.

7 Further Study

BOOKS

Cox, Beverly. *Spirit of the Earth: Native Cooking from Latin America*. New York: Stewart, Tabori, & Chang, 2001.

Essentials of Latin Cooking. Birmingham, AL: Oxmoor, 2010.

Fleetwood, Jenni. *The Illustrated Food and Cooking of the Caribbean, Central, and South America*. London: Lorenz, 2009.

Shields, Charles J. *El Salvador*. Broomall, PA: Mason Crest Publishers, 2005.

Vanderhoof, Ann. *The Spice Necklace*. Boston: Houghton Mifflin Harcourt, 2010.

WEB SITES

El Salvador Travel and Tourism: Gastronomy. http://www.elsalvador.travel/en/category/gastronomia (accessed on February 7, 2012).

Whats4Eats: El Salvador Foods and Recipes. http://www.whats4eats.com/central-america/el-salvador-cuisine (accessed on February 7, 2012).

World Food Programme: El Salvador. http://www.wfp.org/countries/El-Salvador/Overview (accessed on February 7, 2012).

Ethiopia

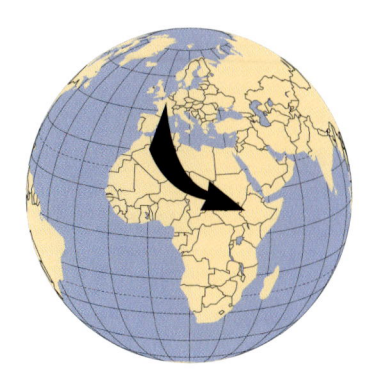

- Kategna 190
- Lab (Ethiopian Cheese) 190
- Berbere (Spice Paste) 192
- Niter Kebbeh or Kibe 192
- Injera (Ethiopian Bread)...............193
- Kitfo (Spiced Raw Beef) 194
- Dabo Kolo (Little Fried Snacks) ...194
- Ethiopian Spice Tea 196
- Aterkek Alecha (Stew) 196
- Gomen Wat (Ethiopian Greens) ..197

① Geographic Setting and Environment

Ethiopia is situated in the area known as the Horn of Africa, in eastern Africa. Ethiopia was once called Abyssinia. It is a large country with an area of approximately 426,373 square miles (1,104,300 square kilometers). Comparatively, the area occupied by Ethiopia is almost twice the size of the state of Texas.

Ethiopia is a country of geographic contrasts, varying from as much as 410 feet (125 meters) below sea level in the Denakil depression to more than 14,872 feet (4,533 meters) above sea level in the mountainous regions. It contains a variety of distinct topographical zones: the Great Rift Valley runs the entire length of the country northeast-southwest; the Ethiopian Highlands are marked by mountain ranges; the Somali Plateau (Ogaden) covers the entire southeastern section of the country; and the Denakil Desert reaches to the Red Sea and the coastal foothills of Eritrea. Ethiopia's largest lake, Lake T'ana, is the source of the Blue Nile River.

The central plateau has a moderate climate with minimal seasonal temperature variation. The mean minimum during the coldest season is 42.8°F (6°C), while the mean maximum rarely exceeds 79°F (26°C). Temperature variations in the lowlands are much greater, and the heat in the desert and Red Sea coastal areas is extreme, with occasional highs of 140°F (60°C).

The countries in Eastern Africa are affected by periodic droughts. In 2011, southern Ethiopia and neighboring countries suffered a severe drought, which caused crops to fail. The government encouraged farmers to move to parts of the country that were not suffering drought conditions.

Droughts hit Ethiopia especially hard since four out of five Ethiopians are employed in agriculture. In 2011, agriculture accounted for about 49 percent of the country's gross domestic product (GDP). According to the World Bank, nearly 39 percent of Ethiopians live in poverty.

Other environmental problems in Ethiopia include poor soil due to improper agricultural

Ethiopia

territory seceded from the inland government, creating the new nation of Eritrea.

Kategna

Ingredients
Large flat bread (flour tortilla, lavosh, or other "wrap" bread)
3 tablespoons Cajun spices
2 teaspoons garlic powder
½ stick (4 tablespoons) unsalted butter, softened

Directions
1. Preheat oven to 250°F.
2. Mix the garlic powder, spices, and butter together to make a spread.
3. Spread a thin layer over a piece of flat bread.
4. Place the bread on a cookie sheet and bake for about 20 minutes, until crispy.

Lab (Ethiopian Cheese)

Ingredients
16 ounces (1 pound) cottage cheese
4 tablespoons plain yogurt
1 tablespoon lemon rind, washed, dried, and grated
2 tablespoons parsley, chopped
1 teaspoon salt
¼ teaspoon black pepper

Directions
1. Combine all the ingredients in a bowl.
2. Place a clean piece of cheesecloth (or a very clean dishtowel) in a colander and pour mixture into the colander to drain off extra liquid.
3. Gather the cheesecloth to make a sack and tie it with clean string or thread.
4. Suspend from the faucet over the sink. (Another option is to suspend the sack over a bowl by tying the string to the knob of a cupboard door.)
5. Allow to drain for several hours until the mixture has the consistency of soft cream cheese.
6. Serve with crackers or injera.

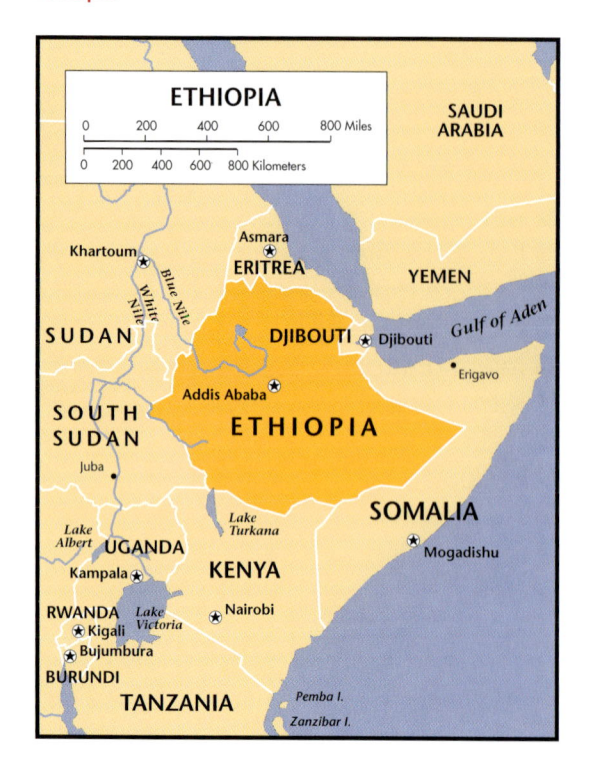

practices. In addition, the land suffers from deforestation and overgrazing.

2 History and Food

Ethiopia was under Italian military control for a period (1935–46) when Benito Mussolini (1883–1945) was in power. Except for that time, Ethiopian culture has been influenced very little by other countries. Ethiopia's mountainous terrain prevented its neighbors from exercising much influence over the country and its customs. Exotic spices were introduced to Ethiopian cooking by traders traveling the trade routes between Europe and the Far East.

Ethiopia went through a period of recurring drought and civil war from 1974 to 1991. In 1991 a new government took over, and civil tensions were relieved somewhat because the coastal

Ethiopia

The Bati market in Ethiopia is considered to be one of the most important because it brings together various ethnic groups. © HECTOR CONESA/SHUTTERSTOCK.COM.

Ethiopia's economy is based on agriculture. Agriculture accounts for more than 80 percent of the country's exports and provides 85 percent of all jobs.

Coffee is the main crop grown for export. In 2000 coffee accounted for 65 percent of export income. The price of coffee dropped during the early 2000s. By 2010, coffee represented only about one-quarter of Ethiopia's export income. Other export crops include pulses (beans and chickpeas) and oilseeds (such as sesame).

Ethiopian farmers also grow a leafy plant called khat. People chew khat leaves as a drug. People say that chewing khat takes away the feeling of hunger. Authorities worry that too much khat use is bad for a person's health. Khat grows better than many other crops during periods of drought.

Ethiopian cooking is very spicy. In addition to flavoring the food, the spices also help to preserve meat in a country where refrigeration is rare.

Berbere (pronounced bare-BARE-ee) is the name of the special spicy paste that Ethiopians use to preserve and flavor foods. According to Ethiopian culture, the woman with the best berbere has the best chance to win a good husband.

Ethiopia

Berbere (Spice Paste)

Ingredients
1 teaspoon ground ginger
½ teaspoon ground cardamom
½ teaspoon ground coriander
½ teaspoon fenugreek seeds
¼ teaspoon ground nutmeg
⅛ teaspoon ground cloves
⅛ teaspoon ground cinnamon
⅛ teaspoon ground allspice
2 tablespoons onion, finely chopped
1 tablespoon garlic, finely chopped
2 tablespoons salt
3 tablespoons red wine vinegar
2 cups paprika
1 to 2 tablespoons red pepper flakes (use larger quantity to make a hotter paste)
½ teaspoon black pepper
1½ cups water
2 tablespoons vegetable oil

Directions
1. Measure the ginger, cardamom, coriander, fenugreek seeds, nutmeg, cloves, cinnamon, and allspice into a large frying pan.
2. Toast the spices over medium-high heat for 1 minute, shaking the pan or stirring with a wooden spoon constantly.
3. Let cool for 10 minutes.
4. Put the spices, onions, garlic, salt, and vinegar in a blender and mix at high speed until the spices form a paste.
5. Toast the paprika, red pepper flakes, and black pepper in the large frying pan for 1 minute, stirring constantly.
6. Add the water slowly to the pan, then add the vegetable oil.
7. Put the blender mixture into the pan as well, and cook everything together for 15 minutes, stirring constantly.
8. Place the paste in a jar and refrigerate.

Makes 2 cups.

Niter Kebbeh or Kibe (Spiced Butter)

Ingredients
4 teaspoons fresh ginger, finely grated
1½ teaspoons turmeric
¼ teaspoon cardamom seeds
1 cinnamon stick, 1-inch long
⅛ teaspoon nutmeg
3 whole cloves
2 pounds salted butter
1 small yellow onion, peeled and coarsely chopped
3 tablespoons garlic, peeled and finely chopped

Directions
1. Melt the butter in a heavy saucepan over moderate heat.
2. Bring the butter up to a light boil.
3. When the surface is covered with a white foam, stir in the remaining ingredients, including the onion and garlic.
4. Reduce the heat to low and cook uncovered for about 45 minutes. Do not stir again. Milk solids will form in the bottom of the pan and they should cook until they are golden brown. The butter will be clear.
5. Strain the mixture through several layers of cheesecloth placed in a strainer.
6. Discard the milk solids left in the cheesecloth.
7. Serve on toast, crackers, or use in cooking.
8. Store the spiced butter in a jar, covered, in the refrigerator (where it can keep up to 3 months).

❸ Foods of the Ethiopians

The national dish of Ethiopia is *wot*, a spicy stew. Wot may be made from beef, lamb, chicken, goat, or even lentils or chickpeas, but it always contains spicy berbere. *Alecha* is a less-spicy stew seasoned with green ginger. For most Ethiopians, who are either Orthodox Christian or Muslim, eating pork is forbidden.

Ethiopian food is eaten with the hands, using pieces of a type of flat bread called *injera*.

Diners tear off a piece of injera, and then use it to scoop up or pinch off mouthfuls of food from a large shared platter. A soft white cheese called *lab* is popular. Although Ethiopians rarely use sugar in their cooking, honey is occasionally used as a sweetener. An Ethiopian treat is injera wrapped around a slab of fresh honeycomb with young honeybee grubs still inside. Injera is usually made from teff, a kind of grain grown in Ethiopia. The bread dough is fermented for several days in a process similar to that used to make sourdough bread. Usually enough bread is made at one time for three days. Little fried snacks called *dabo kolo* are also popular.

Injera (Ethiopian Bread)

Ingredients
1 cup buckwheat pancake mix
¾ cup all-purpose flour
3 teaspoons baking powder
1 cup club soda
½ teaspoon salt
1 beaten egg
2 tablespoons butter

Directions
1. Mix buckwheat pancake mix, all-purpose flour, salt, and baking powder together in a medium bowl.
2. Add egg and club soda, and stir with a wooden spoon to combine.
3. Melt about 1 tablespoon of the butter in a skillet until bubbly.
4. Pour in about 2 tablespoons of batter and cook for 2 minutes on each side until the bread is golden brown on both sides.
5. Remove the bread from the pan carefully to a plate.
6. Repeat, stacking the finished loaves on the plate to cool.

4 Food for Religious and Holiday Celebrations

About 43.5 percent of the Ethiopian population is Orthodox Christian and another 18.6 percent is Protestant Christian. Christians celebrate the holidays of Christmas and Easter. During Lent, the 40 days preceding Easter, Orthodox Christians are prohibited from eating any animal products (no meat, cheese, milk, or butter). (Some Protestants also observe dietary restrictions during Lent.) In place of meat dishes, they may eat a dish called *mitin shiro,* which is a mixture of lentils, peas, field peas, chick peas, peanuts, and berbere. The beans are boiled or roasted and then ground and combined with berbere. This mixture is made into a vegetarian dish by adding vegetable oil. It is then formed into a shape, such as a fish or an egg. It is eaten cold. A vegetable *alecha* may also be eaten during Lent.

During festive times such as marriage feasts, *kwalima*, a kind of beef sausage, is eaten. This sausage is made with beef, onions, pepper, ginger, cumin, basil, cardamom, cinnamon, cloves, and turmeric. It is smoked and dried.

About 34 percent of Ethiopians are Muslim. Harar, a city in eastern Ethiopia, is considered a holy place by Muslims everywhere. In 2006, the United Nations Educational, Scientific and Cultural Organization (UNESCO) designated the historic part of Harar as a World Heritage Site. Harar was founded by an Arab missionary and now has 82 mosques. The old city is surrounded by walls built in the 13th and 16th centuries. UNESCO described Harar as the fourth holy city of Islam.

Ethiopia

Kitfo (Spiced Raw Beef)

Note: This recipe, when finished, contains raw meat. According to the U.S. Food and Drug Administration, raw or undercooked foods such as meat, poultry, fish, shellfish, and eggs can contain harmful bacteria or parasites. Consumption of such food, if improperly refrigerated or prepared, may cause serious illness or death. (http://www.fda.gov/Food/ResourcesForYou/HealthEducators/ucm082294.htm)

Ingredients
⅛ cup niter kebbeh (spiced butter, see earlier recipe)
¼ cup onions, finely chopped
2 tablespoons green pepper, finely chopped
1 tablespoon chili powder
½ teaspoon ginger, ground
¼ teaspoon garlic, finely chopped
¼ teaspoon cardamom, ground
½ tablespoon lemon juice
1 teaspoon berbere (see earlier recipe)
1 teaspoon salt
1 pound ground beef

Directions
1. Melt the niter kebbeh in a large frying pan.
2. Add onions, green pepper, chili powder, ginger, garlic, and cardamom, and cook for 2 minutes while stirring.
3. Let cool for 15 minutes.
4. Add lemon juice, berbere, and salt.
5. Stir in raw beef and serve.

Serves 6.

The most important Muslim holiday is the holy month of Ramadan. It is celebrated during one cycle of the moon, so the dates vary from year to year. (In 2012, it falls from around July 20 to August 20.) The dates rely on the sighting of the phase of the moon, so the beginning of Ramadan may vary by a day from place to place in the world. During Ramadan, Muslims fast (do not eat or drink anything) from sunrise to sunset.

Dabo Kolo (Little Fried Snacks)

Ingredients
2 cups all-purpose flour
½ teaspoon salt
2 tablespoons honey
½ teaspoon cayenne pepper
¼ cup oil
½ cup (approximate) water

Directions
1. Mix flour, salt, honey, cayenne pepper, and oil together in a bowl.
2. Add ½ cup water slowly and gradually to create a stiff dough. Add a little more water if necessary.
3. Knead on a lightly floured board for about 5 minutes. (To knead, flatten the dough, fold in half. Then turn the dough about one-quarter turn, and fold again. Keep turning and folding the dough.)
4. Pull off pieces of dough to fit on the palm of the hand.
5. Press or roll out (using a rolling pin) into a strip about one-half-inch thick on a floured countertop.
6. Cut the strip into squares one-half-inch by one-half-inch.
7. Cook in a frying pan on medium heat until light brown in color on all sides.

Merkato, the mostly Muslim marketplace in the capital, Addis Ababa, is one of the largest markets in Africa. The marketplace is relatively quiet during Ramadan, since many Muslims devote their days to prayer. Some Ethiopian Muslims may make a pilgrimage, known as a hajj, to Mecca in Saudi Arabia. At the end of Ramadan, a festival, known as Eid al-Fitr,

A woman is shown making **injera** *outside her home, over a fire. It is a traditional food of Ethiopia.* © RONNIE JAMES/ALAMY.

celebrates the end of the fasting. In 2011, Eid al-Fitr was celebrated on August 30. On that day, about 1.5 million Muslims celebrated in Addis Ababa by listening to speeches by government officials. On this holiday, Muslims take time to remember the poor. It is common for families to sacrifice a goat, roast it, and share the meat with those in need.

5 Mealtime Customs

Before eating a meal, Ethiopians wash their hands under water poured from a pitcher into a basin. Then a prayer or grace is said. An appetizer of a bowl of curds and whey may be served. At the start of the meal, injera is layered directly on a round, woven basket table called a *mesob*. Different kinds of stews such as wot (spicy) and alecha (mild) are arranged on top of the injera. Sometimes the meal will not begin until the head of the household or guest of honor tears off a piece of bread for each person at the table. The right hand is used to pick up a piece of injera, wrap some meat and vegetables inside, and eat. As a sign of respect, an Ethiopian may find the best piece of food on the table and put it in their guest's mouth. Non-Muslim Ethiopians typically drink *tej* (a honey wine) and *tella* (beer)

Food Terms from Ethiopia

berbere. A paste, composed of hot spices, used to season many foods.

injera. Spongy, fermented bread that tastes similar to sourdough bread and resembles a large flour tortilla or large, thin pancake.

kitfo. Raw beef dish.

teff. A grain used to make teff flour, the basis for the national bread, injera.

tib. Generic name for cooked meat dishes.

wot. Spicy stews. If a dish has "wot" in its name, it will be hot, while "alecha" means mild.

---

with their meals. Coffee, however, the most popular beverage in the country, is usually drunk at the end of a meal. Ethiopia is considered the birthplace of coffee. Coffee is a principal export.

The coffee, or *buna*, ceremony begins by throwing some freshly cut grasses in one corner of the room. Incense is lit in this corner next to a charcoal burner, where charcoal is glowing and ready to roast the coffee. All the guests watch while the raw green coffee beans are roasted. The host shakes the roasting pan to keep the beans from scorching and to release the wonderful aroma of the beans. The beans are then ground with a mortar and pestle (a bowl and pounding tool). A pot is filled with water, the fresh ground coffee is added, and the pot is placed on the charcoal burner until the water boils. The coffee is then served, often with a sprig of rue (a bitter-tasting herb with a small yellow flower). The same grounds may be used for two more rounds of coffee.

Ethiopian Spice Tea

Ingredients
1 teaspoon ground cardamom
½ teaspoon ground cinnamon
⅛ teaspoon ground cloves
1½ cup water
8 slices fresh ginger

Directions
1. Mix all spices together in a small bowl.
2. Bring water to a boil.
3. Add ⅛ teaspoon of the mixture and ginger to the water. Let simmer 4 minutes.
4. Strain the tea through a coffee filter or paper towel.
5. Serve hot.

Serves 8.

Aterkek Alecha (Vegetable Stew)

Ingredients
1 cup vegetable oil (used as ¼ cup and ¾ cup)
2 cups red onion, chopped
2 cups yellow split peas
1 teaspoon salt
½ teaspoon ground ginger
⅛ teaspoon turmeric
3 cups water

Directions
1. Pour ¼ cup oil into a large pot and place over medium heat.
2. Add onion and cook, stirring often, until the onion is golden brown.
3. Add ¾ cup oil and add all other ingredients.
4. Cook over medium heat until the vegetables are tender.
5. Serve with injera. (Flour tortilla, pita, or other flat bread may be substituted.)

Ethiopia has rich farm land in which to grow crops. ©TREVOR KITTELTY/SHUTTERSTOCK.COM.

Gomen Wat (Ethiopian Greens)

Ingredients

1 pound collard greens, chopped
2 cups water
2 tablespoons olive oil, divided
1¾ cups chopped onion
8 cloves garlic, chopped
1½ cups chopped green bell pepper
1 tablespoon lemon juice
1 teaspoon salt
½ teaspoon ground turmeric
½ teaspoon paprika
½ teaspoon ground allspice
2 tablespoons minced fresh ginger root

Directions

1. Boil 2 cups of water and collard greens in a pot. Once brought to a boil, reduce to low heat. Cover and simmer for about 20 minutes.
2. Place a colander over a bowl. Drain collard greens in the colander, but reserve the cooking liquid.
3. Heat 1 tablespoon of olive oil in a large frying pan. Add chopped onions and sauté until golden brown. Stir in garlic, cooked and drained collard greens, and 1 more tablespoon of olive oil.
4. Add reserved cooking water to the pot. Simmer until liquid is almost evaporated, 10 to 15 minutes.
5. Add chopped green pepper, lemon juice, salt, turmeric, paprika, allspice, and ginger root. Cook for about 5 minutes, stirring frequently.

Serves 6.

Ethiopia

Coffee is one of the main crops grown for export in Ethiopia. © PASCAL RATEAU/SHUTTERSTOCK.COM.

6 Politics, Economics, and Nutrition

Approximately 41 percent of the population of Ethiopia is classified as undernourished by the World Bank. This means they do not receive adequate nutrition in their diet. Of children under the age of five, about 35 percent are underweight, and nearly 51 percent are stunted (short for their age).

Wars, drought, political unrest, and population pressures of the 1970s and early 1980s have left their mark on the health of Ethiopians. Hundreds of thousands of people died during a famine (widespread food shortage) in 1973, and as many as one million may have died between 1983 and 1985. Ethiopia's coffee farmers produce one of the largest coffee crops in Africa, but falling coffee prices in the early 2000s have caused hardship.

Food crops are mainly produced by small farmers, known as subsistence farmers, who attempt to grow just enough food to feed their family. These farmers have faced many challenges during the early 2000s and 2010s. Farmers in southern Ethiopia had to cope with the worst drought in more than 60 years in 2010 and 2011.

Ethiopians continue to suffer from malnutrition and a general lack of food. Sanitation (having access to sewers to carry away human waste) is a problem as well. In 2010, only 42 percent of the population had access to safe drinking water. In rural areas, only about one-third of the population had access to safe drinking water. Every year about 230,000 children die from diarrhea and related illnesses, most of which are caused by contaminated water.

In 2010 and 2011, a global food crisis hit Middle Eastern and North African countries, affecting their ability to meet basic food needs. Droughts, resulting in increased food prices, left Ethiopia with many people unable to get enough food. Ethiopia was in close proximity to the famine that plagued Somalia in 2011 and felt many of the effects. During the famine, tens of thousands of refugees fled from Somalia to Ethiopia, Kenya, Eritrea, and Djibouti in search of food and shelter.

7 Further Study

BOOKS

Carillet, Jean-Bernard, Stuart Butler, et al. *Lonely Planet: Ethiopia & Eritrea*. 4th edition. Oakland, CA: Lonely Planet Publications, 2009.

Exotic Ethiopian Cooking. Falls Church, VA: Ethiopian Cookbook Enterprises, 2006.

Harris, Jessica B. *The Africa Cookbook: Tastes of a Continent*. New York: Simon & Schuster, 2010.

McCann, James. *Stirring the Pot: A History of African Cuisine*. Athens: Ohio University Press, 2009.

Montgomery, Bertha Vining. *Cooking the East African Way*. Minneapolis: Lerner Publications 2002.

Sheen. Barbara. *Foods of Ethiopia*. Detroit: KidHaven Press, 2008.

WEB SITES

Ethiopia. http://www.africa.upenn.edu/Cookbook/Ethiopia.html (accessed on February 17, 2012).

Ethiopian Cuisine. http://www.ethiopiancuisine.com/ (accessed on February 12, 2012).

Global Gourmet. http://www.globalgourmet.com/destinations/ethiopia/ (accessed on February 12).

Tourism Ethiopia. http://tourismethiopia.org/ (accessed on February 12, 2012).

United Nations Educational, Scientific and Cultural Organization World Heritage Convention. "Harar Jugol, the Fortified Historic Town." http://whc.unesco.org/en/list/1189 (accessed on February 17, 2012).

Whats4Eats. http://www.whats4eats.com/Africa/ethiopia-cuisine/ (accessed on February 12, 2012).

France

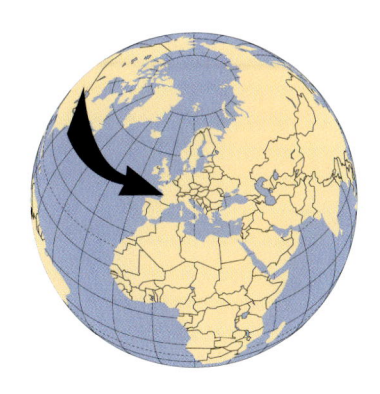

- Baguette (French Bread) 202
- Baguette Sandwich 203
- Croque-Monsieur (Sandwich) 203
- Soupe à l'Oignon Gratinée..........204
- Quiche au Saumon et Crevettes..206
- Nutella-filled Crepes 206
- Fromage (Cheese Board).............207
- Mousse au Chocolat 207
- Steak Frites 208
- Bûche de Noël (Yule Log)............208
- La Galette des Rois (Cake) 210

1 Geographic Setting and Environment

France is the second-largest country in Europe (after Russia). Much of the country is surrounded by mountains. The highest mountain, Mount Blanc, has an elevation of 15,772 feet (14,807 meters). It is near France's border with Italy.

The climate and soil of France create good conditions for farming. Although only about 4 percent of the French earn their living from farming, the country is self-sufficient when it comes to growing its own food. Agriculture was 1.7 percent of the country's gross domestic product (GDP) in 2011.

France ranks second (after the United States) for agricultural output. As of 2010, France's major crops included grains (wheat, barley, and corn), grapes for wine, dairy products, sugar beets, oilseeds (such as sesame), and fruits and vegetables. French farmers also raise livestock and poultry.

2 History and Food

The French have always been proud of their sophisticated way of cooking. Fertile soil provides fresh fruits, vegetables, herbs, grains, and meat, nearly year-round. The soil is also suitable for growing grapes, which are used for making some of the finest wines in the world. Food and alcohol play important roles in French society—the way a person eats often reflects their French heritage, region of birth, social status, and health.

During the reign of Louis XIV (1661–1715), the nobility (upper class citizens) would hold 12-hour feasts with over 10 different dishes served. The presentation of the food was just as important as the taste and quality of the ingredients. Such elaborate feasts were too expensive and required too much time for the common people to prepare for themselves, but others were also able to enjoy exotic foods and spices, such as the kumquat fruit and yellow saffron, brought back from Africa and Asia by explorers. These

France

foods were quickly incorporated into the French diet.

In November 2010, the French gastronomic meal was officially inscribed on the UNESCO Representative List of the Intangible Heritage of Humanity, an offshoot of the World Heritage program. The listing was not based simply on specific foods or recipes, but in consideration of traditional meal rituals that include multiple courses; the pairing of wine with foods; the decoration of the table; the placement of dishware, glasses, and utensils; and food tasting gestures. Such an elaborate meal generally occurs at times of celebration, such as weddings, birthdays, and anniversaries, and it serves to strengthen social and familial ties. This marked the first time that a nation's cuisine was added to the list. To be added, a tradition must be deemed a living tradition by UNESCO, meaning that it is still passed from generation to generation and continues to create a sense of identity and community for those who participate. Such traditions have been approved by UNESCO for special consideration since 2001.

Baguette (French Bread)

Ingredients
1 package dry yeast
1 tablespoon salt
2 tablespoons sugar
2½ cups warm water
7 cups flour
Egg white, lightly beaten

Directions
1. Grease two cookie sheets.
2. Dissolve the yeast, salt, and sugar in water in a large mixing bowl.
3. Stir in the flour until a stiff dough forms. Turn the dough onto a floured surface (countertop or cutting board) and knead for 10 minutes.
4. Clean out the mixing bowl, lightly oil it, and return the dough to the bowl.
5. Cover the bowl with plastic wrap. Let the dough rise until doubled in size, one-half hour or so.
6. Dip your fist in flour and push your fist into the center of the dough to "punch" it down. Remove from the bowl and knead 3 or 4 more times.
7. Separate the dough into 4 equal pieces. Form each piece into a long loaf. Place 2 on each of the greased cookie sheets.
8. Carefully slash the top diagonally every few inches with a knife.
9. Brush the loaves with the egg white. Cover lightly with plastic wrap and let the loaves rise again for about 30 minutes.
10. Preheat oven to 400°F. Bake loaves for 10 minutes.
11. Lower heat to 350°F and bake 20 more minutes.

Baguette Sandwich

Ingredients
- 1 small baguette (purchased or freshly baked; see previous recipe)
- Cheese (may be soft cheese, such as Brie, or hard cheese, such as Gouda)
- Ham
- Tomato
- Leaf lettuce
- Mayonnaise or mustard
- Cornichons (tiny sweet French pickles)

Directions
1. Slice the baguette in half lengthwise.
2. Spread one half with mayonnaise or mustard, depending on preference.
3. Arrange sliced cheese and ham over the mayonnaise.
4. Slice the sweet pickles in half, and arrange on ham.
5. Top with sliced tomato and lettuce.
6. Wrap in plastic wrap and carry for lunch away from home.

Serves 1 or 2.

❸ Foods of the French

The baguette, a long, thin loaf of crusty bread, is the most important part of any French meal. Everyone at the table is expected to eat a piece. It is eaten in a variety of ways, including being used to make sandwiches. Melted cheese spread on a baguette is often presented as part of a meal. A meal of grilled food (called *la raclette*) is sometimes served. Using an open grill, diners melt their own cheese with ham or beef slices, or fry their own egg. The grilled food is accompanied by potatoes. Sometimes diners spear pieces of bread on long-handled forks, and dip the bread into a pot full of melted cheese called *la fondue*.

Croque-Monsieur (Ham and Cheese Sandwich)

Ingredients
- 1 loaf (12 slices) of sandwich bread
- 8 slices of ham
- 8 slices of Swiss cheese
- Swiss cheese, grated
- 1 cup milk
- 1 tablespoon butter
- 2 tablespoons flour
- Salt and pepper

Directions
1. Preheat oven to 400°F.
2. Place a slice of ham and a slice of cheese between two pieces of bread; repeat this step on the same sandwich to make a triple-decker sandwich.
3. Repeat to make 4 sandwiches in all. Arrange the sandwiches in a baking dish.
4. *Make the béchamel:* Combine the flour, milk, butter, salt, and pepper in a saucepan. Heat over low heat, stirring constantly with a wire whisk, until the flour has completely dissolved.
5. Pour the béchamel (white sauce) mixture over the sandwiches and top with the grated Swiss cheese.
6. Bake for 15 minutes, or until the cheese is melted and crusty.
7. Serve on 4 plates. Cut sandwiches into halves or quarters.

Serves 4.

The regions of France have varying cuisine: in Brittany (northwestern France), the main dish is crêpes (thin pancakes) with cider; and in the Alsace region (eastern France near Germany), a popular dish is cabbage with pieces of sausage, called *la choucroute*. The French from the Loire River Valley eat a special dish made of the Lotte fish that can only be found in the Loire River. On

France

the coasts of France, seafood is plentiful, including mussels, clams, oysters, shrimp, and squid. The French enjoy escargots (snails) cooked with garlic and butter, roast duck, and rabbit.

4 Food for Religious and Holiday Celebrations

Major French holidays include Christmas (December 25), New Year's Day (January 1), and Bastille Day (July 14). On Bastille Day, named for the prison that citizens stormed on July 14, 1789, the French celebrate their liberation (freedom) from the monarchy and the beginning of their Republic. There are fireworks, dances, and parties with picnics. Food at picnics almost always includes fromage (cheese), such as Camembert, brie, chevre (goat's milk cheese), or Roquefort.

After floating a slice of bread in the onion soup bowl, top the hot soup with cheese. © ELZBIETA SEKOWSKA/SHUTTERSTOCK.COM.

Soupe à l'Oignon Gratinée (Onion Soup)

Ingredients

½ pound onions, cut into thin slices
3 ounces Swiss cheese, grated
1 tablespoon butter
3 tablespoons olive oil
1 cup white wine (optional) or water
1 tablespoon flour
1 beef bouillon cube and a dash of Worcestershire sauce (optional)
3 cups water
4 slices of bread, ¾-inch thick, cut from a baguette
Salt and pepper

Directions

1. Melt the butter and olive oil in large saucepan over medium heat and add the onions.
2. Brown the onions for about 5 minutes.
3. Sprinkle the flour on onions and stir until dissolved, heating 5 more minutes.
4. Add the wine (if desired) and the water.
5. Add salt and pepper to taste.
6. Add the bouillon cube and dash of Worcestershire sauce (if desired).
7. Simmer for 20 minutes.
8. Pour soup into bowls. Float a slice of bread in each bowl.
9. Top the hot soup with cheese.

Serves 4.

For Christmas, the French have large feasts with many courses, which usually end with a Bûche de Noël, or Yule log. This cake is shaped to look like a log of wood because of the traditional French custom of lighting a real log at Christmas. On the first Sunday of January, the Christian holiday, Epiphany, is celebrated, marking the three kings' visit to the newborn baby Jesus. For this occasion, a special dessert called *la galette des rois* is prepared. A small token, either a bean or porcelain toy, is baked inside. Whoever finds the hidden bean or porcelain toy in their piece gets to be king or queen for the day and wear a golden crown. Traditionally, the king (the

The essential ingredients for a tasty baguette sandwich are assembled and ready to go. © FOODPICS/SHUTTERSTOCK.COM.

man who found the bean in his piece of cake) had to pick a queen and present her with a gift. To avoid this obligation, the "king" would sometimes eat the evidence. To solve this problem, in 1874 French bakers began putting collectible porcelain charms in their cakes instead of beans.

5 Mealtime Customs

When entertaining at home, the hosts pride themselves on making mealtime a memorable and positive experience. For everyday lunches and dinners, four courses are typically served: salad, main dish with meat, cheese with bread, and dessert. Bread and water are always served. Special occasions include even more courses such as an appetizer of savory pastries, or other finger foods. This is normally served with an alcoholic beverage, often French wine. Several bottles of wine may be served with the meal. Coffee is also served.

Restaurants in France are generally more formal than those in the United States. It is expected that patrons are there to have a full meal. Wine is ordered by the half or full carafe (a glass container). Waiters are rarely tipped because a fee for service is added to the bill for the meal. Eating out is a social occasion, and it is a leisurely activity. It is considered rude to ask to have leftover food wrapped to be taken home. Several fast food restaurants such as Quick (a French version of McDonald's) and Pizza Hut

France

are available. Sidewalk vendors and cafés or local *boulangeries* (bakeries) also offer quick food.

Quiche au Saumon et Crevettes (Salmon and Shrimp Quiche)

Ingredients
1 prepared pie crust
4 small pieces of smoked salmon
1 small can of little shrimp
Swiss cheese, grated
½ cup sour cream
3 eggs

Directions
1. Preheat oven to 350°F.
2. Beat the eggs until light and fluffy.
3. Add the sour cream and cheese to the eggs and beat again.
4. Poke holes in the bottom of the pie crust with a fork.
5. Cover the bottom of the crust with the salmon. Arrange the shrimp evenly on top of salmon.
6. Pour the egg mixture over the seafood. Bake for 25 minutes.
7. Cut pie into quarters and serve hot with a salad and crusty bread.

Serves 4.

Many locals and tourists alike visit patisseries and boulangeries in France. A patisserie specializes in pastries while a boulangerie sells breads, rolls, and other baked goods. © PIXACHI/SHUTTERSTOCK.COM.

Nutella-filled Crepes

Ingredients
1 cup flour
3 eggs
1¼ cups milk
½ teaspoon salt
4 tablespoons butter, melted
Nutella (pre-packaged hazelnut spread)

Directions
1. Sift together flour and salt. Whisk in eggs, milk, and butter
2. Coat a skillet with butter or non-stick spray.
3. Pour ½ cup batter onto the heated skillet in a circular motion. Tilt and rotate the skillet until the entire pan is coated.
4. Cook for about 3 minutes, then carefully loosen sides of the crepe and set aside on a paper towel. Repeat until batter is gone.
5. On a plate, place one of the crepes. Place about 2 to 3 spoonfuls of Nutella onto one half of the crepe and spread around. Fold the crepe in half, and then fold it in half again.

Serves 6.

France

Fromage (Cheese Board)

Ingredients
- ¼ to ½ pound of 3 different cheeses: select from Camembert, brie, chevre (goat's milk), Roquefort (bleu cheese)
- 1 loaf of crusty French bread (or 1 package of crackers)
- Wooden cutting board for cheese
- Basket for bread or crackers
- Cheese knife or paring knife

Directions
1. Arrange the cheeses on the wooden cutting board.
2. Line the basket with a napkin (*serviette* in French), and fill it with crackers or bread, sliced into thin rounds.
3. Diners will use the knife to cut their own individual slices of cheese. Serve at room temperature.

Serves 12 or more.

Mousse au Chocolat (Chocolate Mousse)

Packaged instant chocolate mousse mix, simpler to prepare than this traditional recipe, is available at most grocery stores and may be substituted.

Ingredients
- 4 ounces unsweetened cooking chocolate
- 4 eggs, separated
- ½ cup sugar
- 1 cup heavy cream
- Pinch of salt
- Raspberries, strawberries, and ladyfinger cookies as accompaniment

Directions
1. Melt the chocolate over low heat in a saucepan.
2. Remove from heat, add cream and allow mixture to cool.

Chocolate mousse can also be served in individual cups, garnished with a fresh strawberry or another berry on top.
© FRANCESCO83/SHUTTERSTOCK.COM.

3. Separate egg whites from the yolks.
4. Add sugar to the yolks and mix well.
5. Add yolk mixture to chocolate in the saucepan.
6. Add a pinch of salt to egg whites, then beat with an electric mixer until stiff.
7. Stir egg whites gently into chocolate mixture and let cool in the refrigerator for at least 4 hours.
8. To serve, arrange ladyfinger cookies vertically around the mousse.
9. Arrange fresh fruit such as strawberries or raspberries on top. Serve chilled.

Serves 2 to 4.

France

Steak Frites

Ingredients
4 strip steaks, about ¾-inch thick each
Frozen French fries
Salt and pepper
Basil, chopped fine
Oil

Directions
1. Preheat oven to 400°F.
2. Sprinkle basil over French fries, and then cook French fries in oven for about 10 to 15 minutes, until golden brown.
3. Add oil to a large skillet. Season steaks with salt and pepper.
4. Cook steaks for about 2 minutes per side on high heat. Reduce heat and cook for another 8 minutes, until steaks are done.
5. Arrange steak and fries on a plate. Serve with ketchup (if desired).

Serves 4.

Bûche de Noël (Yule Log)

Ingredients
4 eggs
1 cup sugar
3 tablespoons water
1 cup cake flour
1½ teaspoons cornstarch
1½ teaspoons baking powder
¼ teaspoon salt
½ teaspoon almond extract
½ teaspoon vanilla
Large jar of seedless jelly (strawberry or raspberry)
Chocolate frosting, 1 can
Powdered sugar
Optional decorations: holly berries and evergreen leaves (fresh or artificial)

Directions
1. Preheat oven to 400°F.
2. Grease a jelly-roll pan (cookie sheet with a rim all around) and line the bottom with parchment paper. Grease the parchment paper well.
3. Beat the eggs until frothy and pale yellow in a large mixing bowl.
4. Add the sugar and water to the eggs and continue to beat.
5. Mix flour, cornstarch, baking powder, and salt in a separate bowl.
6. Add the flour mixture to egg mixture.
7. Add the vanilla and almond extract.
8. Pour the batter into the prepared pan.
9. Bake for 15 minutes. (Toothpick inserted into the center should come out clean. Do not overbake.)
10. Remove from oven. Cover pan with a clean dishtowel and turn over to remove cake from pan. Remove pan and carefully peel off the parchment paper. (Cake is wrong-side up.) Trim off any crusty edges.
11. Fold one end of towel over the short end of cake and carefully roll cake up inside the towel.
12. Lift the whole roll and place it, seam side down, on a cooling rack.
13. Allow to cool completely. Unroll carefully.
14. Coat the cake completely with jelly.
15. Carefully roll the cake back up again, without the towel.
16. Cut a 2-inch slice from one end and cut in half.
17. Attach these pieces to the sides of the cake to resemble branch stubs on a log.
18. Frost the cake "log" with chocolate icing. Drag a fork along the length of the cake, scoring the frosting to resemble bark. Dust with powdered sugar.
19. Arrange holly berries and evergreen leaves around the cake if desired.

Serves 12 or more.

6 Politics, Economics, and Nutrition

The diet of the French people is generally considered healthy, and most citizens receive adequate nutrition. In 2001 the countries of Europe

French cuisine is particularly noted for its variety of pastries. © AMSIMO/SHUTTERSTOCK.COM.

experienced outbreaks of two diseases, "mad cow disease" and "hoof and mouth disease" that affected the cattle and sheep herds.

Many countries enacted laws and regulations restricting the import and export of meat during that period, until the diseases could be brought under control.

In France, there have been protests at some fast food restaurants in an attempt to drive them out of the country to keep the traditional quality of French food and the French lifestyle.

Obesity levels (the percent of the population that is overweight or obese) increased during the 1990s and first decade of the 2000s.

From 1994 to 2004, the number of people who were obese doubled in France. Since 2006, vending machines selling snacks and soft drinks have been banned from French schools.

The International Obesity Taskforce reported in 2006 that, among French children, the overall overweight and obesity prevalence was about 18 percent (25 percent for boys and 16 percent for girls).

Another research study compared rates of overweight and obesity among children ages seven to nine in 2000 and 2007. It appeared that the obesity rate was holding steady and no longer increasing. Children from lower-income families were more likely to be overweight.

France

La Galette des Rois (King's Cake)

Ingredients

1¼ pounds puff pastry (available in the frozen foods section of the supermarket)
1 dry bean (such as a dried kidney bean or navy bean)
2 eggs
7 ounces almond paste
Paper crown for decoration

Directions

1. Defrost puff pastry according to package directions.
2. Preheat oven to 425°F.
3. Grease a cookie sheet.
4. Take one sheet of puff pastry and lay in on a clean working surface. Using a small plate or saucer as a template, cut an 8-inch circle of pastry.
5. Mix 1 egg with the almond paste until smooth and spread evenly onto the pastry.
6. Place the bean anywhere on the filling.
7. Cut another 8-inch circle of pastry and place it over the almond filling. Press the edges together firmly to seal. Score the top layer lightly with a sharp knife.
8. Beat the other egg lightly and gently brush over the top layer.
9. Bake for 20 minutes. Lower the heat to 400°F and bake for another 25 minutes.
10. Serve warm, with the crown on top.

Serves 8. The person who finds the bean is designated as the queen or king.

7 Further Study

BOOKS

Blaxland, Wendy. *French Food*. Mankato, MN: Smart Apple Media, 2012.

Gioffre, Rosalba. *Fun with French Cooking*. New York: PowerKids Press, 2010.

Greenspan, Dorie. *Around My French Table: More Than 300 Recipes from My Home to Yours*. New York: Houghton Mifflin Harcourt, 2010.

Locricchio, Matthew. *The Cooking of France*. New York: Benchmark Books, 2003.

Wagner, Lisa. *Cool French Cooking*. Minneapolis, MN: ABDO Publishing Company, 2011.

WEB SITES

Easy French Food: Easy Recipes for Kids. http://www.easy-french-food.com/easy-recipes-for-kids.html (accessed on February 15, 2012).

French Food and Cook. http://www.ffcook.com/ (accessed on February 15, 2012).

Global Gourmet. http://www.globalgourmet.com/destinations/france/ (accessed on February 15, 2012).

Whats4Eats. http://www.whats4eats.com/europe/france-cuisine/ (accessed on February 15, 2012).

FILMS

Babette's Feast. Rated G. (1987) This film is set in France in the late 1800s. During an uprising, a French chef named Babette is exiled to Denmark where she becomes maid and cook for two sisters. Babette spends years making simple meals for the sisters until one day she wins the French lottery. Babette uses her winnings to prepare an extravagant seven-course French meal for the sisters and 10 other community members. The film depicts the lavish feast in detail, including the food preparation and consumption.

Germany

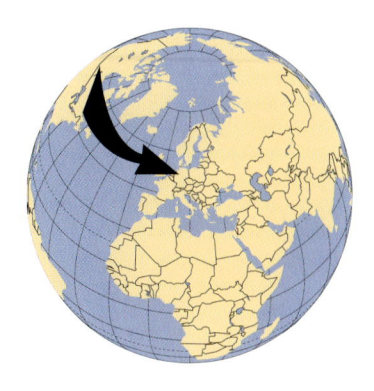

- Weisse Bohnensuppe (Soup) 212
- Spargelgemuse (Asparagus) 213
- Glühwein (Non-alcoholic Drink)..214
- Bratwurst (Sausage) 214
- Eis und Heiss 215
- Apfelschörle 215
- Kartoffelknödeln (Dumplings) 216
- Rye Bread 216
- Lebkuchen 217
- Potato Roesti 218
- Red Coleslaw 218
- Apfelpfannkuchen (Pancakes).....218
- Soft Pretzels................................219

1 Geographic Setting and Environment

Germany is located in Western Europe. The topography of the country is varied and includes regions of deep forest and high mountains, as well as a wide valley surrounding the Rhine, Germany's largest river. The highest mountain peak, the Zugspitze, lies on the border with Austria.

Less than 3 percent of Germans are farmers, and the country must import much of its food. Apples, pears, cherries, and peaches, as well as grapes for wine production, are important crops in Germany.

Agriculture, horticulture, and food are promoted at the International Green Week Berlin fair, which has been held annually since 1926. In addition to presentations about various types of food, the fair also features discussions of renewable resources, climate change's impact on agriculture and vice versa, food safety, and the like.

2 History and Food

Food has always been a major part of German culture. The well-known German fairy tale, Hansel and Gretel, makes reference to food. Hansel and Gretel, brother and sister, discover a house in the forest made of gingerbread and candies.

King Frederick II (King Frederick the Great, 1712–1786) introduced the potato, a staple in the German diet. He gave away seed potatoes and taught the people how to grow them. But wars caused food shortages and hardship twice during the 20th century. After the Germans lost World War I (1914–18), food was scarce. Soldiers trying to get home, and Germans living in towns and villages, were starving. Hundreds

Germany

of thousands of Germans starved to death in the months right after World War I ended.

After World War II (1939–45), the country had even less food available. This time the nations that had defeated Adolf Hitler's Germany, including the United States, helped to feed the Germans and rebuild the country.

In 1949 after World War II, Germany was divided into East Germany and West Germany. This division caused the country's two halves to develop different styles of cooking. East Germany, closely associated with its neighbor, Russia, took on a more Russian style of cooking. West Germans continued the traditional German cuisine. East and West Germany were reunited in the early 1990s, but Germans continue to cook according to their region.

Weisse Bohnensuppe (White Bean Soup)

Ingredients
- 1 pound dry navy beans
- 3 quarts (12 cups) water
- ½ pound ham, cubed
- 2 tablespoons fresh parsley, chopped
- 2 medium onions, chopped
- 1 garlic clove, minced
- 5 stalks of celery, chopped (including the leafy tops)
- 1 teaspoon salt
- Pumpernickel or rye bread or rolls as accompaniment

Directions
1. Rinse beans in a colander and remove any discolored or shriveled beans.
2. Place beans in a large pot, cover with water, and leave to soak overnight.
3. Drain beans in colander, rinse them, and return them to the pot.
4. Measure 3 quarts of water (12 cups) into the pot.
5. Heat the water to boiling, and then lower heat and simmer the beans, uncovered, for about 2 hours, until the beans are tender.
6. Add parsley, onions, garlic, celery, and salt. Simmer for about one hour more.
7. Add chopped ham and heat for about 10 minutes more. Serve hot, accompanied by pumpernickel or rye bread or rolls.

Serves 10 to 12.

There are also differences in cooking style between northern and southern Germany, similar to the northern and southern styles of cooking in the United States. In the north, restaurants in Hamburg and Berlin might feature *aalsuppe* (eel soup) or *eintopf* (seafood stew). Soups of dried beans, such as *weisse bohnensuppe* (white bean soup) are also popular. In the center of the country, menus include breads and cereals made with buckwheat and rye flour. A favorite dish is *birnen, bohnen und speck* (pears, green beans, and bacon). In the middle of the country, a region near the Netherlands known as Westphalia is famous for *spargel* (asparagus), especially white asparagus, and rich, heavy pumpernickel bread. Westphalian ham, served with pungent mustard, is popular with Germans worldwide.

Frankfurt, located in the south, is the home of a sausage known as *Wüstchen*. This sausage is similar to the U.S. hot dog, sometimes called a "frankfurter" after the German city. In the south, a dish mysteriously called *Himmel und erde* (Heaven and Earth) combines potatoes and apples with onions and bacon.

Spargelgemuse (Fresh Asparagus)

Ingredients
- 2 pounds of asparagus
- ¼ cup (½ stick) butter
- 3 tablespoons Parmesan cheese, grated
- 1 large egg, hard-boiled

Directions
1. Wash the asparagus and snap off the hard ends.
2. Cook the asparagus in boiling, salted water for 7 to 10 minutes (until tender) and drain.
3. Melt the butter in a saucepan.
4. Add cheese to butter and cook until melted and lightly browned.
5. Serve asparagus topped with cheese sauce.
6. Garnish with a sliced, hard-boiled egg.

Serves 8 to 10.

The southern region of Bavaria features rugged mountains and the famous Black Forest. Black Forest cherry cake and tortes, as well as Kirschwasser, a clear cherry brandy, are two contributions from this area. Spätzle (tiny dumplings) are the southern version of *knödel* (potato dumplings) of the north. *Lebkuchen* is a spicy cookie prepared especially during the Christmas season.

In all regions of Germany, sausages are popular. In cities, currywurst is a popular kind of fast food, which may be eaten as a meal or a snack. Adults often drink one of the many styles of German beer with meals, but *Apfelsaft* (apple juice) or *Apfelschörle* (sparkling apple juice) are also popular. Germans enjoy many fruit juices as well as combinations such as apple-mango and apple-orange.

3 Foods of the Germans

Germans tend to eat heavy and hearty meals that include ample portions of meat and bread. Potatoes are a staple food, and each region has its own favorite way of preparing them. Some Germans eat potatoes with pears, bacon, and beans. Others prepare a special stew called the *Pichelsteiner*, made with three kinds of meat and potatoes.

Germans from the capital city of Berlin eat potatoes with bacon and spicy sausage. *Sauerbraten* is a large roast made of pork, beef, or veal that is popular throughout Germany, and it is flavored in different ways depending on the region. In the Rhine River area, it is flavored with raisins, but is usually cooked with a variety of savory spices and vinegar. Fruit (instead of vegetables) is often combined with meat dishes to add a sweet-and-sour taste to the meal. Throughout Germany desserts made with apples are very popular.

Knödel, or dumplings, accompany many meals, especially in the north. In the south, a tiny

Germany

Spätzle, a type of egg noodle, is commonly served with various dishes in Germany. Uncooked spätzle is shown here. © BW FOLSOM/SHUTTERSTOCK.COM.

version called spätzle is more common. Knödel may be made either of mashed potatoes or bread (or a mixture of both), and are either boiled or fried. Germans enjoy bread with every meal, with rye, pumpernickel, and sourdough breads more common than white bread. Soft pretzels can be found almost anywhere. *Spargel* (asparagus) served with a sauce or in soup is popular in the spring.

Glühwein (Non-alcoholic Drink)

Note: The orange and lemon should be washed well before the peel is used in this recipe.

Ingredients
4 cups apple juice
2 cups black tea
2 tablespoons sugar
1 lemon
1 orange
1 cinnamon stick
2 cloves

Directions
1. Slowly heat the apple juice and tea in a pan.
2. Squeeze the juice from the lemon and orange, keeping the peels.
3. Add the lemon and orange juices, sugar, peels, and spices to the pan and heat without boiling.
4. Carefully strain the mixture through a sieve and serve.

Serves 4 to 6.

Bratwurst (Sausage)

Ingredients
6 slices bacon
1 small onion, chopped
1 clove garlic, minced
1 can of sauerkraut (32-ounces), drained and rinsed in a strainer
2 medium potatoes, peeled and sliced
1 cup water
½ cup white grape or apple juice
1 tablespoon brown sugar
1 cube chicken bouillon
1 bay leaf
1 teaspoon caraway seed
1 pound bratwurst
1 large apple, cored and sliced

Directions
1. In a deep skillet, cook the bacon, drain most of the fat, and crumble into pieces.
2. In the same skillet, fry the onion and garlic in the remaining bacon fat over medium-low heat until tender.
3. Add the sauerkraut, potatoes, water, white grape (or apple) juice, brown sugar, bouillon, bay leaf, and caraway seed.
4. Add enough water to cover potatoes and bring to a boil.
5. Add the bratwurst to the mixture.
6. Cover and simmer for 20 to 30 minutes.
7. Add apple slices and simmer 5 to 10 more minutes. Remove bay leaf and serve.

Serves 4 to 6.

Eis und Heiss

Ingredients

2 cups frozen fruit (traditionally cherries, raspberries, blackberries, and strawberries)
2 cups fruit juice of your choice
1 tablespoon cornstarch
1 tablespoon water
Vanilla ice cream

Directions

1. Cook frozen fruit and juice in a saucepan. Simmer until fruit is thawed and hot.
2. Dissolve cornstarch in water. Stir into the simmering fruit. The mixture will reach a thicker consistency.
3. Scoop ice cream into a bowl and top with the hot fruit sauce.

Serves 4.

Apfelschörle

Ingredients

4 cups apple juice
1 bottle of club soda (1-liter, 33.8 ounces)

Directions

1. Mix equal parts of apple juice and club soda in a tall drinking glass and serve.

Serves 4.

❹ Food for Religious and Holiday Celebrations

Eis und Heiss, cooked fruit, is often served with vanilla ice cream. Mint leaves may be used as a garnish. © EPD PHOTOS.

Oktoberfest is the German festival of October. It is held, not in October but during the last week of September in Munich. In late summer or early fall in the United States, many cities stage Oktoberfests to celebrate German culture, especially German beer. At German Oktoberfests, beer is traditionally drunk from a large, decorated stone mug called a *bier stein* (beer stein). Germany has some 1,250 breweries, making over 5,000 different kinds of beer.

For Christmas, cut-out honey cakes called *lebkuchen* are baked in squares, hearts, semicircles, or little bear shapes, iced, and decorated with tiny cutouts of cherubs (angels) and bells. One large or five to seven small cakes are then tied together with a bright ribbon and presented by a young lady to a young man of her choice on Christmas Day. *Springerle* (cookies), marzipan candies, and stollen (coffeecake with candied and dried fruit) are also popular Christmas desserts. To accompany the cookies, Germans drink *Glühwein,* a type of mulled wine. A favorite

Germany

drink with teenagers is *Apfelschörle*, a sparkling fruit juice. A traditional Christmas dinner is roast goose with vegetables and *Kartoffelknödeln* (potato dumplings).

5 Mealtime Customs

When eating out in Germany, it is polite to have both hands above the table at all times, but elbows should not rest on the table. It is also considered impolite to leave food on a plate. Waiters expect a 5 to 10 percent tip. An *imbiss* is a food stand that may serve bratwurst or other fast foods. Another type of restaurant is the *bierhall*, which commonly serves bratwursts, accompanied by beer.

Mittagessen (Lunch) Menu

Fleischbrühe (clear soup)

Rollmops (rolled herring fillets)

Königsberger klopse (meatballs in cream sauce)

Sauerkraut

Armer ritter (German French toast, literally "poor knight")

Cheese and crackers

Cookie platter with coffee

Kartoffelknödeln (Potato Dumplings)

Ingredients

- 8 medium potatoes
- 3 egg yolks, beaten
- 3 tablespoons cornstarch
- 1 cup bread crumbs
- ½ teaspoon pepper
- 1½ teaspoons salt
- Flour

Directions

1. Peel the potatoes. Place them into a large pot and fill the pot with enough water to cover them.
2. Bring the water to a boil, lower the heat, and simmer until the potatoes are soft (about 20 to 30 minutes).
3. Drain the potatoes well in a colander, place them in a bowl, and mash them, using a hand mixer or potato masher.
4. Add the egg yolks, cornstarch, bread crumbs, salt, and pepper.
5. Rinse out the pot and refill it with water and heat the water to boiling.
6. While the water is heating, shape the potato mixture into golf-ball sized dumplings.
7. Roll the dumplings in flour, and drop them immediately into boiling water for 15 to 20 minutes.
8. Serve with butter and salt.

Makes about 2 dozen dumplings.

Rye Bread

Ingredients

- ¾ cup water
- 2¼ teaspoons dry yeast (one package)
- 4½ teaspoons sugar (used in varying amounts)
- ¼ cup molasses
- 2 tablespoons honey
- 1 teaspoon salt
- 1 tablespoon shortening
- 1¼ cups whole grain rye flour
- 1¼ cups unbleached flour
- 1½ teaspoons caraway seed
- 1 rind of a small orange, finely grated

Germany

Directions

1. In a large mixing bowl, dissolve yeast in warm water with 1½ teaspoons sugar.
2. Add molasses, honey, shortening, salt, caraway seed, orange rind, and the rest of the sugar.
3. Slowly add both types of flour to mixture and knead until smooth and elastic (about 10 minutes).
4. Clean out the mixing bowl, butter it lightly, and return dough to bowl. Cover with plastic wrap and allow the dough to rise for 1 to 2 hours.
5. Push a fist dipped in flour into the center of the dough. Turn dough out onto a floured countertop or cutting board and shape into a loaf. Transfer the loaf to a greased cookie sheet.
6. Cover the dough with plastic wrap and allow it to rise again for 1 hour.
7. Preheat oven to 375°F.
8. Bake for 30 to 40 minutes.

Lebkuchen, a popular Christmas cookie in Germany, are shown here decorated with white icing. © SHTUKICREW/SHUTTERSTOCK.COM.

Lebkuchen

Ingredients
1 cup margarine
1 cup sugar
1 egg
1 cup honey
1 cup sour milk (add 1 tablespoon vinegar to 1 cup milk and let stand for 10 minutes)
2 tablespoons vinegar
6 cups flour
1½ teaspoons baking powder
½ teaspoon salt
1 teaspoon ginger, ground
½ teaspoon mace
1 tablespoon cinnamon

Directions

1. Preheat oven to 375°F.
2. Cream margarine and sugar together in a bowl. Add the egg and beat until fluffy.
3. Add the honey, sour milk, and vinegar. Add flour, baking powder, salt, ginger, mace, and cinnamon.
4. Chill for 1 hour.
5. Roll out to ¼-inch thickness and cut into shapes, especially hearts.
6. Bake for 6 minutes.
7. Decorate with white frosting and candies.

Breakfast, or *früstück,* consists of rolls with jam, cheese, eggs, and meat. Coffee or tea may also be served. The *zweites früstück* (literally second breakfast) is a mid-morning snack eaten at work or school. Students may have *belegtes brot* (literally covered bread), a small sandwich of meat or cheese, and a piece of fruit. Germans eat their big meal of the day, *mittagessen,* around noon or later, sometimes lasting two hours. The meal almost always begins with *suppe* (soup), and several more courses follow (see sample menu on page 216).

In the afternoon, *kaffee* (snack with coffee) is often served, consisting of pastries and cakes. *Abendbrot* (supper, literally "bread of the evening") is a lighter meal than lunch, usually

Germany

offering an open-faced sandwich of bread with cold cuts and cheese, eaten with a knife and fork, and perhaps some coleslaw or fruit. Pretzels and sweets may be enjoyed, especially by children, any time during the day.

Potato Roesti

Ingredients

3 or 4 medium potatoes
3 tablespoons butter
1 teaspoon salt

Directions

1. Grate raw potatoes into a bowl. Mix in salt.
2. Heat the butter in a frying pan until melted.
3. Add grated potatoes to the pan until there is about a 1-inch deep layer.
4. Stir several times until the potatoes are coated with butter.
5. Once potatoes are coated, pat them down into a cake with a spatula. Cook for about 10 minutes. Once the bottom seems browned, use a spatula to carefully flip the cake. You can also use a plate to flip the cake if it seems to be falling apart with the spatula.
6. Cook for another 5 to 7 minutes.
7. Cut into slices sprinkle with salt, and serve.

Makes 1 potato cake.

Red Coleslaw

Ingredients

1 small head of red cabbage
1 tablespoon salt
2 small onions, chopped
1 Granny Smith apple, peeled, cored, and cut into matchstick-sized slivers
3 tablespoons vinegar
1 teaspoon sugar
3 tablespoons salad oil

Directions

1. Remove the tough outer leaves from the head of a red cabbage.
2. Cut the cabbage into quarters and slice away the tough core.
3. Grate or chop the cabbage coarsely.
4. Put the grated cabbage in a large bowl, sprinkle with salt, and add the chopped onions and slivered apples. Toss gently to combine.
5. In a small bowl, combine the vinegar, sugar, and salad oil.
6. Pour over the cabbage mixture, toss, and serve.

Serves about 8.

Apfelpfannkuchen (Apple Pancakes)

Ingredients

⅔ cup flour
2 teaspoons sugar
¼ teaspoon salt
4 eggs, beaten
½ cup milk
2 large apples, peeled, cored, and cut into thin slices
1½ sticks butter (¾ cup), divided to make four pancakes
2 tablespoons sugar
¼ teaspoon cinnamon
Confectioners' sugar

Directions

1. Combine the flour with 2 teaspoons sugar and salt, then set aside.
2. In a large bowl, beat eggs and milk together.
3. Gradually add flour mixture to the eggs and milk, and beat until smooth.
4. Melt ½ stick (¼ cup) butter in a saucepan.
5. Add apple slices and cook gently until apples are softened.
6. Mix 2 tablespoons sugar and cinnamon together and stir gently into apples.
7. In a 6-inch frying pan, melt 2 tablespoons of butter.
8. Pour in batter so that it is about ¼-inch deep.

9. Cook until the bubbles on top of the batter burst and the pancake begins to set.
10. Spoon about ¼ of the apples over the pancake and cover with more batter.
11. Allow it to set, and then gently turn the pancake to brown it on the other side.
12. Repeat to make 3 more pancakes.
13. Dust with confectioners' sugar and serve.

Serves 4.

Soft Pretzels

Baked soft pretzels, like these available in a Germany bakery, are best served warm. © C12/SHUTTERSTOCK.COM.

Ingredients
1 package active dry yeast
1½ cups warm water
1 teaspoon salt
1 tablespoon sugar
4 cups flour (approximate)
Shortening for greasing bowl and cookie sheet
1 egg, beaten
Coarse salt

Directions
1. Dissolve sugar, salt, and yeast in warm water.
2. Allow to stand for 3 to 4 minutes.
3. Stir in 3 cups of flour.
4. Add the last cup of flour, a little at a time, until a stiff dough forms.
5. Sprinkle flour onto a cutting board or countertop and turn the dough out of the bowl.
6. Using clean hands, knead the dough (fold it over, press down, turn).
7. Repeat this process for about 7 or 8 minutes. Clean out the mixing bowl and coat the inside lightly with oil.
8. Return the dough to the bowl, cover with plastic wrap, and leave the bowl in a warm place for 1 to 2 hours.
9. During this time the dough will expand, or "rise" to about twice its size.
10. Grease two cookie sheets and remove the plastic wrap from the bowl.
11. Cover your fist with flour, and then punch down into the center of the dough.
12. Turn the dough back out onto the floured counter and cut or tear it into about 12 equal pieces.
13. Roll each piece into a long rope (about 12 to 16 inches long).
14. Twist the ropes into pretzel shapes and place them on a greased cookie sheet.
15. Using a clean pastry brush, brush each pretzel with beaten egg and then sprinkle them with coarse salt.
16. Cover the cookie sheets loosely with plastic wrap and allow the pretzels to rise again for about 1 hour.
17. Preheat oven to 425°F. Remove the plastic wrap.
18. Bake the pretzels for 10 to 15 minutes (until lightly browned).
19. Serve immediately with spicy mustard.

Makes about 1 dozen pretzels.

6 Politics, Economics, and Nutrition

Many Germans have begun to modify their eating habits to lower their calorie and cholesterol intake. Since the unification of East and West Germany in the 1990s, the government has faced the challenge of bringing the living conditions in the former East Germany up to the

Germany

Many Germans like to meet for coffee or a snack at sidewalk cafés. © JOYCE SHERWIN/SHUTTERSTOCK.COM.

standard found in the former West Germany. Upgrading housing, schools, and utilities continued after 2001. Despite unequal living conditions, Germans in all parts of the country are well nourished. Only 1 percent of children under the age of five have a low weight for their age or are stunted (short for their age).

In 2007, Germans ranked as the most obese people of Europe. The government launched a program that year, called "Fit Instead of Fat," to improve the quality of school cafeteria and hospital food and to encourage Germans, especially children, to exercise. The government hoped to cut obesity rates by 2020. In 2011, the Gallup-Healthways Well-Being Index found that 13.7 percent of German adults were obese and 36.4 percent were overweight.

7 Further Study

BOOKS

Chamberlain, Lesley. *Classic German Cookbook*. London: Southwater, 2007.

Chamberlain, Lesley, Catherine Atkinson, and Trish Davies. *Cooking around the World: German, Austrian, Czech, and Hungarian*. London: Lorenz, 2005.

Lund, Duane R. *German Home Cooking*. Cambridge, MN: DR Lund, 2008.

Parnell, Helga. *Cooking the German Way*. Revised and expanded ed. Minneapolis: Lerner Publications Company, 2003.

Sheen, Barbara. *Foods of Germany*. Detroit: KidHaven Press, 2007.

Trenkner, Mirko. *The Food and Cooking of Germany*. London: Aquamarine, 2009.

WEB SITES

German Food Guide. http://www.germanfoodguide.com (accessed on February 15, 2012).

Global Gourmet. http://www.globalgourmet.com/destinations/germany/ (accessed on February 15, 2012).

Let's Cook German. http://www.letscookgerman.com (accessed on February 15, 2012).

Whats4Eats. http://www.whats4eats.com/europe/germany-cuisine/ (accessed on February 15, 2012).

Further Study

Books

Abazov, Rafis. *Culture and Customs of Turkey.* Westport, CT: Greenwood Press, 2009.

Abdennour, Samia. *Egyptian Cooking: And Other Middle Eastern Recipes.* New York: American University in Cairo Press, 2005.

African American Foodways: Explorations of History and Culture. Urbana: University of Illinois Press, 2009.

Alejandro, Reynaldo G. *The Food of the Philippines.* London: Periplus, 2000.

Alexander, Heather. *Easy Desserts from Around the World.* Berkeley Heights, NJ: Enslow Publishers, 2012.

Al-Faqih, Kamal. *Classic Lebanese Cuisine.* Guilford, CT: Globe Pequot Press, 2009.

Al-Hamad, Sarah. *Cardamom and Lime: Recipes from the Arabian Gulf.* Northampton, MA: Interlink Books, 2008.

Ali, Barlin. *Somali Cuisine.* Bloomington, IN: Author House, 2007.

Amari, Suad. *Cooking the Lebanese Way.* Minneapolis: Lerner Publications Company, 2003.

Ammon, Richard. *An Amish Year.* Honesdale, PA: Boyds Mills Press, 2007.

Andrews, Colman. *Country Cooking of Ireland.* San Francisco: Chronicle, 2009.

Aranas, Jennifer M., Brian Briggs, and Michael Lande. *The Filipino-American Kitchen.* North Clarendon, VT: Tuttle Publishing, 2006.

Arcaya de Deliot, Flor. *The Food and Cooking of Peru.* London: Aquamarine, 2009.

Aris, Pepita. *The Complete Book of Tapas and Spanish Cooking.* London: Hermes House, 2012.

Arsana, Lother. *Authentic Recipes from Indonesia.* Boston: Tuttle, 2006.

Further Study

Atkinson, Catherine. *From Borsch to Blinis: Great Traditional Cooking from Russia and Poland*. New York: Southwater, 2000.

Atkinson, Greg. *West Coast Cooking*. Seattle: Sasquatch Books, 2006.

Augustin, Byron. *The Food of Mexico*. Tarrytown, NY: Marshall Cavendish Benchmark, 2012.

Ayter, Roman. *Foods of the Middle East*. New York: Gareth Stevens Publishing, 2012.

Bacon, Josephine. *The Complete Illustrated Food and Cooking of Africa and the Middle East*. London: Lorenz, 2009.

Barrenechea, Teresa. *The Cuisines of Spain*. Berkeley, CA: Ten Speed Press, 2005.

Bartell, Karen H. *Fine Filipino Food*. New York: Hippocrene Books, 2009.

Basan, Ghillie. *The Food and Cooking of Malaysia and Singapore, Indonesia and Philippines*. Leicestershire, UK: Lorenz, 2012.

Basan, Ghillie. *Lebanese Food & Cooking*. London: Aquamarine, 2009.

Basan, Ghillie. *The Turkish Kitchen*. London: Southwater, 2010.

Batmanglij, Najmieh. *Food of Life: Ancient Persian and Modern Iranian Cooking and Ceremonies*. Washington, DC: Mage Publishers, 2012.

Behnke, Alison. *Cooking the Central American Way*. Minneapolis: Lerner Publications, 2005.

Behnke, Alison. *Cooking the Mediterranean Way*. Minneapolis: Lerner Publications, 2005.

Behnke, Alison. *Cooking the Middle Eastern Way*. Minneapolis: Lerner Publications, 2005.

Bhumichitr, Vatcharin. *The Big Book of Noodles*. Lanham, MD: Kyle Books, 2011.

Blaxland, Wendy. *French Food*. Mankato, MN: Smart Apple Media, 2012.

Bloomfield, Jill. *Jewish Holidays Cookbook: Festive Meals for Celebrating the Year*. New York: DK Publishing, 2008.

Boetz, Martin. *Modern Thai Food*. Rutland, VT: Tuttle Publishing, 2011.

Bogataj, Janez. *The Food and Cooking of Slovenia*. London: Aquamarine, 2008.

Bone, Eugenia. *At Mesa's Edge: Cooking and Ranching in Colorado's North Fork Valley*. Boston: Houghton Mifflin, 2004.

Booth, George C. *Food and Drink of Mexico*. New York: Dover, 2011.

Brennan, Georgeanne. *The Mediterranean Herb Cookbook*. San Francisco, CA: Chronicle Books, 2000.

Brooks, Shirley Lomax. *Argentina Cooks!: Treasured Recipes from the Nine Regions of Argentina*. New York: Hippocrene Books, 2001.

Brown, Catherine. *Broths to Bannocks: Cooking in Scotland 1690 to Present Day*. Glasgow: Waverley, 2010.

Byler, Linda. *Lizzie's Amish Cookbook: Favorite Recipes from Three Generations of Amish Cooks!* Intercourse, PA: Good Books, 2011.

Camorra, Frank. *Rustica: A Return to Spanish Home Cooking.* San Francisco: Chronicle Books, 2011.

Castella, Krystina. *A World of Cake: 150 Recipes for Sweet Traditions from Cultures Near and Far.* North Adams, MA: Storey Publishing, 2010.

Castro, Lourdes. *Latin Grilling.* Berkeley, CA: Ten Speed Press, 2011.

Chamberlain, Lesley. *Classic German Cookbook.* London: Southwater, 2007.

Chamberlain, Lesley. *Cooking around the World: German, Austrian, Czech, and Hungarian.* London: Lorenz, 2005.

Chamberlain, Lesley. *The Food and Cooking of Eastern Europe.* Lincoln: University of Nebraska Press, 2006.

Christian, Rebecca. *Cooking the Spanish Way.* Minneapolis: Lerner Publications Company, 2002.

Chung, Soon Young. *Korean Home Cooking.* North Clarendon, VT: Periplus, 2006.

Clarke, Philip A. *Aboriginal People and Their Plants.* Dural, NSW, Australia: Rosenberg, 2007.

Cohen, Jayne. *The Gefilte Variations: 200 Inspired Re-creations of Classics from the Jewish Kitchen, with Menus, Stories, and Traditions for the Holidays and Year-round.* New York: Scribner, 2000.

Cornell, Kari A. *Cooking the Southern African Way: Culturally Authentic Foods Including Low-fat and Vegetarian Recipes.* Minneapolis: Lerner Publications, 2005.

Cortina, Martha Abreu. *Authentic Cuban Cuisine.* Gretna, LA: Pelican Publishing, 2011.

Crocker, Pat. *150 Best Tagine Recipes.* Toronto: R. Rose Inc., 2011.

Daft, Rohan. *Menú Del Día: More Than 100 Classic, Authentic Recipes from Across Spain.* New York: Simon & Schuster, 2008.

D'Amico, Joan, and Karen Eich Drummond. *The Coming to America Cookbook: Delicious Recipes and Fascinating Stories from America's Many Cultures.* Hoboken, NJ: Wiley, 2005.

D'Amico, Joan, and Karen Eich Drummond. *The United States Cookbook: Fabulous Foods and Fascinating Facts from All 50 States.* New York: John Wiley & Sons, 2000.

D'Amico, Joan, and Karen Eich Drummond. *The U.S. History Cookbook: Delicious Recipes and Exciting Events from the Past.* New York: John Wiley & Sons, 2000.

Danhi, Robert. *Easy Thai Cooking.* Rutland, VT: Tuttle Publishing, 2011.

Daniels-Zeller, Debra. *The Northwest Vegetarian Cookbook.* Portland, OR: Timber Press, 2010.

DeMers, John. *Authentic Recipes from Jamaica.* Singapore: Periplus, 2005.

Further Study

DePietro, Frank. *Latin American Cuisine*. Philadelphia: Mason Crest Publishers, 2012.

Dresser, Norine. *Multicultural Manners*. Edina, MN: ABDO Publishing Company, 2005.

Dunlop, Fiona. *The North African Kitchen*. Northampton, MA: Interlink Publishing, 2008.

Edge, John T. *Southern Belly: The Ultimate Food Lover's Companion to the South*. Chapel Hill, NC: Algonquin Books of Chapel Hill, 2007.

Ejaz, Khadija. *Recipe and Craft Guide to India*. Hockessin, DE: Mitchell Lane Publishers, 2010.

Elias, Leile Salloum. *The Sweets of Araby*. Woodstock, VT: Countryman Press, 2011.

Esposito, Mary Ann. *Ciao Italia Family Classics*. New York: St. Martin's Press, 2011.

Essentials of Latin Cooking. Birmingham, AL: Oxmoor, 2010.

Evans, Pete. *My Grill: Outdoor Cooking Australian Style*. San Francisco: Welcon Owen, 2011.

Exotic Ethiopian Cooking. Falls Church, VA: Ethiopian Cookbook Enterprises, 2006.

Fajardo, Anika. *The Dish on Food and Farming in Colonial America*. North Mankato: Capstone Press, 2011.

Favish, Melody. *Swedish Cakes and Cookies*. New York: Skyhorse Publishing, 2008.

Fay, Kim. *Communion: A Culinary Journey through Vietnam*. San Francisco: Things Asian Press, 2010.

Fintor, Yolanda. *Hungarian Cookbook*. New York: Hippocrene Books, 2009.

Fleetwood, Jenni. *The Illustrated Food and Cooking of the Caribbean, Central & South America*. London: Lorenz, 2009.

Fleetwood, Jenni. *South American Food and Cooking*. London: Southwater, 2005.

Ford, Jean. *Latino Cuisine and Its Influence on American Foods: The Taste of Celebration*. Philadelphia: Mason Crest, 2006.

Gammon, Shana. *The Great State Cookbook: Recipes from Around the Country for Kids!* Lynchburg, VA: Willow Tree Press, 2003.

George, Charles. *What Makes Me Amish?* Farmington Hills, MI: KidHaven Press, 2006.

Germaine, Elizabeth. *Cooking the Australian Way*. Minneapolis: Lerner Publications, 2004.

Get Cooking! London: Dorling Kindersley, 2012.

Gifford, Clive. *Food and Cooking in Ancient Egypt*. New York: PowerKids Press, 2010.

Gioffre, Rosalba. *Fun with French Cooking*. New York: PowerKids Press, 2010.

Gioffre, Rosalba. *Fun with Italian Cooking*. New York: PowerKids Press, 2010.

Gomes, Tania. *Flavors of Portugal*. San Diego, CA: Thunder Bay Press, 2005.

Goodman, Polly. *Food in India*. New York: PowerKids Press, 2008.

Greenberg, Arnold. *Buenos Aires: And the Best of Argentina Alive!* Edison, NJ: Hunter Publishing, 2000.

Greenspan, Dorie. *Around My French Table: More Than 300 Recipes from My Home to Yours*. New York: Houghton Mifflin Harcourt, 2010.

Grossman, Chaya Feigy. *The Cherry on Top: A Kosher Junior Cookbook*. Nanyuet, NY: Feldheim Publishers, 2009.

Gutterson, Connie. *The New Sonoma Cookbook*. New York: Sterling, 2011.

Han, Bok Jin. *Appreciation of Korean Cuisine*. Seoul, South Korea: Seoul National University Press, 2009.

Harms, Julia. *Recipe and Craft Guide to Italy*. Hockessin, DE: Mitchell Lane, 2012.

Harris, Jessica B. *The Africa Cookbook: Tastes of a Continent*. New York: Simon & Schuster, 2010.

Harris, Jessica B. *High on the Hog: A Culinary Journey from Africa to America*. New York: Bloomsbury, 2011.

Heine, Peter. *Food Culture in the Near East, Middle East, and North Africa*. Westport, CT: Greenwood, Press, 2004.

Hepinstall, Hi Soo Shin. *Growing Up in a Korean Kitchen: A Cookbook*. Berkeley, CA: Ten Speed Press, 2001.

Hofberg, Caroline. *Traditional Swedish Cooking*. New York: Skyhorse Publishing, 2011.

Horn, Ken. *Complete Chinese Cookbook*. Toronto: Firefly Books Ltd., 2011.

Houts, Amy. *Cooking Around the Country with Kids: USA Regional Recipes and Fun Activities*. Maryville, MO: Snaptail Press, 2010.

Hunter, David. *Teen Life among the Amish and Other Alternative Communities*. Philadelphia: Mason Crest, 2008.

Ibrahim, Lamees. *The Iraqi Cookbook*. Northampton, MA: Interlink, 2011.

Ilkin, Nur. *The Turkish Cookbook*. Northampton, MA: Interlink Books, 2010.

Imoisi, Janice. *Cooking Nigerian Style: Delicious African Recipes*. Houston, TX: Gayle Publishing, 2000.

Isaacs, Jennifer. *Bush Food: Aboriginal Food and Herbal Medicine*. Sydney, Australia: Lansdowne, 1996.

Jaffrey, Madhur. *At Home with Madhur Jaffrey: Simple, Delectable Dishes from India, Pakistan, Bangladesh, and Sri Lanka*. New York: Alfred A. Knopf, 2010.

Further Study

Jamison, Cheryl Alters. *Tasting New Mexico: Recipes Celebrating One Hundred Years of Distinctive New Mexican Cooking.* Santa Fe, NM: Museum of New Mexico Press, 2012.

Janer, Zilkia. *Latino Food Culture.* Westport, CT: Greenwood, 2008.

Joelson, Daniel. *Tasting Chile.* New York: Hippocrene Books, 2004.

Jones, Catherine Cheremeteff. *A Year of Russian Feasts.* Bethesda, MD: Jellyroll Press, 2002.

Jordan, Christy. *Southern Plate: Classic Comfort Food That Makes Everyone Feel Like Family.* New York: William Morrow, 2010.

Karam, Michael. *Arak and Mezze: The Taste of Lebanon.* Berkeley, CA: Saqi, 2008.

Karim, Kay. *Iraqi Family Cookbook.* Falls Church, VA: Iraqi Family Cookbook, 2006.

Kazuko, Emi. *The Food and Cooking of Japan & Korea.* London: Lorenz, 2010.

Keoke, Emory Dean. *American Indian Contributions to the World: Food, Farming, and Hunting.* New York: Facts on File, 2005.

Kiros, Tessa. *Food from Many Greek Kitchens.* Kansas City, MO: Andrews McMeel Publishing, 2011.

Knab, Sophie Hodoriwicz. *The Polish Country Kitchen Cookbook.* New York: Hippocrene Books, 2002.

Koosmann, Melissa. *Recipe and Craft Guide to South Africa.* Hockessin, DE: Mitchell Lane, 2012.

Kras, Sara Louise. *Foods of Italy.* Tarrytown, NY: Marshall Cavendish Benchmark, 2012.

Kuiper, Kathleen, ed. *Native American Culture.* New York: Britannica Educational Publishing, 2010.

Kummer, Patricia K. *Foods of Thailand.* Tarrytown, NY: Marshall Cavendish Benchmark, 2012.

Larson, Leah. *The Yaldah Year: Crafts & Recipes for Every Month of the Jewish Year.* London: YM Books, 2009.

Laverty, Maura. *Full and Plenty: Classic Irish Cooking.* Cork, Ireland: Mercier Press, 2009.

Leavitt, Amie Jane. *Southwestern Recipes.* Hockessin, DE: Mitchell Lane, 2012.

Leavitt, Amie Jane. *Western Recipes.* Hockessin, DE: Mitchell Lane, 2012.

Lee, Cecilia Hae-Jin. *Quick & Easy Korean Cooking.* San Francisco: Chronicle Books, 2009.

Lee, Cecilia Hae-Jin. *Quick & Easy Mexican Cooking.* San Francisco: Chronicle Books, 2011.

Lee, Siek-Jung. *Korean Cooking.* London: Aquamarine, 2005.

Leite, David. *The New Portuguese Table.* New York: Clarkson Potter Publishers, 2009.

Further Study

Liao, Yan. *Food and Festivals of China*. Philadelphia: Mason Crest Publishers, 2011.

Locricchio, Matthew. *The 2nd International Cookbook for Kids*. New York: Benchmark Books, 2008.

Locricchio, Matthew. *The Super Chef: Cooking of Brazil*. New York: Marshall Cavendish Benchmark, 2011.

Locricchio, Matthew. *The Super Chef: Cooking of China*. New York: Marshall Cavendish Benchmark, 2011.

Locricchio, Matthew. *The Super Chef: Cooking of France*. New York: Marshall Cavendish Benchmark, 2011.

Locricchio, Matthew. *The Super Chef: Cooking of Greece*. New York: Marshall Cavendish Benchmark, 2011.

Locricchio, Matthew. *The Super Chef: Cooking of India*. New York: Marshall Cavendish Benchmark, 2011.

Locricchio, Matthew. *The Super Chef: Cooking of Mexico*. New York: Marshall Cavendish Benchmark, 2011.

Locricchio, Matthew. *The Super Chef: Cooking of Thailand*. New York: Marshall Cavendish Benchmark, 2011.

Locricchio, Matthew. *Teen Cuisine*. New York: Benchmark Books, 2010.

Low, Bee Yini. *Easy Chinese Recipes*. Rutland, VT: Tuttle Publishing, 2011.

Lund, Duane R. *German Home Cooking*. Cambridge, MN: DR Lund, 2008.

Lynette, Rachel. *Let's Throw a St. Patrick's Day Party!* New York: PowerKids Press, 2012.

Mack, Glenn Randall. *Food Culture in Russia and Central Asia*. Westport, CT: Greenwood Press, 2005.

Mallos, Tess. *North African Cooking*. North Clarendon, VT: Periplus, 2006.

Marsh, Carole. *The Kitchen House: How Yesterday's Black Women Created Today's Most Popular & Famous American Foods*. Peachtree City, GA: Gallopade International, 2003.

Mason, Laura. *Food Culture in Great Britain*. Westport, CT: Greenwood Press, 2004.

Matten, Joanne. *Mid-Atlantic Recipes*. Hockessin, DE: Mitchell Lane, 2012.

McCann, James. *Stirring the Pot: A History of African Cuisine*. Athens: Ohio University Press, 2009.

McCourt, Jeff. *Flavours of Prince Edward Island*. North Vancouver, BC: Whitecap, 2010.

McDougall, Nancy. *We Can Cook!: Kids in the Kitchen*. London: Southwater, 2012.

McNeill, F. Marian. *The Scots Kitchen*. Edinburgh: Birlinn, 2010.

Menard, Valerie. *The Latino Holiday Book*. New York: Marlowe & Company, 2000.

Further Study

Menzel, Peter. *What I Eat: Around the World in 80 Diets*. Berkeley, CA: Material World Books, Ten Speed Press, 2010.

Milhench, Heike. *Flavors of Slovenia*. New York: Hippocrene, 2007.

Montgomery, Bertha Vining, and Constance Nabwire. *Cooking the West African Way*. Minneapolis: Lerner Publications, 2002.

Moore, Sharon. *Native American Foods and Recipes*. New York: Rosen Publishing, 2002.

Morris, Sallie. *A Taste of Asia*. London: Southwater, 2009.

Nayak, Hari. *My Indian Kitchen*. Rutland, VT: Tuttle Publishing, 2011.

Nicholson, Louise. *The Festive Food of India and Pakistan*. London: Kyle Cathie, 2006.

Orr, Tamra. *The Food of China*. Tarrytown, NY: Marshall Cavendish Benchmark, 2012.

Orr, Tamra. *The Food of Greece*. Tarrytown, NY: Marshall Cavendish Benchmark, 2012.

Orr, Tamra. *Pacific Northwest Recipes*. Hockessin, DE: Mitchell Lane, 2012.

Ortins, Ana Patuleia. *Portuguese Homestyle Cooking*. Revised ed. Northampton, MA: Interlink Publishing, 2011.

Osseo-Asare, Fran. *A Good Soup Attracts Chairs: A First African Cookbook for American Kids*. Gretna, LA: Pelican Publishing, 2001.

Owen, Sri. *The Indonesian Kitchen*. Northhampton, MA: Interlink Books, 2009.

Paddleford, Clementine. *The Great American Cookbook: 500 Recipes: Favorite Foods from Every State*. New York: Rizzo Publications, 2011.

Panayi, Panikos. *Spicing Up Britain: The Multicultural History of British Food*. London: Reaktion, 2008.

Parasecoli, Fabio. *Food Culture in Italy*. Westport, CT: Greenwood Press, 2004.

Parnell, Helga. *Cooking the German Way*. Minneapolis: Lerner Publications Company, 2003.

Patent, Greg. *Montana Cooking*. Guilford, CT: Three Forks, 2008.

Perez, Papi. *Food with Attitude: Cooking the Cuban-Rican Way*. River Forest, IL: Wicker Park Press Limited, 2011.

Plotkin, Gregory. *Cooking the Russian Way*. Minneapolis: Lerner, 2003.

Quinn, Lucinda Scala. *Lucinda's Authentic Jamaican Kitchen*. Hoboken, NJ: Wiley, 2006.

Raabe, Emily. *A Kwanzaa Holiday Cookbook*. New York: PowerKids Press, 2002.

Rabade Roque, Raquel. *The Cuban Kitchen*. New York: Alfred A. Knopf, 2011.

The Real Taste of Indonesia. Prahran, Victoria, Australia: Hardie Grant Books, 2009.

Further Study

Reusser, Kayleen. *Recipe and Craft Guide to Indonesia*. Hockessin, DE: Mitchell Lane Publishers, 2010.

Robertson, Carol. *Portuguese Cooking*. Berkeley, CA: North Atlantic Books, 2008.

Roden, Claudia. *Arabesque: A Taste of Morocco, Turkey, and Lebanon*. New York: Knopf, 2006.

Rowe, Silvena. *Purple Citrus and Sweet Perfume*. New York: Ecco, 2011.

Roy, Suman. *From Pemmican to Poutine: A Journey through Canada's Culinary History*. Toronto: Key Publishing House, 2010.

Salfellner, Harald. *Best Czech Recipes*. Prague: Vitalis, 2005.

Salloum, Habeeb. *The Arabian Nights Cookbook: From Lamb Kebabas to Baba Ghanouj*. Rutland, VT: Tuttle Publishing, 2010.

Saul, Laya. *Recipe and Craft Guide to Israel*. Hockessin, DE: Mitchell Lane, 2012.

Schmidt, Darlene Anne. *Knack Thai Cooking*. Guilford, CT: Knack, 2009.

Schwartz, Leticia Moreinos. *The Brazilian Kitchen*. London: Kyle Books, 2010.

Senker, Cath. *A World of Food: Lebanon*. Minneapolis: Clara House Books, 2010.

Sharpless, Rebecca. *Cooking in Other Women's Kitchens: Domestic Workers in the South, 1865-1960*. Chapel Hill: University of North Carolina Press, 2010.

Sheen, Barbara. *Foods of Afghanistan*. Farmington Hills, MI: KidHaven Press, 2011.

Sheen, Barbara. *Foods of Australia*. Farmington Hills, MI: KidHaven Press, 2010.

Sheen, Barbara. *Foods of Brazil*. Farmington Hills, MI: KidHaven Press, 2008.

Sheen, Barbara. *Foods of Canada*. Farmington Hills, MI: KidHaven Press, 2012.

Sheen, Barbara. *Foods of the Caribbean*. Farmington Hills, MI: KidHaven Press, 2008.

Sheen, Barbara. *Foods of China*. Farmington Hills, MI: KidHaven Press, 2006.

Sheen, Barbara. *Foods of Colombia*. Farmington Hills, MI: KidHaven Press, 2012.

Sheen, Barbara. *Foods of Cuba*. Farmington Hills, MI: KidHaven Press, 2011.

Sheen, Barbara. *Foods of Egypt*. Farmington Hills, MI: KidHaven Press, 2010.

Sheen, Barbara. *Foods of Ethiopia*. Farmington Hills, MI: KidHaven Press, 2008.

Sheen, Barbara. *Foods of Germany*. Farmington Hills, MI: KidHaven Press, 2007.

Sheen, Barbara. *Foods of Ghana*. Farmington Hills, MI: KidHaven Press, 2012.

Sheen, Barbara. *Foods of Greece*. Farmington Hills, MI: KidHaven Press, 2006.

Further Study

Sheen, Barbara. *Foods of Iceland*. Farmington Hills, MI: KidHaven Press, 2011.

Sheen, Barbara. *Foods of India*. Farmington Hills, MI: KidHaven Press, 2007.

Sheen, Barbara. *Foods of Indonesia*. Farmington Hills, MI: KidHaven Press, 2012.

Sheen, Barbara. *Foods of Iran*. Farmington Hills, MI: KidHaven Press, 2006.

Sheen, Barbara. *Foods of Ireland*. Farmington Hills, MI: KidHaven Press, 2011.

Sheen, Barbara. *Foods of Israel*. Farmington Hills, MI: KidHaven Press, 2011.

Sheen, Barbara. *Foods of Italy*. Farmington Hills, MI: KidHaven Press, 2006.

Sheen, Barbara. *Foods of Japan*. Farmington Hills, MI: KidHaven Press, 2005.

Sheen, Barbara. *Foods of Kenya*. Farmington Hills, MI: KidHaven Press, 2010.

Sheen, Barbara. *Foods of Korea*. Farmington Hills, MI: KidHaven Press, 2011.

Sheen, Barbara. *Foods of Mexico*. Farmington Hills, MI: KidHaven Press, 2005.

Sheen, Barbara. *Foods of Morocco*. Farmington Hills, MI: KidHaven Press, 2011.

Sheen, Barbara. *Foods of Pakistan*. Farmington Hills, MI: KidHaven Press, 2011.

Sheen, Barbara. *Foods of Peru*. Farmington Hills, MI: KidHaven Press, 2011.

Sheen, Barbara. *Foods of the Philippines*. Farmington Hills, MI: KidHaven Press, 2006.

Sheen, Barbara. *Foods of Poland*. Farmington Hills, MI: KidHaven Press, 2012.

Sheen, Barbara. *Foods of Russia*. Farmington Hills, MI: KidHaven Press, 2006.

Sheen, Barbara. *Foods of Scandinavia*. Farmington Hills, MI: KidHaven Press, 2010.

Sheen, Barbara. *Foods of Thailand*. Farmington Hills, MI: KidHaven Press, 2006.

Sheen, Barbara. *Foods of Vietnam*. Farmington Hills, MI: KidHaven Press, 2006.

Sinclair, Patricia. *Scandinavian Classic Baking*. Gretna, LA: Pelican, 2011.

Smythyman, Kathryn, and Bobbie Kalman. *Native North American Foods and Recipes*. New York: Crabtree Publishing, 2006.

Song, Young Jin. *The Food and Cooking of Korea*. London: Lorenz, 2007.

Spears, Grady. *Cooking the Cowboy Way*. Kansas City: Andrews McMeel Publishing, 2009.

Stewart, Anita, and Robert Wigington. *The Flavors of Canada: A Celebration of the Finest Regional Foods*. Vancouver, BC: Raincoast Books, 2006.

Strybel, Robert. *Polish Holiday Cookery*. New York: Hippocrene, 2003.

Sullivan, Caroline. *Classic Jamaican Cooking*. London: Serif, 2003.

Symons, Michael. *One Continuous Picnic: A Gastronomic History of Australia*. 2nd ed. Carlton, Victoria, Australia: Melbourne University Press, 2007.

Further Study

Taabu, Alice. *Mke Nyumbani: Alice Taabu's Cookery Book*. Nairobi: Kenway Publications, 2001.

Treasured Amish & Mennonite Recipes. East Petersburg, PA: Fox Chapel Publishing, 2011.

Tritenbach, Paul. *Traveling Taste Buds: Delectable Dishes from All Over the U.S. and Canada*. Bishop, CA: Excellence Press, 2000.

Trnka, Peter. *The Best of Czech Cooking*. New York: Hippocrene Books, 2008.

Valladolid, Marcela. *Mexican Made Easy*. New York: Clarkson Potter, 2011.

Vanderhoof, Ann. *The Spice Necklace*. Boston: Houghton Mifflin Harcourt, 2010.

Van Wyk, Magdaleen. *Traditional South African Cooking*. Cape Town: Struik, 2007.

Villios, Lynne W. *Cooking the Greek Way*. Minneapolis: Lerner Publications, 2002.

Visson, Lynn. *The Russian Heritage Cookbook*. New York: Overlook Press, 2009.

Wagner, Lisa. *Cool African Cooking*. Edina, MN: ABDO Publishing, 2011.

Wagner, Lisa. *Cool French Cooking*. Minneapolis, MN: ABDO Publishing Company, 2011.

Wagner, Lisa. *Cool Mexican Cooking*. Minneapolis: ABDO Publishing, 2011.

Webb, Andrew. *Food Britannia*. London: Random House, 2011.

Webb, Lois Sinaiko, and Lindsay Grace Roten. *Holidays of the World Cookbook for Students*. Santa Barbara, CA: Greenwood, 2011.

Weston, Reiko. *Cooking the Japanese Way*. Minneapolis: Lerner, 2001.

White Lennon, Biddy. *Irish Cooking*. London: Southwater, 2007.

Willinsky, Helen. *Jerk from Jamaica*. Berkeley, CA: Ten Speed Press, 2007.

Willis, Virginia. *Bon Appetit, Y'all: Recipes and Stories from Three Generations of Southern Cooking*. Berkeley, CA: Ten Speed Press, 2008.

Wilson, Carol. *The Food and Cooking of Scotland*. London: Southwater, 2008.

Winget, Mary. *Cooking the North African Way*. Minneapolis: Lerner Publications, 2004.

World Hunger. Bronx, NY: H. W. Wilson, 2007.

Yan, Martin. *Chinese Cooking for Dummies*. Foster City, CA: IDG Books, 2000.

Yates, Annette. *A Taste of Wales*. London: Lorenz, 2009.

Zaarour, Monique Bassila. *The Lebanese Kitchen*. Northampton, MA: Interlink Books, 2007.

Zanger, Mark H. *The American Ethnic Cookbook for Students*. Phoenix, AZ: Oryx Press, 2001.

Zoloth, Joan. *Jewish Holiday Treats*. San Francisco: Chronicle Books, 2000.

Further Study

Web Sites

Aboriginal Canada Portal: Food and Recipes. http://www.aboriginalcanada.gc.ca/acp/site.nsf/eng/ao35296.html (accessed on February 5, 2012).

Aboriginal Culture. "Aboriginal Bush Foods: Insect, Animal, and Plant Foods." http://www.aboriginalculture.com.au/bushfoods.shtml (accessed on February 1, 2012).

The African Cookbook http://www.africa.upenn.edu/Cookbook/about_cb_wh.html (accessed on March 21, 2012).

African Cooking and Recipes. http://www.africancooking.org/ (accessed on January 23, 2012).

All Nigerian Recipes.com. http://www.allnigerianrecipes.com/ (accessed on February 20, 2012).

AllRecipes.com: World Cuisine. http://allrecipes.com/Recipes/world-cuisine/ (accessed on March 23, 2012).

Argentour: Argentina Food. http://www.argentour.com/en/argentina/argentina_food.php (accessed on February 2, 2012).

Asia Foods. http://www.asiafoods.com (accessed on February 5, 2012).

Aunt Clara's Kitchen Dominican Cooking. http://www.dominicancooking.com/ (accessed on February 8, 2012).

Caribbean Choice. http://www.caribbeanchoice.com/main.asp (accessed on March 23, 2012).

Celebrate Brazil: Brazil Food. http://www.celebratebrazil.com/brazil-food.html (accessed on January 23, 2012).

Central Asian Online Travel Company (OrexCA.com): Cuisine of Kazakhstan. http://www.kazakhstan.orexca.com/kazakhstan_cuisine.shtml (accessed on February 18, 2012).

Centre for Indigenous Peoples' Nutrition and Environment, McGill University. http://www.mcgill.ca/cine/ (accessed on February 5, 2012).

Chile Guide: Food and Drink. http://www.contactchile.cl/en/chile-food-drink.php (accessed on February 5, 2012).

Cook Brazil. http://www.cookbrazil.com (accessed on January 23, 2012).

Cooking Korean. http://www.cookingkorean.com/ (accessed on February 24, 2012).

Culinary Slovenia. http://www.kulinarika.net/English/English.html (accessed on February 21, 2012).

CzechUnderScope: Czech Sweets Recipes. http://czechunderscope.com/culture/czech-sweets/czech-sweets-recipes/lng/en/ (accessed on February 8, 2012).

Easy French Food: Easy Recipes for Kids. http://www.easy-french-food.com/easy-recipes-for-kids.html (accessed on February 15, 2012).

El Salvador Travel and Tourism: Gastronomy. http://www.elsalvador.travel/en/category/gastronomia (accessed on February 7, 2012).

Further Study

Embassy of the Dominican Republic in the United States: The Dominican Republic Kids Corner. http://www.domrep.org/kids.html (accessed on February 8, 2012).

Embassy of the Kingdom of Morocco in London. http://www.moroccanembassylondon.org.uk/en/Gastronomy.html (accessed on February 19, 2012).

Embassy of Peru: Peruvian Gastronomy. http://www.peruvianembassy.us/do.php?p=507/ (accessed on February 20, 2012).

Embassy of the Republic of Kazakhstan: Cuisine of Kazakhstan. http://www.kazakhembus.com/index.php?page=cuisine/ (accessed on February 18, 2012).

Ethiopian Cuisine. http://www.ethiopiancuisine.com/ (accessed on February 12, 2012).

Filipino Recipes. http://www.filipinofoodrecipes.net/ (accessed on February 21, 2012).

Food.com: Home of the Home Cook. http://www.food.com (accessed on March 23, 2012).

French Food and Cook. http://www.ffcook.com/ (accessed on February 15, 2012).

Friends of Cameroon: Cooking. http://www.friendsofcameroon.org/cooking (accessed on January 23, 2012).

German Food Guide. http://www.germanfoodguide.com (accessed on February 15, 2012).

Ghana Nation: Recipes. http://www.ghananation.com/recipes/ (accessed on February 15, 2012.

Global Gourmet. http://www.globalgourmet.com/destinations/ (accessed on March 21, 2012).

Go Lisbon. http://www.golisbon.com/food/food.html (accessed on February 22, 2012).

Government of Australia Department of Agriculture and Food. http://www.agric.wa.gov.au/ (accessed on February 2, 2012).

GreekCuisine.com. http://www.greekcuisine.com/ (accessed on February 15, 2012).

Guatemala Food and Drink. http://gocentralamerica.about.com/od/guatemalaguide/p/Guatemala_Food.htm/ (accessed on February 15, 2012).

Hansik: The Korean Ministry for Food, Agriculture, Forestry and Fisheries. http://www.hansik.org/en/index.do (accessed on February 24, 2012).

Hawaiian Style Cooking. http://www.hawaiianstylecooking.com/index.htm (accessed on February 15, 2012).

Hungarian Soup. http://www.hungariansoup.com/cook/ (accessed on February 17, 2012).

Further Study

Indian Food Forever. http://www.indianfoodforever.com (accessed on February 16, 2012).

Indigenous Australia: Aboriginal Bush Tucker. http://www.indigenousaustralia.info/food.html (accessed on February 2, 2012).

Indochef: Indonesian Cooking Made Easy. http://www.indochef.com (accessed on February 16, 2012).

Indonesian Cuisine: A Brief Guide. http://www.embassyofindonesia.org/ (accessed on February 16, 2012).

In Mama's Kitchen: Saudi Arabian Cooking. http://www.inmamaskitchen.com/FOOD_IS_ART/mideast/saudi_cooking.html (accessed on February 22, 2012).

Inside Israel: Israeli Food. http://www.ifcj.org/site/PageNavigator/eng/inside/Israeli_food/ (accessed on February 15, 2012).

Iraqi Cookbook. http://www.iraqicookbook.com/ (accessed on February 18, 2012).

Iraqi Food and Cuisine. http://www.iraqimage.com/pages/food/ (accessed on February 18, 2012).

IrelandsEye.com: Irish Recipes and Baking. http://www.irelandseye.com/aarticles/culture/recipes/index.shtm (accessed on February 13, 2012).

Israel Ministry of Foreign Affairs: Israeli Cuisine. http://www.mfa.gov.il/MFA/Facts+About+Israel/Israeli+Cuisine/ (accessed on February 15, 2012).

Italian Food Forever. http://www.italianfoodforever.com (accessed on February 13, 2012).

Italy Link. http://www.italylink.com/food.html (accessed on January 13, 2012).

Jamaica Cooking. http://www.jamaicacooking.com/ (accessed on February 13, 2012).

Jamaican Food. http://foodjamaica.net/ (accessed on February 13, 2012).

Japanese Cuisines. http://www.bento.com/tf-recp.html/ (accessed on February 13, 2012).

Latin American Recipes. http://www.ma.iup.edu/Pueblo/latino_cultures/recipes.html (accessed on March 21, 2012).

Let's Cook German. http://www.letscookgerman.com (accessed on February 15, 2012).

LiberianForum.com. http://www.liberianforum.com/Liberian-Recipes/ (accessed on February 19, 2012).

Lidia's Italy. http://lidiasitaly.com/recipes/ (accessed on January 13, 2012).

Mexconnect. http://www.mexconnect.com/cuisine/ (accessed on February 18, 2012).

My Czech Republic: Czech Food and Drink. http://www.myczechrepublic.com/czech_culture/czech_cuisine.html (accessed on February 8, 2012).

My Filipino Recipes. http://www.myfilipinorecipes.com/ (accessed on February 21, 2012).

My Somali Food. http://www.mysomalifood.com (accessed on February 21, 2012).

Nutrition Australia. http://www.nutritionaustralia.org/ (accessed on February 2, 2012).

OnlineNigeria.com: Nigerian Recipes. http://www.onlinenigeria.com/recipes/ (accessed on February 20, 2012).

Pacific Island and Polynesian Food. http://australianfood.about.com/od/pacificislandpolynesian/Pacific_Island_Polynesian_Food.htm/ (accessed on February 15, 2012).

Pakistani Cookery. http://www.contactpakistan.com/pakfood/ (accessed on February 20, 2012).

Polish Tourist Organisation: Polish Cuisine Epicurean Travels. http://pdf.polska.travel/doc.php?lang=en&doc=kuchnia (accessed on February 21, 2012).

Portuguese Cooking. http://www.portuguesecooking.com (accessed on February 22, 2012).

Prague.net: Traditional Czech Food. http://www.prague.net/traditional-czech-food (accessed on February 8, 2012).

Rainbow Nation: South Africa Recipes. http://www.rainbownation.com/recipes/index.asp (accessed on February 21, 2012).

Recipe Source. http://recipesource.com (accessed on March 23, 2012).

Ruscuisine.com. http://www.ruscuisine.com/ (accessed on February 22, 2012).

Safe Food International. http://safefoodinternational.org/ (accessed on March 21, 2012).

Sally's Place: Ethnic Cuisine: Lebanon. http://www.sallybernstein.com/food/cuisines/lebanon/ (accessed on February 18, 2012).

Slovenia Cuisine. http://www.slovenia.si/en/visit/cuisine/ (accessed on February 21, 2012).

Slovenia Traditions and Customs. http://eslovenia.tapirus.net/ingtradicoes.html (accessed on February 21, 2012).

Slovenian Main Courses. http://easteuropeanfood.about.com/od/slovenianmaincourses/Slovenian_Main_Courses.htm (accessed on February 21, 2012).

Somali Culture: The Food of Somalia. http://www.somaliculture.net/food/index.html (accessed on February 21, 2012).

South African Cuisine. http://www.southafrica.info/travel/food/food.htm (accessed on February 6, 2012).

South America Travel Guide. http://www.southamerica.cl (accessed on March 21, 2012).

Southern African Cooking and Recipes. http://www.africaguide.com/culture/recipes/southernafricanrecipes.htm/destinations/southafrica/ (accessed on February 21, 2012).

Further Study

Sumo Kitchen: Quick, Easy, and Delicious Japanese Recipes. http://sumokitchen.com (accessed on February 13, 2012).

Susan Kaman's Kenyan Kitchen. http://www.kenyankitchen.co.ke/kenyan-kitchen-features3.php (accessed on February 18, 2012).

Taste Hungary. http://hungarian-food.hungaryguide.info/ (accessed on February 17, 2012).

Taste of Cuba. http://www.tasteofcuba.com/(accessed on February 8, 2012).

Taste Portugal: Regional Cuisine. http://www.taste-portugal.com/gastronomia/oporto-and-north (accessed on February 22, 2012).

Tour Egypt: Recipes for Food and Cuisine in Egypt. http://touregypt.net/recipes/ (accessed on February 8, 2012).

Ultimate Guide to Greek Food. http://www.ultimate-guide-to-greek-food.com (accessed on February 15, 2012).

UNICEF: Information by Country and Programme. http://www.unicef.org/infobycountry/ (accessed on March 23, 2012).

Use of Insects by Australian Aborigines, Cultural Entomology Digest 1. http://www.insects.org/ced1/aust_abor.html (accessed on February 2, 2012).

Way to Russia. http://www.waytorussia.net/WhatIsRussia/RussianFood.html (accessed on February 22, 2012).

What's Cooking? http://www.whats-cooking.ca (accessed on March 23, 2012).

Whats4Eats: International Recipes & Cooking Around the World. http://www.whats4eats.com (accessed on March 21, 2012).

World Food Programme: Fighting Hunger Worldwide. http://www.wfp.org/ (accessed on March 21, 2012).

World Health Organization: Global Infobase. https://apps.who.int/infobase/?id=1 (accessed on March 21, 2012).

World Health Organization: Global Strategy on Diet, Physical Activity, and Health. http://www.who.int/dietphysicalactivity/en/index.html (accessed on March 21, 2012).

World Health Organization: Nutrition. http://www.who.int/nutrition/en/index.html (accessed on March 21, 2012).

World Health Organization: Pan American Health Organization: Obesity. http://www.paho.org/Project.asp?SEL=TP&LNG=ENG&ID=196 (accessed on March 21, 2012).

World Health Organization: Regional Office for the Eastern Mediterranean: Obesity. http://www.emro.who.int/nutrition/index.htm (accessed on March 21, 2012).

World Health Organization: Regional Office for the Europe: Obesity. http://www.euro.who.int/en/what-we-do/health-topics/noncommunicable-diseases/obesity (accessed on March 21, 2012).

Your Irish. http://www.yourirish.com/food/ (accessed on February 13, 2012).

Index

This index contains terms and recipes from all four volumes of this encyclopedia. The volume number appears in italics. The volume number is followed by the page number. For example, the reference *4:* 84 means that the indexed term can be found in volume 4 on page 84. Entries in **boldface** type indicate main entries and main recipe categories. Recipe categories include Appetizers, Beverages, Breads, Cookies, Desserts, Main dishes, Salads, Sandwiches, Sauces and relishes, Seasonings, Side dishes, Snacks, Soups, Spreads, and Stews.

A

Aaloo Bukhary Ki Chutney (Plum Chutney, Pakistan), *3:* 39
Aberdeen Buttery (Scotland, United Kingdom), *4:* 62
Aboriginals (Canada), *1:* **85**
    Bannock, *1:* 90
    Bannock on a Stick, *1:* 90
    Man-O-Min (Ojibwa Wild Rice), *1:* 92
    Pemmican Cakes, *1:* 86
    Saskatoon Berry Snack, *1:* 87
    Soapberry Ice Cream, *1:* 87
    Squash Soup, *1:* 88
    Three Sisters Soup, *1:* 89
    Wild Rice Cakes, *1:* 91
Aborigines and Bush Tucker (Australia), *1:* **35**
    Billy Tea, *1:* 38
    Bush Tomato Relish, *1:* 40
    Damper (Aboriginal Style), *1:* 36
    Damper (European Style), *1:* 36
    Macadamia and Fruit Snack, *1:* 37
    Macadamia Nut Cookies, *1:* 38
    Plum Ice Cream, *1:* 39
Abyssinia. *See* Ethiopia
Acaçá (Rice Flour Pudding, Afro-Brazilians, Brazil), *1:* 63

Aceitunas Alinadas (Olives, Cuba), *1:* 143
Adas Bil Hamod (Lentils, Iraq), *2:* 96
Adobong Hiponsa Gata (Philippines), *3:* 68
African Americans (United States), *4:* **65**
    Baked Macaroni and Cheese, *4:* 72
    Chitlins, *4:* 69
    Collard Greens, *4:* 66
    Fried Apples, *4:* 74
    Fried Bologna, *4:* 74
    Hush Puppies, *4:* 70
    Kwanzaa Brownies, *4:* 73
    Molasses Water, *4:* 68
    Okra, *4:* 75
    Peanut Soup, *4:* 75
    Potato Salad, *4:* 71
    Red Beans and Rice, *4:* 70
    Sweet Potato Pie, *4:* 68
    Tomato and Cucumber Salad, *4:* 74
Afro-Brazilians (Brazil), *1:* **55**
    Acaçá (Rice Flour Pudding), *1:* 63
    Angu de Milho (Cornmeal Dish), *1:* 60
    Basic Rice, *1:* 57
    Brazilian Black Beans, *1:* 60
    Carurú, *1:* 57
    Cocada, *1:* 58
    Empanadas (Little Baked Pies), *1:* 61
    Moqueca (Spicy Fish Stew), *1:* 58

xlix

Index

Afro-Brazilians (*continued*)
    Moqueca aos Ovos (Egg Stew), *1:* 59
    Olho de Sogra, *1:* 63
    Quiabo (Okra), *1:* 57
    Quindins (Coconut Macaroons), *1:* 59
Aji de Gallina (Peru), *3:* 60
Akara (Fritters, Ghana), *2:* 8
Alfajores (Peru), *3:* 60
Alfajores de Maizena (Cookies, Argentina), *1:* 20
Algeria, *1:* 1
    Algerian Cooked Carrot Salad, *1:* 7
    Banadura Salata B'Kizbara, *1:* 5
    Chlada Fakya (Fruit Medley), *1:* 8
    Cucumber & Yogurt Soup, *1:* 9
    Etzai (Mint Tea), *1:* 4
    Fresh Sweet Dates, *1:* 4
    M'hajeb, *1:* 8
    Saffron and Raisin Couscous, *1:* 3
    Sahlab, *1:* 5
    Smen Butter, *1:* 3
    Stuffed Dates and Walnuts, *1:* 6
    Sweet Couscous Dessert, *1:* 6
Algerian Cooked Carrot Salad (Algeria), *1:* 7
Almond Cookies (China), *1:* 125
Almond Kisses (Hungary), *2:* 54
"Almost" Ting (Jamaica), *2:* 154
Aloko (Fried Bananas, Côte d'Ivoire), *1:* 128
Ambrosia (Brazil), *1:* 46
Amish and Pennsylvania Dutch (United States), *4:* 79
    Apple Butter, *4:* 87
    Baked Apples, *4:* 85
    Cream of Cabbage Soup, *4:* 81
    Old-Fashioned Spicy Lemonade, *4:* 84
    Peanut Butter Molasses Spread, *4:* 86
    Pork Chops with Sauerkraut, *4:* 80
    Shoofly Pie, *4:* 82
    Snow Ice Cream, *4:* 83
    Spicy Oven-Fried Chicken, *4:* 83
    Strawberry Jam, *4:* 86
    Sugar Cookies, *4:* 85
    Whoopie Pie, *4:* 87
Amlou (Almond Butter, Morocco), *3:* 10
Angu de Milho (Cornmeal Dish, Afro-Brazilians, Brazil), *1:* 60
Ansalaato (Salad, Somalia), *3:* 144

ANZAC Biscuits (Australia), *1:* 26
Apfelpfannkuchen (Pancakes, Germany), *1:* 218
Apfelschörle (Germany), *1:* 215
Appetizers
    Bajiya (Black Eyed Pea Fritter, Somalia), *3:* 141
    Baked Papas (Potato Skins, Peru), *3:* 51
    Buffalo Chicken Wings (Great Lakes Region, United States), *4:* 96
    Cheese and Vegetable Tray (Iran), *2:* 90
    Deviled Eggs (Midwest Region, United States), *4:* 127
    Eggplant Appetizer (Israel), *2:* 134
    French-Canadian Creton (Pate, French Canadians, Canada), *1:* 96
    Fromage (Cheese Board, France), *1:* 207
    Gebna Makleyah (Egypt), *1:* 175
    Hummus (Egypt), *1:* 173
    Hummus (Great Lakes Region, United States), *4:* 95
    Hummus (Saudi Arabia), *3:* 120
    Hummus be Tahini (Lebanon), *2:* 202
    Hungarian Cold Plate (Hungary), *2:* 50
    Jansson's Frestelse (Sweden), *3:* 193
    Kutya (Sweet Porridge, Ukraine), *4:* 33
    Lab (Ethiopian Cheese, Ethiopia), *1:* 190
    Marinated Artichokes (Western Region, United States), *4:* 178
    Pepinos Rellenos (Guatemala), *2:* 29
    Poa Pee (Thai Egg Rolls, Thailand), *4:* 6
    Quesadillas (Latino Americans, United States), *4:* 122
    Quesadillas (Mexico), *2:* 222
    Spring Rolls (Vietnam), *4:* 196
    Stuffed Eggs (Poland), *3:* 88
    Tabbouleh (Bulgur Wheat Salad, Saudi Arabia), *3:* 120
    Tabbouleh (Lebanon), *2:* 196
    Tapa: Aceitunas Aliñadas (Spain), *3:* 185
    Tapa: Crema de Cabrales (Spain), *3:* 184
    Tapa: Tartaletas de Champiñón (Spain), *3:* 185
Apple and Carrot Tsimmes (Jewish Americans, United States), *4:* 105
Apple Butter (Amish and Pennsylvania Dutch, United States), *4:* 87
Apple Cake (Ireland), *2:* 114
Apple Chutney (Pakistan), *3:* 45

Index

Apple Crisp (Western Region, United States), *4:* 180
Apple Sauerkraut (Great Lakes Region, United States), *4:* 95
Arachid Sauce (Côte d'Ivoire), *1:* 135
Argentina, *1:* **13**
    Alfajores de Maizena (Cookies), *1:* 20
    Bocaditos (Finger Sandwiches), *1:* 18
    Carbonada Criolla (Stew), *1:* 15
    Chimichurri (Dipping Sauce), *1:* 16
    Dulce de Leche (Milk Jam), *1:* 21
    Empanadas (Little Meat Pies), *1:* 16
    Fruit Salad with Frozen Yogurt, *1:* 18
    Milanesa, *1:* 19
    Ñoquis, *1:* 14
    Submarino, *1:* 20
Arni Souvlakia (Lamb Skewers, Greece), *2:* 15
Arroz Blanco (White Rice, Mexico), *2:* 225
Arroz con Leche (Rice and Milk, Peru), *3:* 54
Arroz con Leche (Rice Pudding, Chile), *1:* 112
Arroz con Leche (Rice Pudding, Cuba), *1:* 143
Arroz Doce (Rice Pudding, Portugal), *3:* 95
Arroz Guatemalteco (Rice, Guatemala), *2:* 26
Artsoppa (Pea Soup, Sweden), *3:* 200
Ash-e Jo (Barley Stew, Iran), *2:* 91
Aterkek Alecha (Vegetable Stew, Ethiopia), *1:* 196
Australia, *1:* **23**
    Aborigines and Bush Tucker (Australia), *1:* **35**
    ANZAC Biscuits, *1:* 26
    Australian Meat Pie, *1:* 27
    Billy Tea (Aborigines and Bush Tucker), *1:* 38
    Bush Tomato Relish (Aborigines and Bush Tucker), *1:* 40
    Carrot, Apple, and Raisin Salad, *1:* 26
    Chocolate Crackles, *1:* 31
    Christmas Shortbread, *1:* 29
    Damper (Aboriginal Style, Aborigines and Bush Tucker), *1:* 36
    Damper (European Style, Aborigines and Bush Tucker), *1:* 36
    Lamingtons, *1:* 28
    Macadamia and Fruit Snack (Aborigines and Bush Tucker), *1:*37
    Macadamia Nut Cookies (Aborigines and Bush Tucker), *1:* 37
    Macadamia Nut Dukkah, *1:* 24
    Pavlova, *1:* 30
    Pikelets, *1:* 27
    Plum Ice Cream (Aborigines and Bush Tucker), *1:* 39
    Quick No-Cook Mini-Pavlova, *1:* 30
    Toast with Vegemite, *1:* 32
Australian Meat Pie (Australia), *1:* 27
Avgolemono (Soup, Greece), *2:* 14
Avocado with Dressing (Côte d'Ivoire), *1:* 135
Avocado with Peanut Dressing (Ghana), *2:* 9

B

Baasto (Somalia), *3:* 138
Baat Bo Fon (Rice Pudding, China), *1:* 120
Babka (Poland), *3:* 86
Badam Pistaz Barfi (Nut Candy, Islands of the Pacific), *2:* 123
Baguette (French Bread, France), *1:* 202
Baguette Sandwich (France), *1:* 203
Baharat (Spice Blend, Saudi Arabia), *3:* 114
Baigan Bhartha (India), *2:* 58
Baingan Ka Raita (Pakistan), *3:* 42
Bajiya (Black Eyed Pea Fritter, Somalia), *3:* 141
Baked Apples (Amish and Pennsylvania Dutch, United States), *4:* 85
Baked Kibbeh (Lebanon), *2:* 198
Baked Macaroni and Cheese (African Americans, United States), *4:* 72
Baked Mushrooms with Cheese (Slovenia), *3:* 129
Baked Papas (Potato Skins, Peru), *3:* 51
Baked Papaya Dessert (Islands of the Pacific), *2:* 126
Baked Ripe Banana (Jamaica), *2:* 156
Baked Yams (Côte d'Ivoire), *1:* 132
Bamia (Sweet and Sour Okra, Egypt), *1:* 174
Banadura Salata B'Kizbara (Algeria), *1:* 5
Banana and Pineapple Salad (Cameroon), *1:* 70
Banana Frita (Fried Bananas, Brazil), *1:* 50
Banana with Coconut Milk (Thailand), *4:* 8
Bananas and Sweet Potatoes (Islands of the Pacific), *2:* 122
Banann Peze (Fried Plantains, Haiti), *2:* 38
Banh Chuoi Nuong (Cake, Vietnam), *4:* 192
Banh Mi Tom Chien (Vietnam), *4:* 197
Bannock (Aboriginals, Canada), *1:* 90
Bannock on a Stick (Aboriginals, Canada), *1:* 90

Index

Barbeque Sauce (Southern Region, United States), *4:* 171
Barley Pudding (Scotland, United Kingdom), *4:* 63
Barm Brack (Ireland), *2:* 112
Barriga de freira ("Nun's Belly," Portugal), *3:* 92
Barros Jarpa (Chile), *1:* 113
Basic Rice (Afro-Brazilians, Brazil), *1:* 57
Basturma (Kazakhstan), *2:* 176
Baursaki (Fried Doughnuts, Kazakhstan), *2:* 178
Bean Soup (Slovenia), *3:* 133
Beef Sukiyaki (Japan), *2:* 165
Beef with Fruit (Iraq), *2:* 94
Beetroot Salad (Turkey), *4:* 21
Belila (Egypt), *1:* 173
Berbere (Spice Paste, Ethiopia), *1:* 192

Beverages
  "Almost" Ting (Jamaica), *2:* 154
  Apfelschörle (Germany), *1:* 215
  Billy Tea (Aborigines and Bush Tucker, Australia), *1:* 38
  Café de Olla (Spiced Coffee, Mexico), *2:* 218
  Caphe (Vietnamese Coffee, Vietnam), *4:* 195
  Chai (Indian Tea, India), *2:* 62
  Chai (Tea, Tanzania), *3:* 207
  Chai Po-Russki (Tea, Russia), *3:* 110
  Chocolate a la Española (Spain), *3:* 179
  Chocolate Mexicana (Mexico), *2:* 225
  Coconut Milk (Islands of the Pacific), *2:* 120
  Coconut Milk (Philippines), *3:* 65
  Coffee Milkshake (Northeast Region, United States), *4:* 153
  Cola de Mono (Eggnog, Chile), *1:* 110
  Crème de Vie (Cuban Eggnog, Cuba), *1:* 144
  Dugh (Sparkling Yogurt Drink, Iran), *2:* 87
  Es Pokat (Avocado Drink, Indonesia), *2:* 74
  Ethiopian Spice Tea (Ethiopia), *1:* 196
  Etzai (Mint Tea, Algeria), *1:* 4
  Frozen Orange Delight (Peru), *3:* 56
  Ginger Beer (Liberia), *2:* 208
  Glühwein (Non-alcoholic Drink, Germany), *1:* 214
  Green Tea (Japan), *2:* 170
  Horchata (El Salvador), *1:* 185
  Hot Christmas Punch (Guatemala), *2:* 28
  Hot Cranberry Punch (Northeast Region, United States), *4:* 155
  'Irea (Cinnamon Beverage, Egypt), *1:* 176
  Iroquois Strawberry Drink (Native Americans, United States), *4:* 142
  Jamaican Fruit Drink (Jamaica), *2:* 154
  Jasmine Bubble Tea (China), *1:* 116
  Jengibre (Ginger Tea, Dominican Republic), *1:* 166
  Kahweh (Arabic Coffee, Lebanon), *2:* 199
  Kelapa Susu (Coconut Milk, Indonesia), *2:* 71
  Laban Drink (Yogurt Drink, Saudi Arabia), *3:* 117
  Lassi (Yogurt Drink, Pakistan), *3:* 42
  Lemon Grass Tea (Liberia), *2:* 211
  Limoonada (Lemonade, Lebanon), *2:* 202
  Mango Juice (Haiti), *2:* 35
  Mango-Orange Drink (Tanzania), *3:* 209
  Milk Tea (Portugal), *3:* 99
  Molasses Water (African Americans, United States), *4:* 68
  Morir Soñando (Dominican Republic), *1:* 167
  Moroccan Mint Tea (Morocco), *3:* 4
  Naneli Limonata (Lemonade, Turkey), *4:* 20
  Old-Fashioned Spicy Lemonade (Amish and Pennsylvania Dutch, United States), *4:* 84
  Pineapple Nog (Haiti), *2:* 36
  Pineapple-Orange Drink (Brazil), *1:* 48
  Pineapple Sherbet (Smoothie, South Africa), *3:* 157
  Pinole (Cornmeal Drink, Native Americans, United States), *4:* 144
  Ponche (Berry Punch, Chile), *1:* 112
  Qahwa (Arabic Coffee, Saudi Arabia), *3:* 122
  Rock Shandy (Zimbabwe), *4:* 204
  Sbiten (Winter Beverage, Russia), *3:* 107
  Shaah Hawaash (Spiced Tea, Somalia), *3:* 143
  Shai (Mint Tea, Egypt), *1:* 171
  Soda Chanh (Lemon Soda, Vietnam), *4:* 195
  Soo Chunkwa (Ginger Drink, South Korea), *3:* 163
  Spiced Cocoa (Haiti), *2:* 35
  Submarino (Argentina), *1:* 20
  Svart Vinbärsglögg (Sweden), *3:* 197
  Sweet Tea (Southern Region, United States), *4:* 168
  Té con Leche (Tea with Milk, Chile), *1:* 108
  Tea with Milk (United Kingdom), *4:* 51
  Teh Halia (Hot Ginger Tea, Indonesia), *2:* 78

Tropical Fruit Shake (Islands of the Pacific), *2:* 124
Tsokolate (Hot Chocolate, Philippines), *3:* 70
Wassail (United Kingdom), *4:* 48
Bigos (Polish Hunter's Stew, Poland), *3:* 78
Billy Tea (Aborigines and Bush Tucker, Australia), *1:* 38
Biltong and Dried Fruit Snack (South Africa), *3:* 152
Birria (Mexico), *2:* 221
Birthday Noodles with Sauce (China), *1:* 122
Biscotti (Italy), *2:* 146
Bisteeya (Morocco), *3:* 6
Blandad Fruktsoppa (Soup, Sweden), *3:* 194
Blintzes (Israel), *2:* 130
Bliny (Russian Pancakes, Russia), *3:* 102
Bliny Filling (Russia), *3:* 102
Blueberry Muffins (Western Region, United States), *4:* 181
Bobotie (South Africa), *3:* 154
Bocadillo (Morocco), *3:* 10
Bocaditos (Finger Sandwiches, Argentina), *1:* 18
Boerewors (South Africa), *3:* 158
Boiled Cassava (Cameroon), *1:* 70
Boiled Fruitcake (United Kingdom), *4:* 49
Bolinho de Chuva (Brazil), *1:* 52
Bolo Polana (Mozambique), *3:* 21
Bolo Rei (King's Cake, Portugal), *3:* 98
Borscht (Beet Soup, Jewish Americans, United States), *4:* 110
Borscht (Beet Soup, Russia), *3:* 108
Boston Baked Beans (Northeast Region, United States), *4:* 152
Boston Cream Pie (Northeast Region, United States), *4:* 156
Boxty (Potato Pancakes, Ireland), *2:* 115
Bratwurst (Sausage, Germany), *1:* 214

Brazil, *1:* 45
Acaçá (Rice Flour Pudding, Afro-Brazilians), *1:* 63
Afro-Brazilians, *1:* 55
Ambrosia, *1:* 46
Angu de Milho (Cornmeal Dish, Afro-Brazilians), *1:* 60
Banana Frita (Fried Bananas), *1:* 50
Basic Rice (Afro-Brazilians), *1:* 57
Bolinho de Chuva, *1:* 52

Brazilian Black Beans (Afro-Brazilians), *1:* 60
Carurú (Afro-Brazilians), *1:* 57
Cocada (Afro-Brazilians), *1:* 58
Corn Cake, *1:* 49
Empanadas (Little Baked Pies, Afro-Brazilians), *1:* 61
Feijoada (Meat Stew), *1:* 48
Moqueca (Spicy Fish Stew, Afro-Brazilians), *1:* 58
Moqueca aos Ovos (Egg Stew, Afro-Brazilians), *1:* 59
Olho de Sogra (Afro-Brazilians), *1:* 63
Orange Salad, *1:* 46
Pão de Queijo, *1:* 51
Pepper-Scented Rice, *1:* 49
Pineapple-Orange Drink, *1:* 48
Polenta (Fried Corn Mush), *1:* 47
Pudim (Thick Custard), *1:* 50
Quejadinhas, *1:* 51
Quiabo (Okra, Afro-Brazilians), *1:* 57
Quindins (Coconut Macaroons, Afro-Brazilians), *1:* 59
Brazilian Black Beans (Afro-Brazilians, Brazil), *1:* 60
Bread Pudding (Midwest Region, United States), *4:* 127

Breads
Aberdeen Buttery (Scotland, United Kingdom), *4:* 62
Babka (Poland), *3:* 86
Baguette (French Bread, France), *1:* 202
Bannock (Aboriginals, Canada), *1:* 90
Bannock on a Stick (Aboriginals, Canada), *1:* 90
Barm Brack (Ireland), *2:* 112
Blueberry Muffins (Western Region, United States), *4:* 181
Bruschetta (Garlic Bread, Italy), *2:* 147
Canjeero (Flatbread, Somalia), *3:* 141
Chapati (Fried Flatbread, Tanzania), *3:* 210
Cherry Muffins (Great Lakes Region, United States), *4:* 93
Chili Corn Bread (Latino Americans, United States), *4:* 122
Chinchin (Nigeria), *3:* 32
Corn Cake (Brazil), *1:* 49
Cornbread (Southern Region, United States), *4:* 162

Index

Breads (*continued*)
- Damper (Aboriginal Style, Aborigines and Bush Tucker, Australia), *1:* 36
- Damper (European Style, Aborigines and Bush Tucker, Australia), *1:* 36
- Date Nut Bread (Tanzania), *3:* 212
- Ensaymada (Philippines), *3:* 69
- Fatir (Flat Bread, Saudi Arabia), *3:* 115
- Gari Biscuits (Ghana), *2:* 6
- Hunza Bread (Hungary), *2:* 54
- Indian Fry-Bread (Native Americans, United States), *4:* 143
- Injera (Ethiopian Bread, Ethiopia), *1:* 193
- Irish Soda Bread (Ireland), *2:* 108
- Italian Easter Bread (Italy), *2:* 144
- Johnnycake (Jamaica), *2:* 157
- Kac-Kac (Sweet Bread, Somalia), *3:* 146
- Khachapuri (Cheesy Boats, Russia), *3:* 111
- Khubaz (Pita with Jelly, Iraq), *2:* 98
- Kimaje (Flat Bread, Saudi Arabia), *3:* 119
- Lambropsoma (Easter Bread, Greece), *2:* 16
- Lefse (Midwest Region, United States), *4:* 131
- Lussekatter (Saffron Buns, Sweden), *3:* 197
- Muufo Baraawe (Bread Rolls, Somalia), *3:* 144
- Naan (India), *2:* 65
- Nachynka (Cornbread Stuffing, Ukraine), *4:* 38
- Pain Haïtien (Haitian Bread, Haiti), *2:* 41
- Pan de Banano (Banana Bread, Guatemala), *2:* 30
- Pan de Maiz (Dominican Republic), *1:* 160
- Pan de Sal (Philippines), *3:* 68
- Panettone (Christmas Bread, Italy), *2:* 145
- Pao de Banana (Mozambique), *3:* 23
- Pão de Queijo (Brazil), *1:* 51
- Pãozinho (Portuguese Rolls, Mozambique), *3:* 15
- Paska (Easter Bread, Ukraine), *4:* 37
- Pita Bread (Lebanon), *2:* 195
- Potato Lefse (Great Lakes Region, United States), *4:* 96
- Potica (Slovenia), *3:* 132
- Pumpkin Bread (Native Americans, United States), *4:* 142
- Rågbröd (Swedish Rye Bread, Sweden), *3:* 201
- Rice Bread (Liberia), *2:* 208
- Rosca de Reyes (Sweet Bread, Mexico), *2:* 218
- Rye Bread (Germany), *1:* 217
- Scones (Ireland), *2:* 110
- Scones (United Kingdom), *4:* 46
- Simit (Sesame Rings, Turkey), *4:* 20
- Warqa (Morocco), *3:* 5
- Broiled Salmon (Japan), *2:* 168
- Broiled Salmon Steaks (Western Region, United States), *4:* 180
- Brown Stew Fish (Jamaica), *2:* 152
- Bruschetta (Garlic Bread, Italy), *2:* 147
- Bûche de Noël (Yule Log, France), *1:* 208
- Buffalo Chicken Wings (Great Lakes Region, United States), *4:* 96
- Buffalo Stew (Native Americans, United States), *4:* 140
- Bulgogi (Korean Beef, South Korea), *3:* 171
- Bulgur Pilavi (Pilaf, Turkey), *4:* 25
- Bunuelos (Fried Fritters, Guatemala), *2:* 28
- Bush Tomato Relish (Aborigines and Bush Tucker, Australia), *1:* 40
- Butter Mochi (Islands of the Pacific), *2:* 124
- Butter Tarts (French Canadians, Canada), *1:* 98

C

- Cabbage Borshch (Ukraine), *4:* 32
- Cabbage Pirozhki or Piroghi (Russia), *3:* 104
- Café de Olla (Spiced Coffee, Mexico), *2:* 218
- Cajeya de Almendra (Chile), *1:* 114
- Calalou (Vegetable Stew, Côte d'Ivoire), *1:* 134
- Caldo Verde (Kale Soup, Portugal), *3:* 97
- California-style Pizza (Western Region, United States), *4:* 182
- Calzone (Midwest Region, United States), *4:* 132
- Cambuulo (Somalia), *3:* 144
- **Cameroon,** *1:* **65**
  - Banana and Pineapple Salad, *1:* 70
  - Boiled Cassava, *1:* 70
  - Coconut Rice, *1:* 71
  - Easy Fufu, *1:* 68
  - Koki, *1:* 68
  - Ndolé (Bitterleaf Stew), *1:* 70
  - Safou a la Sauce Tomate, *1:* 67
  - Traditional Fufu, *1:* 68
- Camote (Sweet Potatoes, Mexico), *2:* 222
- **Canada,** *1:* **75**
  - **Aboriginals (Canada),** *1:* **85**

Bannock (Aboriginals, Canadian), *1:* 90
Bannock on a Stick (Aboriginals, Canadian), *1:* 90
Butter Tarts (French Canadians), *1:* 98
Canada Day Cake, *1:* 79
Canadian Bacon, *1:* 78
Cock-a-Leekie Soup, *1:* 80
Crêpes de la Chandeleur (French Canadians) , *1:* 100
Doughboys (Dumplings, French Canadians), *1:* 97
French-Canadian Creton (Pate, French Canadians)), *1:* 96
French-Canadian Pea Soup (French Canadians), *1:* 97
French Canadians, *1:* 95
Fish and Brewis, *1:* 82
Man-O-Min (Ojibwa Wild Rice, Aboriginals, Canadian), *1:* 92
Maple Sundae, *1:* 82
Maple Syrup Upside-Down Cake, *1:* 82
Nanaimo Bars, *1:* 81
Pemmican Cakes (Aboriginals, Canadian), *1:* 86
Pizza-ghetti (French Canadians), *1:* 100
Pudding au Chomeur (French Canadians), *1:* 99
Quebec Poutine (French Canadians), *1:* 103
Ragoût de Boulettes (French Canadians), *1:* 101
St. Catherine's Taffy (French Canadians), *1:* 102
Saskatoon Berry Snack (Aboriginals, Canadian), *1:* 87
Sautéed Fiddleheads, *1:* 77
Soapberry Ice Cream (Aboriginals, Canadian), *1:* 87
Squash Soup (Aboriginals, Canadian), *1:* 88
Sweet Corn Pancakes, *1:* 78
Tarte au Sucre (Sugar Pie, French Canadians), *1:* 99
Three Sisters Soup (Aboriginals, Canadian), *1:* 89
Tourtière (Meat Pie, French Canadians), *1:* 98
Wild Rice Cakes (Aboriginals, Canadian), *1:* 91
Yorkshire Pudding, *1:* 77
Canada Day Cake (Canada), *1:* 79
Canadian Bacon (Canada), *1:* 78
Canh Bi Ro Ham Dua (Vietnam), *4:* 192
Canjeero (Flatbread, Somalia), *3:* 141
Cannoli (Italy), *2:* 145
Caphe (Vietnamese Coffee, Vietnam), *4:* 195

Caramel Corn (Midwest Region, United States), *4:* 131
Carbonada Criolla (Stew, Argentina), *1:* 15
Carne Asada Fries (Western Region, United States), *4:* 183
Carrot, Apple, and Raisin Salad (Australia), *1:* 26
Carrot Bredie (South Africa), *3:* 153
Carurú (Afro-Brazilians, Brazil), *1:* 57
Casamiento (El Salvador), *1:* 182
Ceviche (Marinated Seafood, Peru), *3:* 57
Chai (Indian Tea, India), *2:* 62
Chai (Tea, Tanzania), *3:* 207
Chai Po-Russki (Tea, Russia), *3:* 110
Champ (Ireland), *2:* 109
Chancho en Piedra (Chile), *1:* 111
Chap Ch'ae (South Korea), *3:* 166
Chapati (Fried Flatbread, Tanzania), *3:* 210
Charoset (Jewish Americans, United States), *4:* 105
Charoseth (Israel), *2:* 131
Cheese and Vegetable Tray (Iran), *2:* 90
Cheesecake (Poland), *3:* 82
Cherry Muffins (Great Lakes Region, United States), *4:* 93
Chess Pie (Southern Region, United States), *4:* 161
Chicago Deep Dish Pizza (Great Lakes Region, United States), *4:* 98
Chicken and Sausage Gumbo (Southern Region, United States), *4:* 165
Chicken Biryani (Pakistan), *3:* 45
Chicken Karahi (Pakistan), *3:* 41
Chicken Satay (Thailand), *4:* 5
Chicken Tajine (Morocco), *3:* 2
Chicken Teriyaki (Japan), *2:* 164
Chickpea, Feta, and Olive Salad (Morocco), *3:* 8
Chile, *1:* 105
Arroz con Leche (Rice Pudding), *1:* 112
Barros Jarpa, *1:* 113
Cajeya de Almendra, *1:* 114
Chancho en Piedra, *1:* 111
Cola de Mono (Eggnog), *1:* 110
Ensalada Campesina, *1:* 106
Ensalada Chilena (Salad), *1:* 108
Pastel de Choclo, *1:* 107
Ponche (Berry Punch), *1:* 112
Té con Leche (Tea with Milk), *1:* 108

Index

Chile (*continued*)
   Tomaticán (Stew), *1:* 109
   Torta de Cumpleaños (Cake), *1:* 111
Chile Rellenos Casserole (Guatemala), *2:* 31
Chili Corn Bread (Latino Americans, United States), *4:* 122
Chilled Avocado Soup (Côte d'Ivoire), *1:* 134
Chimichurri (Dipping Sauce, Argentina), *1:* 16
China, *1:* 115
   Almond Cookies, *1:* 125
   Baat Bo Fon (Rice Pudding), *1:* 120
   Birthday Noodles with Sauce, *1:* 122
   Chinese Mooncakes, *1:* 121
   Egg Drop Soup, *1:* 117
   Fried Rice, *1:* 120
   Fried Wonton, *1:* 124
   Fu Yung Don (Egg Fu Yung), *1:* 123
   Jasmine Bubble Tea, *1:* 116
   Spiced Chicken, *1:* 126
   Sweet and Sour Pork, *1:* 119
   Wonton Soup, *1:* 119
Chinchin (Nigeria), *3:* 32
Chinese Mooncakes (China), *1:* 121
Chinese Peanut Sauce (Western Region, United States), *4:* 181
Chitlins (African Americans, United States), *4:* 69
Chlada Fakya (Fruit Medley, Algeria), *1:* 8
Ch'o Kanjang (Vinegar Soy Sauce, South Korea), *3:* 171
Choclo con Queso (Peru), *3:* 53
Chocolate a la Española (Spain), *3:* 179
Chocolate Crackles (Australia), *1:* 31
Chocolate-dipped Shortbread (Scotland, United Kingdom), *4:* 59
Chocolate Mexicana (Mexico), *2:* 225
Chopped Chicken Liver (Jewish Americans, United States), *4:* 103
Christmas Shortbread (Australia), *1:* 29
Chuck Wagon Brisket (Western Region, United States), *4:* 175
Churros (Spain), *3:* 182
Cocada (Afro-Brazilians, Brazil), *1:* 58
Cock-a-Leekie Soup (Canada), *1:* 80
Cock-a-Leekie Soup (Scotland, United Kingdom), *4:* 61
Coconut Bean Soup (Tanzania), *3:* 208

Coconut-Chicken Soup (Thailand), *4:* 10
Coconut Chips (Jamaica), *2:* 151
Coconut Custard (Vietnam), *4:* 191
Coconut Milk (Islands of the Pacific), *2:* 120
Coconut Milk (Philippines), *3:* 65
Coconut Pie (Liberia), *2:* 210
Coconut Pudding (Ghana), *2:* 10
Coconut Rice (Cameroon), *1:* 71
Coffee Milkshake (Northeast Region, United States), *4:* 153
Cola de Mono (Eggnog, Chile), *1:* 110
Colcannon (Ireland), *2:* 110
Collard Greens (African Americans, United States), *4:* 66
Collard Greens with Ham Hocks (Southern Region, United States), *4:* 168
Collards with Cabbage (Liberia), *2:* 211
Cookies
   Alfajores (Peru), *3:* 60
   Alfajores de Maizena (Cookies, Argentina), *1:* 20
   Almond Cookies (China), *1:* 125
   Almond Kisses (Hungary), *2:* 54
   ANZAC Biscuits (Australia), *1:* 26
   Biscotti (Italy), *2:* 146
   Butter Tarts (French Canadians, Canada), *1:* 98
   Chocolate Crackles (Australia), *1:* 31
   Chocolate-dipped Shortbread (Scotland, United Kingdom), *4:* 59
   Christmas Shortbread (Australia), *1:* 29
   Cornmeal Cookies (Côte d'Ivoire), *1:* 129
   Drommar (Swedish Cookies, Sweden), *3:* 198
   Flapjacks (Oatmeal Biscuits, Scotland, United Kingdom), *4:* 57
   Fortune Cookies (Western Region, United States), *4:* 177
   Hungarian Butter Cookies (Hungary), *2:* 49
   Ka'ak Cookies (Lebanon), *2:* 200
   Kichlach (Cookies, Israel), *2:* 136
   Kourabiethes (Butter Cookies, Greece), *2:* 18
   Lamingtons (Australia), *1:* 28
   Lebkuchen (Germany), *1:* 217
   Macadamia Nut Cookies (Aborigines and Bush Tucker, Australia), *1:* 38
   Mandelbrot (Almond Cookies, Israel), *2:* 136
   Mathis (Spicy Cookie, India), *2:* 65
   Mescouta (Date Cookies, Morocco), *3:* 8

Moravske Vano ni Kukyse (Czech Republic), *1:* 156
Nanaimo Bars (Canada), *1:* 81
Pepparkakor (Ginger Cookies, Sweden), *3:* 198
Quindins (Coconut Macaroons, Afro-Brazilians, Brazil), *1:* 59
St. Catherine's Taffy (French Canadians, Canada), *1:* 102
Slovenian Almond Bars (Slovenia), *3:* 130
Springerle (Christmas Cookies, Great Lakes Region, United States), *4:* 96
Strawberry Cookie Bars (Czech Republic), *1:* 151
Sugar Cookies (Amish and Pennsylvania Dutch, United States), *4:* 85
Sweet Potato Cookies (Zimbabwe), *4:* 205
Tea Biscuits (United Kingdom), *4:* 50
Corn Cake (Brazil), *1:* 49
Corn on the Cob (Midwest Region, United States), *4:* 128
Corn on the Cob (South Africa), *3:* 157
Corn Pudding (Haiti), *2:* 35
Cornbread (Southern Region, United States), *4:* 162
Corned Beef with Cabbage (Ireland), *2:* 109
Cornhusker's Casserole (Midwest Region, United States), *4:* 132
Cornish Pasties (United Kingdom), *4:* 45
Cornish Pasty (Great Lakes Region, United States), *4:* 98
Cornmeal Cake (Zimbabwe), *4:* 203
Cornmeal Cookies (Côte d'Ivoire), *1:* 129
Cornmeal Porridge (Haiti), *2:* 39
Côte d'Ivoire, *1:* 127
　Aloko (Fried Bananas), *1:* 128
　Arachid Sauce, *1:* 135
　Avocado with Dressing, *1:* 135
　Baked Yams, *1:* 132
　Calalou (Vegetable Stew), *1:* 134
　Chilled Avocado Soup, *1:* 134
　Cornmeal Cookies, *1:* 129
　Fufu, *1:* 130
　Kedjenou, *1:* 132
　Melon Fingers with Lime, *1:* 131
　Pineapple Salad, *1:* 129
　Sauce Pimente, *1:* 128
Couscous (Morocco), *3:* 8
Cozido (Beef Stew, Portugal), *3:* 94

Cranachan (Scotland, United Kingdom), *4:* 62
Cranberry Salsa (Western Region, United States), *4:* 178
Cream of Cabbage Soup (Amish and Pennsylvania Dutch, United States), *4:* 81
Creamy Dipping Sauce (Sweden), *3:* 191
Crème de Vie (Cuban Eggnog, Cuba), *1:* 144
Creole Seasoning (Southern Region, United States), *4:* 160
Crêpes de la Chandeleur (French Canadians, Canada), *1:* 100
Croque-Monsieur (Sandwich, France), *1:* 203
Cuba, *1:* 137
　Aceitunas Alinadas (Olives), *1:* 143
　Arroz con Leche (Rice Pudding), *1:* 143
　Crème de Vie (Cuban Eggnog), *1:* 144
　Cubano, *1:* 146
　Ensalada Cubana Tipica (Salad), *1:* 141
　Flan (Baked Custard), *1:* 140
　Fried Plantains, *1:* 140
　Helado de Mango (Sherbet), *1:* 142
　Moors and Christians, *1:* 139
　Pastelitos, *1:* 144
　Piña Asada, *1:* 143
　Tuna in Sauce, *1:* 139
　Yucca (Cassava), *1:* 141
Cuban Avocado Salad (Latino Americans, United States), *4:* 122
Cuban Beans and Rice (Latino Americans, United States), *4:* 117
Cubano (Cuba), *1:* 146
Cucumber & Yogurt Soup (Algeria), *1:* 9
Cucumber Salad (Thailand), *4:* 7
Cucumber Sandwiches (United Kingdom), *4:* 44
Cucumber Soup (Guatemala), *2:* 27
Cucumber with Yogurt (Lebanon), *2:* 196
Cullen Skink (Scotland, United Kingdom), *4:* 60
Curried Okra (Nigeria), *3:* 32
Curry Chicken (Jamaica), *2:* 155
Czech Republic, *1:* 149
　Fazolovy Gulás, *1:* 154
　Houbova Polevka Myslivecka, *1:* 151
　Knedlíky (Czech Dumplings), *1:* 152
　Kure Na Paprice, *1:* 155
　Mala Sousta Se Syre, *1:* 157
　Moravske Vano ni Kukyse, *1:* 156

Index

Czech Republic (*continued*)
  Sour Cream Cucumber Salad, *1:* 151
  Strawberry Cookie Bars, *1:* 151
  Topinky S Vejci (Eggs on Toast), *1:* 152

D

Dabo Kolo (Little Fried Snacks, Ethiopia), *1:* 194
Dal (Lentils, India), *2:* 61
Damper (Aboriginal Style, Aborigines and Bush Tucker, Australia), *1:* 36
Damper (European Style, Aborigines and Bush Tucker, Australia), *1:* 36
Dandelion Salad (Slovenia), *3:* 132
Date Nut Bread (Tanzania), *3:* 212
Deep-Fried Potatoes (Slovenia), *3:* 129
Desser Miveh (Fruit Salad, Iran), *2:* 89
Desserts
  Acaçá (Rice Flour Pudding, Afro-Brazilians, Brazil), *1:* 63
  Akara (Fritters, Ghana), *2:* 8
  Ambrosia (Brazil), *1:* 46
  Apple Cake (Ireland), *2:* 114
  Apple Crisp (Western Region, United States), *4:* 180
  Arroz con Leche (Rice and Milk, Peru), *3:* 54
  Arroz con Leche (Rice Pudding, Chile), *1:* 112
  Arroz con Leche (Rice Pudding, Cuba), *1:* 143
  Arroz Doce (Rice Pudding, Portugal), *3:* 95
  Baat Bo Fon (Rice Pudding, China), *1:* 120
  Babka (Poland), *3:* 86
  Badam Pistaz Barfi (Nut Candy, Islands of the Pacific), *2:* 123
  Baked Apples (Amish and Pennsylvania Dutch, United States), *4:* 85
  Baked Papaya Dessert (Islands of the Pacific), *2:* 126
  Banana with Coconut Milk (Thailand), *4:* 8
  Banh Chuoi Nuong (Cake, Vietnam), *4:* 192
  Barley Pudding (Scotland, United Kingdom), *4:* 63
  Barriga de freira ("Nun's Belly," Portugal), *3:* 92
  Baursaki (Fried Doughnuts, Kazakhstan), *2:* 178
  Belila (Egypt), *1:* 173
  Blintzes (Israel), *2:* 130
  Boiled Fruitcake (United Kingdom), *4:* 49
  Bolinho de Chuva (Brazil), *1:* 52
  Bolo Polana (Mozambique), *3:* 21
  Bolo Rei (King's Cake, Portugal), *3:* 98
  Boston Cream Pie (Northeast Region, United States), *4:* 156
  Bread Pudding (Midwest Region, United States), *4:* 127
  Bûche de Noël (Yule Log, France), *1:* 208
  Bunuelos (Fried Fritters, Guatemala), *2:* 28
  Butter Mochi (Islands of the Pacific), *2:* 124
  Cajeya de Almendra (Chile), *1:* 114
  Canada Day Cake (Canada), *1:* 79
  Cannoli (Italy), *2:* 145
  Charoset (Jewish Americans, United States), *4:* 105
  Cheesecake (Poland), *3:* 82
  Chess Pie (Southern Region, United States), *4:* 161
  Chinchin (Nigeria), *3:* 32
  Chinese Mooncakes (China), *1:* 121
  Chlada Fakya (Fruit Medley, Algeria), *1:* 8
  Churros (Spain), *3:* 182
  Cocada (Afro-Brazilians, Brazil), *1:* 58
  Coconut Custard (Vietnam), *4:* 191
  Coconut Pie (Liberia), *2:* 210
  Coconut Pudding (Ghana), *2:* 10
  Corn Pudding (Haiti), *2:* 35
  Cranachan (Scotland, United Kingdom), *4:* 62
  Doughnuts Awwamaat (Lebanon), *2:* 203
  Dried Fruit Compote (Poland), *3:* 85
  Dulce de Leche (Milk Jam, Argentina), *1:* 21
  Easy Lebanese Baklava (Lebanon), *2:* 199
  Eis und Heiss (Germany), *1:* 215
  Ensaymada (Philippines), *3:* 69
  Filhos de Natal (Mozambique), *3:* 19
  Firifiri (Sugared Doughnuts, Islands of the Pacific), *2:* 125
  Flan (Baked Custard, Cuba), *1:* 140
  Flan (Custard, Spain), *3:* 182
  Flan (Peru), *3:* 58
  Fresh Sweet Dates (Algeria), *1:* 4
  Fried Apples (African Americans, United States), *4:* 74
  Fruit Medley (Native Americans, United States), *4:* 144

Index

Fruit Salad with Frozen Yogurt (Argentina), *1:* 18
Gibanica (Slovenia), *3:* 134
Gizzada (Jamaica), *2:* 157
Gooseberry Crumble (Ireland), *2:* 111
Groundnut Toffee (Ghana), *2:* 5
G'shur Purtaghal (Iraq), *2:* 101
Guavas in Syrup (Dominican Republic), *1:* 162
Habichuelas con Dulce (Dominican Republic), *1:* 166
Halva (Turkey), *4:* 23
Helado de Mango (Sherbet, Cuba), *1:* 142
Honey-Baked Apples (Northeast Region, United States), *4:* 155
Indian Pudding (Northeast Region, United States), *4:* 149
Individual Mincemeat Pies (United Kingdom), *4:* 47
Irish Christmas Cake (Ireland), *2:* 113
Jalalo (Dominican Republic), *1:* 167
Jamaican Christmas Cake (Jamaica), *2:* 154
Kaymakli Kuru Kayisi (Turkey), *4:* 17
Kheer (Rice Pudding, Pakistan), *3:* 42
Kheer (Sweet Rice Pudding, India), *2:* 59
Khoshaf (Egypt), *1:* 176
Klyukva S Sakharom (Russia), *3:* 112
Kuping Gajah (Elephant Ears, Indonesia), *2:* 79
Kwanzaa Brownies (African Americans, United States), *4:* 73
La Galette des Rois (Cake, France), *1:* 210
Lebanese Rice Pudding (Lebanon), *2:* 195
Leche Flan (Caramel Custard, Philippines), *3:* 66
Leche Frita (Spain), *3:* 186
Leche Poleada (El Salvador), *1:* 186
Locum (Turkish Candy, Turkey), *4:* 24
Lokma (Golden Fritters, Turkey), *4:* 26
Ma'mounia (Wheat Pudding, Iraq), *2:* 97
Maja Blanco (Coconut Cake, Philippines), *3:* 66
Makiwnyk (Poppy Seed Cake, Ukraine), *4:* 36
Malasadas (Doughnuts, Mozambique), *3:* 17
Malva Pudding (South Africa), *3:* 150
Maná (Peru), *3:* 56
Maple Sundae (Canada), *1:* 82
Maple Syrup Upside-Down Cake (Canada), *1:* 82
Mapopo (Papaya) Candy (Zimbabwe), *4:* 200
Mardi Gras King Cake (Southern Region, United States), *4:* 166
Matzo Brie (Jewish Americans, United States), *4:* 106
Mazapanes (Almond Candies, Spain), *3:* 181
Melon Fingers with Lime (Côte d'Ivoire), *1:* 131
Melopitta (Honey Pie, Greece), *2:* 17
Mexican Fried Ice Cream (Latino Americans, United States), *4:* 119
Mhalbi (Morocco), *3:* 9
Mousse au Chocolat (France), *1:* 207
Muhallabi (Rice Pudding, Turkey), *4:* 18
Muhallabia (Pudding, Saudi Arabia), *3:* 123
New Year's Honey Cake (Israel), *2:* 134
New York Cheesecake (Jewish Americans, United States), *4:* 108
Noodle Pudding (Hungary), *2:* 52
Nutella-filled Crepes (France), *1:* 206
Old Fashioned Bread Pudding (Southern Region, United States), *4:* 170
Olho de Sogra (Afro-Brazilians, Brazil), *1:* 63
Paleta de Coco (Dominican Republic), *1:* 161
Pashka (Russia), *3:* 106
Pasteis de nata (Custard Tarts, Portugal), *3:* 94
Patbingsu (Korean Shaved Ice, South Korea), *3:* 172
Pavlova (Australia), *1:* 30
Picarones (Pumpkin Fritters, Peru), *3:* 50
Pineapple with Honey & Coconut (Tanzania), *3:* 214
Pisang Goreng (Banana Cakes, Indonesia), *2:* 75
Pitepalt (Potato Pastries, Sweden), *3:* 195
Plum Ice Cream (Aborigines and Bush Tucker, Australia), *1:* 39
Polvoron (Milk Candy, Philippines), *3:* 73
Potica (Slovenia), *3:* 132
Pralines (Southern Region, United States), *4:* 170
Prince William's Groom's Cake (United Kingdom), *4:* 48
Pudding au Chomeur (French Canadians, Canada), *1:* 99
Pudim (Thick Custard, Brazil), *1:* 50
Puto Maya (Rice Cake, Philippines), *3:* 74
Qatayef (Iraq), *2:* 102
Quick No-Cook Mini-Pavlova (Australia), *1:* 30
Rosh Hashanah Honey Cake (Jewish Americans, United States), *4:* 110
Sahlab (Algeria), *1:* 5

Index

Desserts (*continued*)
    Sang Ka Ya (Coconut Custard, Thailand), *4:* 9
    Sarikayo Telor (Pudding, Indonesia), *2:* 73
    Sesame Candy (Israel), *2:* 130
    Shahi Tukra (Pakistan), *3:* 39
    Sharlotka (Apple Cake, Russia), *3:* 110
    Sheer Korma (Dates with Milk, Pakistan), *3:* 46
    Shir-Berenj (Rice Pudding, Iran), *2:* 87
    Shoofly Pie (Amish and Pennsylvania Dutch, United States), *4:* 82
    Shuku Shuku (Coconut Balls, Nigeria), *3:* 33
    Snow Ice Cream (Amish and Pennsylvania Dutch, United States), *4:* 83
    Soapberry Ice Cream (Aboriginals, Canada), *1:* 87
    "String of Doughnuts" (Morocco), *3:* 9
    Stuffed Dates and Walnuts (Algeria), *1:* 6
    Sugared Almonds (Lebanon), *2:* 200
    Sweet Couscous Dessert (Algeria), *1:* 6
    Sweet Peanut Mochi (Japan), *2:* 170
    Sweet Potato Pie (African Americans, United States), *4:* 68
    Sweet Potato Pie (Southern Region, United States), *4:* 164
    Sweet Potato Pudding (Tanzania), *3:* 213
    Tarte au Sucre (Sugar Pie, French Canadians, Canada), *1:* 99
    Torta de Cumpleaños (Cake, Chile), *1:* 111
    Tropical Fruit Dessert (Islands of the Pacific), *2:* 124
    Uli Petataws (Potato Fritters, Indonesia), *2:* 73
    Whoopie Pie (Amish and Pennsylvania Dutch, United States), *4:* 87
Deviled Eggs (Midwest Region, United States), *4:* 127
Dhal (Lentil Stew, Pakistan), *3:* 40
Dilly Beans (Southern Region, United States), *4:* 162
Dodo (Fried Plantains, Nigeria), *3:* 31
Dolma (Stuffed Grape Leaves, Iran), *2:* 84
Dominican Republic, *1:* 159
    Guavas in Syrup, *1:* 162
    Habichuelas con Dulce, *1:* 166
    Jalalo, *1:* 167
    Jengibre (Ginger Tea), *1:* 166
    Mangú, *1:* 161
    Morir Soñando, *1:* 167

    Paleta de Coco, *1:* 161
    Pan de Maiz, *1:* 160
    Rainbow Rice, *1:* 164
    Sancocho, *1:* 164
    Tostones, *1:* 166
Dotorimuk (Acorn Curd, South Korea), *3:* 167
Doughboys (Dumplings, French Canadians, Canada), *1:* 97
Doughnuts Awwamaat (Lebanon), *2:* 203
Dovi (Peanut Butter Stew, Zimbabwe), *4:* 201
Dried Fruit Compote (Poland), *3:* 85
Drommar (Swedish Cookies, Sweden), *3:* 198
Dublin Coddle (Ireland), *2:* 114
Dugh (Sparkling Yogurt Drink, Iran), *2:* 87
Dulce de Leche (Milk Jam, Argentina), *1:* 21
Dutch Pancakes (Great Lakes Region, United States), *4:* 91

E

Easy Fufu (Cameroon), *1:* 68
Easy Lebanese Baklava (Lebanon), *2:* 199
Efo (Greens Stew, Nigeria), *3:* 31
Egg Drop Soup (China), *1:* 117
Eggplant Appetizer (Israel), *2:* 134
Egypt, *1:* 169
    Bamia (Sweet and Sour Okra), *1:* 174
    Belila, *1:* 173
    Ful Mudammas, *1:* 170
    Gebna Makleyah, *1:* 175
    Hummus, *1:* 173
    'Irea (Cinnamon Beverage), *1:* 176
    Khoshaf, *1:* 176
    Koushari, *1:* 172
    Lemon and Garlic Potato Salad, *1:* 174
    Lettuce Salad, *1:* 176
    Shai (Mint Tea), *1:* 171
    Spinach with Garlic, *1:* 177
Eis und Heiss (Germany), *1:* 215
El Salvador, *1:* 179
    Casamiento, *1:* 182
    Fried Plantains, *1:* 180
    Fried Yucca with Curtido, *1:* 185
    Horchata, *1:* 185
    Leche Poleada, *1:* 186

Pupusas, *1:* 181
Riguas, *1:* 182
Empanadas (Little Baked Pies, Afro-Brazilians, Brazil), *1:* 61
Empanadas (Little Meat Pies, Argentina), *1:* 16
Ensalada Campesina (Chile), *1:* 106
Ensalada Chilena (Salad, Chile), *1:* 108
Ensalada Cubana Tipica (Salad, Cuba), *1:* 141
Ensalada de Pallares (Salad, Peru), *3:* 55
Ensaymada (Philippines), *3:* 69
Es Pokat (Avocado Drink, Indonesia), *2:* 74
Ethiopia, *1:* 189
Aterkek Alecha (Stew), *1:* 196
Berbere (Spice Paste), *1:* 192
Dabo Kolo (Little Fried Snacks), *1:* 194
Ethiopian Spice Tea, *1:* 196
Gomen Wat (Ethiopian Greens), *1:* 197
Injera (Ethiopian Bread), *1:* 193
Kategna, *1:* 190
Kitfo (Spiced Raw Beef), *1:* 194
Lab (Ethiopian Cheese), *1:* 190
Niter Kebbeh or Kibe, *1:* 192
Ethiopian Spice Tea (Ethiopia), *1:* 196
Etzai (Mint Tea, Algeria), *1:* 4

F

Falafel (Israel), *2:* 133
Fancy Rice (India), *2:* 63
Fatir (Flat Bread, Saudi Arabia), *3:* 115
Fatoosh (Lebanon), *2:* 203
Fava Bean Spread (Israel), *2:* 129
Fazolovy Gulás (Czech Republic), *1:* 154
Feijoada (Meat Stew, Brazil), *1:* 48
Fettucine Alfredo (Italy), *2:* 142
Filhos de Natal (Mozambique), *3:* 19
Firifiri (Sugared Doughnuts, Islands of the Pacific), *2:* 125
Fish and Brewis (Canada), *1:* 82
Fish and Chips (United Kingdom), *4:* 51
Fish Boil (Great Lakes Region, United States), *4:* 91
Flan (Baked Custard, Cuba), *1:* 140
Flan (Custard, Spain), *3:* 182
Flan (Peru), *3:* 58
Flapjacks (Oatmeal Biscuits, Scotland, United Kingdom), *4:* 57
Fortune Cookies (Western Region, United States), *4:* 177
France, *1:* 201
Baguette (French Bread), *1:* 202
Baguette Sandwich, *1:* 203
Bûche de Noël (Yule Log), *1:* 208
Croque-Monsieur (Sandwich), *1:* 203
Fromage (Cheese Board), *1:* 207
La Galette des Rois (Cake), *1:* 210
Mousse au Chocolat, *1:* 207
Nutella-filled Crepes, *1:* 206
Quiche au Saumon et Crevettes, *1:* 206
Soupe à l'Oignon Gratinée, *1:* 204
Steak Frites, *1:* 208
Frango a Cafrial (Mozambique), *3:* 23
French-Canadian Creton (Pate, French Canadians, Canada), *1:* 96
French-Canadian Pea Soup (French Canadians, Canada), *1:* 97
French Canadians, *1:* 95
Butter Tarts, *1:* 98
Crêpes de la Chandeleur, *1:* 100
Doughboys (Dumplings), *1:* 97
French-Canadian Creton (Pate), *1:* 96
French-Canadian Pea Soup, *1:* 97
Pizza-ghetti, *1:* 100
Pudding au Chomeur, *1:* 99
Quebec Poutine, *1:* 103
Ragoût de Boulettes, *1:* 101
St. Catherine's Taffy, *1:* 102
Tarte au Sucre (Sugar Pie), *1:* 99
Tourtière (Meat Pie), *1:* 98
French-Style Lettuce Salad (Haiti), *2:* 34
Fresh Grated Coconut (Islands of the Pacific), *2:* 119
Fresh Oranges (Israel), *2:* 129
Fresh Sweet Dates (Algeria), *1:* 4
Fried Apples (African Americans, United States), *4:* 74
Fried Baby Carrots (Morocco), *3:* 12
Fried Bologna (African Americans, United States), *4:* 74
Fried Plantains (Cuba), *1:* 140
Fried Plantains (El Salvador), *1:* 180

Index

Fried Plantains (Latino Americans, United States), *4:* 118
Fried Rice (China), *1:* 120
Fried Wonton (China), *1:* 124
Fried Yucca with Curtido (El Salvador), *1:* 185
Frijoles (Beans, Mexico), *2:* 217
Frijoles Negros Volteados (Guatemala), *2:* 26
Frijoles Refritos (Refried Beans, Mexico), *2:* 217
Frittata (Italy), *2:* 143
Fromage (Cheese Board, France), *1:* 207
Frouta Ke Yaourti (Fruit Salad, Greece), *2:* 17
Frozen Orange Delight (Peru), *3:* 56
Frtalja (Slovenia), *3:* 128
Fruit Medley (Native Americans, United States), *4:* 144
Fruit Salad (Philippines), *3:* 72
Fruit Salad (Saudi Arabia), *3:* 122
Fruit Salad with Frozen Yogurt (Argentina), *1:* 18
Fu Yung Don (Egg Fu Yung, China), *1:* 123
Fufu (Côte d'Ivoire), *1:* 130
Fufu (Ghana), *2:* 4
Ful Mudammas (Egypt), *1:* 170

G

Gado-Gado (Vegetable Salad, Indonesia), *2:* 77
Garam Masala (Spice Mixture, India), *2:* 59
Gari Biscuits (Ghana), *2:* 6
Gazpacho (Cold Tomato Soup, Spain), *3:* 177
Gazpacho (Latino Americans, United States), *4:* 119
Gebna Makleyah (Egypt), *1:* 175
Geel Rys (Yellow Rice, South Africa), *3:* 155
German Potato Salad (Great Lakes Region, United States), *4:* 93

Germany, *1:* **211**
  Apfelpfannkuchen (Pancakes), *1:* 218
  Apfelschörle, *1:* 215
  Bratwurst (Sausage), *1:* 214
  Eis und Heiss, *1:* 215
  Glühwein (Non-alcoholic Drink), *1:* 214
  Kartoffelknödeln (Dumplings), *1:* 216
  Lebkuchen, *1:* 217
  Potato Roesti, *1:* 218
  Red Coleslaw, *1:* 218
  Rye Bread, *1:* 216
  Soft Pretzels, *1:* 219
  Spargelgemuse (Asparagus), *1:* 213
  Weisse Bohnensuppe (Soup), *1:* 212

Ghana, *2:* **1**
  Akara (Fritters), *2:* 8
  Avocado with Peanut Dressing, *2:* 9
  Coconut Pudding, *2:* 10
  Fufu, *2:* 4
  Gari Biscuits, *2:* 6
  Groundnut Stew, *2:* 8
  Groundnut Toffee, *2:* 5
  Jollof Rice, *2:* 3
  Kelewele (Fried Plantains), *2:* 4
  Kenkey (Ground Cornmeal), *2:* 7
  Oto (Yams & Eggs), *2:* 5
  Pepper Soup, *2:* 8
  Yams, *2:* 2

Gibanica (Slovenia), *3:* 134
Ginger Beer (Liberia), *2:* 208
Githeri (Kenya), *2:* 189
Gizzada (Jamaica), *2:* 157
Glazed Carrots (Sweden), *3:* 191
Glühwein (Non-alcoholic Drink, Germany), *1:* 214
Goat Soup (Liberia), *2:* 209
Gohan (Boiled Rice, Japan), *2:* 163
Golabki (Stuffed Cabbage Rolls, Poland), *3:* 81
Golaz (Goulash, Slovenia), *3:* 127
Gomen Wat (Ethiopian Greens, Ethiopia), *1:* 197
Gooseberry Crumble (Ireland), *2:* 111

Great Lakes Region (United States), *4:* **89**
  Apple Sauerkraut, *4:* 95
  Buffalo Chicken Wings, *4:* 96
  Cherry Muffins, *4:* 93
  Chicago Deep Dish Pizza, *4:* 98
  Cornish Pasty, *4:* 98
  Dutch Pancakes, *4:* 91
  Fish Boil, *4:* 91
  German Potato Salad, *4:* 93
  Hummus, *4:* 95
  Macaroni and Cheese, *4:* 94
  Ojibwa Wild Rice, *4:* 92
  Polish Boy Sandwich, *4:* 97
  Potato Lefse, *4:* 96
  Springerle (Christmas Cookies), *4:* 96
  Swedish Meatballs, *4:* 97

Index

Greece, *2:* 13
    Arni Souvlakia (Lamb Skewers), *2:* 15
    Avgolemono (Soup), *2:* 14
    Frouta Ke Yaourti (Fruit Salad), *2:* 17
    Greek Salad, *2:* 18
    Greek Salad Dressing, *2:* 19
    Kourabiethes (Butter Cookies), *2:* 18
    Lambropsoma (Easter Bread), *2:* 16
    Melitzanosalata, *2:* 21
    Melopitta (Honey Pie), *2:* 17
    Moussaka (Casserole), *2:* 15
    Olive Tapenade, *2:* 22
    Patates Fourno Riganates , *2:* 19
    Tzatziki (Sauce), *2:* 20
Greek Salad (Greece), *2:* 18
Greek Salad Dressing (Greece), *2:* 19
Green Bean Casserole (Midwest Region, United States), *4:* 129
Green Bean Salad (South Africa), *3:* 153
Green Tea (Japan), *2:* 170
Griby Marinovannye (Russia), *3:* 109
Griots (Haiti), *2:* 41
Grits (Southern Region, United States), *4:* 166
Groundnut Stew (Ghana), *2:* 8
Groundnut Toffee (Ghana), *2:* 5
G'shur Purtaghal (Iraq), *2:* 101
Guacamole (Guatemala), *2:* 26
Guacamole (Latino Americans, United States), *4:* 116
Guacamole (Mexico), *2:* 223
Guatemala, *2:* 23
    Arroz Guatemalteco (Rice), *2:* 26
    Bunuelos (Fried Fritters), *2:* 28
    Chile Rellenos Casserole, *2:* 31
    Cucumber Soup, *2:* 27
    Frijoles Negros Volteados, *2:* 26
    Guacamole, *2:* 26
    Hot Christmas Punch, *2:* 28
    Mantequilla de ajo casera, *2:* 30
    Pan de Banano (Banana Bread), *2:* 30
    Pepinos Rellenos, *2:* 29
    Picado de Rabano (Salad), *2:* 24
    Spanish Tortilla, *2:* 24
    Torrejas, *2:* 31
Guavas in Syrup (Dominican Republic), *1:* 162
Gulyás (Hungarian Goulash, Hungary), *2:* 46
Gundel Pancakes (Hungary), *2:* 53

H

Habichuelas con Dulce (Dominican Republic), *1:* 166
Haggis (Scotland, United Kingdom), *4:* 56
Haiti, *2:* 33
    Banann Peze (Fried Plantains), *2:* 38
    Corn Pudding, *2:* 35
    Cornmeal Porridge, *2:* 39
    French-Style Lettuce Salad, *2:* 34
    Griots, *2:* 41
    Haitian Fruit Salad, *2:* 36
    Mango Juice, *2:* 35
    Pain Haïtien (Haitian Bread), *2:* 41
    Pineapple Nog, *2:* 36
    Riz Djon-Djon, *2:* 36
    Riz et Pois Rouges, *2:* 38
    Spiced Cocoa, *2:* 35
    Sweet Potato Casserole, *2:* 40
    Ti-Malice (Spicy Haitian Sauce), *2:* 39
Haitian Fruit Salad (Haiti), *2:* 36
Halva (Iran), *2:* 87
Halva (Turkey), *4:* 23
Harira (Morocco), *3:* 7
Hasselbackspotatis (Sweden), *3:* 200
Hawayij (Spice Blend, Saudi Arabia), *3:* 114
Haysa Al-Tumreya (Dip, Saudi Arabia), *3:* 117
Helado de Mango (Sherbet, Cuba), *1:* 142
Herring Dip (Jewish Americans, United States), *4:* 107
Hin Pap (White Rice, South Korea), *3:* 165
Holubtsi (Cabbage Rolls, Ukraine), *4:* 32
Honey-Baked Apples (Northeast Region, United States), *4:* 155
Horchata (El Salvador), *1:* 185
Hot Christmas Punch (Guatemala), *2:* 28
Hot Cranberry Punch (Northeast Region, United States), *4:* 155
Houbova Polevka Myslivecka (Czech Republic), *1:* 151
Hrechana Kasha (Ukraine), *4:* 33
Huevos Rancheros (Eggs, Mexico), *2:* 225
Hummus (Egypt), *1:* 173
Hummus (Great Lakes Region, United States), *4:* 95
Hummus (Saudi Arabia), *3:* 120
Hummus and Chicken (Turkey), *4:* 26

Index

Hummus be Tahini (Lebanon), *2:* 202
Hungarian Butter Cookies (Hungary), *2:* 49
Hungarian Cold Plate (Hungary), *2:* 50
Hungary, *2:* 45
    Almond Kisses, *2:* 54
    Gulyás (Hungarian Goulash), *2:* 46
    Gundel Pancakes, *2:* 53
    Hungarian Butter Cookies, *2:* 49
    Hungarian Cold Plate, *2:* 50
    Hunza Bread, *2:* 54
    Noodle Pudding, *2:* 52
    Paprika Chicken, *2:* 48
    Pork Cutlets with Potatoes, *2:* 49
    Pörkölt (Hungarian Stew), *2:* 47
    Small Dumplings, *2:* 50
    Stuffed Green Peppers, *2:* 48
    Summer Cucumber Soup, *2:* 52
Hunza Bread (Hungary), *2:* 54
Hush Puppies (African Americans, United States), *4:* 70

I

India, *2:* 57
    Baigan Bhartha, *2:* 58
    Chai (Indian Tea), *2:* 62
    Dal (Lentils), *2:* 61
    Fancy Rice, *2:* 63
    Garam Masala (Spice Mixture), *2:* 59
    Kheer (Sweet Rice Pudding), *2:* 59
    Mathis (Spicy Cookie), *2:* 65
    Naan, *2:* 65
    Palak Bhaji (Fried Spinach), *2:* 60
    Palak Paneer, *2:* 66
    Tamatar Salat (Tomato Salad), *2:* 63
    Tandoori Chicken, *2:* 60
    Vegetable Sandwich, *2:* 62
Indian Fry-Bread (Native Americans, United States), *4:* 143
Indian Pudding (Northeast Region, United States), *4:* 149
Individual Mincemeat Pies (United Kingdom), *4:* 47
Indonesia, *2:* 69
    Es Pokat (Avocado Drink), *2:* 74
    Gado-Gado (Vegetable Salad), *2:* 77

Indonesian Spiced Rice, *2:* 79
Kelapa Susu (Coconut Milk), *2:* 71
Kuping Gajah (Elephant Ears), *2:* 79
Nasi Goreng (Fried Rice), *2:* 71
Nasi Jagung (Corn Rice), *2:* 78
Nasi Kuning (Yellow Rice), *2:* 77
Pisang Goreng (Banana Cakes), *2:* 75
Rujak (Spicy Fruit Salad), *2:* 72
Sambal Kecap (Sauce), *2:* 74
Sarikayo Telor (Pudding), *2:* 73
Tahu Goreng (Fried Tofu), *2:* 74
Teh Halia (Hot Ginger Tea), *2:* 78
Uli Petataws (Potato Fritters), *2:* 73
Indonesian Spiced Rice (Indonesia), *2:* 79
Ingoho (Kenya), *2:* 185
Injera (Ethiopian Bread, Ethiopia), *1:* 193
Insalata Caprese (Italy), *2:* 148
Iran, *2:* 81
    Ash-e Jo (Barley Stew), *2:* 91
    Cheese and Vegetable Tray, *2:* 90
    Desser Miveh (Fruit Salad), *2:* 89
    Dolma (Stuffed Grape Leaves), *2:* 84
    Dugh (Sparkling Yogurt Drink), *2:* 87
    Halva, *2:* 87
    Iranian Rice Cakes, *2:* 88
    Kebab Morgh (Grilled Chicken), *2:* 86
    Kookoo Sabzi (Persian Omelet), *2:* 90
    Lettuce Dipped in Dressing, *2:* 88
    Maast (Homemade Yogurt), *2:* 88
    Shirazi (Salad), *2:* 82
    Shir-Berenj (Rice Pudding), *2:* 87
    Yogurt and Mint Sauce, *2:* 84
Iranian Rice Cakes (Iran), *2:* 88
Iraq, *2:* 93
    Adas Bil Hamod (Lentils), *2:* 96
    Beef with Fruit, *2:* 94
    G'shur Purtaghal, *2:* 101
    Jajeek (Yogurt Salad), *2:* 100
    Kebabs, *2:* 100
    Khubaz (Pita with Jelly), *2:* 98
    Kibbe Batata (Casserole), *2:* 99
    Ma'mounia (Wheat Pudding), *2:* 97
    Qatayef, *2:* 102
    Red Lentil Soup, *2:* 96
    Yalanchi (Stuffed Tomatoes), *2:* 97
'Irea (Cinnamon Beverage, Egypt), *1:* 176

Index

Ireland, *2:* 105
    Apple Cake, *2:* 114
    Barm Brack, *2:* 112
    Boxty (Potato Pancakes), *2:* 115
    Champ, *2:* 109
    Colcannon, *2:* 110
    Corned Beef with Cabbage, *2:* 109
    Dublin Coddle, *2:* 114
    Gooseberry Crumble, *2:* 111
    Irish Christmas Cake, *2:* 113
    Irish Soda Bread, *2:* 108
    Scones, *2:* 110
    Traditional Irish Stew, *2:* 106
Irio (Kenya), *2:* 185
Irish Christmas Cake (Ireland), *2:* 113
Irish Soda Bread (Ireland), *2:* 108
Iroquois Strawberry Drink (Native Americans, United States), *4:* 142
Irtysh Fish (Kazakhstan), *2:* 174
Islands of the Pacific, *2:* 117
    Badam Pistaz Barfi (Nut Candy), *2:* 123
    Baked Papaya Dessert, *2:* 126
    Bananas and Sweet Potatoes, *2:* 122
    Butter Mochi, *2:* 124
    Coconut Milk, *2:* 120
    Firifiri (Sugared Doughnuts), *2:* 125
    Fresh Grated Coconut, *2:* 119
    Papaya Chicken, *2:* 121
    Poi, *2:* 125
    Poisson Cru, *2:* 120
    Roast Pork, *2:* 122
    Tropical Fruit Dessert, *2:* 124
    Tropical Fruit Shake, *2:* 124
Israel, *2:* 127
    Blintzes, *2:* 130
    Charoseth, *2:* 131
    Eggplant Appetizer, *2:* 134
    Falafel, *2:* 133
    Fava Bean Spread, *2:* 129
    Fresh Oranges, *2:* 129
    Israeli Vegetable Salad, *2:* 132
    Kichlach (Cookies), *2:* 136
    Mandelbrot (Almond Cookies), *2:* 136
    New Year's Honey Cake, *2:* 134
    Pita Sandwiches, *2:* 136
    Sesame Candy, *2:* 130
    Shakshooka, *2:* 129
    Tahini Sauce, *2:* 133
Israeli Vegetable Salad (Israel), *2:* 132
Isu (Spiced Boiled Yams, Nigeria), *3:* 27
Italian Easter Bread (Italy), *2:* 144
Italy, *2:* 139
    Biscotti, *2:* 146
    Bruschetta (Garlic Bread), *2:* 147
    Cannoli, *2:* 145
    Fettucine Alfredo, *2:* 142
    Frittata, *2:* 143
    Insalata Caprese, *2:* 148
    Italian Easter Bread, *2:* 144
    Panettone (Christmas Bread), *2:* 145
    Pasta e Fagioli (Soup), *2:* 141
    Pizza Margherita, *2:* 146
    Polenta, *2:* 141
    Saltimbocca alla Romana, *2:* 143
Ivory Coast. *See* Côte d'Ivoire
Iyan (Pounded Yams, Nigeria), *3:* 28

J

Jajeek (Yogurt Salad, Iraq), *2:* 100
Jalalo (Dominican Republic), *1:* 167
Jamaica, *2:* 149
    "Almost" Ting, *2:* 154
    Baked Ripe Banana, *2:* 156
    Brown Stew Fish, *2:* 152
    Coconut Chips, *2:* 151
    Curry Chicken, *2:* 155
    Gizzada, *2:* 157
    Jamaican Christmas Cake, *2:* 154
    Jamaican Fruit Drink, *2:* 154
    Jerk Chicken, *2:* 153
    Johnnycake, *2:* 157
    Rice and Peas, *2:* 150
    Sweet Potato Pone, *2:* 158
Jamaican Christmas Cake (Jamaica), *2:* 154
Jamaican Fruit Drink (Jamaica), *2:* 154
Jansson's Frestelse (Sweden), *3:* 193
Japan, *2:* 161
    Beef Sukiyaki, *2:* 165
    Broiled Salmon, *2:* 168
    Chicken Teriyaki, *2:* 164

Index

Japan (*continued*)
    Gohan (Boiled Rice), *2:* 163
    Green Tea, *2:* 170
    Miso Soup, *2:* 166
    Onigiri (Rice Ball), *2:* 163
    Ozoni (New Year's Soup), *2:* 167
    Ramen (Noodle Soup), *2:* 171
    Sushi, *2:* 164
    Sweet Peanut Mochi, *2:* 170
    Tamagoyaki (Rolled Omelet), *2:* 167
    Yaki-Soba (Fried Noodles), *2:* 166
    Yakitori (Chicken on Skewers), *2:* 169
Jasmine Bubble Tea (China), *1:* 116
Jengibre (Ginger Tea, Dominican Republic), *1:* 166
Jerk Chicken (Jamaica), *2:* 153
Jewish Americans (United States), *4:* 101
    Apple and Carrot Tsimmes, *4:* 105
    Borscht (Beet Soup), *4:* 110
    Charoset, *4:* 105
    Chopped Chicken Liver, *4:* 103
    Herring Dip, *4:* 107
    Matzo Balls, *4:* 109
    Matzo Brie, *4:* 106
    Mother's Chicken Soup, *4:* 103
    New York Cheesecake, *4:* 108
    Noodle Kugel (Noodle Casserole), *4:* 104
    Potato Latkes (Potato Pancakes), *4:* 106
    Rosh Hashanah Honey Cake, *4:* 110
Johnnycake (Jamaica), *2:* 157
Johnnycakes (Northeast Region, United States), *4:* 151
Jollof Rice (Ghana), *2:* 3
Jollof Rice (Liberia), *2:* 207
Jollof Rice (Nigeria), *3:* 28
Jota (Slovenia), *3:* 126
Julgröt (Christmas Porridge, Sweden), *3:* 196

K

Ka Nom Jeen Sour Nam (Thailand), *4:* 11
Ka'ak Cookies (Lebanon), *2:* 200
Kabsa (Lamb with Rice, Saudi Arabia), *3:* 116
Kachumbari Salad (Kenya), *2:* 190
Kac-Kac (Sweet Bread, Somalia), *3:* 146
Kahweh (Arabic Coffee, Lebanon), *2:* 199
Kamja Guk (Potato Soup, South Korea), *3:* 164
Kanom Krok (Pancakes, Thailand), *4:* 8
Kapsa (Chicken and Rice, Saudi Arabia), *3:* 118
Kartoffelknödeln (Dumplings, Germany), *1:* 216
Kartoplia Solimkoi (Potatoes, Ukraine), *4:* 34
Kategna (Ethiopia), *1:* 190
Kaymakli Kuru Kayisi (Turkey), *4:* 17
Kazakhstan, *2:* 173
    Basturma, *2:* 176
    Baursaki (Fried Doughnuts), *2:* 178
    Irtysh Fish, *2:* 174
    Kazakhstan Salad, *2:* 177
    Manti, *2:* 180
    Mutton Kespe, *2:* 176
    Plov (Rice Pilaf), *2:* 175
    Pumpkin Samsa, *2:* 180
    Rice Sorpa, *2:* 181
Kazakhstan Salad (Kazakhstan), *2:* 177
Kebab Morgh (Grilled Chicken, Iran), *2:* 86
Kebabs (Iraq), *2:* 100
Kedjenou (Côte d'Ivoire), *1:* 132
Kelapa Susu (Coconut Milk, Indonesia), *2:* 71
Kelewele (Fried Plantains, Ghana), *2:* 4
Kenkey (Ground Cornmeal, Ghana), *2:* 7
Kenya, *2:* 183
    Githeri, *2:* 189
    Ingoho, *2:* 185
    Irio, *2:* 185
    Kachumbari Salad, *2:* 190
    Kenyan Cabbage, *2:* 189
    Matoke (Mashed Plantains), *2:* 188
    Nyama Choma, *2:* 189
    Sukuma Wiki, *2:* 186
    Ugali, *2:* 187
    Wali wa Nazi (Coconut Rice), *2:* 190
    Western Kenya Cabbage and Egg, *2:* 186
    Yogurt Chutney, *2:* 188
Kenyan Cabbage (Kenya), *2:* 189
Khachapuri (Cheesy Boats, Russia), *3:* 111
Kheer (Rice Pudding, Pakistan), *3:* 42
Kheer (Sweet Rice Pudding, India), *2:* 59
Khoshaf (Egypt), *1:* 176
Khubaz (Pita with Jelly, Iraq), *2:* 98
Kibbe Batata (Casserole, Iraq), *2:* 99
Kichlach (Cookies, Israel), *2:* 136
Kielbasa and Cabbage (Poland), *3:* 80

Index

Kimaje (Flat Bread, Saudi Arabia), *3:* 119
Kimchi (South Korea), *3:* 164
Kitfo (Spiced Raw Beef, Ethiopia), *1:* 194
Klimp (Dumplings, Sweden), *3:* 194
Klobasa and Kisdo Zelje (Slovenia), *3:* 129
Klyukva S Sakharom (Russia), *3:* 112
Knedlíky (Czech Dumplings, Czech Republic), *1:* 152
Köfte (Turkish Meatballs, Turkey), *4:* 22
Koki (Cameroon), *1:* 68
Komkomer Sambal (South Africa), *3:* 155
Kookoo Sabzi (Persian Omelet, Iran), *2:* 90
Korea. *See* South Korea
Kotleta Po-Kyivsky (Ukraine), *4:* 35
Köttbulla (Swedish Meatballs, Sweden), *3:* 194
Kourabiethes (Butter Cookies, Greece), *2:* 18
Koushari (Egypt), *1:* 172
Kuping Gajah (Elephant Ears, Indonesia), *2:* 79
Kure Na Paprice (Czech Republic), *1:* 155
Kutya (Russia), *3:* 107
Kutya (Sweet Porridge, Ukraine), *4:* 33
Kwanzaa Brownies (African Americans, United States), *4:* 73

L

La Galette des Rois (Cake, France), *1:* 210
Lab (Ethiopian Cheese, Ethiopia), *1:* 190
Laban Drink (Yogurt Drink, Saudi Arabia), *3:* 117
Lahmacun (Turkish Pizza, Turkey), *4:* 27
Lambropsoma (Easter Bread, Greece), *2:* 16
Lamingtons (Australia), *1:* 28
Lassi (Yogurt Drink, Pakistan), *3:* 42
Latino Americans (United States), *4:* 113
    Chili Corn Bread, *4:* 122
    Cuban Avocado Salad, *4:* 122
    Cuban Beans and Rice, *4:* 117
    Fried Plantains, *4:* 118
    Gazpacho, *4:* 119
    Guacamole, *4:* 116
    Mexican Fried Ice Cream, *4:* 119
    Puerto Rican Christmas Salad, *4:* 120
    Quesadillas, *4:* 122
    Salsa Cruda, *4:* 116
    Tacos, *4:* 123
    Tropical Fruit Salad, *4:* 123

Lebanese Beet Salad (Lebanon), *2:* 202
Lebanese Eggplant (Lebanon), *2:* 196
Lebanese Fresh Fruit Salad (Lebanon), *2:* 200
Lebanese Rice Pudding (Lebanon), *2:* 195
Lebanon, *2:* 193
    Baked Kibbeh, *2:* 198
    Cucumber with Yogurt, *2:* 196
    Doughnuts Awwamaat, *2:* 203
    Easy Lebanese Baklava, *2:* 199
    Fatoosh, *2:* 203
    Hummus be Tahini, *2:* 202
    Ka'ak Cookies, *2:* 200
    Kahweh (Arabic Coffee), *2:* 199
    Lebanese Beet Salad, *2:* 202
    Lebanese Eggplant, *2:* 196
    Lebanese Fresh Fruit Salad, *2:* 200
    Lebanese Rice Pudding, *2:* 195
    Limoonada (Lemonade), *2:* 202
    Pita Bread, *2:* 195
    Sugared Almonds, *2:* 200
    Tabbouleh, *2:* 196
Lebkuchen (Germany), *1:* 217
Leche Flan (Caramel Custard, Philippines), *3:* 66
Leche Frita (Spain), *3:* 186
Leche Poleada (El Salvador), *1:* 186
Lefse (Midwest Region, United States), *4:* 131
Lemon and Garlic Potato Salad (Egypt), *1:* 174
Lemon and Herb Salad Dressing (Mozambique), *3:* 21
Lemon Curd (United Kingdom), *4:* 44
Lemon Grass Tea (Liberia), *2:* 211
Lettuce Dipped in Dressing (Iran), *2:* 88
Lettuce Salad (Egypt), *1:* 176
Liberia, *2:* 205
    Coconut Pie, *2:* 210
    Collards with Cabbage, *2:* 211
    Ginger Beer, *2:* 208
    Goat Soup, *2:* 209
    Jollof Rice, *2:* 207
    Lemon Grass Tea, *2:* 211
    Palava, *2:* 206
    Pumpkin Soup, *2:* 210
    Rice Bread, *2:* 208
    Stewed Mangoes with Cloves, *2:* 209
    Sweet Potato Pone, *2:* 207
Limoonada (Lemonade, Lebanon), *2:* 202

Index

Ljubljana Egg Dish (Slovenia), *3:* 131
Lobster Roll (Northeast Region, United States), *4:* 156
Locum (Turkish Candy, Turkey), *4:* 24
Lokma (Golden Fritters, Turkey), *4:* 26
Lor Köftesi (Ricotta Patties, Turkey), *4:* 19
Lussekatter (Saffron Buns, Sweden), *3:* 197

M

M'hajeb (Algeria), *1:* 8
Ma'mounia (Wheat Pudding, Iraq), *2:* 97
Maast (Homemade Yogurt, Iran), *2:* 88
Macadamia and Fruit Snack (Aborigines and Bush Tucker, Australia), *1:* 37
Macadamia Nut Cookies (Aborigines and Bush Tucker, Australia), *1:* 38
Macadamia Nut Dukkah (Australia), *1:* 24
Macaroni and Cheese (Great Lakes Region, United States), *4:* 94

Main dishes
    Adobong Hiponsa Gata (Philippines), *3:* 68
    Aji de Gallina (Peru), *3:* 60
    Apfelpfannkuchen (Pancakes, Germany), *1:* 218
    Arni Souvlakia (Lamb Skewers, Greece), *2:* 15
    Arroz Guatemalteco (Rice, Guatemala), *2:* 26
    Ash-e Jo (Barley Stew, Iran), *2:* 91
    Australian Meat Pie (Australia), *1:* 27
    Baasto (Somalia), *3:* 138
    Baked Kibbeh (Lebanon), *2:* 198
    Baked Macaroni and Cheese (African Americans, United States), *4:* 72
    Basturma (Kazakhstan), *2:* 176
    Beef Sukiyaki (Japan), *2:* 165
    Beef with Fruit (Iraq), *2:* 94
    Birria (Mexico), *2:* 221
    Birthday Noodles with Sauce (China), *1:* 122
    Bisteeya (Morocco), *3:* 6
    Bliny (Russian Pancakes, Russia), *3:* 102
    Bobotie (South Africa), *3:* 154
    Boerewors (South Africa), *3:* 158
    Boxty (Potato Pancakes, Ireland), *2:* 115
    Bratwurst (Sausage, Germany), *1:* 214
    Broiled Salmon (Japan), *2:* 168

    Broiled Salmon Steaks (Western Region, United States), *4:* 180
    Brown Stew Fish (Jamaica), *2:* 152
    Buffalo Chicken Wings (Great Lakes Region, United States), *4:* 96
    Buffalo Stew (Native Americans, United States), *4:* 140
    Bulgogi (Korean Beef, South Korea), *3:* 171
    Cabbage Pirozhki or Piroghi (Russia), *3:* 104
    California-style Pizza (Western Region, United States), *4:* 182
    Calzone (Midwest Region, United States), *4:* 132
    Cambuulo (Somalia), *3:* 144
    Canadian Bacon (Canada), *1:* 78
    Carurú (Afro-Brazilians, Brazil), *1:* 57
    Casamiento (El Salvador), *1:* 182
    Ceviche (Marinated Seafood, Peru), *3:* 57
    Chap Ch'ae (South Korea), *3:* 166
    Chicago Deep Dish Pizza (Great Lakes Region, United States), *4:* 98
    Chicken and Sausage Gumbo (Southern Region, United States), *4:* 165
    Chicken Biryani (Pakistan), *3:* 45
    Chicken Karahi (Pakistan), *3:* 41
    Chicken Satay (Thailand), *4:* 5
    Chicken Tajine (Morocco), *3:* 2
    Chicken Teriyaki (Japan), *2:* 164
    Chile Rellenos Casserole (Guatemala), *2:* 31
    Chopped Chicken Liver (Jewish Americans, United States), *4:* 103
    Chuck Wagon Brisket (Western Region, United States), *4:* 175
    Corned Beef with Cabbage (Ireland), *2:* 109
    Cornish Pasties (United Kingdom), *4:* 45
    Cornish Pasty (Great Lakes Region, United States), *4:* 98
    Cornmeal Porridge (Haiti), *2:* 39
    Crêpes de la Chandeleur (French Canadians, Canada), *1:* 100
    Cuban Beans and Rice (Latino Americans, United States), *4:* 117
    Curry Chicken (Jamaica), *2:* 155
    Dolma (Stuffed Grape Leaves, Iran), *2:* 84
    Dovi (Peanut Butter Stew, Zimbabwe), *4:* 201
    Dublin Coddle (Ireland), *2:* 114

Dutch Pancakes (Great Lakes Region, United States), *4:* 91
Easy Fufu (Cameroon), *1:* 68
Efo (Greens Stew, Nigeria), *3:* 31
Empanadas (Little Meat Pies, Argentina), *1:* 16
Fazolovy Gulás (Czech Republic), *1:* 154
Fettucine Alfredo (Italy), *2:* 142
Fish and Brewis (Canada), *1:* 82
Fish and Chips (United Kingdom), *4:* 51
Fish Boil (Great Lakes Region, United States), *4:* 91
Frango a Cafrial (Mozambique), *3:* 23
Fried Bologna (African Americans, United States), *4:* 74
Fried Rice (China), *1:* 120
Frittata (Italy), *2:* 143
Frtalja (Slovenia), *3:* 128
Fu Yung Don (Egg Fu Yung, China), *1:* 123
Fufu (Côte d'Ivoire), *1:* 130
Fufu (Ghana), *2:* 4
Ful Mudammas (Egypt), *1:* 170
Golabki (Stuffed Cabbage Rolls, Poland), *3:* 81
Golaz (Goulash, Slovenia), *3:* 127
Griots (Haiti), *2:* 41
Gulyás (Hungarian Goulash, Hungary), *2:* 46
Gundel Pancakes (Hungary), *2:* 53
Haggis (Scotland, United Kingdom), *4:* 56
Holubtsi (Cabbage Rolls, Ukraine), *4:* 32
Houbova Polevka Myslivecka (Czech Republic), *1:* 151
Huevos Rancheros (Eggs, Mexico), *2:* 225
Hummus and Chicken (Turkey), *4:* 26
Ingoho (Kenya), *2:* 185
Irtysh Fish (Kazakhstan), *2:* 174
Jerk Chicken (Jamaica), *2:* 153
Johnnycakes (Northeast Region, United States), *4:* 151
Jollof Rice (Ghana), *2:* 3
Jollof Rice (Liberia), *2:* 207
Jollof Rice (Nigeria), *3:* 28
Jota (Slovenia), *3:* 126
Julgröt (Christmas Porridge, Sweden), *3:* 196
Ka Nom Jeen Sour Nam (Thailand), *4:* 11
Kabsa (Lamb with Rice, Saudi Arabia), *3:* 116
Kanom Krok (Pancakes, Thailand), *4:* 8
Kapsa (Chicken and Rice, Saudi Arabia), *3:* 118

Kebab Morgh (Grilled Chicken, Iran), *2:* 86
Kebabs (Iraq), *2:* 100
Kedjenou (Côte d'Ivoire), *1:* 132
Kibbe Batata (Casserole, Iraq), *2:* 99
Kielbasa and Cabbage (Poland), *3:* 80
Kimchi (South Korea), *3:* 164
Kitfo (Spiced Raw Beef, Ethiopia), *1:* 194
Klobasa and Kisdo Zelje (Slovenia), *3:* 129
Köfte (Turkish Meatballs, Turkey), *4:* 22
Koki (Cameroon), *1:* 68
Kookoo Sabzi (Persian Omelet, Iran), *2:* 90
Kotleta Po-Kyivsky (Ukraine), *4:* 35
Köttbulla (Swedish Meatballs, Sweden), *3:* 194
Koushari (Egypt), *1:* 172
Kure Na Paprice (Czech Republic), *1:* 155
Kutya (Russia), *3:* 107
Lahmacun (Turkish Pizza, Turkey), *4:* 27
Ljubljana Egg Dish (Slovenia), *3:* 131
Lobster Roll (Northeast Region, United States), *4:* 156
M'hajeb (Algeria), *1:* 8
Macaroni and Cheese (Great Lakes Region, United States), *4:* 94
Maize Porridge (Mozambique), *3:* 16
Mala Sousta Se Syre (Czech Republic), *1:* 157
Manti (Kazakhstan), *2:* 180
Matata (Stew, Mozambique), *3:* 18
Matzo Balls (Jewish Americans, United States), *4:* 109
Midwestern Chili (Midwest Region, United States), *4:* 128
Midwestern Pork Chop Dinner (Midwest Region, United States), *4:* 132
Milanesa (Argentina), *1:* 19
Moors and Christians (Cuba), *1:* 139
Moqueca (Spicy Fish Stew, Afro-Brazilians, Brazil), *1:* 58
Moqueca aos Ovos (Egg Stew, Afro-Brazilians, Brazil), *1:* 59
Moussaka (Casserole, Greece), *2:* 15
Mutton Kespe (Kazakhstan), *2:* 176
Ndolé (Bitterleaf Stew, Cameroon), *1:* 70
New England Boiled Dinner (Northeast Region, United States), *4:* 154
Noodles with Poppy Seeds (Poland), *3:* 84
Ñoquis (Argentina), *1:* 14

Index

Main dishes (*continued*)
  Nyama Choma (Kenya), *2:* 189
  Omelet with Ground Pork (Vietnam), *4:* 197
  Oto (Yams & Eggs, Ghana), *2:* 5
  Pad See Ew (Thailand), *4:* 5
  Pad Thai (Thailand), *4:* 10
  Palak Paneer (India), *2:* 66
  Pansit Mami (Noodles in Broth, Philippines), *3:* 72
  Papaya Chicken (Islands of the Pacific), *2:* 121
  Paprika Chicken (Hungary), *2:* 48
  Pasta with Yogurt-Mint Sauce (Turkey), *4:* 18
  Pastel de Choclo (Chile), *1:* 107
  Pierogi (Dumplings, Poland), *3:* 82
  Pikelets (Australia), *1:* 27
  Pisto Manchego with Eggs (Spain), *3:* 178
  Pizza-ghetti (French Canadians, Canada), *1:* 100
  Pizza Margherita (Italy), *2:* 146
  Plättar (Swedish Pancakes, Sweden), *3:* 200
  Plov (Rice Pilaf, Kazakhstan), *2:* 175
  Poisson Cru (Islands of the Pacific), *2:* 120
  Pork Chops with Sauerkraut (Amish and Pennsylvania Dutch, United States), *4:* 80
  Pork Cutlets with Potatoes (Hungary), *2:* 49
  Pörkölt (Hungarian Stew, Hungary), *2:* 47
  Potato Latkes (Potato Pancakes, Jewish Americans, United States), *4:* 106
  Pumpkin Samsa (Kazakhstan), *2:* 180
  Pupusas (El Salvador), *1:* 181
  Putupap (Cornmeal Porridge, South Africa), *3:* 158
  Quiche au Saumon et Crevettes (France), *1:* 206
  Ragoût de Boulettes (French Canadians, Canada), *1:* 101
  Rårakor (Potato Pancakes, Sweden), *3:* 202
  Rebenadas (French Toast, Portugal), *3:* 96
  Red Beans and Rice (African Americans, United States), *4:* 70
  Rice and Peas (Jamaica), *2:* 150
  Rice Sorpa (Kazakhstan), *2:* 181
  Rice with Peanut Sauce (Zimbabwe), *4:* 204
  Rice with Shrimp (Spain), *3:* 186
  Riz Djon-Djon (Haiti), *2:* 36
  Riz et Pois Rouges (Haiti), *2:* 38
  Roast Pork (Islands of the Pacific), *2:* 122
  Sadza (Zimbabwe), *4:* 202
  Safou a la Sauce Tomate (Cameroon), *1:* 67
  Salmon Kedgeree (United Kingdom), *4:* 43
  Saltimbocca alla Romana (Italy), *2:* 143
  Sancocho (Dominican Republic), *1:* 164
  Shakshooka (Israel), *2:* 129
  Shrimp Mozambique (Mozambique), *3:* 22
  Shu Mai Dumplings (Thailand), *4:* 12
  Somali Lamb and Rice (Somalia), *3:* 145
  Southern Fried Chicken (Southern Region, United States), *4:* 165
  Spanish Tortilla (Guatemala), *2:* 24
  Spiced Chicken (China), *1:* 126
  Spicy Oven-Fried Chicken (Amish and Pennsylvania Dutch, United States), *4:* 83
  Spinach and Peanut Butter Stew (South Africa), *3:* 157
  Stuffed Green Peppers (Hungary), *2:* 48
  Succotash (Corn and Bean Stew, Native Americans, United States), *4:* 138
  Suqaar (Somalia), *3:* 140
  Sushi (Japan), *2:* 164
  Swedish Meatballs (Great Lakes Region, United States), *4:* 97
  Sweet and Sour Pork (China), *1:* 119
  Sweet Corn Pancakes (Canada), *1:* 78
  Tacos (Latino Americans, United States), *4:* 123
  Tahu Goreng (Fried Tofu, Indonesia), *2:* 74
  Tamagoyaki (Rolled Omelet, Japan), *2:* 167
  Tandoori Chicken (India), *2:* 60
  Thai Beef Curry (Thailand), *4:* 4
  Toad-in-the-Hole (United Kingdom), *4:* 45
  Topinky S Vejci (Eggs on Toast, Czech Republic), *1:* 152
  Torrejas (Guatemala), *2:* 31
  Tortilla Española (Omelet, Spain), *3:* 179
  Tourtière (Meat Pie, French Canadians, Canada), *1:* 98
  Traditional Fufu (Cameroon), *1:* 68
  Traditional Irish Stew (Ireland), *2:* 106
  Tuna in Sauce (Cuba), *1:* 139
  Veal Meatballs with Dill (Poland), *3:* 88
  Vegetable Curry (United Kingdom), *4:* 52
  Welsh Rarebit (United Kingdom), *4:* 42
  Western Kenya Cabbage and Egg (Kenya), *2:* 186
  Yaki-Soba (Fried Noodles, Japan), *2:* 166
  Yakitori (Chicken on Skewers, Japan), *2:* 169
  Yalanchi (Stuffed Tomatoes, Iraq), *2:* 97

Maize Porridge (Mozambique), *3:* 16
Maja Blanco (Coconut Cake, Philippines), *3:* 66
Makiwnyk (Poppy Seed Cake, Ukraine), *4:* 36
Makiwnyk Glaze (Cake Glaze, Ukraine), *4:* 36
Makubi (Tanzania), *3:* 214
Mala Sousta Se Syre (Czech Republic), *1:* 157
Malasadas (Doughnuts, Mozambique), *3:* 17
Malva Pudding (South Africa), *3:* 150
Maná (Peru), *3:* 56
Mandelbrot (Almond Cookies, Israel), *2:* 136
Mandu (Korean Dumplings, South Korea), *3:* 169
Mango and Sticky Rice (Thailand), *4:* 12
Mango Juice (Haiti), *2:* 35
Mango-Orange Drink (Tanzania), *3:* 209
Mangú (Dominican Republic), *1:* 161
Man-O-Min (Ojibwa Wild Rice, Aboriginals, Canada), *1:* 92
Mantequilla de ajo casera (Guatemala), *2:* 30
Manti (Kazakhstan), *2:* 180
Maple Baked Beans (Native Americans, United States), *4:* 139
Maple Butter (Northeast Region, United States), *4:* 151
Maple Sundae (Canada), *1:* 82
Maple Syrup Upside-Down Cake (Canada), *1:* 82
Mapopo (Papaya) Candy (Zimbabwe), *4:* 200
Mardi Gras King Cake (Southern Region, United States), *4:* 166
Marinated Artichokes (Western Region, United States), *4:* 178
Matata (Stew, Mozambique), *3:* 18
Mathis (Spicy Cookie, India), *2:* 65
Matoke (Mashed Plantains, Kenya), *2:* 188
Matzo Balls (Jewish Americans, United States), *4:* 109
Matzo Brie (Jewish Americans, United States), *4:* 106
Mazapanes (Almond Candies, Spain), *3:* 181
Mchicha (Tanzania), *3:* 213
Mealie Soup (Corn Soup, South Africa), *3:* 151
Melitzanosalata (Greece), *2:* 21
Melon Fingers with Lime (Côte d'Ivoire), *1:* 131
Melopitta (Honey Pie, Greece), *2:* 17
Mescouta (Date Cookies, Morocco), *3:* 8
Mexican Fried Ice Cream (Latino Americans, United States), *4:* 119

Mexico, *2:* 215
    Arroz Blanco (White Rice), *2:* 225
    Birria, *2:* 221
    Café de Olla (Spiced Coffee), *2:* 218
    Camote (Sweet Potatoes), *2:* 222
    Chocolate Mexicana, *2:* 225
    Frijoles (Beans), *2:* 217
    Frijoles Refritos (Refried Beans), *2:* 217
    Guacamole, *2:* 223
    Huevos Rancheros (Eggs), *2:* 225
    Pico de Gallo (Mexican Salsa), *2:* 224
    Quesadillas, *2:* 222
    Rosca de Reyes (Sweet Bread), *2:* 218
    Tortilla Chips, *2:* 223
Mhalbi (Morocco), *3:* 9
Midwest Region (United States), *4:* 125
    Bread Pudding, *4:* 127
    Calzone, *4:* 132
    Caramel Corn, *4:* 131
    Corn on the Cob, *4:* 128
    Cornhusker's Casserole, *4:* 132
    Deviled Eggs, *4:* 127
    Green Bean Casserole, *4:* 129
    Lefse, *4:* 131
    Midwestern Chili, *4:* 128
    Midwestern Pork Chop Dinner, *4:* 132
    Reuben Sandwich, *4:* 130
Midwestern Chili (Midwest Region, United States), *4:* 128
Midwestern Pork Chop Dinner (Midwest Region, United States), *4:* 132
Milanesa (Argentina), *1:* 19
Milk Tea (Portugal), *3:* 99
Miso Soup (Japan), *2:* 166
Molasses Water (African Americans, United States), *4:* 68
Moors and Christians (Cuba), *1:* 139
Moos Bukaani (Fried Plantains, Somalia), *3:* 142
Moqueca (Spicy Fish Stew, Afro-Brazilians, Brazil), *1:* 58
Moqueca aos Ovos (Egg Stew, Afro-Brazilians, Brazil), *1:* 59
Moravske Vano ni Kukyse (Czech Republic), *1:* 156
Morir Soñando (Dominican Republic), *1:* 167
Moroccan Mint Tea (Morocco), *3:* 4

Index

Morocco, *3:* 1
   Amlou (Almond Butter), *3:* 10
   Bisteeya, *3:* 6
   Bocadillo, *3:* 10
   Chicken Tajine, *3:* 2
   Chickpea, Feta, and Olive Salad, *3:* 8
   Couscous, *3:* 8
   Fried Baby Carrots, *3:* 12
   Harira, *3:* 7
   Mescouta (Date Cookies), *3:* 8
   Mhalbi, *3:* 9
   Moroccan Mint Tea, *3:* 4
   "String of Doughnuts," *3:* 9
   Sweet Grated Carrot Salad, *3:* 10
   Warqa, *3:* 5
Mother's Chicken Soup (Jewish Americans, United States), *4:* 103
Moussaka (Casserole, Greece), *2:* 15
Mousse au Chocolat (France), *1:* 207
Mozambique, *3:* 13
   Bolo Polana, *3:* 21
   Filhos de Natal, *3:* 19
   Frango a Cafrial, *3:* 23
   Lemon and Herb Salad Dressing, *3:* 21
   Maize Porridge, *3:* 16
   Malasadas (Doughnuts), *3:* 17
   Matata (Stew), *3:* 18
   Pao de Banana, *3:* 23
   Pãozinho (Portuguese Rolls), *3:* 15
   Piri-Piri Sauce, *3:* 15
   Rice with Papaya, *3:* 22
   Salada Pera de Abacate (Salad), *3:* 21
   Sandes de Queijo (Sandwich), *3:* 16
   Shrimp Mozambique, *3:* 22
   Sopa de Feijao Verde (Soup), *3:* 22
Muhallabi (Rice Pudding, Turkey), *4:* 18
Muhallabia (Pudding, Saudi Arabia), *3:* 123
Mushroom Barley Soup (Poland), *3:* 85
Mutton Kespe (Kazakhstan), *2:* 176
Muufo Baraawe (Bread Rolls, Somalia), *3:* 144

N

Naan (India), *2:* 65
Nachynka (Cornbread Stuffing, Ukraine), *4:* 38
Nam Pla Prig (Dipping Sauce, Thailand), *4:* 6
Nanaimo Bars (Canada), *1:* 81
Naneli Limonata (Lemonade, Turkey), *4:* 20
Nasi Goreng (Fried Rice, Indonesia), *2:* 71
Nasi Jagung (Corn Rice, Indonesia), *2:* 78
Nasi Kuning (Yellow Rice, Indonesia), *2:* 77
Native Americans (United States), *4:* 135
   Buffalo Stew, *4:* 140
   Fruit Medley, *4:* 144
   Indian Fry-Bread, *4:* 143
   Iroquois Strawberry Drink, *4:* 142
   Maple Baked Beans, *4:* 139
   Pemmican, *4:* 144
   Pinole (Cornmeal Drink), *4:* 144
   Popcorn, *4:* 136
   Popped Wild Rice, *4:* 143
   Pumpkin Bread, *4:* 142
   Pumpkin-Corn Sauce, *4:* 140
   Succotash (Corn and Bean Stew), *4:* 138
Ndizi Kaanga (Fried Plantains, Tanzania), *3:* 209
Ndolé (Bitterleaf Stew, Cameroon), *1:* 70
New England Boiled Dinner (Northeast Region, United States), *4:* 154
New England Clam Chowder (Northeast Region, United States), *4:* 152
New Year's Honey Cake (Israel), *2:* 134
New York Cheesecake (Jewish Americans, United States), *4:* 108
Nigeria, *3:* 25
   Chinchin, *3:* 32
   Curried Okra, *3:* 32
   Dodo (Fried Plantains), *3:* 31
   Efo (Greens Stew), *3:* 31
   Isu (Spiced Boiled Yams), *3:* 27
   Iyan (Pounded Yams), *3:* 28
   Jollof Rice, *3:* 28
   Nigerian Stew, *3:* 29
   Obe Ata (Pepper Soup), *3:* 33
   Ojojo, *3:* 32
   Shuku Shuku (Coconut Balls), *3:* 33
Nigerian Stew (Nigeria), *3:* 29
Niter Kebbeh or Kibe (Ethiopia), *1:* 192
Noodle Kugel (Noodle Casserole, Jewish Americans, United States), *4:* 104
Noodle Pudding (Hungary), *2:* 52
Noodles with Poppy Seeds (Poland), *3:* 84

Index

Northeast Region (United States), *4:* 147
    Boston Baked Beans, *4:* 152
    Boston Cream Pie, *4:* 156
    Coffee Milkshake, *4:* 153
    Honey-Baked Apples, *4:* 155
    Hot Cranberry Punch, *4:* 155
    Indian Pudding, *4:* 149
    Johnnycakes, *4:* 151
    Lobster Roll, *4:* 156
    Maple Butter, *4:* 151
    New England Boiled Dinner, *4:* 154
    New England Clam Chowder, *4:* 152
    Succotash, *4:* 150
Ñoquis (Argentina), *1:* 14
Nuoc Cham (Dipping Sauce, Vietnam), *4:* 188
Nutella-filled Crepes (France), *1:* 206
Nyama Choma (Kenya), *2:* 189

O

Obe Ata (Pepper Soup, Nigeria), *3:* 33
Ojibwa Wild Rice (Great Lakes Region, United States), *4:* 92
Ojojo (Nigeria), *3:* 32
Okra (African Americans, United States), *4:* 75
Old Fashioned Bread Pudding (Southern Region, United States), *4:* 170
Old-Fashioned Spicy Lemonade (Amish and Pennsylvania Dutch, United States), *4:* 84
Old Fashioned Turnip Soup (Southern Region, United States), *4:* 161
Olho de Sogra (Afro-Brazilians, Brazil), *1:* 63
Olive Tapenade (Greece), *2:* 22
Omelet with Ground Pork (Vietnam), *4:* 197
Onigiri (Rice Ball, Japan), *2:* 163
Orange Salad (Brazil), *1:* 46
Oto (Yams & Eggs, Ghana), *2:* 5
Ozoni (New Year's Soup, Japan), *2:* 167

P

Pad See Ew (Thailand), *4:* 5
Pad Thai (Thailand), *4:* 10
Pain Haïtien (Haitian Bread, Haiti), *2:* 41

Pakistan, *3:* 37
    Aaloo Bukhary Ki Chutney, *3:* 39
    Apple Chutney, *3:* 45
    Baingan Ka Raita, *3:* 42
    Chicken Biryani, *3:* 45
    Chicken Karahi, *3:* 41
    Dhal (Lentil Stew), *3:* 40
    Kheer (Rice Pudding), *3:* 42
    Lassi (Yogurt Drink), *3:* 42
    Raita (Salad), *3:* 41
    Shahi Tukra, *3:* 39
    Sheer Korma (Dates with Milk), *3:* 46
Palak Bhaji (Fried Spinach, India), *2:* 60
Palak Paneer (India), *2:* 66
Palava (Liberia), *2:* 206
Paleta de Coco (Dominican Republic), *1:* 161
Palta Aji Sauce (Peru), *3:* 53
Pan de Banano (Banana Bread, Guatemala), *2:* 30
Pan de Maiz (Dominican Republic), *1:* 160
Pan de Sal (Philippines), *3:* 68
Panettone (Christmas Bread, Italy), *2:* 145
Pansit Mami (Noodles in Broth, Philippines), *3:* 72
Pao de Banana (Mozambique), *3:* 23
Pão de Queijo (Brazil), *1:* 51
Pãozinho (Portuguese Rolls, Mozambique), *3:* 15
Papas a la Huancaína (Peru), *3:* 55
Papaya Chicken (Islands of the Pacific), *2:* 121
Paprika Chicken (Hungary), *2:* 48
Parsley New Potatoes (Western Region, United States), *4:* 182
Pashka (Russia), *3:* 106
Paska (Easter Bread, Ukraine), *4:* 37
Pasta e Fagioli (Soup, Italy), *2:* 141
Pasta with Yogurt-Mint Sauce (Turkey), *4:* 18
Pasteis de nata (Custard Tarts, Portugal), *3:* 94
Pastel de Choclo (Chile), *1:* 107
Pastelitos (Cuba), *1:* 144
Patatas Bravas (Spain), *3:* 184
Patates Fourno Riganates (Greece), *2:* 19
Patbingsu (Korean Shaved Ice, South Korea), *3:* 172
Pavlova (Australia), *1:* 30
Peanut Butter Molasses Spread (Amish and Pennsylvania Dutch, United States), *4:* 86
Peanut Soup (African Americans, United States), *4:* 75

Index

Pemmican (Native Americans, United States), *4:* 144
Pemmican Cakes (Aboriginals, Canada), *1:* 86
Pennsylvania Dutch. See Amish and Pennsylvania Dutch (United States)
Pepinos Rellenos (Guatemala), *2:* 29
Pepparkakor (Ginger Cookies, Sweden), *3:* 198
Pepper Soup (Ghana), *2:* 8
Pepper-Scented Rice (Brazil), *1:* 49
Peru, *3:* 49
    Aji de Gallina, *3:* 60
    Alfajores, *3:* 60
    Arroz con Leche (Rice and Milk), *3:* 54
    Baked Papas (Potato Skins), *3:* 51
    Ceviche (Marinated Seafood), *3:* 57
    Choclo con Queso, *3:* 53
    Ensalada de Pallares (Salad), *3:* 55
    Flan, *3:* 58
    Frozen Orange Delight, *3:* 56
    Maná, *3:* 56
    Palta Aji Sauce, *3:* 53
    Papas a la Huancaína, *3:* 55
    Picarones (Pumpkin Fritters), *3:* 50
Philippines, *3:* 63
    Adobong Hiponsa Gata, *3:* 68
    Coconut Milk, *3:* 65
    Ensaymada, *3:* 69
    Fruit Salad, *3:* 72
    Leche Flan (Caramel Custard), *3:* 66
    Maja Blanco (Coconut Cake), *3:* 66
    Pan de Sal, *3:* 68
    Pansit Mami (Noodles in Broth), *3:* 72
    Polvoron (Milk Candy), *3:* 73
    Puto Maya (Rice Cake), *3:* 74
    Sinangag (Garlic Rice), *3:* 71
    Tsokolate (Hot Chocolate), *3:* 70
Pho Bo (Beef Noodle Soup, Vietnam), *4:* 191
Picado de Rabano (Salad, Guatemala), *2:* 24
Picarones (Pumpkin Fritters, Peru), *3:* 50
Pico de Gallo (Mexican Salsa, Mexico), *2:* 224
Pierogi (Dumplings, Poland), *3:* 82
Pikelets (Australia), *1:* 27
Piña Asada (Cuba), *1:* 143
Pineapple Nog (Haiti), *2:* 36
Pineapple-Orange Drink (Brazil), *1:* 48
Pineapple Salad (Côte d'Ivoire), *1:* 129

Pineapple Sherbet (Smoothie, South Africa), *3:* 157
Pineapple with Honey & Coconut (Tanzania), *3:* 214
Pinole (Cornmeal Drink, Native Americans, United States), *4:* 144
Piri-Piri Sauce (Mozambique), *3:* 15
Piri Piri Sauce (Portugal), *3:* 93
Pisang Goreng (Banana Cakes, Indonesia), *2:* 75
Pisto Manchego with Eggs (Spain), *3:* 178
Pita Bread (Lebanon), *2:* 195
Pita Sandwiches (Israel), *2:* 136
Pitepalt (Potato Pastries, Sweden), *3:* 195
Pizza-ghetti (French Canadians, Canada), *1:* 100
Pizza Margherita (Italy), *2:* 146
Plättar (Swedish Pancakes, Sweden), *3:* 200
Plov (Rice Pilaf, Kazakhstan), *2:* 175
Plum Ice Cream (Aborigines and Bush Tucker, Australia), *1:* 39
Poa Pee (Thai Egg Rolls, Thailand), *4:* 6
Poi (Islands of the Pacific), *2:* 125
Poisson Cru (Islands of the Pacific), *2:* 120
Poland, *3:* 77
    Babka, *3:* 86
    Bigos (Polish Hunter's Stew), *3:* 78
    Cheesecake, *3:* 82
    Dried Fruit Compote, *3:* 85
    Golabki (Stuffed Cabbage Rolls), *3:* 81
    Kielbasa and Cabbage, *3:* 80
    Mushroom Barley Soup, *3:* 85
    Noodles with Poppy Seeds, *3:* 84
    Pierogi (Dumplings), *3:* 82
    Salatka, *3:* 86
    Stuffed Eggs, *3:* 88
    Uszka, *3:* 84
    Veal Meatballs with Dill, *3:* 88
    Zupa Koperkowa (Dill Soup), *3:* 80
Polenta (Fried Corn Mush, Brazil), *1:* 47
Polenta (Italy), *2:* 141
Polish Boy Sandwich (Great Lakes Region, United States), *4:* 97
Polvoron (Milk Candy, Philippines), *3:* 73
Ponche (Berry Punch, Chile), *1:* 112
Popcorn (Native Americans, United States), *4:* 136
Popped Wild Rice (Native Americans, United States), *4:* 143

Pork Chops with Sauerkraut (Amish and Pennsylvania Dutch, United States), *4:* 80
Pork Cutlets with Potatoes (Hungary), *2:* 49
Pörkölt (Hungarian Stew, Hungary), *2:* 47
Portugal, *3:* **91**
   Arroz Doce (Rice Pudding), *3:* 95
   Barriga de freira ("Nun's Belly"), *3:* 92
   Bolo Rei (King's Cake), *3:* 98
   Caldo Verde (Kale Soup), *3:* 97
   Cozido (Beef Stew), *3:* 94
   Milk Tea, *3:* 99
   Pasteis de nata (Custard Tarts), *3:* 94
   Piri Piri Sauce, *3:* 93
   Rebenadas (French Toast), *3:* 96
Potato Latkes (Potato Pancakes, Jewish Americans, United States), *4:* 106
Potato Lefse (Great Lakes Region, United States), *4:* 96
Potato Roesti (Germany), *1:* 218
Potato Salad (African Americans, United States), *4:* 71
Potato Varenyky (Dumplings, Ukraine), *4:* 31
Potica (Slovenia), *3:* 132
Pralines (Southern Region, United States), *4:* 170
Prince William's Groom's Cake (United Kingdom), *4:* 48
Pudding au Chomeur (French Canadians, Canada), *1:* 99
Pudim (Thick Custard, Brazil), *1:* 50
Puerto Rican Christmas Salad (Latino Americans, United States), *4:* 120
Pumpkin Bread (Native Americans, United States), *4:* 142
Pumpkin-Corn Sauce (Native Americans, United States), *4:* 140
Pumpkin Samsa (Kazakhstan), *2:* 180
Pumpkin Soup (Liberia), *2:* 210
Pupusas (El Salvador), *1:* 181
Puto Maya (Rice Cake, Philippines), *3:* 74
Putupap (Cornmeal Porridge, South Africa), *3:* 158

Q

Qahwa (Arabic Coffee, Saudi Arabia), *3:* 122
Qatayef (Iraq), *2:* 102
Quebec Poutine (French Canadians, Canada), *1:* 103
Quejadinhas (Brazil), *1:* 51
Quesadillas (Latino Americans, United States), *4:* 122
Quesadillas (Mexico), *2:* 222
Quiabo (Okra, Afro-Brazilians, Brazil), *1:* 57
Quiche au Saumon et Crevettes (France), *1:* 206
Quick No-Cook Mini-Pavlova (Australia), *1:* 30
Quindins (Coconut Macaroons, Afro-Brazilians, Brazil), *1:* 59

R

Rågbröd (Swedish Rye Bread, Sweden), *3:* 201
Ragoût de Boulettes (French Canadians, Canada), *1:* 101
Rainbow Rice (Dominican Republic), *1:* 164
Raita (Salad, Pakistan), *3:* 41
Ramen (Noodle Soup, Japan), *2:* 171
Rårakor (Potato Pancakes, Sweden), *3:* 202
Rebenadas (French Toast, Portugal), *3:* 96
Red Beans and Rice (African Americans, United States), *4:* 70
Red Coleslaw (Germany), *1:* 218
Red Lentil Soup (Iraq), *2:* 96
Reuben Sandwich (Midwest Region, United States), *4:* 130
Rice and Peas (Jamaica), *2:* 150
Rice Bread (Liberia), *2:* 208
Rice Sorpa (Kazakhstan), *2:* 181
Rice with Papaya (Mozambique), *3:* 22
Rice with Peanut Sauce (Zimbabwe), *4:* 204
Rice with Shrimp (Spain), *3:* 186
Rice, Saudi Style (Saudi Arabia), *3:* 119
Riguas (El Salvador), *1:* 182
Riz Djon-Djon (Haiti), *2:* 36
Riz et Pois Rouges (Haiti), *2:* 38
Roast Pork (Islands of the Pacific), *2:* 122
Roasted Butternut Squash (Zimbabwe), *4:* 202
Roasted Eggplant Salad (Turkey), *4:* 27
Rock Shandy (Zimbabwe), *4:* 204
Rosca de Reyes (Sweet Bread, Mexico), *2:* 218
Rose Hip Soup (Sweden), *3:* 192

Index

Rosh Hashanah Honey Cake (Jewish Americans, United States), *4:* 110
Rujak (Spicy Fruit Salad, Indonesia), *2:* 72
Russia, *3:* 101
   Bliny (Russian Pancakes), *3:* 102
   Bliny Filling, *3:* 102
   Borscht (Beet Soup), *3:* 108
   Cabbage Pirozhki or Piroghi, *3:* 104
   Chai Po-Russki (Tea), *3:* 110
   Griby Marinovannye, *3:* 109
   Khachapuri (Cheesy Boats), *3:* 111
   Klyukva S Sakharom , *3:* 112
   Kutya, *3:* 107
   Pashka, *3:* 106
   Salat Olivier (Russian Salad), *3:* 103
   Sbiten (Winter Beverage), *3:* 107
   Semechki (Sunflower Seeds), *3:* 110
   Sharlotka (Apple Cake), *3:* 110
   Shchi (Cabbage Soup), *3:* 105
Rye Bread (Germany), *1:* 216

S

Sadza (Zimbabwe), *4:* 202
Saffron and Raisin Couscous (Algeria), *1:* 3
Safou a la Sauce Tomate (Cameroon), *1:* 67
Sahlab (Algeria), *1:* 5
St. Catherine's Taffy (French Canadians, Canada), *1:* 102
Salada Pera de Abacate (Salad, Mozambique), *3:* 21
Salads
   Algerian Cooked Carrot Salad (Algeria), *1:* 7
   Ansalaato (Salad, Somalia), *3:* 144
   Banadura Salata B'Kizbara (Algeria), *1:* 5
   Banana and Pineapple Salad (Cameroon), *1:* 70
   Beetroot Salad (Turkey), *4:* 21
   Carrot, Apple, and Raisin Salad (Australia), *1:* 26
   Chickpea, Feta, and Olive Salad (Morocco), *3:* 8
   Cuban Avocado Salad (Latino Americans, United States), *4:* 122
   Cucumber Salad (Thailand), *4:* 7
   Dandelion Salad (Slovenia), *3:* 132
   Desser Miveh (Fruit Salad, Iran), *2:* 89
   Ensalada Campesina (Chile), *1:* 106
   Ensalada Chilena (Salad, Chile), *1:* 108
   Ensalada Cubana Tipica (Salad, Cuba), *1:* 141
   Ensalada de Pallares (Salad, Peru), *3:* 55
   Fatoosh (Lebanon), *2:* 203
   French-Style Lettuce Salad (Haiti), *2:* 34
   Frouta Ke Yaourti (Fruit Salad, Greece), *2:* 17
   Fruit Salad (Philippines), *3:* 72
   Fruit Salad (Saudi Arabia), *3:* 122
   Gado-Gado (Vegetable Salad, Indonesia), *2:* 77
   German Potato Salad (Great Lakes Region, United States), *4:* 93
   Greek Salad (Greece), *2:* 18
   Green Bean Salad (South Africa), *3:* 153
   Haitian Fruit Salad (Haiti), *2:* 36
   Insalata Caprese (Italy), *2:* 148
   Israeli Vegetable Salad (Israel), *2:* 132
   Jajeek (Yogurt Salad, Iraq), *2:* 100
   Kachumbari Salad (Kenya), *2:* 190
   Kazakhstan Salad (Kazakhstan), *2:* 177
   Lebanese Beet Salad (Lebanon), *2:* 202
   Lebanese Fresh Fruit Salad (Lebanon), *2:* 200
   Lemon and Garlic Potato Salad (Egypt), *1:* 174
   Lettuce Dipped in Dressing (Iran), *2:* 88
   Lettuce Salad (Egypt), *1:* 176
   Orange Salad (Brazil), *1:* 46
   Picado de Rabano (Salad, Guatemala), *2:* 24
   Pineapple Salad (Côte d'Ivoire), *1:* 129
   Potato Salad (African Americans, United States), *4:* 71
   Puerto Rican Christmas Salad (Latino Americans, United States), *4:* 120
   Raita (Salad, Pakistan), *3:* 41
   Red Coleslaw (Germany), *1:* 218
   Roasted Eggplant Salad (Turkey), *4:* 27
   Rujak (Spicy Fruit Salad, Indonesia), *2:* 72
   Salada Pera de Abacate (Salad, Mozambique), *3:* 21
   Salat Olivier (Russian Salad, Russia), *3:* 103
   Salatka (Poland), *3:* 86
   Shirazi (Salad, Iran), *2:* 82
   Sillsallad (Herring Salad, Sweden), *3:* 203
   Sour Cream Cucumber Salad (Czech Republic), *1:* 151
   Sweet Grated Carrot Salad (Morocco), *3:* 10
   Tabbouleh (Bulgur Wheat Salad, Saudi Arabia), *3:* 120
   Tabbouleh (Lebanon), *2:* 196

Tamatar Salat (Tomato Salad, India), *2:* 63
Tomato and Cucumber Salad (African Americans, United States), *4:* 74
Tropical Fruit Salad (Latino Americans, United States), *4:* 123
Salat Olivier (Russian Salad, Russia), *3:* 103
Salatka (Poland), *3:* 86
Salmon Kedgeree (United Kingdom), *4:* 43
Salsa Cruda (Latino Americans, United States), *4:* 116
Saltimbocca alla Romana (Italy), *2:* 143
Sambal Kecap (Sauce, Indonesia), *2:* 74
Samgyetang (Chicken Soup, South Korea), *3:* 165
Sancocho (Dominican Republic), *1:* 164
Sandes de Queijo (Sandwich, Mozambique), *3:* 16

Sandwiches
Baguette Sandwich (France), *1:* 203
Banh Mi Tom Chien (Vietnam), *4:* 197
Barros Jarpa (Chile), *1:* 113
Bocadillo (Morocco), *3:* 10
Bocaditos (Finger Sandwiches, Argentina), *1:* 18
Croque-Monsieur (Sandwich, France), *1:* 203
Cubano (Cuba), *1:* 146
Cucumber Sandwiches (United Kingdom), *4:* 44
Falafel (Israel), *2:* 133
Pita Sandwiches (Israel), *2:* 136
Polish Boy Sandwich (Great Lakes Region, United States), *4:* 97
Reuben Sandwich (Midwest Region, United States), *4:* 130
Sandes de Queijo (Sandwich, Mozambique), *3:* 16
Smörgås med ost och päron (Sweden), *3:* 202
Vegetable Sandwich (India), *2:* 62

Sang Ka Ya (Coconut Custard, Thailand), *4:* 9
Sarikayo Telor (Pudding, Indonesia), *2:* 73
Saskatoon Berry Snack (Aboriginals, Canada), *1:* 87
Sauce Pimente (Côte d'Ivoire), *1:* 128

Sauces and relishes
Aaloo Bukhary Ki Chutney (Pakistan), *3:* 39
Apple Butter (Amish and Pennsylvania Dutch, United States), *4:* 87
Apple Chutney (Pakistan), *3:* 45
Arachid Sauce (Côte d'Ivoire), *1:* 135
Baigan Bhartha (India), *2:* 58
Barbeque Sauce (Southern Region, United States), *4:* 171
Bush Tomato Relish (Aborigines and Bush Tucker, Australia), *1:* 40
Chimichurri (Dipping Sauce, Argentina), *1:* 16
Chinese Peanut Sauce (Western Region, United States), *4:* 181
Ch'o Kanjang (Vinegar Soy Sauce, South Korea), *3:* 171
Cranberry Salsa (Western Region, United States), *4:* 178
Creamy Dipping Sauce (Sweden), *3:* 191
Greek Salad Dressing (Greece), *2:* 19
Guacamole (Guatemala), *2:* 26
Guacamole (Latino Americans, United States), *4:* 116
Guacamole (Mexico), *2:* 223
Haysa Al-Tumreya (Dip, Saudi Arabia), *3:* 117
Herring Dip (Jewish Americans, United States), *4:* 107
Komkomer Sambal (South Africa), *3:* 155
Lemon and Herb Salad Dressing (Mozambique), *3:* 21
Lemon Curd (United Kingdom), *4:* 44
Maast (Homemade Yogurt, Iran), *2:* 88
Makiwnyk Glaze (Cake Glaze, Ukraine), *4:* 36
Maple Butter (Northeast Region, United States), *4:* 151
Nam Pla Prig (Dipping Sauce, Thailand), *4:* 6
Nuoc Cham (Dipping Sauce, Vietnam), *4:* 188
Olive Tapenade (Greece), *2:* 22
Palava (Liberia), *2:* 206
Palta Aji Sauce (Peru), *3:* 53
Pico de Gallo (Mexican Salsa, Mexico), *2:* 224
Piña Asada (Cuba), *1:* 143
Piri-Piri Sauce (Mozambique), *3:* 15
Piri Piri Sauce (Portugal), *3:* 93
Pumpkin-Corn Sauce (Native Americans, United States), *4:* 140
Salsa Cruda (Latino Americans, United States), *4:* 116
Sambal Kecap (Sauce, Indonesia), *2:* 74
Sauce Pimente (Côte d'Ivoire), *1:* 128
Stewed Mangoes with Cloves (Liberia), *2:* 209
Tahini Sauce (Israel), *2:* 133
Ti-Malice (Spicy Haitian Sauce, Haiti), *2:* 39
Tzatziki (Sauce, Greece), *2:* 20

Index

Sauces and relishes (*continued*)
  Yogurt and Mint Sauce (Iran), *2:* 84
  Yogurt Chutney (Kenya), *2:* 188
Saudi Arabia, *3:* 113
  Baharat (Spice Blend), *3:* 114
  Fatir (Flat Bread), *3:* 115
  Fruit Salad, *3:* 122
  Hawayij (Spice Blend), *3:* 114
  Haysa Al-Tumreya (Dip), *3:* 117
  Hummus, *3:* 120
  Kabsa (Lamb with Rice), *3:* 116
  Kapsa (Chicken and Rice), *3:* 118
  Kimaje (Flat Bread), *3:* 119
  Laban Drink (Yogurt Drink), *3:* 117
  Muhallabia (Pudding), *3:* 123
  Qahwa (Arabic Coffee), *3:* 122
  Rice, Saudi Style, *3:* 119
  Tabbouleh (Bulgur Wheat Salad), *3:* 120
Sautéed Fiddleheads (Canada), *1:* 77
Sbiten (Winter Beverage, Russia), *3:* 107
Scones (Ireland), *2:* 110
Scones (United Kingdom), *4:* 46
Scotland (United Kingdom), *4:* 55
  Aberdeen Buttery, *4:* 62
  Barley Pudding, *4:* 63
  Chocolate-dipped Shortbread, *4:* 59
  Cock-a-Leekie Soup, *4:* 61
  Cranachan, *4:* 62
  Cullen Skink, *4:* 60
  Flapjacks (Oatmeal Biscuits), *4:* 57
  Haggis, *4:* 56
  Skirlie, *4:* 58
  Tattie Soup, *4:* 57
  Tatties n' Neeps, *4:* 57
Seasonings
  Baharat (Spice Blend, Saudi Arabia), *3:* 114
  Berbere (Spice Paste, Ethiopia), *1:* 192
  Creole Seasoning (Southern Region, United States), *4:* 160
  Fresh Grated Coconut (Islands of the Pacific), *2:* 119
  Garam Masala (Spice Mixture, India), *2:* 59
  Hawayij (Spice Blend, Saudi Arabia), *3:* 114
  Macadamia Nut Dukkah (Australia), *1:* 24
  Toasted Sesame Seeds (South Korea), *3:* 169
Semechki (Sunflower Seeds, Russia), *3:* 110

Sesame Candy (Israel), *2:* 130
Shaah Hawaash (Spiced Tea, Somalia), *3:* 143
Shahi Tukra (Pakistan), *3:* 39
Shai (Mint Tea, Egypt), *1:* 171
Shakshooka (Israel), *2:* 129
Sharlotka (Apple Cake, Russia), *3:* 110
Shchi (Cabbage Soup, Russia), *3:* 105
Sheer Korma (Dates with Milk, Pakistan), *3:* 46
Shigumch'i Namul (Spinach, South Korea), *3:* 170
Shirazi (Salad, Iran), *2:* 82
Shir-Berenj (Rice Pudding, Iran), *2:* 87
Shoofly Pie (Amish and Pennsylvania Dutch, United States), *4:* 82
Shrimp Mozambique (Mozambique), *3:* 22
Shu Mai Dumplings (Thailand), *4:* 12
Shuku Shuku (Coconut Balls, Nigeria), *3:* 33
Side dishes
  Adas Bil Hamod (Lentils, Iraq), *2:* 96
  Aloko (Fried Bananas, Côte d'Ivoire), *1:* 128
  Angu de Milho (Cornmeal Dish, Afro-Brazilians, Brazil), *1:* 60
  Apple and Carrot Tsimmes (Jewish Americans, United States), *4:* 105
  Apple Sauerkraut (Great Lakes Region, United States), *4:* 95
  Arroz Blanco (White Rice, Mexico), *2:* 225
  Arroz Guatemalteco (Rice, Guatemala), *2:* 26
  Avocado with Dressing (Côte d'Ivoire), *1:* 135
  Avocado with Peanut Dressing (Ghana), *2:* 9
  Baingan Ka Raita (Pakistan), *3:* 42
  Baked Macaroni and Cheese (African Americans, United States), *4:* 72
  Baked Mushrooms with Cheese (Slovenia), *3:* 129
  Baked Ripe Banana (Jamaica), *2:* 156
  Bamia (Sweet and Sour Okra, Egypt), *1:* 174
  Banana Frita (Fried Bananas, Brazil), *1:* 50
  Bananas and Sweet Potatoes (Islands of the Pacific), *2:* 122
  Banann Peze (Fried Plantains, Haiti), *2:* 38
  Basic Rice (Afro-Brazilians, Brazil), *1:* 57
  Boiled Cassava (Cameroon), *1:* 70
  Boston Baked Beans (Northeast Region, United States), *4:* 152
  Brazilian Black Beans (Afro-Brazilians, Brazil), *1:* 60
  Bulgur Pilavi (Pilaf, Turkey), *4:* 25

Camote (Sweet Potatoes, Mexico), *2:* 222
Canh Bi Ro Ham Dua (Vietnam), *4:* 192
Carne Asada Fries (Western Region, United States), *4:* 183
Carrot Bredie (South Africa), *3:* 153
Champ (Ireland), *2:* 109
Charoset (Jewish Americans, United States), *4:* 105
Charoseth (Israel), *2:* 131
Chitlins (African Americans, United States), *4:* 69
Choclo con Queso (Peru), *3:* 53
Coconut Rice (Cameroon), *1:* 71
Colcannon (Ireland), *2:* 110
Collard Greens (African Americans, United States), *4:* 66
Collard Greens with Ham Hocks (Southern Region, United States), *4:* 168
Collards with Cabbage (Liberia), *2:* 211
Corn on the Cob (Midwest Region, United States), *4:* 128
Corn on the Cob (South Africa), *3:* 157
Cornhusker's Casserole (Midwest Region, United States), *4:* 132
Cornmeal Cake (Zimbabwe), *4:* 203
Couscous (Morocco), *3:* 8
Curried Okra (Nigeria), *3:* 32
Dal (Lentils, India), *2:* 61
Deep-Fried Potatoes (Slovenia), *3:* 129
Dilly Beans (Southern Region, United States), *4:* 162
Dodo (Fried Plantains, Nigeria), *3:* 31
Doughboys (Dumplings, French Canadians, Canada), *1:* 97
Fancy Rice (India), *2:* 63
Fried Baby Carrots (Morocco), *3:* 12
Fried Plantains (Cuba), *1:* 140
Fried Plantains (El Salvador), *1:* 180
Fried Plantains (Latino Americans, United States), *4:* 118
Fried Rice (China), *1:* 120
Fried Wonton (China), *1:* 124
Fried Yucca with Curtido (El Salvador), *1:* 185
Frijoles (Beans, Mexico), *2:* 217
Frijoles Refritos (Refried Beans, Mexico), *2:* 217
Ful Mudammas (Egypt), *1:* 170
Geel Rys (Yellow Rice, South Africa), *3:* 155

German Potato Salad (Great Lakes Region, United States), *4:* 93
Githeri (Kenya), *2:* 189
Glazed Carrots (Sweden), *3:* 191
Gohan (Boiled Rice, Japan), *2:* 163
Gomen Wat (Ethiopian Greens, Ethiopia), *1:* 197
Green Bean Casserole (Midwest Region, United States), *4:* 129
Griby Marinovannye (Russia), *3:* 109
Grits (Southern Region, United States), *4:* 166
Hasselbackspotatis (Sweden), *3:* 200
Hin Pap (White Rice, South Korea), *3:* 165
Hrechana Kasha (Ukraine), *4:* 33
Hush Puppies (African Americans, United States), *4:* 70
Indonesian Spiced Rice (Indonesia), *2:* 79
Iranian Rice Cakes (Iran), *2:* 88
Irio (Kenya), *2:* 185
Kartoffelknödeln (Dumplings, Germany), *1:* 216
Kartoplia Solimkoi (Potatoes, Ukraine), *4:* 34
Kelewele (Fried Plantains, Ghana), *2:* 4
Kenkey (Ground Cornmeal, Ghana), *2:* 7
Kenyan Cabbage (Kenya), *2:* 189
Klimp (Dumplings, Sweden), *3:* 194
Knedlíky (Czech Dumplings, Czech Republic), *1:* 152
Koki (Cameroon), *1:* 68
Kutya (Sweet Porridge, Ukraine), *4:* 33
Lebanese Eggplant (Lebanon), *2:* 196
Lor Köftesi (Ricotta Patties, Turkey), *4:* 19
M'hajeb (Algeria), *1:* 8
Makubi (Tanzania), *3:* 214
Mandu (Korean Dumplings, South Korea), *3:* 169
Mango and Sticky Rice (Thailand), *4:* 12
Mangú (Dominican Republic), *1:* 161
Man-O-Min (Ojibwa Wild Rice, Aboriginals, Canada), *1:* 92
Maple Baked Beans (Native Americans, United States), *4:* 139
Matoke (Mashed Plantains, Kenya), *2:* 188
Mchicha (Tanzania), *3:* 213
Moos Bukaani (Fried Plantains, Somalia), *3:* 142
Nasi Goreng (Fried Rice, Indonesia), *2:* 71
Nasi Jagung (Corn Rice, Indonesia), *2:* 78
Nasi Kuning (Yellow Rice, Indonesia), *2:* 77
Ndizi Kaanga (Fried Plantains, Tanzania), *3:* 209

Index

Side dishes (*continued*)
- Noodle Kugel (Noodle Casserole, Jewish Americans, United States), *4:* 104
- Ojibwa Wild Rice (Great Lakes Region, United States), *4:* 92
- Okra (African Americans, United States), *4:* 75
- Papas a la Huancaína (Peru), *3:* 55
- Parsley New Potatoes (Western Region, United States), *4:* 182
- Patatas Bravas (Spain), *3:* 184
- Patates Fourno Riganates (Greece), *2:* 19
- Pepper-Scented Rice (Brazil), *1:* 49
- Pierogi (Dumplings, Poland), *3:* 82
- Poa Pee (Thai Egg Rolls, Thailand), *4:* 6
- Poi (Islands of the Pacific), *2:* 125
- Polenta (Fried Corn Mush, Brazil), *1:* 47
- Polenta (Italy), *2:* 141
- Popped Wild Rice (Native Americans, United States), *4:* 143
- Potato Latkes (Potato Pancakes, Jewish Americans, United States), *4:* 106
- Potato Roesti (Germany), *1:* 218
- Potato Varenyky (Dumplings, Ukraine), *4:* 31
- Pumpkin Samsa (Kazakhstan), *2:* 180
- Quebec Poutine (French Canadians, Canada), *1:* 103
- Quiabo (Okra, Afro-Brazilians, Brazil), *1:* 57
- Rainbow Rice (Dominican Republic), *1:* 164
- Red Beans and Rice (African Americans, United States), *4:* 70
- Rice with Papaya (Mozambique), *3:* 22
- Rice with Peanut Sauce (Zimbabwe), *4:* 204
- Rice, Saudi Style (Saudi Arabia), *3:* 119
- Riguas (El Salvador), *1:* 182
- Riz Djon-Djon (Haiti), *2:* 36
- Riz et Pois Rouges (Haiti), *2:* 38
- Roasted Butternut Squash (Zimbabwe), *4:* 202
- Sadza (Zimbabwe), *4:* 202
- Saffron and Raisin Couscous (Algeria), *1:* 3
- Sautéed Fiddleheads (Canada), *1:* 77
- Shu Mai Dumplings (Thailand), *4:* 12
- Sinangag (Garlic Rice, Philippines), *3:* 71
- Skirlie (Scotland, United Kingdom), *4:* 58
- Small Dumplings (Hungary), *2:* 50
- Spargelgemuse (Asparagus, Germany), *1:* 213
- Spiced Couscous (Somalia), *3:* 145
- Spicy Braised Cabbage (Tanzania), *3:* 214
- Spring Rolls (Vietnam), *4:* 196
- Steak Frites (France), *1:* 208
- Stuffed Eggs (Poland), *3:* 88
- Succotash (Northeast Region, United States), *4:* 150
- Sugared Almonds (Lebanon), *2:* 200
- Sukuma Wiki (Kenya), *2:* 186
- Sunday Lunch Cauliflower Cheese (United Kingdom), *4:* 52
- Surbiyaan (Somali Rice, Somalia), *3:* 140
- Sweet Potato Casserole (Haiti), *2:* 40
- Sweet Potato Pone (Jamaica), *2:* 158
- Sweet Potato Pone (Liberia), *2:* 207
- Tahu Goreng (Fried Tofu, Indonesia), *2:* 74
- Tatties n' Neeps (Scotland, United Kingdom), *4:* 57
- Tostones (Dominican Republic), *1:* 166
- Ugali (Kenya), *2:* 187
- Ugali (Tanzania), *3:* 209
- Uszka (Poland), *3:* 84
- Wali wa Nazi (Coconut Rice, Kenya), *2:* 190
- Wali wa Nazi (Tanzania), *3:* 211
- Wild Rice Cakes (Aboriginals, Canada), *1:* 91
- Yorkshire Pudding (Canada), *1:* 77
- Yucca (Cassava, Cuba), *1:* 141
- Zimbabwe Greens (Zimbabwe), *4:* 204

Sillsallad (Herring Salad, Sweden), *3:* 203
Simit (Sesame Rings, Turkey), *4:* 20
Sinangag (Garlic Rice, Philippines), *3:* 71
Skirlie (Scotland, United Kingdom), *4:* 58
Slovenia, *3:* **125**
- Baked Mushrooms with Cheese, *3:* 129
- Bean Soup, *3:* 133
- Dandelion Salad, *3:* 132
- Deep-Fried Potatoes, *3:* 129
- Frtalja, *3:* 128
- Gibanica, *3:* 134
- Golaz (Goulash), *3:* 127
- Jota, *3:* 126
- Klobasa and Kisdo Zelje, *3:* 129
- Ljubljana Egg Dish, *3:* 131
- Potica, *3:* 132
- Slovenian Almond Bars, *3:* 130

Slovenian Almond Bars (Slovenia), *3:* 130
Small Dumplings (Hungary), *2:* 50

Smen Butter (Algeria), *1:* 3
Smörgås med ost och päron (Sweden), *3:* 202
Snacks
   Biltong and Dried Fruit Snack (South Africa), *3:* 152
   California-style Pizza (Western Region, United States), *4:* 182
   Calzone (Midwest Region, United States), *4:* 132
   Caramel Corn (Midwest Region, United States), *4:* 131
   Cheese and Vegetable Tray (Iran), *2:* 90
   Chicago Deep Dish Pizza (Great Lakes Region, United States), *4:* 98
   Churros (Spain), *3:* 182
   Coconut Chips (Jamaica), *2:* 151
   Cornish Pasties (United Kingdom), *4:* 45
   Cornish Pasty (Great Lakes Region, United States), *4:* 98
   Dabo Kolo (Little Fried Snacks, Ethiopia), *1:* 194
   Deviled Eggs (Midwest Region, United States), *4:* 127
   Empanadas (Little Baked Pies, Afro-Brazilians, Brazil), *1:* 61
   Fresh Oranges (Israel), *2:* 129
   Fried Bologna (African Americans, United States), *4:* 74
   Fromage (Cheese Board, France), *1:* 207
   Fruit Medley (Native Americans, United States), *4:* 144
   G'shur Purtaghal (Iraq), *2:* 101
   Halva (Iran), *2:* 87
   Hungarian Cold Plate (Hungary), *2:* 50
   Indian Fry-Bread (Native Americans, United States), *4:* 143
   Kategna (Ethiopia), *1:* 190
   Lab (Ethiopian Cheese, Ethiopia), *1:* 190
   Lahmacun (Turkish Pizza, Turkey), *4:* 27
   Locum (Turkish Candy, Turkey), *4:* 24
   Macadamia and Fruit Snack (Aborigines and Bush Tucker, Australia), *1:* 37
   Mapopo (Papaya) Candy (Zimbabwe), *4:* 200
   Mazapanes (Almond Candies, Spain), *3:* 181
   Ojojo (Nigeria), *3:* 32
   Onigiri (Rice Ball, Japan), *2:* 163
   Pastelitos (Cuba), *1:* 144
   Pemmican (Native Americans, United States), *4:* 144
   Pemmican Cakes (Aboriginals, Canada), *1:* 86
   Pepinos Rellenos (Guatemala), *2:* 29
   Pizza Margherita (Italy), *2:* 146
   Popcorn (Native Americans, United States), *4:* 136
   Pralines (Southern Region, United States), *4:* 170
   Quejadinhas (Brazil), *1:* 51
   Quesadillas (Latino Americans, United States), *4:* 122
   Quesadillas (Mexico), *2:* 222
   Saskatoon Berry Snack (Aboriginals, Canada), *1:* 87
   Semechki (Sunflower Seeds, Russia), *3:* 110
   Soft Pretzels (Germany), *1:* 219
   Sweet Potato Cookies (Zimbabwe), *4:* 205
   Tapa: Aceitunas Aliñadas (Spain), *3:* 185
   Tapa: Crema de Cabrales (Spain), *3:* 184
   Tapa: Tartaletas de Champiñón (Spain), *3:* 185
   Toast with Tomatoes (Ukraine), *4:* 36
   Toast with Vegemite (Australia), *1:* 32
   Tortilla Chips (Mexico), *2:* 223
   Tropical Fruit Salad (Latino Americans, United States), *4:* 123
   Whoopie Pie (Amish and Pennsylvania Dutch, United States), *4:* 87
Snow Ice Cream (Amish and Pennsylvania Dutch, United States), *4:* 83
Soapberry Ice Cream (Aboriginals, Canada), *1:* 87
Soda Chanh (Lemon Soda, Vietnam), *4:* 195
Soft Pretzels (Germany), *1:* 219
Somali Lamb and Rice (Somalia), *3:* 145
Somalia, *3:* 137
   Ansalaato (Salad), *3:* 144
   Baasto, *3:* 138
   Bajiya (Black Eyed Pea Fritter), *3:* 141
   Cambuulo, *3:* 144
   Canjeero (Flatbread), *3:* 141
   Kac-Kac (Sweet Bread), *3:* 146
   Moos Bukaani (Fried Plantains), *3:* 142
   Muufo Baraawe (Bread Rolls), *3:* 144
   Shaah Hawaash (Spiced Tea), *3:* 143
   Somali Lamb and Rice, *3:* 145
   Spiced Couscous, *3:* 145
   Suqaar, *3:* 140
   Surbiyaan (Somali Rice), *3:* 140

Index

Soo Chunkwa (Ginger Drink, South Korea), *3:* 163
Sopa de Feijao Verde (Soup, Mozambique), *3:* 22
Soupe à l'Oignon Gratinée (France), *1:* 204

Soups
  Artsoppa (Pea Soup, Sweden), *3:* 200
  Avgolemono (Soup, Greece), *2:* 14
  Bean Soup (Slovenia), *3:* 133
  Blandad Fruktsoppa (Soup, Sweden), *3:* 194
  Borscht (Beet Soup, Jewish Americans, United States), *4:* 110
  Borscht (Beet Soup, Russia), *3:* 108
  Cabbage Borshch (Ukraine), *4:* 32
  Caldo Verde (Kale Soup, Portugal), *3:* 97
  Chilled Avocado Soup (Côte d'Ivoire), *1:* 134
  Cock-a-Leekie Soup (Canada), *1:* 80
  Cock-a-Leekie Soup (Scotland, United Kingdom), *4:* 61
  Coconut Bean Soup (Tanzania), *3:* 208
  Coconut-Chicken Soup (Thailand), *4:* 10
  Cream of Cabbage Soup (Amish and Pennsylvania Dutch, United States), *4:* 81
  Cucumber & Yogurt Soup (Algeria), *1:* 9
  Cucumber Soup (Guatemala), *2:* 27
  Cullen Skink (Scotland, United Kingdom), *4:* 60
  Egg Drop Soup (China), *1:* 117
  French-Canadian Pea Soup (French Canadians, Canada), *1:* 97
  Gazpacho (Cold Tomato Soup, Spain), *3:* 177
  Gazpacho (Latino Americans, United States), *4:* 119
  Goat Soup (Liberia), *2:* 209
  Harira (Morocco), *3:* 7
  Kamja Guk (Potato Soup, South Korea), *3:* 164
  Mealie Soup (Corn Soup, South Africa), *3:* 151
  Miso Soup (Japan), *2:* 166
  Mother's Chicken Soup (Jewish Americans, United States), *4:* 103
  Mushroom Barley Soup (Poland), *3:* 85
  New England Clam Chowder (Northeast Region, United States), *4:* 152
  Obe Ata (Pepper Soup, Nigeria), *3:* 33
  Old Fashioned Turnip Soup (Southern Region, United States), *4:* 161
  Ozoni (New Year's Soup, Japan), *2:* 167
  Pasta e Fagioli (Soup, Italy), *2:* 141
  Peanut Soup (African Americans, United States), *4:* 75
  Pepper Soup (Ghana), *2:* 8
  Pho Bo (Beef Noodle Soup, Vietnam), *4:* 191
  Pumpkin Soup (Liberia), *2:* 210
  Ramen (Noodle Soup, Japan), *2:* 171
  Red Lentil Soup (Iraq), *2:* 96
  Rose Hip Soup (Sweden), *3:* 192
  Samgyetang (Chicken Soup, South Korea), *3:* 165
  Shchi (Cabbage Soup, Russia), *3:* 105
  Sopa de Feijao Verde (Soup, Mozambique), *3:* 22
  Soupe à l'Oignon Gratinée (France), *1:* 204
  Squash Soup (Aboriginals, Canada), *1:* 88
  Summer Cucumber Soup (Hungary), *2:* 52
  Supu Ya Ndizi (Plantain Soup, Tanzania), *3:* 211
  Tattie Soup (Scotland, United Kingdom), *4:* 57
  Three Sisters Soup (Aboriginals, Canada), *1:* 89
  Weisse Bohnensuppe (Soup, Germany), *1:* 212
  Wonton Soup (China), *1:* 119
  Zupa Koperkowa (Dill Soup, Poland), *3:* 80

Sour Cream Cucumber Salad (Czech Republic), *1:* 151

South Africa, *3:* 149
  Biltong and Dried Fruit Snack, *3:* 152
  Bobotie, *3:* 154
  Boerewors, *3:* 158
  Carrot Bredie, *3:* 153
  Corn on the Cob, *3:* 157
  Geel Rys (Yellow Rice), *3:* 155
  Green Bean Salad, *3:* 153
  Komkomer Sambal, *3:* 155
  Malva Pudding, *3:* 150
  Mealie Soup (Corn Soup), *3:* 151
  Pineapple Sherbet (Smoothie), *3:* 157
  Putupap (Cornmeal Porridge), *3:* 158
  Spinach and Peanut Butter Stew, *3:* 157

South Korea, *3:* 161
  Bulgogi (Korean Beef), *3:* 171
  Chap Ch'ae, *3:* 166
  Ch'o Kanjang (Vinegar Soy Sauce), *3:* 171
  Dotorimuk (Acorn Curd), *3:* 167
  Hin Pap (White Rice), *3:* 165
  Kamja Guk (Potato Soup), *3:* 164
  Kimchi, *3:* 164
  Mandu (Korean Dumplings), *3:* 169
  Patbingsu (Korean Shaved Ice), *3:* 172

Samgyetang (Chicken Soup), *3:* 165
Shigumch'i Namul (Spinach), *3:* 170
Soo Chunkwa (Ginger Drink), *3:* 163
Toasted Sesame Seeds, *3:* 169
Southern Fried Chicken (Southern Region, United States), *4:* 165
Southern Region (United States), *4:* 159
Barbeque Sauce, *4:* 171
Chess Pie, *4:* 161
Chicken and Sausage Gumbo, *4:* 165
Collard Greens with Ham Hocks, *4:* 168
Cornbread, *4:* 162
Creole Seasoning, *4:* 160
Dilly Beans, *4:* 162
Grits, *4:* 166
Mardi Gras King Cake, *4:* 166
Old Fashioned Bread Pudding, *4:* 170
Old Fashioned Turnip Soup, *4:* 161
Pralines, *4:* 170
Southern Fried Chicken, *4:* 165
Sweet Potato Pie, *4:* 164
Sweet Tea, *4:* 168
Spain, *3:* 175
Chocolate a la Española, *3:* 179
Churros, *3:* 182
Flan (Custard), *3:* 182
Gazpacho (Cold Tomato Soup), *3:* 177
Leche Frita, *3:* 186
Mazapanes (Almond Candies), *3:* 181
Patatas Bravas, *3:* 184
Pisto Manchego with Eggs, *3:* 178
Rice with Shrimp, *3:* 186
Tapa: Aceitunas Aliñadas, *3:* 185
Tapa: Crema de Cabrales, *3:* 184
Tapa: Tartaletas de Champiñón, *3:* 185
Tortilla Española (Omelet), *3:* 179
Spanish Tortilla (Guatemala), *2:* 24
Spargelgemuse (Asparagus, Germany), *1:* 213
Spiced Chicken (China), *1:* 126
Spiced Cocoa (Haiti), *2:* 35
Spiced Couscous (Somalia), *3:* 145
Spicy Braised Cabbage (Tanzania), *3:* 214
Spicy Oven-Fried Chicken (Amish and Pennsylvania Dutch, United States), *4:* 83
Spinach and Peanut Butter Stew (South Africa), *3:* 157

Spinach with Garlic (Egypt), *1:* 177
Spreads
Amlou (Almond Butter, Morocco), *3:* 10
Apple Butter (Amish and Pennsylvania Dutch, United States), *4:* 87
Baigan Bhartha (India), *2:* 58
Berbere (Spice Paste, Ethiopia), *1:* 192
Bliny Filling (Russia), *3:* 102
Chancho en Piedra (Chile), *1:* 111
Dotorimuk (Acorn Curd, South Korea), *3:* 167
Fava Bean Spread (Israel), *2:* 129
French-Canadian Creton (Pate, French Canadians, Canada), *1:* 96
Frijoles Negros Volteados (Guatemala), *2:* 26
Guacamole (Guatemala), *2:* 26
Guacamole (Latino Americans, United States), *4:* 116
Guacamole (Mexico), *2:* 223
Hummus (Egypt), *1:* 173
Hummus (Great Lakes Region, United States), *4:* 95
Hummus (Saudi Arabia), *3:* 120
Hummus be Tahini (Lebanon), *2:* 202
Kategna (Ethiopia), *1:* 190
Lemon Curd (United Kingdom), *4:* 44
Mantequilla de ajo casera (Guatemala), *2:* 30
Melitzanosalata (Greece), *2:* 21
Niter Kebbeh or Kibe (Ethiopia), *1:* 192
Peanut Butter Molasses Spread (Amish and Pennsylvania Dutch, United States), *4:* 86
Smen Butter (Algeria), *1:* 3
Strawberry Jam (Amish and Pennsylvania Dutch, United States), *4:* 86
Spring Rolls (Vietnam), *4:* 196
Springerle (Christmas Cookies, Great Lakes Region, United States), *4:* 96
Squash Soup (Aboriginals, Canada), *1:* 88
Steak Frites (France), *1:* 208
Stewed Mangoes with Cloves (Liberia), *2:* 209
Stews
Aji de Gallina (Peru), *3:* 60
Ash-e Jo (Barley Stew, Iran), *2:* 91
Aterkek Alecha (Stew, Ethiopia), *1:* 196
Bigos (Polish Hunter's Stew, Poland), *3:* 78
Birria (Mexico), *2:* 221

Index

Stews (*continued*)
    Buffalo Stew (Native Americans, United States), *4:* 140
    Calalou (Vegetable Stew, Côte d'Ivoire), *1:* 134
    Carbonada Criolla (Stew, Argentina), *1:* 15
    Carurú (Afro-Brazilians, Brazil), *1:* 57
    Cozido (Beef Stew, Portugal), *3:* 94
    Dhal (Lentil Stew, Pakistan), *3:* 40
    Dovi (Peanut Butter Stew, Zimbabwe), *4:* 201
    Efo (Greens Stew, Nigeria), *3:* 31
    Feijoada (Meat Stew, Brazil), *1:* 48
    Groundnut Stew (Ghana), *2:* 8
    Matata (Stew, Mozambique), *3:* 18
    Moqueca (Spicy Fish Stew, Afro-Brazilians, Brazil), *1:* 58
    Moqueca aos Ovos (Egg Stew, Afro-Brazilians, Brazil), *1:* 59
    Ndolé (Bitterleaf Stew, Cameroon), *1:* 70
    Nigerian Stew (Nigeria), *3:* 29
    Pörkölt (Hungarian Stew, Hungary), *2:* 47
    Sancocho (Dominican Republic), *1:* 164
    Spinach and Peanut Butter Stew (South Africa), *3:* 157
    Succotash (Corn and Bean Stew, Native Americans, United States), *4:* 138
    Tomaticán (Stew, Chile), *1:* 109
    Traditional Irish Stew (Ireland), *2:* 106
Strawberry Cookie Bars (Czech Republic), *1:* 151
Strawberry Jam (Amish and Pennsylvania Dutch, United States), *4:* 86
"String of Doughnuts" (Morocco), *3:* 9
Stuffed Dates and Walnuts (Algeria), *1:* 6
Stuffed Eggs (Poland), *3:* 88
Stuffed Green Peppers (Hungary), *2:* 48
Submarino (Argentina), *1:* 20
Succotash (Corn and Bean Stew, Native Americans, United States), *4:* 138
Succotash (Northeast Region, United States), *4:* 150
Sugar Cookies (Amish and Pennsylvania Dutch, United States), *4:* 85
Sugared Almonds (Lebanon), *2:* 200
Sukuma Wiki (Kenya), *2:* 186
Summer Cucumber Soup (Hungary), *2:* 52
Sunday Lunch Cauliflower Cheese (United Kingdom), *4:* 52
Supu Ya Ndizi (Plantain Soup, Tanzania), *3:* 211

Suqaar (Somalia), *3:* 140
Surbiyaan (Somali Rice, Somalia), *3:* 140
Sushi (Japan), *2:* 164
Svart Vinbärsglögg (Sweden), *3:* 197
Sweden, *3:* 189
    Artsoppa (Pea Soup), *3:* 200
    Blandad Fruktsoppa (Soup), *3:* 194
    Creamy Dipping Sauce, *3:* 191
    Drommar (Swedish Cookies), *3:* 198
    Glazed Carrots, *3:* 191
    Hasselbackspotatis, *3:* 200
    Jansson's Frestelse, *3:* 193
    Julgröt (Christmas Porridge), *3:* 196
    Klimp (Dumplings), *3:* 194
    Köttbulla (Swedish Meatballs), *3:* 194
    Lussekatter (Saffron Buns), *3:* 197
    Pepparkakor (Ginger Cookies), *3:* 198
    Pitepalt (Potato Pastries), *3:* 195
    Plättar (Swedish Pancakes), *3:* 200
    Rågbröd (Swedish Rye Bread), *3:* 201
    Rårakor (Potato Pancakes), *3:* 202
    Rose Hip Soup, *3:* 192
    Sillsallad (Herring Salad), *3:* 203
    Smörgås med ost och päron, *3:* 202
    Svart Vinbärsglögg, *3:* 197
Swedish Meatballs (Great Lakes Region, United States), *4:* 97
Sweet and Sour Pork (China), *1:* 119
Sweet Corn Pancakes (Canada), *1:* 78
Sweet Couscous Dessert (Algeria), *1:* 6
Sweet Grated Carrot Salad (Morocco), *3:* 10
Sweet Peanut Mochi (Japan), *2:* 170
Sweet Potato Casserole (Haiti), *2:* 40
Sweet Potato Cookies (Zimbabwe), *4:* 205
Sweet Potato Pie (African Americans, United States), *4:* 68
Sweet Potato Pie (Southern Region, United States), *4:* 164
Sweet Potato Pone (Jamaica), *2:* 158
Sweet Potato Pone (Liberia), *2:* 207
Sweet Potato Pudding (Tanzania), *3:* 213
Sweet Tea (Southern Region, United States), *4:* 168

Index

T

Tabbouleh (Bulgur Wheat Salad, Saudi Arabia), *3:* 120
Tabbouleh (Lebanon), *2:* 196
Tacos (Latino Americans, United States), *4:* 123
Tahini Sauce (Israel), *2:* 133
Tahu Goreng (Fried Tofu, Indonesia), *2:* 74
Tamagoyaki (Rolled Omelet, Japan), *2:* 167
Tamatar Salat (Tomato Salad, India), *2:* 63
Tandoori Chicken (India), *2:* 60
Tanzania, *3:* 205
    Chai (Tea), *3:* 207
    Chapati (Fried Flatbread), *3:* 210
    Coconut Bean Soup, *3:* 208
    Date Nut Bread, *3:* 212
    Makubi, *3:* 214
    Mango-Orange Drink, *3:* 209
    Mchicha, *3:* 213
    Ndizi Kaanga (Fried Plantains), *3:* 209
    Pineapple with Honey & Coconut, *3:* 214
    Spicy Braised Cabbage, *3:* 214
    Supu Ya Ndizi (Plantain Soup), *3:* 211
    Sweet Potato Pudding, *3:* 213
    Ugali, *3:* 209
    Wali wa Nazi, *3:* 211
Tapa: Aceitunas Aliñadas (Spain), *3:* 185
Tapa: Crema de Cabrales (Spain), *3:* 184
Tapa: Tartaletas de Champiñón (Spain), *3:* 185
Tarte au Sucre (Sugar Pie, French Canadians, Canada), *1:* 99
Tattie Soup (Scotland, United Kingdom), *4:* 57
Tatties n' Neeps (Scotland, United Kingdom), *4:* 57
Té con Leche (Tea with Milk, Chile), *1:* 108
Tea Biscuits (United Kingdom), *4:* 50
Tea with Milk (United Kingdom), *4:* 51
Teh Halia (Hot Ginger Tea, Indonesia), *2:* 78
Thai Beef Curry (Thailand), *4:* 4
Thailand, *4:* 1
    Banana with Coconut Milk, *4:* 8
    Chicken Satay, *4:* 5
    Coconut-Chicken Soup, *4:* 10
    Cucumber Salad, *4:* 7
    Ka Nom Jeen Sour Nam, *4:* 11
    Kanom Krok (Pancakes), *4:* 8
    Mango and Sticky Rice, *4:* 12

    Nam Pla Prig (Dipping Sauce), *4:* 6
    Pad See Ew, *4:* 5
    Pad Thai, *4:* 10
    Poa Pee (Thai Egg Rolls), *4:* 6
    Sang Ka Ya (Coconut Custard), *4:* 9
    Shu Mai Dumplings, *4:* 12
    Thai Beef Curry, *4:* 4
Three Sisters Soup (Aboriginals, Canada), *1:* 89
Ti-Malice (Spicy Haitian Sauce, Haiti), *2:* 39
Toad-in-the-Hole (United Kingdom), *4:* 45
Toast with Tomatoes (Ukraine), *4:* 36
Toast with Vegemite (Australia), *1:* 32
Toasted Sesame Seeds (South Korea), *3:* 169
Tomaticán (Stew, Chile), *1:* 109
Tomato and Cucumber Salad (African Americans, United States), *4:* 74
Topinky S Vejci (Eggs on Toast, Czech Republic), *1:* 152
Torrejas (Guatemala), *2:* 31
Torta de Cumpleaños (Cake, Chile), *1:* 111
Tortilla Chips (Mexico), *2:* 223
Tortilla Española (Omelet, Spain), *3:* 179
Tostones (Dominican Republic), *1:* 166
Tourtière (Meat Pie, French Canadians, Canada), *1:* 98
Traditional Fufu (Cameroon), *1:* 68
Traditional Irish Stew (Ireland), *2:* 106
Tropical Fruit Dessert (Islands of the Pacific), *2:* 124
Tropical Fruit Salad (Latino Americans, United States), *4:* 123
Tropical Fruit Shake (Islands of the Pacific), *2:* 124
Tsokolate (Hot Chocolate, Philippines), *3:* 70
Tuna in Sauce (Cuba), *1:* 139
Turkey, *4:* 15
    Beetroot Salad, *4:* 21
    Bulgur Pilavi (Pilaf), *4:* 25
    Halva, *4:* 23
    Hummus and Chicken, *4:* 26
    Kaymakli Kuru Kayisi, *4:* 17
    Köfte (Turkish Meatballs), *4:* 22
    Lahmacun (Turkish Pizza), *4:* 27
    Locum (Turkish Candy), *4:* 24
    Lokma (Golden Fritters), *4:* 26
    Lor Köftesi (Ricotta Patties), *4:* 19
    Muhallabi (Rice Pudding), *4:* 18
    Naneli Limonata (Lemonade), *4:* 20

Index

Turkey (*continued*)
    Pasta with Yogurt-Mint Sauce, *4:* 18
    Roasted Eggplant Salad, *4:* 27
    Simit (Sesame Rings), *4:* 20
Tzatziki (Sauce, Greece), *2:* 20

U

Ugali (Kenya), *2:* 187
Ugali (Tanzania), *3:* 209
Ukraine, *4:* **29**
    Cabbage Borshch, *4:* 32
    Holubtsi (Cabbage Rolls), *4:* 32
    Hrechana Kasha, *4:* 33
    Kartoplia Solimkoi (Potatoes), *4:* 34
    Kotleta Po-Kyivsky, *4:* 35
    Kutya (Sweet Porridge), *4:* 33
    Makiwnyk (Poppy Seed Cake), *4:* 36
    Makiwnyk Glaze (Cake Glaze), *4:* 36
    Nachynka (Cornbread Stuffing), *4:* 38
    Paska (Easter Bread), *4:* 37
    Potato Varenyky (Dumplings), *4:* 31
    Toast with Tomatoes, *4:* 36
Uli Petataws (Potato Fritters, Indonesia), *2:* 73
United Kingdom, *4:* **41**
    Aberdeen Buttery (Scotland), *4:* 62
    Barley Pudding (Scotland), *4:* 63
    Boiled Fruitcake, *4:* 49
    Chocolate-dipped Shortbread (Scotland), *4:* 59
    Cock-a-Leekie Soup (Scotland), *4:* 61
    Cornish Pasties, *4:* 45
    Cranachan (Scotland), *4:* 62
    Cucumber Sandwiches, *4:* 44
    Cullen Skink (Scotland), *4:* 60
    Fish and Chips, *4:* 51
    Flapjacks (Oatmeal Biscuits, Scotland), *4:* 57
    Haggis (Scotland), *4:* 56
    Individual Mincemeat Pies, *4:* 47
    Lemon Curd, *4:* 44
    Prince William's Groom's Cake, *4:* 48
    Salmon Kedgeree, *4:* 43
    Scones, *4:* 46
    Scotland, *4:* **55**
    Skirlie (Scotland), *4:* 58
    Sunday Lunch Cauliflower Cheese, *4:* 52
    Tattie Soup (Scotland), *4:* 57
    Tatties n' Neeps (Scotland), *4:* 57
    Tea Biscuits, *4:* 50
    Tea with Milk, *4:* 51
    Toad-in-the-Hole, *4:* 45
    Vegetable Curry, *4:* 52
    Wassail, *4:* 48
    Welsh Rarebit, *4:* 42
United States
    African Americans, *4:* **65**
    Amish and Pennsylvania Dutch, *4:* **79**
    Apple and Carrot Tsimmes (Jewish Americans), *4:* 105
    Apple Butter (Amish and Pennsylvania Dutch), *4:* 87
    Apple Crisp (Western Region), *4:* 180
    Apple Sauerkraut (Great Lakes Region), *4:* 95
    Baked Apples (Amish and Pennsylvania Dutch), *4:* 85
    Baked Macaroni and Cheese (African Americans), *4:* 72
    Barbeque Sauce (Southern Region), *4:* 171
    Blueberry Muffins (Western Region), *4:* 181
    Borscht (Beet Soup, Jewish Americans), *4:* 110
    Boston Baked Beans (Northeast Region), *4:* 152
    Boston Cream Pie (Northeast Region), *4:* 156
    Bread Pudding (Midwest Region), *4:* 127
    Broiled Salmon Steaks (Western Region), *4:* 180
    Buffalo Chicken Wings (Great Lakes Region), *4:* 96
    Buffalo Stew (Native Americans), *4:* 140
    California-style Pizza (Western Region), *4:* 182
    Calzone (Midwest Region), *4:* 132
    Caramel Corn (Midwest Region), *4:* 131
    Carne Asada Fries (Western Region), *4:* 183
    Charoset (Jewish Americans), *4:* 105
    Cherry Muffins (Great Lakes Region), *4:* 93
    Chess Pie (Southern Region), *4:* 161
    Chicago Deep Dish Pizza (Great Lakes Region), *4:* 98
    Chicken and Sausage Gumbo (Southern Region), *4:* 165
    Chili Corn Bread (Latino Americans), *4:* 122
    Chinese Peanut Sauce (Western Region), *4:* 181
    Chitlins (African Americans), *4:* 69

Chopped Chicken Liver (Jewish Americans), *4:* 103
Chuck Wagon Brisket (Western Region), *4:* 175
Coffee Milkshake (Northeast Region), *4:* 153
Collard Greens (African Americans), *4:* 66
Collard Greens with Ham Hocks (Southern Region), *4:* 168
Corn on the Cob (Midwest Region), *4:* 128
Cornbread (Southern Region), *4:* 162
Cornhusker's Casserole (Midwest Region), *4:* 132
Cornish Pasty (Great Lakes Region), *4:* 98
Cranberry Salsa (Western Region), *4:* 178
Cream of Cabbage Soup (Amish and Pennsylvania Dutch), *4:* 81
Creole Seasoning (Southern Region), *4:* 160
Cuban Avocado Salad (Latino Americans), *4:* 122
Cuban Beans and Rice (Latino Americans), *4:* 117
Deviled Eggs (Midwest Region), *4:* 127
Dilly Beans (Southern Region), *4:* 162
Dutch Pancakes (Great Lakes Region), *4:* 91
Fish Boil (Great Lakes Region), *4:* 91
Fortune Cookies (Western Region), *4:* 177
Fried Apples (African Americans), *4:* 74
Fried Bologna (African Americans), *4:* 74
Fried Plantains (Latino Americans), *4:* 118
Fruit Medley (Native Americans), *4:* 144
Gazpacho (Latino Americans), *4:* 119
German Potato Salad (Great Lakes Region), *4:* 93
Great Lakes Region, *4:* 89
Green Bean Casserole (Midwest Region), *4:* 129
Grits (Southern Region), *4:* 166
Guacamole (Latino Americans), *4:* 116
Herring Dip (Jewish Americans), *4:* 107
Honey-Baked Apples (Northeast Region), *4:* 155
Hot Cranberry Punch (Northeast Region), *4:* 155
Hummus (Great Lakes Region), *4:* 95
Hush Puppies (African Americans), *4:* 70
Indian Fry-Bread (Native Americans), *4:* 143
Indian Pudding (Northeast Region), *4:* 149
Iroquois Strawberry Drink (Native Americans), *4:* 142
Jewish Americans, *4:* 101
Johnnycakes (Northeast Region), *4:* 151
Kwanzaa Brownies (African Americans), *4:* 73
Latino Americans, *4:* 113
Lefse (Midwest Region), *4:* 131

Lobster Roll (Northeast Region), *4:* 156
Macaroni and Cheese (Great Lakes Region), *4:* 94
Maple Baked Beans (Native Americans), *4:* 139
Maple Butter (Northeast Region), *4:* 151
Mardi Gras King Cake (Southern Region), *4:* 166
Marinated Artichokes (Western Region), *4:* 178
Matzo Balls (Jewish Americans), *4:* 109
Matzo Brie (Jewish Americans), *4:* 106
Mexican Fried Ice Cream (Latino Americans), *4:* 119
Midwest Region, *4:* 125
Midwestern Chili (Midwest Region), *4:* 128
Midwestern Pork Chop Dinner (Midwest Region), *4:* 132
Molasses Water (African Americans), *4:* 68
Mother's Chicken Soup (Jewish Americans), *4:* 103
Native Americans, *4:* 135
New England Boiled Dinner (Northeast Region), *4:* 154
New England Clam Chowder (Northeast Region), *4:* 152
New York Cheesecake (Jewish Americans), *4:* 108
Noodle Kugel (Noodle Casserole, Jewish Americans), *4:* 104
Northeast Region, *4:* 147
Ojibwa Wild Rice (Great Lakes Region), *4:* 92
Okra (African Americans), *4:* 75
Old Fashioned Bread Pudding (Southern Region), *4:* 170
Old-Fashioned Spicy Lemonade (Amish and Pennsylvania Dutch), *4:* 84
Old Fashioned Turnip Soup (Southern Region), *4:* 161
Parsley New Potatoes (Western Region), *4:* 182
Peanut Butter Molasses Spread (Amish and Pennsylvania Dutch), *4:* 86
Peanut Soup (African Americans), *4:* 75
Pemmican (Native Americans), *4:* 144
Pinole (Cornmeal Drink, Native Americans), *4:* 144
Polish Boy Sandwich (Great Lakes Region), *4:* 97
Popcorn (Native Americans), *4:* 136
Popped Wild Rice (Native Americans), *4:* 143
Pork Chops with Sauerkraut (Amish and Pennsylvania Dutch), *4:* 80

Index

United States (*continued*)

Potato Latkes (Potato Pancakes, Jewish Americans), *4:* 106
Potato Lefse (Great Lakes Region), *4:* 96
Potato Salad (African Americans), *4:* 71
Pralines (Southern Region), *4:* 170
Puerto Rican Christmas Salad (Latino Americans), *4:* 120
Pumpkin Bread (Native Americans), *4:* 142
Pumpkin-Corn Sauce (Native Americans), *4:* 140
Quesadillas (Latino Americans), *4:* 122
Red Beans and Rice (African Americans), *4:* 70
Reuben Sandwich (Midwest Region), *4:* 130
Rosh Hashanah Honey Cake (Jewish Americans), *4:* 110
Salsa Cruda (Latino Americans), *4:* 116
Shoofly Pie (Amish and Pennsylvania Dutch), *4:* 82
Snow Ice Cream (Amish and Pennsylvania Dutch), *4:* 83
Southern Fried Chicken (Southern Region), *4:* 165
Southern Region, *4:* 159
Spicy Oven-Fried Chicken (Amish and Pennsylvania Dutch), *4:* 83
Springerle (Christmas Cookies, Great Lakes Region), *4:* 96
Strawberry Jam (Amish and Pennsylvania Dutch), *4:* 86
Succotash (Corn and Bean Stew, Native Americans), *4:* 138
Succotash (Northeast Region), *4:* 150
Sugar Cookies (Amish and Pennsylvania Dutch), *4:* 85
Swedish Meatballs (Great Lakes Region), *4:* 97
Sweet Potato Pie (African Americans), *4:* 68
Sweet Potato Pie (Southern Region), *4:* 164
Sweet Tea (Southern Region), *4:* 168
Tacos (Latino Americans), *4:* 123
Tomato and Cucumber Salad (African Americans), *4:* 74
Tropical Fruit Salad (Latino Americans), *4:* 123
Western Region, *4:* 173
Whoopie Pie (Amish and Pennsylvania Dutch), *4:* 87
Uszka (Poland), *3:* 84

V

Veal Meatballs with Dill (Poland), *3:* 88
Vegetable Curry (United Kingdom), *4:* 52
Vegetable Sandwich (India), *2:* 62

Vegetables

Aceitunas Alinadas (Olives, Cuba), *1:* 143
Algerian Cooked Carrot Salad (Algeria), *1:* 7
Apple and Carrot Tsimmes (Jewish Americans, United States), *4:* 105
Baingan Ka Raita (Pakistan), *3:* 42
Baked Papas (Potato Skins, Peru), *3:* 51
Baked Yams (Côte d'Ivoire), *1:* 132
Bamia (Sweet and Sour Okra, Egypt), *1:* 174
Banadura Salata B'Kizbara (Algeria), *1:* 5
Beetroot Salad (Turkey), *4:* 21
Camote (Sweet Potatoes, Mexico), *2:* 222
Canh Bi Ro Ham Dua (Vietnam), *4:* 192
Carne Asada Fries (Western Region, United States), *4:* 183
Carrot Bredie (South Africa), *3:* 153
Champ (Ireland), *2:* 109
Choclo con Queso (Peru), *3:* 53
Colcannon (Ireland), *2:* 110
Collard Greens (African Americans, United States), *4:* 66
Collard Greens with Ham Hocks (Southern Region, United States), *4:* 168
Collards with Cabbage (Liberia), *2:* 211
Corn on the Cob (Midwest Region, United States), *4:* 128
Corn on the Cob (South Africa), *3:* 157
Cornhusker's Casserole (Midwest Region, United States), *4:* 132
Cucumber Salad (Thailand), *4:* 7
Cucumber with Yogurt (Lebanon), *2:* 196
Curried Okra (Nigeria), *3:* 32
Deep-Fried Potatoes (Slovenia), *3:* 129
Dilly Beans (Southern Region, United States), *4:* 162
Eggplant Appetizer (Israel), *2:* 134
Fried Baby Carrots (Morocco), *3:* 12
Glazed Carrots (Sweden), *3:* 191
Gomen Wat (Ethiopian Greens, Ethiopia), *1:* 197
Green Bean Casserole (Midwest Region, United States), *4:* 129

Griby Marinovannye (Russia), *3:* 109
Hasselbackspotatis (Sweden), *3:* 200
Israeli Vegetable Salad (Israel), *2:* 132
Isu (Spiced Boiled Yams, Nigeria), *3:* 27
Iyan (Pounded Yams, Nigeria), *3:* 28
Kartoplia Solimkoi (Potatoes, Ukraine), *4:* 34
Kenyan Cabbage (Kenya), *2:* 189
Lebanese Eggplant (Lebanon), *2:* 196
Makubi (Tanzania), *3:* 214
Marinated Artichokes (Western Region, United States), *4:* 178
Mchicha (Tanzania), *3:* 213
Okra (African Americans, United States), *4:* 75
Palak Bhaji (Fried Spinach, India), *2:* 60
Papas a la Huancaína (Peru), *3:* 55
Parsley New Potatoes (Western Region, United States), *4:* 182
Patatas Bravas (Spain), *3:* 184
Patates Fourno Riganates (Greece), *2:* 19
Potato Roesti (Germany), *1:* 218
Potato Salad (African Americans, United States), *4:* 71
Quiabo (Okra, Afro-Brazilians, Brazil), *1:* 57
Roasted Butternut Squash (Zimbabwe), *4:* 202
Roasted Eggplant Salad (Turkey), *4:* 27
Shigumch'i Namul (Spinach, South Korea), *3:* 170
Spargelgemuse (Asparagus, Germany), *1:* 213
Spicy Braised Cabbage (Tanzania), *3:* 214
Spinach with Garlic (Egypt), *1:* 177
Steak Frites (France), *1:* 208
Succotash (Corn and Bean Stew, Native Americans), *4:* 138
Succotash (Northeast Region, United States), *4:* 150
Sukuma Wiki (Kenya), *2:* 186
Sunday Lunch Cauliflower Cheese (United Kingdom), *4:* 52
Sweet Grated Carrot Salad (Morocco), *3:* 10
Sweet Potato Casserole (Haiti), *2:* 40
Tatties n' Neeps (Scotland, United Kingdom), *4:* 57
Toast with Tomatoes (Ukraine), *4:* 36
Tomato and Cucumber Salad (African Americans, United States), *4:* 74
Vegetable Curry (United Kingdom), *4:* 52
Yalanchi (Stuffed Tomatoes, Iraq), *2:* 97
Yams (Ghana), *2:* 2
Zimbabwe Greens (Zimbabwe), *4:* 204

Vietnam, *4:* 185
Banh Chuoi Nuong (Cake), *4:* 192
Banh Mi Tom Chien, *4:* 197
Canh Bi Ro Ham Dua, *4:* 192
Caphe (Vietnamese Coffee), *4:* 195
Coconut Custard, *4:* 191
Nuoc Cham (Dipping Sauce), *4:* 188
Omelet with Ground Pork, *4:* 197
Pho Bo (Beef Noodle Soup), *4:* 191
Soda Chanh (Lemon Soda), *4:* 195
Spring Rolls, *4:* 196

W

Wales. *See* United Kingdom
Wali wa Nazi (Coconut Rice, Kenya), *2:* 190
Wali wa Nazi (Tanzania), *3:* 211
Warqa (Morocco), *3:* 5
Wassail (United Kingdom), *4:* 48
Weisse Bohnensuppe (Soup, Germany), *1:* 212
Welsh Rarebit (United Kingdom), *4:* 42
Western Kenya Cabbage and Egg (Kenya), *2:* 186
Western Region (United States), *4:* 173
Apple Crisp, *4:* 180
Blueberry Muffins, *4:* 181
Broiled Salmon Steaks, *4:* 180
California-style Pizza, *4:* 182
Carne Asada Fries, *4:* 183
Chinese Peanut Sauce, *4:* 181
Chuck Wagon Brisket, *4:* 175
Cranberry Salsa, *4:* 178
Fortune Cookies, *4:* 177
Marinated Artichokes, *4:* 178
Parsley New Potatoes, *4:* 182
Whoopie Pie (Amish and Pennsylvania Dutch, United States), *4:* 87
Wild Rice Cakes (Aboriginals, Canada), *1:* 91
Wonton Soup (China), *1:* 119

Y

Yaki-Soba (Fried Noodles, Japan), *2:* 166
Yakitori (Chicken on Skewers, Japan), *2:* 169
Yalanchi (Stuffed Tomatoes, Iraq), *2:* 97
Yams (Ghana), *2:* 2

Index

Yogurt and Mint Sauce (Iran), *2:* 84
Yogurt Chutney (Kenya), *2:* 188
Yorkshire Pudding (Canada), *1:* 77
Yucca (Cassava, Cuba), *1:* 141

Z

Zanzibar. *See* Tanzania
Zimbabwe, *4:* 199
   Cornmeal Cake, *4:* 203

Dovi (Peanut Butter Stew), *4:* 201
Mapopo (Papaya) Candy, *4:* 200
Rice with Peanut Sauce, *4:* 204
Roasted Butternut Squash, *4:* 202
Rock Shandy, *4:* 204
Sadza, *4:* 202
Sweet Potato Cookies, *4:* 205
Zimbabwe Greens, *4:* 204
Zimbabwe Greens (Zimbabwe), *4:* 204
Zupa Koperkowa (Dill Soup, Poland), *3:* 80

MAR 1 2 2013
307-